WOMEN ON NATURE

WOMEN
ON NATURE

*An anthology of women's writing about the
natural world in the east Atlantic archipelago*

Edited by Katharine Norbury

unbound

First published in 2021

Unbound
TC Group, Level 1, Devonshire House, One Mayfair Place, London W1J 8AJ
www.unbound.com

Text design by PDQ Digital Media Solutions Ltd

A CIP record for this book is available from the British Library

ISBN 978-1-80018-041-3 (hardback)
ISBN 978-1-80018-042-0 (ebook)

Printed in Great Britain by CPI Group (UK)

1 3 5 7 9 8 6 4 2

To Eva Rae Thomson
and
Rupert Thomson

In memory of beloved
Anna Norbury
1994–2020

Editor's Note

The majority of pieces in this collection are extracted from previously published works and the date of first publication is given in brackets. The book is for a general readership and I have forgone the tens of pages that full citations would have demanded; all the source material is readily accessible. It is only comparatively recently that English orthography has become standardised and I have occasionally modernised spelling in order to enhance clarity. Material that is original to this anthology is marked with a dagger †.

CONTENTS

INTRODUCTION

When Unbound first asked me to curate this anthology, I was hesitant. The words 'women' and 'nature' have both, in different ways, shifted their meaning in the first quarter of the twenty-first century. The simple dictionary definitions no longer seem to cover it. 'Women', in English, is the plural form of 'woman', a Middle English term that grew from the Old English 'wiman', or 'wifmann', and is given in most dictionaries to mean an adult female human. But it's hard to ignore the implication of an adjunct, or 'spare rib', in those three letters: 'wif'. My relaxed and supportive parents didn't impart to me an awareness of being a 'female human'. Perhaps because Mum was, in her own words, a tomboy, and though there were dresses for Sunday best, hand-tailored by older female relatives, I was usually to be found in slacks, often climbing the pear tree in our garden or hiding in the shrub-house I had constructed with my friends in a massive rhododendron bush. While my brother and I had different interests – he played golf, I played the flute – neither of these pastimes were especially associated with either maleness or femaleness, as a result of which I grew up without any particular awareness of having a gender. With hindsight, I have come to regard the laissez-faire attitude of my parents in relation to who or what I perceived myself to be as having been a great luxury.

'Nature' is an equally slippery notion. The online dictionary describes 'nature' as 'the phenomena of the physical world collectively, including plants, animals, the landscape, and other features and products of the earth, as opposed to humans or human creations'. This idea of 'the other' was something that I struggled with. Many of you will be too young to remember the 'I Spy' books: *I Spy in the Country*, *I Spy Birds*, with their alluring tick boxes for stag beetles and hayricks, chiffchaffs and mallards – even for different kinds of gate openings. The 'I Spy' books were perfect for negotiating and giving form to the endless summer holidays, both as a solitary child and as one accompanied by friends. There was a reassuring, football-card nerdiness in ticking off the natural features or species of moths and comparing them with your friends' or cousins' achievements. During school term time, our formidable deputy head, Mrs Ames, ran the Young Ornithologists' Club, then the junior branch of the RSPB. Seventeen species of bird appeared regularly at the bird table Dad had made for our garden. I had once hand-reared a baby thrush after some boys plucked the nest from the hedgerow. These things were the stuff of everyday life, growing up as I did at the edge of a Green Belt, and I certainly didn't think of them as 'other', or see 'nature' as something separate or different from myself.

Looking at that dictionary definition – what does it actually mean? Does 'nature' only include things that have evolved naturally, without our intervention? Should it include domestic animals, cats and dogs, cows and sheep? And what about the things that are wild? Where does the hand-reared thrush, Jimmy, fit in? Was he still wild? What does 'wild' mean? Also, as anyone who has spent time outdoors will have learned, humans and 'other than human critters', to borrow Donna Haraway's term, have a tendency to domesticate one another, if left in too close proximity for any length of time. When I returned this evening and put the light on in my study here at RSPB Haweswater, there was a quick 'Agh!' and a metallic tap at the window. A great spotted woodpecker – something of a martinet – had observed my return to the house, and specifically to the room where a plastic bird feeder was attached by suction discs to the window. 'Agh!' meant, 'Go and get those sunflower hearts you know I love,' or, at the very least, 'Where are they?' This bird will enter the room if I leave the window open. I haven't 'tamed' it. It has simply come to associate me with 1) no danger to itself and 2) a thus-far endless supply of sunflower hearts. It doesn't come into the room to be my friend, but to try to find the stash (they're in a filing cabinet, in a sack labelled 'RSPB Sunflower Hearts').

Carl Safina, in his ground-breaking study of animal behaviour, *Becoming Wild: How Animal Cultures Raise Families, Create Beauty, and Achieve Peace*, seeks to open our eyes to the largely unacknowledged cultural common ground shared by whales, scarlet macaws, chimpanzees and humans, among others, and the extent to which we are all taught by our elders, to 'become'. Animals learn and share with us cultural attributes such as the desire to nurture one's family, in the case of whales, or to live in peace with one's neighbours, despite a natural war-like proclivity, in the case of chimpanzees.

My real issue with the word 'nature' is that it is implicitly anthropocentric. It is, by definition, 'them' and 'us'. The philosopher Timothy Morton prefers not to use the word, favouring 'ecology' instead. Ecology – and here's another dictionary term – is 'the branch of biology that deals with the relations of organisms to one another and to their physical surroundings'; or put another way, we too are part of the whole. And yet even the term 'ecology' takes no cognisance of a spiritual or other-than-physical aspect that which we are seeking to describe. The unseen, the unquantifiable, and the sublime slips through the net. How many of us respond to something elusive, something mysterious, about the natural world?

Given my own discomfort at the concepts of both gender and nature, it may seem an odd decision for me to have called this collection *Women on Nature*, even, perhaps, something of a retrograde step. But, the thing is, you know what I mean! If you are reading this now, then those two words have clearly conveyed enough for you to have picked up and possibly bought this book. In reality I chose the title as a playful acknowledgement of Susan Griffin's controversial

1978 feminist polemic *Woman and Nature: The Roaring Inside Her*, in which Griffin disputed the patriarchal and somewhat patronising position that 'women' are 'intuitive', 'closer to nature' (Mother Nature, Father God) and therefore inherently 'wild' or 'volatile' and in need of 'taming' or 'civilising'. And until really very recently, in our east Atlantic archipelago at any rate, it is true that what we think of as nature writing has been associated almost exclusively with men. As a fledgling writer, I was very much influenced by the work of Bruce Chatwin, Roger Deakin, Robert Macfarlane and Peter Matthiessen. At a certain level these writers may be thought of as travel writers, and nature writing, as we often find it, bears a familial relationship to travel writing. A writer goes out into a landscape and records what they see. Yet this kind of endeavour, writing that is born out of a journey, has often been undertaken, and for sound cultural and economic reasons, by men, who for one reason or another have had the time and resources to do both the travelling and the writing. We are stumbling into a trap, therefore, if we assume that women have traditionally not written about the natural world because they have not been writing these kinds of books.

What would happen, I wondered, if I simply missed out the 50 per cent of the population whose voices have been credited with shaping this particular cultural form? If I coppiced the woodland and allowed the light to shine down to the forest floor and illuminate countless saplings now that a gap has opened in the canopy?

But it isn't only male voices that are hushed in this volume. I have also focused exclusively on writing in English about the eastern islands of the Atlantic Ocean. This is because if you ask someone to name well-known nature writers who are women, the names Annie Dillard, Gretel Ehrlich, Rebecca Solnit, Terry Tempest Williams and Robin Wall Kimmerer – all US writers – are likely to be among the first to come up,, and the American tradition, for want of a better term, and its east

4

Atlantic equivalent, have had different formative influences, and have emerged in different ways. So, having cut away half the population and much of the English-speaking world, this volume focuses on what is left.

I have presented the authors in alphabetical order, which means that Dorothy Wordsworth, who opens the collection through the medium of Kathryn Aalto's twenty-first-century essay, also closes it through the nineteenth-century words of her own journal. The words of Scotland's current Makar, Jackie Kay, sit between the words of the fourteenth-century anchorite Julian of Norwich and the author of the first autobiography written in English, Margery Kempe. (As it happened, Margery Kempe had visited Mother Julian in her cell in Norwich to ask her advice, so these two extraordinary women knew one another.) While this means that the reader is constantly shifting in time and space from Ireland, to Wales, from the fourteenth century to the twenty-first, it also means that if you want to find, for example, Naoko Abe, or Emily Brontë, you just open the book quite near the beginning, and if you're looking for Anita Sethi or Dorothy Wellesley, then you can work your way backwards from the end. There are a great number of voices ranging, unevenly, over 700 years, and the writing shifts in form through essay, fiction, journal, letter, life writing, poetry, recipe book to travelogue, and its subjects stretch from fishing to gardening, mysticism to natural history. Many pieces are fragments of greater works, and in this respect *Women on Nature* has something of the feel of a commonplace book, and I encourage the reader to seek out the originals for themselves, or find other works by the writers here presented. The word 'anthology' does, after all, mean a collection of flowers, so it is fitting that there is something of the field notebook here, with blooms of varying provenance pressed between its pages. The collection could easily have been twice the size, with double the number of contributors, but time and available funding have determined the present volume.

Virginia Woolf famously observed in *A Room of One's Own* that in order for a woman to write she needs independent means and a place in which to do it. I have drawn together this collection during the coronavirus 'lockdown' of 2020. You, the reader, have generously funded the physical making of the book. I am funded by Chancellor Rishi Sunak's emergency bailout scheme for the self-employed, because my ordinary work has vanished as a direct consequence of the pandemic. An unexpected side effect of this eventuality has been the much-needed time in which to compile this anthology.

For a room, I am indebted to Lee Schofield of RSPB Haweswater who has invited me to come and write at the society's remote and exquisitely located headquarters in ancient Naddle Forest while the regular staff are furloughed. The view from my room is of two mighty, creaking ash trees. When I first arrived here the air was bright with cuckoos and the sunlight seemingly interminable. As the long days have slipped into shortening weeks, the soft breath of the canopy has displaced the clattering din of morning birds, until only an occasional curlew, or the giggle of a green woodpecker, or the bleat of a disgruntled lamb interrupt the ear-stopping, tinnitus-inducing silence. A combination of circumstances has enabled me to compile this anthology. Several of the women in this book fulfil Woolf's exacting criteria in a more direct way. In other words, many of these writers, certainly until the last third of the twentieth century, enjoyed a high degree of privilege, though by no means all of them.

In searching for contributions to the anthology I have been interested by how many times the words 'island', 'garden' and 'tree' have appeared. Domestic animals are referred to interchangeably with their wild counterparts. There is an emphasis on the lived experience of 'being outside', rather than on the elusive term 'nature'. Perhaps that is what this book is: a collection of writing by women about the experience of being under the permissive sky rather than beneath a man-made ceiling. And it usually was made by a man or men.

Several of the writers here are gardeners, while others are artists, beekeepers, biologists, farmers, cooks, geologists, mountaineers, natural historians, poets, teachers, theologians and travel writers. Visual artists have also contributed to the anthology, and their work is interleaved throughout the collection. The experience of a working and interactive relationship with the natural world characterises the pages of this book alongside more familiar aesthetic or conservation-weighted responses. Perhaps this is in part because of the size of these islands, where the sea – which for any of us is at most a two-hour drive away – is one of the last unruly places. On land there is little sense of a pristine 'baseline' to which we might return. After all, our islands are mapped, ravaged, evaluated and known. The future of our other-than-human neighbours – animal, vegetable and mineral – is clearly in our hands. Exciting and important choices beckon about how we manage our natural resources, how we farm, where and how we build. It is imperative that we live in 'right relationship', as the eighteenth-century Quaker John Woolman put it, with the world that sustains us, on both the micro and macro level, from our choice of washing powder to the restoration of upland hay meadows.

I often find myself returning to the words of the American writer Emma Marris: 'We are already influencing the whole Earth, whether we admit it or not. To influence it consciously and effectively, we must admit our role and even embrace it. We must temper our romantic notion of untrammelled wilderness and find room next to it for the more nuanced notion of a global, half-wild rambunctious garden, tended by us.' While I still believe in an inclusive ecology, or enfolding net, of which we are but a part, it is also apparent that of all the creatures, plants and features of our land, sky and seas it is our species that has the greatest capacity to act consciously for the good of the whole. To act to conserve, to shape, to change, to renew, to invigorate that which we encounter, not merely to observe and catalogue its fall.

Katharine Norbury
Naddle Farm, Haweswater, August 2020

KATHRYN AALTO

From *Writing Wild* (2020)

I left my sole companion-friend,
To wander out alone.
Lured by a little winding path,
I quitted soon the public road,
A smooth and tempting path it was,
By sheep and shepherds trod.

Dorothy Wordsworth, *Grasmere, A Fragment*

Our journey begins in Wasdale, one of the wildest and most remote valleys in England's Lake District. In the pink predawn light of midsummer, I set out on a narrow lane lined in drystone walls overflowing in fragrant wild honeysuckle and mustard lichen. I pass St Olaf's, possibly England's smallest church, a stone structure set amid a grove of yews in ancient Viking fields.

I lift the latch at a path marked Scafell Pike, step through the gate, and hear the metallic clink break the morning silence. I cross a pasture toward a wooden bridge and onto a narrow ascending gravel trail. The way is up, but Scafell Pike – the peak I'm aiming for and England's tallest – is hidden for the moment by Goat Crag. I walk through Brackenclose then rise along the rocky cascades of Lingmell Gill and higher, through alpine meadows of purple saxifrage and carpets of moss along Brown Tongue. Above me is Black Crag, a peak shorter than my destination, and I stop here to appreciate the pleasures of total silence. When I begin hiking again, I can hear my breath, my feet crunching in the gravel, and somewhere in the clear air above me, a ring ouzel calls, pauses, then sings a warbled song that sounds like marbles in

9

hand. An hour passes, 1,500 feet climbed. Higher up at Lingmell Col, the saddle between Broad Crag and Scafell Pike, Herdwick sheep rest in boulder shadows, where they leave tufts of black and white wool in the parsley fern. Above me, a sharp ping, ping, ping of a buzzard against the fingernail moon. The sun is rising, and soon it will be hot. My legs are strong and I travel light. I don't mean to overtake two sets of highly kitted men – but I do. And I wink at them.

I reach a large debris field of scree and shattered rock and look for cairns to lead me in the final steep climb. I leap across rocks and boulders. There are some final steps onto a platform, and I'm finally standing at the 3,209-foot summit. For a little while, before less early risers make their way up, I am alone on one of the world's most rapturous stages. I take a deep breath, a study in blues all around me. Dark blue lakes. Indigo mountain shadows. Robin-egg sky. It's seven in the morning, and the sun is spreading golden light into these blue hues. I see Helvellyn and Skiddaw and can just make out the Mourne Mountains across the Irish Sea and Snowdonia in Wales to the south. Somewhere in the hills below me is Grasmere, the home of England's most famous poet.

Here on top of Scafell Pike, it's easy to understand why few landscapes are more steeped in literary history than this. It's a place celebrated over 200 years ago by the enraptured band of brothers known as the Lake Poets – Robert Southey, Samuel Taylor Coleridge and William Wordsworth – who all walked and wrote among these hills and vales. In their landmark 1798 *Lyrical Ballads*, Wordsworth and Coleridge sought to overturn the pompous epic poetry that came before them. They were their generation's Sex Pistols and Dead Kennedys, and this was poetry's punk moment. Old subjects were thrown out – sensations were celebrated. In ordinary language and in folk-ballad form, these poets celebrated their own memories, their own emotions, and their own experiences in nature. Their work represents the start of what is known as English Romanticism, the artistic celebration of the individual, nature and the past that extended from the late 1700s to the early 1800s. It was a reaction to the Industrial Revolution and the new faith in reason, science and mathematics embodied by the Enlightenment. Romantics sought a return to individual experiences like awe, horror and fear as a way to cultivate mystery and wonder in an increasingly mechanistic society. In simple terms, you could say that a Romantic preferred to wake to a cockerel than to a clock.

Squinting in the direction of Grasmere, I think of Glencoyne Bay near Ullswater, where Wordsworth and his younger sister Dorothy often walked together. But I haven't climbed all this way to celebrate him – 170 years after his death, he still has his fame, and rightly so. Instead, I'm thinking of Dorothy.

She was born in 1771 in Cockermouth, a market town on the western edge of the Lake District, the middle child and only girl of the five Wordsworth children. Tall and slender, radiating intelligence and kindness, Dorothy's natural disposition and sensibilities mirrored the wild and emotive traits the Romantics esteemed. As a little girl, she wept at first sight of the sea – as an adult, contrasts of colour and texture in fields also moved her deeply. Their mother and father died when the Wordsworth children were young, and the four brothers bounced between relatives, while Dorothy was sent to Yorkshire to live with her mother's cousin. There was 'life before', with her family. And there was 'life after', a time that cut into her well-being and caused a deep sense of abandonment and rejection. Though only 100 miles separated her from them, Dorothy did not see her brothers for ten years. When at last she did, she and William discovered they shared an especially close poetic companionability. They began to walk great distances together, and she became his sensitive sounding board, inspiration, and eventual amanuensis.

One immortal walk took place in the green hills near Ullswater on 15 April 1802. As they strolled around Glencoyne Bay, they encountered a scene of wild English daffodils flouncing with effervescence in the wind along the water. After stopping to marvel at it in the manner of true Romantics, they continued to Dove Cottage, their rose-covered home, surrounded with wild strawberries, primroses, dandelions and foxgloves, all collected by Dorothy on walks in nearby woods. That evening, Dorothy recorded the scene in her journal:

> When we were in the woods beyond Gowbarrow park we saw a few daffodils close to the water side, we fancied that the lake had floated the seed ashore and that the little colony had so sprung up – But as we went along there were more and yet more and at last under the boughs of the trees, we saw that there was a long belt of them along the shore, about the breadth of a country turnpike road. I never saw daffodils so beautiful they grew among the mossy stones about and about them, some rested their heads upon these stones as on a pillow for weariness and the rest tossed and reeled and danced and seemed as if they verily laughed with the wind that blew upon them over the Lake, they looked so gay ever glancing ever changing.

Known today as the *Grasmere Journal*, this collection is one of four small diaries that captured Dorothy's own lyrical voice and acute observations of the natural world from 1800 to 1803. And yet, two years later, William Wordsworth wrote 'Daffodils', arguably one of the most famous poems in the English language:

> I wandered lonely as a cloud,
> That floats on high o'er vales and hills,
> When all at once I saw a crowd,
> A host, of golden daffodils;

Beside the lake, beneath the trees,

Fluttering and dancing in the breeze.

In twenty-four breezy lines, the future poet laureate praises the purity and beauty of nature, reflecting the gospel of Romanticism that 'all good poetry is the spontaneous overflow of powerful feelings'. Beloved around the world, 'Daffodils' captures the essence of the Romantic era – but it doesn't entirely belong to him. How this came to be reveals much about what has changed from the Wordsworths' time to now.

William's Cambridge University education was out of the question for Dorothy as a woman, but her talent and urge to create would not be stifled. She penned poetry, kept journals, and wrote thousands of letters, including 700 we can still read today, which are marked by an acute and cultivated power of observation equal to the many educated men who visited Dove Cottage. She wrote so well that both her brother and Coleridge are known to have lifted phrases from her journals, but Dorothy was more than the wind beneath their wings, and her own work deserves to be celebrated as distinct from her famous brother and his peers.

Dorothy's poetic sensibilities flow throughout her unpretentious journals – both the experimental, sublunary *Alfoxden Journal* and the more revealing *Grasmere Journal*. Neither were intended for publication. Rather, she wrote pieces to share with family and friends about walks and travel to Scotland, the Alps, the Isle of Man, and more. Ernest de Selincourt, one of her earliest posthumous editors and biographers, remarked that Dorothy was 'probably the most remarkable and the most distinguished of English prose writers who never wrote a line for the general public'. But more people have read her uncredited work than they know. In a revision of his book *A Guide through the District of the Lakes*, William Wordsworth includes a letter Dorothy wrote to a friend about her 1818 ascent of Scafell Pike, now considered one of the most notable ascents of a mountain by a woman during the Romantic era. However, he didn't attribute the letter to Dorothy, giving the appearance that it was his own climb and he wrote the piece.

Call it what you will – plagiarism, borrowing, lifting – what was Mr Wordsworth thinking? But we must give some thought to circumstance. Casting a glance back to that time, my guess is that Dorothy simply did not mind – maybe she considered the experiences she wrote about to be mutual. She never sought out notoriety or publication, and brother and sister had a long, respectful and loving sibling relationship. But, as many Romantic scholars have done, we can mind for her and make sure she gets credit where it is due. Her essay enticed me to climb Scafell myself, to see what she saw, and I believe Harriet Martineau, Victorian feminist icon and Britain's first sociologist, would have wanted to know that the ascent, which she republished in her famous 1855 *A Complete Guide to the English Lakes* – the book that eclipsed Wordsworth's as the seminal Lake District walking book – belonged not to William, but Dorothy.

From the village of Rosthwaite, Dorothy set out with her friend, painter and poet Mary Barker, along with Barker's maid, a hired porter, and a Borrowdale shepherd to act as guide, to ascend the mountain. In her signature picturesque and phenomenological style, she observed and recorded the hike as it unfolded in the moment:

> Cushions or tufts of moss, parched and brown, appear between the blocks and stones that lie in heaps on all sides to a great distance, like skeletons or bones of the earth not needed at the creation, and there left to be covered with never-dying lichens, which the clouds and dews nourish and adorn with colours of vivid and exquisite beauty.

On reaching the summit, she burst with delight, 'But how shall I speak of the deliciousness of the . . . prospect! At this time, that

was most favoured by sunshine and shade. The green Vale of Esk –
deep and green, with its glittering serpent stream, lay below us . . .
We were far above the reach of the cataracts of Scaw Fell; and not an
insect there was to hum in the air.' In the delicious silence, her group
begins a conversation about what they see in the distance. Dorothy's
effervescent wonder is contagious.

> While we were gazing around, 'Look,' I exclaimed, 'at yon ship upon
> the glittering sea!' 'Is it a ship?' replied our shepherd-guide. 'It can be
> nothing else,' interposed my companion; 'I cannot be mistaken, I am
> so accustomed to the appearance of ships at sea.' The guide dropped
> the argument; but, before a minute was gone, he quietly said, 'Now
> look at your ship; it is changed into a horse.' So indeed it was; – a horse
> with a gallant neck and head. We laughed heartily; and I hope, when
> again inclined to be positive, I may remember the ship and the horse
> upon the glittering sea; and the calm confidence, yet submissiveness, of
> our wise Man of the Mountains, who certainly had more knowledge
> of clouds than we, whatever might be our knowledge of ships.

After my own summit of Scafell, I stay a few days at an inn near
Wasdale then travel on to Dove Cottage. In one of the front rooms,
I notice the small 1806 silhouette of Dorothy. Like that illusory ship,
which turned out to be something else entirely, this portrait feels
indistinct, an ironic representation for a woman who was, in fact, at
her critical and poetic peak and in her strongest body. Hoping to see
beyond the illusion, I read her original letters sitting in the sunshine in
the garden she tended.

I think how Dorothy was an outlier among women for climbing
the tallest mountain in England, but she was not alone. Women
explored in the company of mothers, aunts and sisters, as well as
husbands, fathers, uncles and brothers. Some climbed with a guide

because they felt threatened, were subject to verbal abuse, and could experience 'reputational anxiety' about walking alone and what that conveyed to others. Dorothy herself received a steady stream of letters from a disapproving aunt and grandmother reprimanding her for her daring habit of walking in the moonlight and at twilight. Women of this era were often trapped by marriage and society into states of dependency, but Dorothy seemed to escape this fate, at least until the end of her long life.

In my visit to Rydal Mount, the house where Dorothy lived with William and his wife and children, I am finally able to shake off the gauzy veil of passing time and sort of lock eyes with this remarkable woman. An oil painting shows Dorothy in her early sixties, seated in a vibrant orange chair with a white terrier at her feet, a scenic lake and mountain just over her shoulder. Her grey-blue eyes are lively. Like many women who spent decades walking, Dorothy lived long, to age eighty-three, and though she was not without health problems, her eyes retained their twinkle. On her lap is a paper notebook, to her side a collection of inkwells and perhaps a canister of opium. She feels vibrant and alive. This woman treaded and recorded our literary landscapes before they were iconic, and she helped make them so. Far more than 'the poet's sister', she is a woman worth her own words: Dorothy Wordsworth, 'mountaineer, diarist, and poet'.

NAOKO ABE

From *'Cherry' Ingram: The Englishman
Who Saved Japan's Blossoms* (2019)

One day in 1923, three years after Ingram had begun his quest to
collect as many different cherry-tree varieties as he could find, he
visited the Greyfriars Estate in Winchelsea, a coastal town in East
Sussex fifteen miles south-east of Benenden. There a fellow cherry
enthusiast called Annie Freeman lived with her barrister husband,
George Mallows Freeman, and their three children. In 1899, when
Annie was visiting Provence, she had met a Frenchman who described
some outstandingly beautiful cherries that he had seen in Japan.
Annie, who had already imported several rare flowering cherries from
Asia, contacted a friend of this Frenchman in Japan. Through him,
she imported another small collection of cherries that matched the
Frenchman's description of these trees.

Among the plants that Annie Freeman had bought were four
cherries, from which Ingram took scions back to the Grange. One was
a variety with large pink, almost purplish, double-blossom flowers that
Ingram later named *Daikoku*. Two others were *Tora-no-o* — a cherry
with single light-pink petals, also known as the Tiger's Tale cherry —
and another single-petalled variety called *Chōshū-hizakura*.

Yet what most attracted Ingram was a fourth cherry with
exceptionally large snow-white blossoms, whose name was unknown.
Growing in Annie's shrubbery, the tree was in a sad state, although a
couple of its boughs were still alive. The blossoms, Ingram reported,
were huge: up to 2.4 inches in diameter, with leaves as long as 7.5
inches. Ingram had never seen this cherry before, but he immediately
recognised 'the rarity and remarkable beauty of this variety' and took
home a few twigs for grafting.

The results were spectacular. And when Ingram's friend, Duke Nobosuke Takatsukasa visited the Grange in the spring of 1925 he dubbed the tree *Taihaku* – the 'Great White Cherry'. The name – '*tai*' (great) and '*haku*' (white) – summed up the size and colour of the blossom, although it didn't quite capture the beauty or sense of tranquillity that had attracted Ingram.

A year later, on the afternoon of Tuesday 20 April 1926, Ingram was sitting in the living room of the cherry expert Seisaku Funatsu, near the Arakawa river in Tokyo. Eating *wagashi,* traditional Japanese sweets, and drinking green tea with his kimono-clad host, he had carefully studied Funatsu's prized album of local cherry blossoms, called *Kōhoku Ōfu* (*Cherry Trees of the* Kōhoku *Region*). It consisted of fifty-seven watercolours of the cherry trees planted along the riverbank.

One by one, Funatsu explained the characteristics of each variety as Ingram, himself an adept painter, marvelled at the minute details in each sketch. Reaching the end of the album, Funatsu left the room and returned carrying a long and narrow *kakemono*, or scroll, which had been hanging elsewhere in his house. He unrolled the scroll carefully. It bore a vivid painting of a cherry plant with immense white blossoms. Funatsu said that the plant was a variety called *Akatsuki*, a relative of the *Ōshima* cherry. But he added wistfully, 'This is the cherry that my great-grandfather painted more than 130 years ago. We used to see it near Kyoto, but it seems to be extinct. I can't find it anywhere any more.'

Ingram gasped. From the size and colour of the flowers to its young copper-red leaves, the blossom on the scroll was undoubtedly *Taihaku*. 'This cherry is growing in my garden in Kent!' Ingram blurted out. It seemed like fate. Funatsu 'was clearly incredulous, but his good manners forbade any open expression of doubt', Ingram wrote.

Funatsu said nothing. He just smiled and bowed deeply and courteously towards the Englishman. 'Piqued by his obvious doubt, I there and then resolved to convince him,' Ingram wrote. He swore to himself that he would return the blossom to Japan, even if Funatsu didn't believe his story. A week later, in his speech to the Cherry Association in Tokyo, Ingram repeated his vow to reintroduce *Taihaku*. He also said he would return *Daikoku*, which he had named after a Buddhist deity featured on Japan's one-yen note. Like *Taihaku*, this variety no longer existed in Japan.

KITTY ALDRIDGE

From *Cryers Hill* (2007)

If he is to enter deep space, Sean must practise being weightless. They walk, Sean and Ann, to the pond by Cockshoot Wood and he throws himself in. Ann waits for him to surface. She hurls in a stone to get his attention but there is no sign of him. She waits, bored. She wonders if he has drowned.

Up he comes then, spluttering like an amateur, half strangled in his blue tubing. Ann loses interest and watches the pond for movement. The surface is grey-green and busy with insects and there is a lapping at the far end.

Legend says the Hughenden Dragon lives here, though no one has ever seen it. Though it is impossible to know what to expect, chances are it won't respond kindly to the arrival of a small trainee astronaut in its depths. The dragon had to be at least 400 years old. One day, in its youth probably, it was said to have frightened a farm girl as she collected water and the girl's neighbours hatched a plan to kill it. The story was well known locally. It was decided the girl would sit at the water's edge, tempting it to the surface, and when it appeared they would leap out from behind briars and set about the serpent with axes. It was said the unfortunate creature let out piteous cries. A woman and a baby were swallowed by a dragon from this very same pond some years after; that is the rumour. It remains unclear whether the original creature had survived or if another was in residence. Nobody took any chances, all the same, until eventually a lack of fresh occurrences faded the collective memory and turned the tales into local legend.

No one on the new Gabbett housing estate knows anything of tales, rumours or legends. On the dust-blown estate there is no collective memory. But for the long-term residents the dragon is a source of civic pride these days – not every village had one, after all. At the Village Association it had become their very own heritage item, their motif, and nobody thought to be fearful, not now in the twentieth century, what with two blokes hoofing about on the moon and a nuclear reactor just a few miles up the A40.

Sean paddles frantically towards the bank, his chin held high out of the water, de-streamlining him, turning his eyes wild; green stuff slimes his hair. It is doubtful at this stage that he will ever manage to break free of the Earth's gravitational field to find himself orbiting around anything other than his own imagination. He scrabbles at the bank, strangled by tubing, tearing at pond rushes, while Ann closes her eyes against the sun. She knows it is best not to interfere with his preliminary training. She senses this would be detrimental in the long run; sometimes you have to be cruel to be kind. She holds out her palms to the butterflies tumbling around the tall weeds. A small blue one lands on her thumb and she calls out to Sean to look and see. She sidles over, cupping her other hand over it. 'Look! Look! It likes me, see?' Sean has managed to get himself onto the bank, and is wet and dazed and wrapped in blue tube like an alien birth. He is on his back, gazing up at Ann through his slimed fringe. 'Ahh, look, Sean, look.' Sean stares up at the inverted vision of her bare legs and softly astonished face, at her curled hands, and the bright blue butterfly growing out of her thumb. 'Ahh, look. I love you, do you love me?' she asks the insect. 'It loves me, look.' And Sean looks and sees. But he loved her first; he loved her before the butterfly; he loves her more than any insect ever could; he loves her so much he cannot speak to tell her.

MONICA ALI

From *In the Kitchen* (2009)

The morning sun scattered sugar here and there across the moors, which stretched out ahead, white glowing spills among the russet tones of green and brown. Gabriel squinted into the distant cut and swathe. This gently sloping, ever-reaching land was filled with a vague kind of longing. The peaty ground was soft beneath his boots. The red winter bracken shouldered the wind.

It was Christmas Eve. They used to walk up to the tower on Christmas Eve and the whole of Blantwhistle, it seemed, would be there, airing the children, the old folk, the dog.

'Where's everyone gone?' said Gabe.

Ted leaned two-handed on his walking stick. 'Shops. Shopping, I'll be bound.'

'We can stop here if you like.'

Gabriel had driven them up (raised Ted's old Rover from under her shroud) and parked in a lay-by. They'd walked scarcely a third of a mile.

'Give over wi' that fussing,' said Ted. But he stayed where he was.

Gabriel drifted off the path. He crossed some rocky ground. 'Back in a minute,' he called to Ted, and hoped the words weren't blown away.

It was all bracken. Where was the heather? When he was a boy there was bell heather here, and cross-leaved heath and of course there was ling – common heather – everywhere. In summer there'd be great purple carpets of the stuff. After they'd moved to Plodder Lane, they'd march out of the garden, him and Jen, across the cow fields, across Marsh End, over by Sleepwater Farm, and run on the moors. They'd not be missed till Dad got home. He'd take a stick to the nodding cotton-wool heads of the cotton grass. Jenny collected bilberries and tart little cloudberries and sometimes she found crowberries, hard and black, and didn't eat them but drew with them on a rock. And there was lime-green sphagnum that sprang up when you pushed it down and the scattered yellow stars of the bog asphodel, and the sundew that ate insects, and if you were lucky you could lie on your belly in the soft and soggy ground and watch a butterfly slowly dissolving in the plant's red and yellow hairy mouth.

There was nothing now but coarse grass and ferns. Nothing to keep a boy here. When they were kids they'd spend a summer's day. If he came back in the summer maybe he'd find berries and flowers.

They'd always keep Twistle Tower in view because they knew the way home from there, and it was easy to get lost on the moors. There was a proper name for the tower but he couldn't remember it. He remembered pretending it was a space rocket, eighty-five feet of stone topped with a glass-domed cockpit. You could see Morecambe Bay from up there. You could see Blackpool and the Isle of Man. When the mist wasn't in, which it usually was. He'd smoked his first cigarette in the dank stairwell, French-kissed Catherine Dyer against the two-feet-thick stone wall, counted the eight sides, sixteen windows, ninety-two steps, one hundred and fifteen rivets so many times he would take the numbers to his grave.

Sometimes Mum forgot they were playing in the garden and went out and locked all the doors. There was always Twistle Tower and they'd go in out of the rain, though you could sit there a month and not get dry. If he planned ahead he'd take his binoculars and look for birds. In summer you'd see all sorts – curlews, skylarks, lapwings. They didn't interest him so much. Of course he liked the merlins, the buzzards and peregrines, the thrill of spotting a hen harrier or sparrow hawk. He'd seen a golden eagle once.

Today he'd not seen so much as a pipit, not heard the red grouse call go-back-go-back. In London he hardly saw a sparrow, a blackbird. From pigeons there was no escape.

Gabriel thought he should turn, find Ted, but the moor pulled him on a little further and a little further yet. He saw that there was heather among the bracken and large stands up ahead. Now that he had stopped looking, he saw the place was not so barren after all. Creeping dogwood in its purple winter foliage ran under his feet, and there was a clump of bog rosemary, here a juniper bush. He reached a track and looked down the spine of a shallow valley, the moors rising like soft gold wings, and the sun beat white-pale in the sky, sending flurries of light down on the hillsides and over the far clouds that started to roll in now, dark and low.

Gabe breathed deeply and gave himself to a single thought. *Yes, I am alive.*

ELIZABETH VON ARNIM

From *All the Dogs of My Life* (1936)

Pincher took me to London, and Knobbie brought me away. It looked as if I were beginning to be led about by dogs.

My relations, indeed, pointed this out, and expressed regret. They used the word infatuation, and said infatuation was always a pity. But I paid no heed, for he who heeds relations won't get anywhere, not even into the country, and on getting into the country I was absolutely bent.

This time, though, I didn't go farther than twenty miles out, so that I would still be able to visit friends for a few hours, should I have a relapse into gregariousness; yet, although so near London, the effect of being in pure country was complete, because the house, standing alone, faced golf links, and on its other three sides was surrounded by woods.

In these woods were endless safe paths for Knobbie, where she would never meet a soul, while for Pincher there was a roomy garden in which he could lie and pant comfortably, with ancient trees to shade him should he be inconvenienced by the sun. The day we took possession there was no sun, but since sun, sooner or later, is bound to shine, its absence didn't at the moment disturb me, and we settled in in good humour – at least, Knobbie and I did, and I think Pincher too must have been in some sort of good spirits beneath his outer apathy, for the first thing he got was an extra-big dinner.

I thought it a very charming little house. It breathed peace and silence. The woods, dressed for autumn, brooded close over it at the back, and in front stretched the golf course, empty that day because of a fog. Outside the sitting-room window was a dovecote, filled, by the same friend who had given me my dogs, with doves whose cooings were to soothe me while I worked; and on the hearth-rug, also a present from this same — ought I to call him zoological? — friend, sat a coal-black cat for luck, which at once took to Knobbie, and began diligently tidying and washing her ears.

Tea was brought; curtains were drawn; the firelight danced; the urn hissed. We might have been a picture in a romance, when the pen, swerving a moment aside from high life, pauses on a simple cottage interior. And while I ate muffins — things I had never been able even to look at in London, but now swallowed with complacence — and Pincher sat in front of me watching every mouthful, just as though he hadn't had an enormous dinner a few minutes before, and the cat, finished with Knobbie's ears, deftly turned her over and began tidying her stomach, I did feel that my feet were set once more in the path of peace, and that all I had to do was to continue steadily along it.

POLLY ATKIN

'Fell' (2021)†

The stars come back in the early morning,
in the half light. Corrupted by the rain.
They look for a moment through the broken window
like the fells themselves, just where they should be, with that
rectangular look of theirs, that air of miniature.

A fallen city from a long dead people.

A tumbled henge. Shackles risen.

I am new in my body, suddenly storied.
The idea of asterism mapped onto asterism.
Visually obvious. Distinct in the season.
Ludicrous, unrepeatable myth.

JANE AUSTEN

From *Pride and Prejudice* (1813)

Before they were separated by the conclusion of the play, she had the unexpected happiness of an invitation to accompany her uncle and aunt in a tour of pleasure, which they proposed taking in the summer.

'We have not determined how far it shall carry us,' said Mrs Gardiner, 'but, perhaps, to the Lakes.'

No scheme could have been more agreeable to Elizabeth, and her acceptance of the invitation was most ready and grateful. 'Oh, my dear, dear aunt,' she rapturously cried, 'what delight! what felicity! You give me fresh life and vigour. Adieu to disappointment and spleen. What are young men to rocks and mountains? Oh! what hours of transport we shall spend! And when we *do* return, it shall not be like other travellers, without being able to give one accurate idea of anything. We *will* know where we have gone – we *will* recollect what we have seen. Lakes, mountains, and rivers shall not be jumbled together in our imaginations; nor when we attempt to describe any particular scene, will we begin quarrelling about its relative situation. Let *our* first effusions be less insupportable than those of the generality of travellers.'

ANNA LAETITIA BARBAULD

'Inscription for an Ice House' (1795)

Stranger, approach within this iron door
Thrice locked and bolted, this rude arch beneath
That vaults with ponderous stone the cell; confined
By man, the great magician, who controuls
Fire, earth and air, and genii of the storm,
And bends the most remote and opposite things
To do him service and perform his will,
A giant sits; stern Winter; here he piles,
While summer glows around, and southern gales
Dissolve the fainting world, his treasured snows
Within the rugged cave. Stranger, approach!
He will not cramp thy limbs with sudden age,
Nor wither with his touch the coyest flower
That decks thy scented hair. Indignant here,
Like fettered Sampson when his might was spent
In puny feats to glad the festive halls
Of Gaza's wealthy sons; or he who sat
Midst laughing girls submiss, and patient twirled
The slender spindle in his sinewy grasp;
The rugged power, fair Pleasure's minister,
Exerts his art to deck the genial board;
Congeals the melting peach, the nectarine smooth,
Burnished and glowing from the sunny wall:
Darts sudden frost into the crimson veins
Of the moist berry; moulds the sugared hail:
Cools with his icy breath our flowing cups;
Or gives to the fresh dairy's nectared bowls

A quicker zest. Sullen he plies his task,
And on his shaking fingers counts the weeks
Of lingering Summer, mindful of his hour
To rush in whirlwinds forth, and rule the year.

CICELY M. BARKER

'The Daisy Fairy' (1923)

Come to me and play with me,
I'm the babies' flower;
Make a necklace gay with me,
Spend the whole long day with me,
Till the sunset hour.

I must say Good-night, you know,
Till tomorrow's playtime;
Close my petals tight, you know,
Shut the red and white, you know,
Sleeping till the daytime.

ELIZABETH BARRETT BROWNING

'Flush or Faunus' (1850)*

You see this dog. It was but yesterday
I mused forgetful of his presence here
Till thought on thought drew downward tear on tear,
When from the pillow, where wet-cheeked I lay
A head as hairy as Faunus, thrust its way
Right sudden against my face, – two golden-clear
Great eyes astonished mine, – a drooping ear
Did flap me on either cheek to dry the spray!
I started first, as some Arcadian,
Amazed by goatly god in twilight grove;
But, as the bearded vision closelier ran
My tears off, I knew Flush, and rose above
Surprise and sadness; thanking the true PAN,
Who, by low creatures, leads to heights of love.

---

* In 1933 Virginia Woolf published *Flush: A Biography*, being a fictional account of the world through the eyes of Barrett Browning's beloved cocker spaniel.

AMY-JANE BEER

From *The Flow: A Return to the River* (2022)

Compared to their craggy Lakeland neighbours, the Howgill Fells are voluptuous. Where they stretch out between the valleys of the Lune and Rawthey, the bones of the Earth seem well fleshed, despite every curve along the tops being shaven by grazing. Lower down there are steep gills – damp, intimate, inguinal crevices, where life sprouts, water seeps and rivers fill.

On a cold, poster-bright morning, I step off tarmac onto a farm track and head downhill. The change in gradient shifts tension from one set of walking muscles to another and, almost immediately, I hear running water. It's just a tiny rush-lined beck, but now I'm following it, I feel as though this thing I've resisted for nearly seven years has begun.

Autumn is well advanced here. The dog roses and hawthorns, heavy with fruit, have shed their leaves and the house sparrows in the farm hedges are unusually quiet. While the rosehips are scarlet and vital-looking, the haws are the colour of blood spilled in the dirt, with a scabby crust on each little gout. I wonder if the sinister reputation of hawthorn stems in part from the appearance of the fruit. The contrast between wholesome hip and ominous haw intrigues me – I know I'm not the first to notice – and I pocket a little bunch of each as a reminder to read up on their multi-faceted symbolism.

I continue around a bend, and reach the river. There's a footbridge next to a ford, and a yellow sign reading 'Danger of Death', a warning about overhead power lines. I turn my head so I don't have to see it, and give my attention instead to the water. It's sliding under the bridge, all of a piece and so smoothly it seems a solid, impossible thing. Staring too long at the ceaseless issuing of water, you could fear that the Earth is running herself dry.

The water level is low, way too low to navigate by boat. It takes heavy rain to bring the levels up here and plans to paddle these small catchment rivers always had to be made at the last minute, mooted twelve hours ahead on the basis of a weather forecast, but not firmed up until we gathered, early, kayaks strapped ready on roof-racks. Then we'd agree a destination and drive, hopping out to gauge water levels. In ten years of running rivers all over the north of England, however, the Rawthey eluded me. It was never quite in condition, or its sister, the Clough, looked better, or we'd end up heading downstream to the Lune. This always remained a river for another day.

I'm approaching my destination from upriver, because I don't want to take the route the emergency services took, from a layby, across a field, lugging their equipment. I want to go the way my friend Kate did, when she and three friends, all experienced kayakers, passed this way downstream on the first of January, 2012.

Kate was larger than life without trying. Brown eyes, hair she never grew long, though her fringe sometimes swept past her brows, prompting her to rake it back often. Her hands were large and strong, the nails neatly manicured but unvarnished and she had the seemingly effortless good posture that befits a physiotherapist and Pilates devotee. She made clothes look good but wore the same few, well-chosen items nearly all the time. Her smile was huge and easy.

I pass dense thickets of gorse, some of it in flower – dazzlingly yellow in the strong light. The hawthorns on the other side of the path mark a field boundary, and they are *old* – without their leaves they look sparse and windbitten, but sturdy, having grown slowly, carefully. Several have lost their bark, and the wood is bleached and skeletal. A robin is singing. Robins are always singing.

The river below me is silver in the sunshine. I can hear it – the continuous background rush of fast-flowing water. I pass another farmhouse and the path heads downhill. It's steep and gravity tugs until I'm among trees again. The oaks, beeches and sycamores are still in leaf, golden and fox red, but the air pings with the alarm calls of blackbird and wren.

The river has entered a gorge below me. I know this is close to the place, that the water I can hear must be *that* rapid. The birds keep shouting.

Why don't you just *go away?*

And then I'm past the gorge, still walking, telling myself I'll find a bridge, and go back up the other side. I cross a field, and negotiate a farm gate where a shepherd is expertly manhandling recalcitrant sheep. I fuss his dog.

A grand day.

Aye, have to make the most of 'em.

Yes, we do.

When I rejoin the river, it's quiet, with no sign of any turmoil upstream, and I imagine that on New Year's Day, it must have looked much the same. Flowing on, with the light gleaming, just as beautifully as before. The sound as consistent as before.

I cross a stone bridge and hike back up the valley road. I'm resigned now to walking from where the paramedics parked, across the field where the air ambulance must have landed. It's easy enough to clamber over a fence and slither down the riverbank. Before I've gathered my thoughts I'm in the gorge. The birds on the wooded crag opposite might still be calling, but I can't hear them over the rush of the water. Shafts of sun still reach down though, lending brilliance to the flow.

This should be the place. The river is constricted – only about five metres wide. But there's more than one rapid and I'm confused because I thought I'd just *know*. From a kayaking perspective they're not steep, but intricate and technical. But the lack of water today makes it hard to read the flow. I can picture Kate in the eddy above, enjoying the winter greenery of moss and fern and lichen and woodrush. Maybe she'd have scooped up a handful of water to splash her face.

It's not just water though. You can see that simply by looking. Little by little, the hills are letting themselves go, and relinquishing life they have fostered. The peaty tint is a geological and biological essence of what was once living matter, but which no longer belongs to anything other than the river.

Kate had announced she was pregnant around the time my husband Roy and I started trying for our own baby, but there ended up being a two-year age gap between our children. I sought her advice often, and two pieces of wisdom stuck. The first was 'Embrace the mess', and has stood us in good stead, applied to all aspects of life, not just the sticky and exhausting business of childrearing. The second was, and is, harder. 'When a baby is born,' she once said, 'that's only the start of your separation, so you have to start getting used to it. You have to put your baby in the arms of others and let them love him too. Because though our kids feel like part of us, they are people in their own right and they need us to teach them how to be that. Our job as mothers is partly to make ourselves redundant, when our hearts want the opposite.' I definitely wanted the opposite. I still do. I want my son to stay close. To know he is loved beyond measure. But, like Kate's daughter, he's an only child. And seeing them both grow and connect at their root-tips like trees in a forest, befriending the world beyond their immediate family, I know Kate would be proud.

Kate had a heart like a rising sun: huge, touching everything, but her eye was always on the horizon, which she had sailed around the world in pursuit of – racing, not cruising. After my son Lochy was born, I wanted to start exercising as soon as possible, and I sought her advice about regaining some shape. I remember her guiding my fingers so I could feel the gaps where my abdominal muscles had separated to accommodate the baby, and warning me against running until they rejoined. There was nothing to stop me paddling though, within reason, and I was back on the water as soon as the C-section scar had healed. Several others in our circle were managing the same juggling act. Roy and I took our regular summer trip to the French Alps when Lochy was seven months – friends took turns to mind him while we paddled. Babies and kayaking – we could have both. We did have both.

As I confront the bones of the rapids in the gorge, my gaze is drawn from feature to feature, trying to make sense of it, envisaging ways things might have gone wrong. That rock? That crease? Or that one? In this low water I can't even see what the line – the optimal route – might be. Everything is flowing easily, little swirls of spume making patterns on the surface, as though it's being stirred by an invisible wand.

I don't really know what to do, now I'm here. I didn't bring flowers. It seems I didn't even bring words. But there are the two small bunches of berries in my pocket. Scarlet hips and crimson haws. I weigh them in my hand, then toss them into the water. The hips glow so brightly in the sun I can see them bobbing until the river curves slightly and they are carried out of sight. I start picking my way downstream. It's not easy. The bank is too steep to move on, so I'm climbing over mossy rocks at the water's edge, grasping roots. I pass the end of the second rapid, and realise only then that there is another below. The gorge narrows though, and I can't get to it, so I climb up and around, descending towards a wide pool a little further on. As I begin to scramble down again, I glimpse the rapid below, and it stops me in my tracks because I know that *this* is it. It's a mean, tight space, with water piling in, relentlessly beating itself up, with a whole tree trunk stuck in it, roots uppermost. Sunlight doesn't reach in there and individual sounds are kettled by rock walls and subsumed into white noise.

Kate was under there for ten minutes.

I flinch and swear. I don't want to be here and I wonder what good I thought coming would do.

I turn my back but I can't unsee it.

I find my way to the edge of the pool, and crouch on a rock shelf at the edge. This must be where they got her out, though how they managed it I can hardly fathom. They didn't stop CPR until the paramedics came.

I wash my face, smelling the cold water and feeling it tingle on my skin. There's almost more nostalgia in the sensations than I can bear. I realise how much I miss the water – *this* kind of water, icy, earthy and aerated, fresh and yet so very old.

I have tried to go back. We've used the open canoe on placid water. But when it comes to white water, the paddling that always had my heart, I can't trust my vision to stay clear, my muscles not to flood with adrenaline, my heart not to race. For years, my kayak sat in the garage. Then it went to a friend's barn; I guess it's still there.

As the water trickles down my neck and evaporates from my face, I look down… and there is something strange. At first I think it's a fine thread – fishing line, or a strand of spider silk maybe, floating on the water. It moves slowly, sinuously, then disappears. I cock my head and there it is again, catching the light. I reach out to touch it, but there's only water. But I can still see it, very clearly now, and I realise that it's not just on the surface. It's a veil, visible only as a perturbation of light, extending down into the depths. It has no substance and fragments of detritus in the water pass through it, as do my fingers, and it reforms when I take my hand away.

It dawns on me that I'm seeing an interface between flows – an eddyline. In my kayak, I used to visualise eddylines as curtains or walls – obstacles that required carefully judged power and angle to cross safely, without the tension between one flow and the other forcing me off line, or even into a capsize. But I don't recall ever *seeing* one. I've seen surface flows colliding, curtains of bubbles, swirls and humps of water – other clues to where the flows meet. But never this perfect, precise boundary between flow and return. The currents here are slow, so slow that the water appears almost still. There's no disturbance at the surface to disrupt the slight refractions that are allowing me to perceive something that is normally invisible. It's like seeing the join between past and present, life and death. The tiniest nothing between enormities. The longer I look, the more of these subtle features I see. Micro-eddies, upwellings, swirls and little dimples. The latter must be the result of vortices, tiny ones, tugging at the surface from below. They look like fingerprints, as though someone had just touched the water and it remembered. They move slowly, sometimes bumping into each other as they drift downstream. It's mesmerising, weird and comforting, this layering, mobile architecture.

I remember the few hours just before the call that New Year's Day, when I didn't know. There was a pearly pink sunrise, a run up Arnside Knott, and lunch in a pub in Ambleside. For some reason I always picture the carpet there, from which I'd done an inadequate job of cleaning up the pasta and vegetables scattered by a less-than-cooperative eleven-month-old. But then there was a phone call, a drive back to Yorkshire in the dark, to a house packed with a lot of the people we loved best, and the waiting for news of a miracle from the intensive care unit. Cold water can slow things down, can't it? We'd all heard stories of hypothermia lending a lifeline, reducing the brain's roaring demand for oxygen. And this was Kate. Kate who never gave up.

Kate who would never dream of leaving early.

We waited two days, dossing down together. Candles burned to stubs, more were lit. We cuddled our babies and hugged each other. We drank a lot. Then the call came from Kate's husband. A few strangled words, two unfinishable sentences. The world changed shape. Important parts ripped and splintered.

For a few weeks it seemed we just trod water. Did what had urgently to be done. The funeral was a riot of colour, a river of stories, an ocean of love. Weeks became months and by the time I realised life was moving on, it was like coming ashore after a long time at sea, landmarks in familiar places, solid ground under my feet, gravity doing what it always does. But by then I had sea-legs, and solid ground felt insecure. And of course I didn't have the worst of it. Kate's family were all doing her proud, leading by example. And while I felt sure that there must be more I could do for them, and for the friends who had tried so hard to keep Kate with us, the best I could manage was curb the rage at my inability to intervene in events that had already happened, to make things better.

Kate's husband shared a letter with us many months later, from one of the recipients of Kate's donated organs. And then I wept properly, privately, almost gratefully. Because there she was, somehow, making things better herself.

I've always meant to visit the place. I thought that it might be on an anniversary of some sort – that a *right* time would somehow suggest itself. But it never has, or I haven't been brave enough. Today I just happened to be in the area and it seemed easier somehow, for not being planned and not telling anyone. I've tricked myself into it. But the fact that it's autumn does feel apt. Fecundity and decay press in from either side, channelling life into a silver stream with death on one bank, renewal on the other.

I'm halfway back to the car when I realise I didn't do the thing I think I must have meant to do. I didn't say goodbye. And I didn't say it because Kate wasn't there. Of course she wasn't. There was just water, moving on.

She'd regret that I've barely sat in my boat since, but perhaps she'd understand why, after years of seeking adventure with a spring in my step, I started baulking. Partly of course, it's being a parent, partly it's growing older, and becoming much less fit. There are plenty of adventurous mums out there, still hitting it hard. Maybe I've just come to a point from which I don't need to be pushing further, daring more. I can look back on the endorphin-soaked days with pleasure. I can see where I've been, and yes, it's a great view. But Kate I believe, would tell me not to spend too much time looking back. She would insist that the more intriguing vista is the new one just coming into view. It's hummocky and cryptic, and something is pulling, gently, but insistently, like gravity. Resisting gravity is easier than you might imagine. You can do it with a puff of breath that keeps thistledown aloft. But for now, the river and I seem to want to just go with it.

To just flow.

ISABELLA BEETON

From *Mrs Beeton's Book of Household Management* (1861)

MUSHROOM KETCHUP.

Ingredients.—7 lbs. of flap mushrooms, ½ a lb. of salt. To 1 quart of mushroom liquor add ½ an oz. of allspice, ½ an oz. of ground ginger, ¼ of a teaspoonful of pounded mace, ¼ of a teaspoonful of cayenne.

Method.—Mushrooms intended for this purpose should be gathered on a dry day, otherwise the ketchup will not keep. Trim the tips of the stalks, but do not wash nor peel the mushrooms; simply rub any part not quite clean with a little salt. Place them in a large jar, sprinkling each layer liberally with salt. Let them remain for 3 days, stirring them at least 3 times daily. At the end of that time, cook them very gently either on the stove or in a cool oven, until the juice flows freely, then strain the mushrooms through a clean cloth, and drain well, but do not squeeze them.

Replace the liquor in the jar, add allspice, ginger, cayenne and mace as stated above, place the jar in a saucepan of boiling water, and cook very gently for 3 hours. Strain 2 or 3 times through fine muslin when quite cold, pour into small bottles, cork securely, and store for use.

How to Distinguish Mushrooms from Toadstools.—The cultivated mushroom, known as *Agaricus campestris*, may be distinguished from the poisonous kinds of fungi by its having pink or flesh-coloured gills, or under side, and by its having invariably an agreeable smell, which the toadstool has not. Mushrooms are like a small round button, both the stalk and head being white. As they grow larger they expand their heads by degrees into a flat form, the gills underneath being first of a pale flesh colour, but becoming, as they stand longer, dark-brown or blackish. Nearly all the poisonous kinds are brown, and have in general a rank and putrid smell. Edible mushrooms are found in closely fed pastures, but seldom grow in woods, where most of the poisonous sorts flourish.

GERTRUDE BELL

Letter to her father, Sir Hugh Bell (1874)[†]

July 21st 1874 Red Barns Coatham, Redcar.

My dearest Papa.

Pilcher has got on very well with our garden, he has done half the kitchen garden. The hens are not laying us any eggs. We went and waded yesterday and we are going to wade today. Stevie was here yesterday. We waded in the morning and Stevie came in the afternoon and he had tea with us. The rabbits are getting on very well. Will you write us a letter in return? We have been very good while you have been away. Maurice every day at dinner asks why the pineapple isn't coming in. Stevie stayed to have tea with us. He soon after went away[;] a little time before tea we tried to harness Sherwyn[?] in the cart but we didn't succeed. After we wash this evening we are going to run in the sands barefoot. We shall go out with our spades and pails and boats and we shall dig a hole and let the water run in: before that when we have dug our hole we shall put water in to make it muddy, cause we think its better to have our own water first before the sea runs in with its own strength and power. Stevie was very amused with the Kittens. We had the Rabbits as well and they stayed very quiet in the cart all tea time: we had tea out of doors. We put them on to Stevies crib too. He was very amused with them – one thing particuly [sic] we put the Kittens in and directly we'd got them in they ran away and Stevie laughed very much.

FRANCES BELLERBY

'All Soul's Day' (1970)

Let's go our old way
by the stream, and kick the leaves
as we always did to make
the rhythm of breaking waves.

This day draws no breath –
shows no colour anywhere
except for the leaves – in their death
brilliant as never before.

Yellow of Brimstone Butterfly,
brown of Oak Eggar Moth –
you'd say. And I'd be wondering why
a summer never seems lost

if two have been together
witnessing the variousness of light,
and the same two in lustreless November
enter the year's night...

The slow-worm stream – how still!
Above that spider's unguarded door,
look – dull pearls... Time's full,
brimming, can hold no more.

Next moment (we well know,
my darling, you and I)
what the small day cannot hold
must spill into eternity.

So perhaps we should move cat-soft
meanwhile, and leave everything unsaid,
until no shadow of risk can be left
of disturbing the scatheless dead.

Ah, but you were always leaf-light.
And you so seldom talk
as we go. But there at my side
through the bright leaves you walk.

And yet – touch my hand
that I may be quite without fear,
for it seems as if a mist descends,
and the leaves where you walk do not stir.

CLAIRE-LOUISE BENNETT

From *Pond* (2015)

A leaf came in through the window and dropped directly onto the water between my knees as I sat in the bath looking out. It was a thoroughly square window and I had it open completely, with the pane pushed right back against the wall. It was there, level with the rim of the bath – I didn't have to stretch or lean; it was almost as if I were in the coniferous tree that continued upwards, how tall. There was a storm, an old storm, going around and around the mountain, visiting the mountains again perhaps after who knows how long, trying to get somewhere, going nowhere.

And to begin with nothing, just a storm, nothing original, nothing I hadn't heard before. I went about my business for a while until it struck me I should disconnect the cables and thus the lights went out on those small matters I endeavour to attend to and I didn't mind very much because the matters were straightforward and already composed and yet were at the same time quite beyond me at that moment. It was of no great consequence really. I got into the water which had been waiting for some time, the temperature loosening, and then I had the idea about opening the window wide, which I did with no difficulty despite the rigid appearance of the clasp.

And then, from there, it was possible, unavoidable really, to listen to the storm going around and around, and I knew it was an old one that had come back – it seemed to know exactly where it was and there was such intimacy in its movement and in the sound it made as it went along and around and around. Yes, I thought, you know these mountains and the mountains are familiar with you also. No – it was not raging, it was not simply raging – I heard no element of anger in fact. How loud it was and yet so fragile, stopping and starting for a long time – it didn't know where to begin, but it was by no means frantic, either, not at all. I moved a web of lather about the roots of my hair and became immersed in the body of the storm; I knew its structure, saw its eyes, felt its past, and I empathised with its entreaty. It had style, it was experienced; and it came back, and it came back again.

Going around and around, trying to get somewhere, going nowhere. And even though the mountain did nothing the mountain was not impervious to the storm and in fact dreaded its retreat and longed for it always to come back, and to come back again. Then it turned in closer still and the rain came in slants through the wide-open window so I slipped further down into the clouded milky water and held my book way up. It was a book that made me long for men so so far away. The storm carried on into dusk and I stood in my bathrobe at the big window and held onto a cup and saucer with both hands. I knew exactly what was going on. I reconnected the lamps and eventually confronted the row of dresses that hung so very readily along the Japanese screen.

SHARON BLACKIE

'Peregrina' (2019)

O mother of the sea
lend me a wave that is strong and true
to carry me from this Age which unbinds me.

I do not need a ship, mother,
but make it a buoyant swell
to bear me up and float me on the sea's dreaming
then beach me on some lighter shore.

When I land there, mother, give me warp and weft again,
and an urchin quill to remind me
how the prettiest barb can lodge under your skin
and leave you undone.

Only lend me a loom and I will
take up the threads of this unravelled life.
I will weave a braid from three strands of seaweed
I will wind it three times around my finger
I will dig my salt-encrusted hands into the soil
and wed myself to the thirsty
brown roots of a new beginning.

ENID BLYTON

From *The Mountain of Adventure* (1949)

They went up the steep little path. The sun was up higher now and was hot. The children wore only thin blouses or shirts, and shorts, but they felt very warm. They came to a spring gushing out of the hillside and sat down to drink, and to cool their hands and feet. Snowy drank too, and then capered about lightly on his strong little legs, leaping from place to place almost as if he had wings.

'I wish I could leap like a goat,' said Jack lazily. 'It looks so lovely and easy to spring up high into the air like that, and land wherever you want to.'

Philip suddenly made a grab at something that was slithering past him on the warm bank. Dinah sat up at once. 'What is it, what is it?'

'This,' said Philip, and showed the others a silvery-grey, snake-like creature, with bright little eyes.

Dinah screamed at once. 'A snake! Philip, put it down. Philip, it'll bite you.'

'It won't,' said Philip scornfully. 'It's not a snake – and anyway British snakes don't bite unless they're adders. I've told you that before. This is a slow-worm – and a very fine specimen too!'

The children looked in fascination as the silvery slow-worm wriggled over Philip's knees. It certainly looked like a snake, but it wasn't. Lucy-Ann and Jack knew that, but Dinah always forgot. She was so terrified of snakes that to her anything that glided along must belong to the snake family.

'It's horrible,' she said with a shudder. 'Let it go, Philip. How do you know it's not a snake?'

'Well – for one thing it blinks its eyes and no snake does that,' said

Philip. 'Watch it. It blinks like a lizard – and no wonder, because it belongs to the lizard family.'

As he spoke the little creature blinked its eyes. It stayed still on Philip's knee and made no further attempt to escape. Philip put his hand over it and it stayed there quite happy.

'I've never had a slow-worm for a pet,' said Philip. 'I've a good mind…'

'Philip! If you dare to keep that snake for a pet I'll tell Mother to send you home!' said Dinah in great alarm.

'Dinah, it's *not* a snake!' said Philip impatiently. 'It's a lizard – a legless lizard – quite harmless and very interesting. I'm going to keep it for a pet if it'll stay with me.'

'Stay with you! Of course it will,' said Jack. 'Did you ever know an animal that wouldn't? I should hate to go to a jungle with you, Philip – you'd have monkeys hanging round your neck, and tigers purring at you, and snakes wrapping themselves round your legs, and…'

Dinah gave a little scream. 'Don't say such horrible things! Philip, make that slow-worm go away.'

Instead he slipped it into his pocket. 'Now don't make such a fuss, Dinah,' he said. 'You don't need to come near me. I don't expect it will stay with me because it won't like my pocket – but I'll just see.'

They set off up the hill once more, Dinah hanging back sulkily. Oh dear! Philip *would* go and spoil the holiday by keeping something horrible again!

TESSA BOASE

From *Mrs Pankhurst's Purple Feather* (2018)

Etta Lemon

For fifty years, from the 1870s to the 1920s, wild bird species from around the world were systematically slaughtered for the millinery trade in one of the most lucrative commodity markets on earth. At its peak, the trade was worth a staggering £20 million a year to Britain; around £200 million in today's money. In 1891, as the insatiable fashion for feathers stepped up yet another gear, two exclusively women's groups – one in Croydon, one in Manchester – banded together to save the birds. They gave themselves an ambitious title – the Society for the Protection of Birds – and their determination was rewarded with a Royal Charter in 1904. As the RSPB grew in scale and stature, so the men involved attempted to take charge.

One remarkable woman drove the anti-plumage campaign of the RSPB – and she did so quietly and heroically for half a century, leading it to eventual victory. She campaigned so doggedly, and for so long, against what she called 'murderous millinery' that she became known as Mother of the Birds. Her struggle to get the world to care about birds met with as much derision, contempt and indifference as Emmeline Pankhurst's fight for the vote. The millinery and the plumage trade demonised her as a 'frothy fanatic', a 'feather faddist'. Right up until the First World War, the idea of bird protection was as laughable to the general population as the concept of female emancipation.

She stuck to her convictions though, and she won her fight. The law was changed, plumage imports were banned and the strange female fashion for avian adornment receded into the unimaginable past.

Unlike Mrs Pankhurst, she is today a forgotten figure – even within the RSPB. Not a plaque, not a portrait at headquarters, not a mention in the canon of those women who helped shape the twentieth century. Yet she has proved, in her way, to be as deeply influential to the modern psyche.

Her name is Etta Lemon. She was militant right from the start.

Young Etta: 1887
Each little flower that opens
Each little bird that sings
He made their glowing colours
He made their tiny wings . . .

As the congregation of St Margaret's Church warbled its way to the end of 'All Things Bright and Beautiful', a young woman slipped a small notebook and silver pencil from her purse. She surveyed the pews around her. Bonnets, she noted, appeared to be in decline among the fashionable ladies of Blackheath, a fast expanding suburb south of the capital. Hats, on the other hand, were becoming more and more outlandish. The riding bowler, favourite look of the Princess of Wales, had risen upwards into a flowerpot shape, its brim now jutting out over the face. As for the trimmings... Soaring above the congregation was an extraordinary display of nature. Once you honed in on the hats, it really became impossible to look at anything else.

In 1887, the year of Queen Victoria's Golden Jubilee, trimmings included spiders, water beetles, caterpillars, lizards and toads. The hat itself had become an irrelevance: 'simply an excuse for a feather, a pretext for a spray of flowers, the support for an aigrette, the fastening for a plume of Russian cock's feathers', wrote the French art critic and arbiter of taste Charles Blanc. A subtle shift was occurring, away from mid-century modesty to late-century New Woman chutzpah. The hat was becoming a provocative thing of sexuality. 'It is placed on the head, not to protect it, but that it may be seen better,' wrote Blanc. 'Its great use is to be charming.'

Miss Margaretta 'Etta' Smith wasn't one for high fashion. She noted the hats in her church with a dispassionate, forensic eye. Her interest lay in feathers – or rather, in birds. As the congregation filed down the aisle and milled out onto the crest of Belmont Hill, she opened her pocketbook and wrote three words at the top of the page: 'Feather Bedecked Women'. She then jotted rapidly a list of names and species. Peacock, Asian pheasant, eagle, grebe and heron. Hummingbird, swallow, robin, blue tit and chaffinch.

Whole owls' heads with staring glass eyes were all the rage that season, along with the breasts and wings of brightly coloured parrots. Native seabirds, ducks, doves and blackbirds were used to create 'Mercury wings', placed skittishly on either side of a woman's head. Birds-of-paradise were everywhere: whole, halved or simply the flame-coloured, softly cascading tail of the Raggiana species. Miss Smith had a passion for the paradise.

The 'unkempt' look was also in vogue that jubilee year. *Harper's Magazine* suggested rearranging old bird pieces in new positions – perhaps splayed on the crown of the hat, as if fallen straight out of the sky, an 'appealing expression' on its taxidermied face; or else peering over the brim as if in 'earnest incubation' on a nest. *Myra's Journal* was featuring hats 'nearly concealed by their feather ornaments', with green or gold plumes as the favourite colour. Miss Smith's pencil noted other travesties: tiny songbirds trimming bodices, decorating 'novelty' capes or flying out of fur collars.

Once back at the large family home at 46 Lee Terrace, Blackheath, Margaretta Smith would peel off her gloves, sit down at her desk and devote the rest of the morning to her task. Each lady on her list –

and it was always the same offenders – would be written a personal letter describing the horrors behind their fashion accessories. The birds they wore had in all probability been slaughtered during the mating season, she explained. This meant starvation and death for their orphaned fledglings. All but the African ostrich feather met with Miss Smith's condemnation, for ostriches did not (it was hoped) die for their plumes.

Margaretta Smith's admonitory letters fell, one by one, through polished brass letter boxes onto waxed hall floors, where parlour maids or butlers picked them up and placed them on silver trays. They were delivered at breakfast – in bed or in dining rooms – throughout the prosperous parish of St Margaret's.

DOROTHY BONARJEE

'Immensity' (1919)

To-day a little wind is in the grass
So dim you hardly see it pass
Or feel its faint soft lips.
Yet, if you part the slender bright grass-tips
And stooping look quite silently awhile,
You see small insects swiftly file
Along mysterious twisting ways,
Like men in some great thick-meshed forest's maze,
Where closely woven branches hide the sky
And giant trees toss terribly.
So do the grasses toss and sway
And giant blades shut out the day.

ALISON BRACKENBURY

''75' (2019)

The summer that I married
I found the pond which would
be dry one fierce year later,
fish flapping, snatched from mud.
I lay face down on grass.
The evening rose in flies,
cloud deepened on still waters.
It swam straight at my eyes,
from hidden bank or hole,
small whisker, endless ripple.
It was the water vole.

KATE BRADBURY

From *The Bumblebee Flies Anyway* (2018)

She sticks her bum in the air to tell the boys she has mated. Bright orange, it is, orange for Leave Me Alone. It's not a bum, really, but a scopa on the underside of her abdomen, a patch of hairs, or a 'brish', used to collect pollen. And with it held high, like Mary Poppins in full bustle, she flies, unmolested, from one flower to another, gathering food to feed her young.

She visits drumstick alliums and sweet peas, ornamental thistles and perennial wallflower, she's not fussy. She dives down into a thistle head and all you see is a wiggling orange bum as she swims across its anthers. She takes deep drinks of nectar. She doesn't rest, launches herself into the air again, now back to her nest where she regurgitates the nectar and brushes the pollen off her scopa. Mixes them together. She backs out of the nest and then backs into it, lays an egg. Then she returns to the garden. She's looking for something else now. She flies around a bit, lands on a rose leaf. She clasps the leaf between her legs and chews into it, working her way around it as a pair of scissors. She takes seconds to do this, cutting and rolling as she goes, the perfect elliptical disc. Heavy now, her wings have to work harder. She lifts off like a helicopter, brrrrrrrr, the disc of leaf rolled up between her legs, the weight of it pulling her down before she gains enough momentum to lift herself skyward again. She carries it to her nest and fumbles with it, unrolls it and pushes it in. She makes it wet with something like spit, wallpapers it to the sides. She pastes it into the corners. She's locking her baby in. Locking her egg with its parcel of pollen mixed with nectar into its little leafy hollow. She works in a circle, sealing the leaf to the wall so nothing can get in. She inspects her work thoroughly. And then she backs out again, chews a piece of leaf again, flies back again and begins building again. In front of the egg with its pollen and nectar, in front of the leafy hollow, she starts making another cell, another little nest for another little babe. The first section of cylinder is made from four leaves pasted together, like a closed daisy capped off two thirds of the way along its petals, in which the first egg lies. Now she pastes four more leaves to the existing ones, lengthening the daisy. Sometimes she ignores 'Frances' and takes a disc from an evening primrose leaf or even its bloom. The new nest cell is prettier than the last, yellow and green. She returns now to the drumstick alliums and the ornamental thistles, wiggles her abdomen to gather pollen, fills her belly with nectar. She flies back to the nest, deposits her load, flies again to the flowers for more. A few trips now. Then, when the nest is ready, she backs in and lays the third egg. Cut leaves, gather pollen, lay egg, repeat. It takes all day and she's barely started. It takes all day to lay three eggs.

I wait until dusk before I sneak a peek in the bee hotel. It's not nice to disturb them during the day and they can abandon the nest if they feel unsafe. I peel back the viewing panel and see her cylinder of leaves, beautifully arranged in a variety of colours. She's resting in the newest one, pops her head out to see what's going on. It's just me, little leafcutter bee. I'm just seeing how you're doing. She shrinks back into her cylinder and I gently close the door on her, return her to darkness.

There's no way of knowing where she came from. A bee hotel in someone else's garden or an undisturbed cavity in a wall or tree. Only red and blue mason bees nested with me until now, this leafcutter is a pioneer. I'm so happy. The rose, 'Frances E. Lester', is barely six months in the soil, the thistles and alliums there flowering first. Yet here she is, oblivious to the bareness and the smallness, the ungerminated grass seed, the expanse of stones. There's pollen and nectar, the right type of rose leaf, a bee hotel to nest in. She's here, only a few months after the garden was released from the prison of decking. My first leafcutter bee in this half-made mess. My heart swells with pride.

CHARLOTTE BRONTË

From *Jane Eyre* (1847)

October, November, December passed away. One afternoon in
January, Mrs Fairfax had begged a holiday for Adele, because she had a
cold; and, as Adele seconded the request with an ardour that reminded
me how precious occasional holidays had been to me in my own
childhood, I accorded it, deeming that I did well in showing pliability
on the point. It was a fine, calm day, though very cold; I was tired of
sitting still in the library through a whole long morning: Mrs Fairfax
had just written a letter which was waiting to be posted, so I put on my
bonnet and cloak and volunteered to carry it to Hay; the distance, two
miles, would be a pleasant winter afternoon walk. Having seen Adele
comfortably seated in her little chair by Mrs Fairfax's parlour fireside,
and given her her best wax doll (which I usually kept enveloped in
silver paper in a drawer) to play with, and a story-book for change of
amusement; and having replied to her '*Revenez bientôt, ma bonne amie,
ma chère Mdlle Jeannette,*' with a kiss I set out.

The ground was hard, the air was still, my road was lonely; I walked
fast till I got warm, and then I walked slowly to enjoy and analyse
the species of pleasure brooding for me in the hour and situation. It
was three o'clock; the church bell tolled as I passed under the belfry:
the charm of the hour lay in its approaching dimness, in the low-
gliding and pale-beaming sun. I was a mile from Thornfield, in a lane
noted for wild roses in summer, for nuts and blackberries in autumn,
and even now possessing a few coral treasures in hips and haws, but
whose best winter delight lay in its utter solitude and leafless repose.
If a breath of air stirred, it made no sound here; for there was not
a holly, not an evergreen to rustle, and the stripped hawthorn and
hazel bushes were as still as the white, worn stones which causewayed

the middle of the path. Far and wide, on each side, there were only fields, where no cattle now browsed; and the little brown birds, which stirred occasionally in the hedge, looked like single russet leaves that had forgotten to drop.

This lane inclined up-hill all the way to Hay; having reached the middle, I sat down on a stile which led thence into a field. Gathering my mantle about me, and sheltering my hands in my muff, I did not feel the cold, though it froze keenly; as was attested by a sheet of ice covering the causeway, where a little brooklet, now congealed, had overflowed after a rapid thaw some days since. From my seat I could look down on Thornfield: the grey and battlemented hall was the principal object in the vale below me; its woods and dark rookery rose against the west. I lingered till the sun went down amongst the trees, and sank crimson and clear behind them. I then turned eastward.

On the hill-top above me sat the rising moon; pale yet as a cloud, but brightening momentarily, she looked over Hay, which, half lost in trees, sent up a blue smoke from its few chimneys: it was yet a mile distant, but in the absolute hush I could hear plainly its thin murmurs of life. My ear, too, felt the flow of currents; in what dales and depths I could not tell: but there were many hills beyond Hay, and doubtless many becks threading their passes. That evening calm betrayed alike the tinkle of the nearest streams, the sough of the most remote.

A rude noise broke on these fine ripplings and whisperings, at once so far away and so clear: a positive tramp, tramp, a metallic clatter, which effaced the soft wave-wanderings; as, in a picture, the solid mass of a crag, or the rough boles of a great oak, drawn in dark and strong on the foreground, efface the aerial distance of azure hill, sunny horizon, and blended clouds where tint melts into tint.

The din was on the causeway: a horse was coming; the windings of the lane yet hid it, but it approached. I was just leaving the stile; yet, as the path was narrow, I sat still to let it go by. In those days I was young, and all sorts of fancies bright and dark tenanted my mind: the memories of nursery stories were there amongst other rubbish; and when they recurred, maturing youth added to them a vigour and vividness beyond what childhood could give. As this horse approached, and as I watched for it to appear through the dusk, I remembered certain of Bessie's tales, wherein figured a North-of-England spirit called a 'Gytrash', which, in the form of horse, mule, or large dog, haunted solitary ways, and sometimes came upon belated travellers, as this horse was now coming upon me.

It was very near, but not yet in sight; when, in addition to the tramp, tramp, I heard a rush under the hedge, and close down by the hazel stems glided a great dog, whose black and white colour made him a distinct object against the trees. It was exactly one form of Bessie's Gytrash – a lion-like creature with long hair and a huge head: it passed me, however, quietly enough; not staying to look up, with strange pretercanine eyes, in my face, as I half expected it would. The horse followed, – a tall steed, and on its back a rider. The man, the human being, broke the spell at once. Nothing ever rode the Gytrash: it was always alone; and goblins, to my notions, though they might tenant the dumb carcasses of beasts, could scarce covet shelter in the commonplace human form. No Gytrash was this, – only a traveller taking the short cut to Millcote. He passed, and I went on; a few steps, and I turned: a sliding sound and an exclamation of 'What the deuce is to do now?' and a clattering tumble, arrested my attention. Man and horse were down; they had slipped on the sheet of ice which glazed the causeway. The dog came bounding back, and seeing his master in a predicament, and hearing the horse groan, barked till the evening hills echoed the sound, which was deep in proportion to his magnitude. He snuffed round the prostrate group, and then he ran up to me; it was all he could do, – there was no other help at hand to summon. I obeyed him, and walked down to the traveller, by this time struggling himself free of his steed. His efforts were so vigorous, I thought he could not be much hurt; but I asked him the question –

'Are you injured, sir?'

I think he was swearing, but am not certain; however, he was pronouncing some formula which prevented him from replying to me directly.

'Can I do anything?' I asked again.

'You must just stand on one side,' he answered as he rose, first to his knees, and then to his feet. I did; whereupon began a heaving, stamping, clattering process, accompanied by a barking and baying which removed me effectually some yards' distance; but I would not be driven quite away till I saw the event. This was finally fortunate; the horse was re-established, and the dog was silenced with a 'Down, Pilot!' The traveller now, stooping, felt his foot and leg, as if trying whether they were sound; apparently something ailed them, for he halted to the stile whence I had just risen, and sat down. I was in the mood for being useful, or at least officious, I think, for I now drew near him again.

'If you are hurt, and want help, sir, I can fetch some one either from Thornfield Hall or from Hay.'

'Thank you: I shall do: I have no broken bones, – only a sprain;' and again he stood up and tried his foot, but the result extorted an involuntary 'Ugh!'

Something of daylight still lingered, and the moon was waxing bright: I could see him plainly. His figure was enveloped in a riding cloak, fur collared and steel clasped; its details were not apparent, but I traced the general points of middle height and considerable breadth of chest. He had a dark face, with stern features and a heavy brow; his eyes and gathered eyebrows looked ireful and thwarted just now; he was past youth, but had not reached middle-age; perhaps he might be thirty-five. I felt no fear of him, and but little shyness. Had he been a handsome, heroic-looking young gentleman, I should not have dared to stand thus questioning him against his will, and offering my services unasked. I had hardly ever seen a handsome youth; never in my life spoken to one. I had a theoretical reverence and homage for beauty, elegance, gallantry, fascination; but had I met those qualities incarnate in masculine shape, I should have known instinctively that they neither had nor could have sympathy with anything in me, and should have shunned them as one would fire, lightning, or anything else that is bright but antipathetic.

If even this stranger had smiled and been good-humoured to me when I addressed him; if he had put off my offer of assistance gaily and with thanks, I should have gone on my way and not felt any vocation to renew inquiries: but the frown, the roughness of the traveller, set me at my ease: I retained my station when he waved to me to go, and announced –

'I cannot think of leaving you, sir, at so late an hour, in this solitary lane, till I see you are fit to mount your horse.'

He looked at me when I said this; he had hardly turned his eyes in my direction before.

'I should think you ought to be at home yourself,' said he, 'if you have a home in this neighbourhood: where do you come from?'

'From just below; and I am not at all afraid of being out late when it is moonlight: I will run over to Hay for you with pleasure, if you wish it: indeed, I am going there to post a letter.'

'You live just below – do you mean at that house with the battlements?' pointing to Thornfield Hall, on which the moon cast a hoary gleam, bringing it out distinct and pale from the woods that, by contrast with the western sky, now seemed one mass of shadow.

'Yes, sir.'

'Whose house is it?'

'Mr Rochester's.'

'Do you know Mr Rochester?'

'No, I have never seen him.'

'He is not resident, then?'

'No.'

'Can you tell me where he is?'

'I cannot.'

'You are not a servant at the hall, of course. You are—' He stopped, ran his eye over my dress, which, as usual, was quite simple: a black merino cloak, a black beaver bonnet; neither of them half fine enough for a lady's-maid. He seemed puzzled to decide what I was; I helped him.

'I am the governess.'

'Ah, the governess!' he repeated; 'deuce take me, if I had not forgotten! The governess!' and again my raiment underwent scrutiny. In two minutes he rose from the stile: his face expressed pain when he tried to move.

'I cannot commission you to fetch help,' he said; 'but you may help me a little yourself, if you will be so kind.'

'Yes, sir.'

'You have not an umbrella that I can use as a stick?'

'No.'

'Try to get hold of my horse's bridle and lead him to me: you are not afraid?'

I should have been afraid to touch a horse when alone, but when told to do it, I was disposed to obey. I put down my muff on the stile, and went up to the tall steed; I endeavoured to catch the bridle, but it was a spirited thing, and would not let me come near its head; I made effort on effort, though in vain: meantime, I was mortally afraid of its trampling fore-feet. The traveller waited and watched for some time, and at last he laughed.

'I see,' he said, 'the mountain will never be brought to Mahomet, so all you can do is to aid Mahomet to go to the mountain; I must beg of you to come here.'

I came. 'Excuse me,' he continued: 'necessity compels me to make you useful.' He laid a heavy hand on my shoulder, and leaning on me with some stress, limped to his horse. Having once caught the bridle, he mastered it directly and sprang to his saddle; grimacing grimly as he made the effort, for it wrenched his sprain.

'Now,' said he, releasing his under lip from a hard bite, 'just hand me my whip; it lies there under the hedge.'

I sought it and found it.

'Thank you; now make haste with the letter to Hay, and return as fast as you can.'

A touch of a spurred heel made his horse first start and rear, and then bound away; the dog rushed in his traces; all three vanished, 'Like heath that, in the wilderness, The wild wind whirls away.'

I took up my muff and walked on. The incident had occurred and was gone for me: it WAS an incident of no moment, no romance, no interest in a sense; yet it marked with change one single hour of a monotonous life. My help had been needed and claimed; I had given it: I was pleased to have done something; trivial, transitory though the deed was, it was yet an active thing, and I was weary of an existence all passive. The new face, too, was like a new picture introduced to the gallery of memory; and it was dissimilar to all the others hanging there: firstly, because it was masculine; and, secondly, because it was dark, strong, and stern. I had it still before me when I entered Hay, and slipped the letter into the post-office; I saw it as I walked fast down-hill all the way home. When I came to the stile, I stopped a minute, looked round and listened, with an idea that a horse's hoofs might ring on the causeway again, and that a rider in a cloak, and a Gytrash-like Newfoundland dog, might be again apparent: I saw only the hedge and a pollard willow before me, rising up still and straight to meet the moonbeams; I heard only the faintest waft of wind roaming fitful among the trees round Thornfield, a mile distant; and when I glanced down in the direction of the murmur, my eye, traversing the hall-front, caught a light kindling in a window: it reminded me that I was late, and I hurried on.

EMILY BRONTË

'Stars' (1846)

Ah! Why, because the dazzling sun
    Restored our Earth to joy,
Have you departed, every one,
    And left a desert sky?

All through the night, your glorious eyes
    Were gazing down in mine,
And with a full heart's thankful sighs,
    I blessed that watch divine.

I was at peace, and drank your beams
    As they were life to me;
And revelled in my changeful dreams,
    Like petrel on the sea.

Thought followed thought, star followed star,
    Through boundless regions, on;
While one sweet influence, near and far,
    Thrilled through, and proved us one!

Why did the morning dawn to break
    So great, so pure a spell;
And scorch with fire the tranquil cheek,
    Where your cool radiance fell?

Blood-red, he rose, and arrow-straight,
His fierce beams struck my brow;
The soul of nature sprang, elate,
But *mine* sank sad and low!

My lids closed down, yet through their veil,
I saw him, blazing still,
And steep in gold the misty dale,
And flash upon the hill.

I turned me to the pillow, then,
To call back night, and see
Your worlds of solemn light, again,
Throb with my heart, and me!

It would not do – the pillow glowed,
And glowed both roof and floor;
And birds sang loudly in the wood,
And fresh winds shook the door;

The curtains waved, the wakened flies
Were murmuring round my room,
Imprisoned there, till I should rise,
And give them leave to roam.

Oh, stars, and dreams, and gentle night;
Oh, night and stars return!
And hide me from the hostile light,
That does not warm, but burn;

That drains the blood of suffering men;
Drinks tears, instead of dew;
Let me sleep through his blinding reign,
And only wake with you!

NANCY CAMPBELL

'Beachcombers' (2021)[†]

They are prospecting for cowrie beads
amongst green glints of glass salted by years at sea,
flecks of white shell, cartilage splinters,
dangerous fragments of ship shrapnel,
garlands cast for the drowned,
rusted things once useful,
barnacle dust, amber rocks,
stones scored with arteries,
mollusc speckles, iridescent slivers,
squat cochleae polished by hourly washing,
small mouths opening into infinity.
The shell gatherers, mismatched pair
bundled in dark cast-offs
bend down to scan the shingle:
What happened last night on the drifting shale?
Edging forwards – standing up – stooping again –
looking aside at random
they are prisoned between work and hope
and the conflicting scale of the horizon.

Did they find the right curve of the bay,
the very crook of Lothian land
between Eyemouth and the Head,
that legendary place where year on year
the cowries gather?
Grey tides slurp the red rocks
promising, promising

that salt-dusted early whorls
will be held in the hand as labour's solace;
eroded fingerprints, lost seven-years' skin.

KEGGIE CAREW
'The Heron Blood Tulips' (2021)[†]

I am a river monitor. A few years ago the Wiltshire Wildlife Trust advertised for volunteers to attend a training course and I applied. This, I knew, would be my perfect vocation, aside from the joy of poking around in rivers in waders, I would be able to *say* I was a river monitor, removing the dilemma I faced when people asked me what I did. I could tell them about taking three-minute kick samples of the river and counting specific species of invertebrates to give an indication of the health of the ecosystem and water quality. Far more interesting than explaining how most of the time I sat in my shed trying to write books. Even better, I could avoid having to answer the awful question: What's your book about?

So I went on the river-monitoring course and learned to identify the cased caddisfly larvae and the caseless caddis, the mayfly, the blue-winged olive, the olive, the flat-bodied mayfly, the gammarus (freshwater shrimp) and stoneflies. These, apart from the gammarus, were the aquatic larvae forms that would later hatch out into river flies, the food of many freshwater fish. They were also sensitive to pollution, so if their numbers fell below a certain level, an investigation by the Environment Agency would be triggered; they were like canaries of the river. The Welshman who taught our group gave an example of stretch of a river in Wales, where samples were showing no gammarus present after heavy rain. They set up gammarus traps (a netted cage from which the shrimps can't escape), and after every heavy rainfall the gammarus would be dead. This baffled them. Until they traced the cause to a nearby woodyard with uncovered piles of tanalised timber. When the rain washed through the stacks, the toxic chemicals leached out, and straight into the river. Milk was another problem if dairy farms had a spill or cleaned equipment. One teaspoon of milk in your garden pond, he said, can kill everything. The natural bacteria that break down milk use up the oxygen in the water more quickly than it can be replaced – so aquatic life suffocates. Fishermen of course have a particular interest in a healthy river, because lots of river flies mean lots of fish.

So it transpired the next time someone asked me what I did, I was able to say I was a river monitor. We talked about chalk streams, which interested him a great deal because he had one. Let's call him Roger Swift. A few days later an email came in with the subject line: River A— AGM. Roger Swift was inviting me to attend his river association's AGM to 'give us an overview of your interest and work on river entomology'. A ten-minute talk was all he required, and there would be other guest speakers talking about chalk streams, fishing, ecology, hydrology and wild trout. The meeting would be held at a schtonking great house with its own river, lake and cricket ground, even its own chapel, and there would be lunch and wine afterwards. Chalk streams, ecology, wine, lunch… I was in.

A few days later the association's secretary sent me the Agenda, the list of invitees, the address and directions. I checked out the invitees: blimey, two lords and a sir. A doubt crept in… The meeting was to be held in the Shoot Room.

The day before the meeting I decided to take a sample of the River A—. I cleaned my kit and drove to a bridge I knew where a footpath crossed an old water meadow. I scouted for a good entry spot, filled a bucket of river water, set up my inspection tray, grabbed my net and stopwatch and clambered in. I held my net on the bed of the river and gently roughed the gravel upstream with the toe of my boot for a minute, then emptied my catch into the inspection tray. Another

minute sweeping under the river weed, then a minute along the bank
and under some stones. I crouched over the inspection tray, waiting
for it to settle and for its occupants to reveal themselves. I never tire of
it. The rocking-horse motion of the blue-winged olive; the fluttery
leaf-like gills along the body of the olive; the swaying cobra motion
of the flatworms and leeches; the comical shrimps buzzing about the
place, swimming on their sides; their transparent amber bodies, their
whizzing legs. The cased caddis were my favourites. These soft-bodied
creatures make mobile homes from tiny stones and twig debris, which
they stick together with silk from their salivary glands. The minuscule
tubes have a studded, jewel-like quality. They live inside and lug them
about, like a hermit crab. Some enterprising human jewellers provide
caddisfly larvae with precious gem chips, pearls and crumbs of gold to
make their cases, which they collect after metamorphosis and flog for
a fortune. Which has nothing to do with this story, which needs to get
me into the Shoot Room.

I drove through the big iron gates, down the grand drive flanked by
battalions of blood-red tulips, *swish*, onto the sea of gravel outside the
stable block, where I parked amongst the Range Rovers. A man in a
flat cap directed me up some wooden stairs to a long, elegant room.
I glanced around. My shoulders sank, for everyone else was in the
uniform: bracken-tweed shooting coats, green waistcoats, gingham and
Barbours and brushed-cotton Viyella checked shirts, smart blazers and
club ties. Good God, one guy was wearing breeks, those short tweed
trousers with woollen stockings and garters. There was a silver tray
loaded with glasses of elderflower cordial. The long table was set with
water carafes and twenty-five places laid with a single-page agenda by
our name tags. Mine, embarrassingly, read: 'Keggie Carew, Riparian
Entomologist'. I made a circuit of the table. There was a 'Game &
River Keeper', another 'River Keeper', a hydrologist, someone from

the water company, a fish-farm manager, an estate manager, the head gardener, someone from the Angling Trust, the Wildlife Trust, the Wild Trout Trust. One label read, 'Retiring Cormorant Licensee'. All men, but for me and the secretary taking the minutes.

By now of course I had realised I was in a country 'sports' room. I scanned the agenda: Apologies; Chairman's Introduction; Matters arising from last year's meeting; Accounts; Subscriptions; River Reports from the various estates in the area (we're not talking council); then Reports from Guest Attendees. No. 9 on the list was: Cormorants & Predation. I could feel my skin cool with foreboding in the overwhelming knowledge that I was in The Wrong Place.

We began. This river was divided into beats. Of course it was. The first anglers had been through and caught 'reasonable numbers'. One river keeper reported that one fisherman caught nothing and complained, but then he discovered the man was using a dry fly! Ho, ho. (I have no idea, but can imagine.) A stoat had been spotted. I was quickly getting the picture. A stoat in this company was most probably bad. A cormorant did a fly-by. Also bad. A pair of swans were resident but not causing any damage, so the keeper was happy for them to stay. There were three 'persistently active' herons. Uh-oh. And a kayaker. I piped up. What was the problem with a kayaker? He might carry the spores of the crayfish plague. Otters, it was noted, carry them too. Double-bad. And there were a few incidents of poachers...

I began my spiel telling them for the purposes of the meeting I had done a kick sample of the River A— the day before. The red-faced river keeper three seats down shuffled loudly in his seat.

'If I may...' he coughed.

I stopped and turned. I suspected what was coming.

'If I may ask *where* you took this sample and *how* you accessed the river?' he said, his red face reddening.

I told him where.

'Did you have permission?' he asked.

'From whom?' I replied.

'From the landowner,' he snarled politely.

'I did not,' I said. 'I accessed the river from a path by a public bridge at a place where some schoolboys were fishing for minnows.' (I knew that information would annoy him.)

'I don't know if you understand,' he proceeded, 'that the river is easily contaminated by dirty nets, your waders and the like.'

'I was *very* careful, as I was taught, to make sure *everything* was scrupulously clean,' I replied, thinking of all the flying ducks and other creatures that travelled to and from the rivers, along the banks.

Roger Swift motioned me to continue.

I gave my results, explained what invertebrates I was looking for and why, then sat down, a little red-faced myself.

Ten minutes later we got to No. 9: Cormorants & Predation. This began with mink traps. Minks have wiped out the water-vole population, so fair enough; and fair enough too, the man from the Angling Trust who donated a 200-yard stretch to offending poachers – to be managed and stocked by them – and has not suffered any poaching for three years. The thing that was exercising them most was 'cormorant trouble'. There was a simple solution, of course. Shoot them. A licence to shoot ten cormorants had been granted, but this was a drop in the ocean to the 120 reported.

My jaw was beginning to lock. I understood cormorants were supposed to be coastal birds, but they were only up the river because there was nothing for them to eat on the coast, because *we'd* buggered that up for them. I felt for these fine birds, trying to survive, trying to feed their one brood a year, trying to cut out some niche in their impoverished world. But the next thing on the troublesome list was herons. And herons bloody live here. They, as far as I was concerned, were entitled to be on their river. Herons *were* the river, for it was in their bones, and river light filled their eyes. Monitoring the river and keeping it healthy was, I thought, for *all* the indigenous wildlife. For the well-being of the ecosystem and the complex web of life that we were trying to put back together again. Because now we understood that to mess with bits of it messed with the whole thing. And things got out of kilter, and these were fine-tuned, beautiful, elaborate systems where everything was interlinked and had impacts on everything else.

It was noted, eyes cast down, that the authorities required 'proof of evidence' to grant a licence to shoot herons. The red-faced river keeper tittered. I saw a knowing look flicker around the room. Lips folded firmly over smirks. The estate manager opposite me smiled a smile with thunder playing around the edges. And I knew. I shrank into my expensive wooden chair, scanning the men in the circle. Proof of what evidence? That they were herons? That herons ate fish? I looked across at the guy from the Wildlife Trust, but he wasn't saying anything.

In Margaret Atwood's novel *Surfacing,* a dead heron hangs upside down in a tree. The abiding image is of two grey wings wide open as if flight had fallen out of them. Trappers had snared the bird. Tied his feet to a branch with a nylon rope. But why had they strung him up like a lynch victim? Crucified upside-down, until his life had fallen out of his wings.

I love herons. Their bigness, their patience, their creaking pterodactyl flight. Old Franky is his Sussex name, from the sound of his cry: *Frarnk, Fraarnk!* We have a small pond in our garden. Last winter, each morning for a fortnight in the coldest, shortest days, a heron stood hunched over it. She was there at 7.00 a.m. and still there an hour later. Waiting. With her own spear. Even when the pond was frozen, as it often was after a bitterly cold night. Every day the heron flew away empty beaked, for the frogs were staying below, comatose in the mud. I watched from our bedroom window and my heart ached for her. Her sharp round yellow eye with its fathomless black pupil, fixed on the bare larder of our pond. I imagined her stomach twisting in tighter knots. She waited, motionless, except when the breeze picked up her long, soft, grey over feathers.

I left dog food out in vain hope. But herons need heron food and it is hard to conjure it up. I watched heron videos on YouTube to see if there was anything I could do. The babies have mohawk hairdos. In one of the films a young heron, fallen out of its nest, climbed all the way back up the tree, pulling itself up with its unformed wings through the branches. A feat of wonder, and the indomitable instinct for survival. This is what always amazes me: the lionhearts around us, that anything survives at all on the leftover crumbs of our dominion. Atwood's heron was valueless to those who took his life. Here, the value was in what the heron was perceived to be taking from these river keepers and landowners. That the heron's magnificence was not seen, or valued as part of the experience, that eradication was the default, never cohabitation, or that we couldn't factor in the loss from – let's face it – very fat pockets indeed. At least stop playing 'guardians of the countryside', please. For there is little guarded that is not to be murdered later. I could understand the attraction of fishing. I really could. What can be more lovely in this world than a river? Its rush flowing around you, the quiet contemplation, the long braids of crowsfoot with its trapped buttercup flowers, the flash of a kingfisher, the azure blue of a damsel, or a sudden cloud of emerging mayfly – once so common, now such a rare sight. (Us again – phosphate and silt.) There was skill in catching a fish, and it didn't involve gunpowder. The fascination, the knowledge, learning to think like a trout. I got it.

Dry-fly tying was a mysterious art. And frequently the fish got away with their lives – I appreciated it wasn't great being dragged into a suffocating atmosphere by a hook in your mouth, but at least you lived to get dragged out another day. I got fishing. And it has a vested interest in keeping the rivers clean. But I didn't get killing a four-and-a-half-foot-tall feather-boa-ed heron for it. I didn't get that at all.

Three months after the heron's winter visits I came across a skull in the meadow. I held the long stabbing bill, imagining the missile speed of its dagger strike. Heron cell upon heron cell, built up in the nest by both parents' ministrations. The bone had a shell-like lustre. In the eye cavity was the stretched meniscus of dry meat. Tiny feathers were stuck above the eye socket where her long, black extended eyebrow once flicked over the back of her head. I contemplated the heron's skull, remembering her patience and cold hunger. She didn't touch the lifeless dog food, of course. The place I feel this is the centre of my chest. It rises up and clenches its fist tightly, then stays like that in silence.

In the harsh winter of 1963 the heron population fell to just 2,000 pairs.

I sat, quiet as a mole, slunk into myself. Eyes down, fingers fingering my pen. Herons are protected under the Wildlife and Countryside Act, 1981, but that doesn't mean much on private land, where herons and otters mysteriously disappear for no one to know and no one to miss them. I toyed with the notion of speaking out, but I knew my voice would only climb to an alarmingly high register. My tongue would clog in my throat, my brain would forget words, and what, anyway, would be the use of it? I was outflanked and outnumbered. I took the English path and kept my counsel.

The chairman wrapped the meeting up. If anyone saw a silver Subaru Forester and four large guys, the estate manager would like the registration number. And what to do with all the money in the River Association's coffers? *Feed the herons?* He thanked the lord (human, I think) for having us. To a rustling and scraping of chairs we funnelled out towards a table groaning with sandwiches. I love sandwiches. I've always loved sandwiches. And there were cakes and vol-au-vents. A longing look was all they got from me.

'Not staying for lunch?' Roger Swift had caught me speed-walking for the door.

I fumbled an apology, looking at my watch. My legs sped me out into the fresh air and into my little car, which sped me up the long drive, flanked by battalions of blood-red tulips.

•

NATASHA CARTHEW

From *All Rivers Run Free* (2018)

Coast

The first time it happened it was the worst of all times; the young woman told herself it was important not to forget this. The first show of red when it wasn't meant the first moment she glimpsed a chance at happiness, since then it had gotten easier. Familiarity was all; failure a used-to thing another blood-drop in the ocean.

She stood on the furthest stretch of rocks and bent to the surf to place the tiny raft into the water. Floating in the ebb tide the bit of meat didn't look like much at all, the kerosene-soaked rag made more of it than what it was what was it? Not a baby not life in any recognisable form except it came from life: this was the best she could do. The only part of her she could ever hope to leave the cove, she would set it free with fire and water same as all the other little creatures that had come before; she would help it evade the grip of that prison place.

One strike of match she flicked the flame spot on, a practised shot and she returned to the beach the fire she had lit and sat to watch the thing the solitary star be gone be burnt and washed; it was better this way better than leaving a piece of herself in the cold creek ground.

'Easy come,' said Ia. 'Easily another.' She didn't mean this she didn't know what else to say if she was respectable she would have said something sacred she wasn't.

When the last wink of light flashed out on the horizon and full dark down she waited for the cove to fill with night its shackles tight around her its weight like bog water until she could no longer breathe; she lay down and searched the sky for stars kicked her boot into the driftwood flames to make her own.

She could hear her heart beat in her ears it split the silence one atom at a time. A little wind the last of tide water the ocean taken away, this the only sound it didn't count she endured it every day.

'You come back to me,' she said. 'Bring me somethin for the baby; a gift for a gift.' She sat up and put her hands to the fire; it wasn't cold not yet but warmth meant small comfort; she caught it and put it into her hoodie pocket took it with her as she walked the short stretch of sand. She reached the cliff-path steps the short climb without light knew the place better than she knew herself; when her feet hit the stony ridge she didn't stop headed toward home a quiet place without hope it would be the quietest. What else to do but go to bed; in the morning she would forget this night like a dream she would overlook the detail of loss find a place to put it somewhere less lonely, imaginary, gone.

The first thing to wash up on the shore next morning was a crate of oranges, just that. Tiny pools of sunlight scattered on the shingle-sand, the rock pools spread golden, happy to be tricked into summer. Ia had watched them come in from the caravan window at the sink; she had been looking at her reflection, the contrasting blond hair black-eye bruise, she was about to contemplate worse when she saw it. A slick of colour being and then split, the oranges were one thing and then a hundred things; she wondered if the dots connected they would reveal their true meaning. She took her first pill of the day rinsed her mug and wiped the laminate sides like always each morning and kept the spectacle at the corner of her eye for as long as she could bear. This magic thing this secret moment that had drifted into the bay and Ia watching alone she was always alone.

She stretched to open the window to smell the fruit and fill the caravan with sweet notes not the usual sour and stood with the breeze pressed to her cheeks. This was colour no paint no palette could replicate; thrown against the slate grey sea the sand the bastard rocks it was the sun come down heaven fallen upon earth. The sea had listened, a hundred gifts for a gift.

'OK,' she said. 'You remain forever it's a straight swop this life I can do.'

She put on her coat and buttoned and slipped the leather journal that she was never without into her pocket and she wished for colours not the usual Cornish slate so she could record this phenomenon draw it for her sister Evie a present for when she saw her again. She stamped her wellie boots in the lean-to porch and amongst the pile of soft-maybes she found a hessian sack worthy of collecting fruit.

Outside the morning was coming good, mizzle just and a light wind threatening clouds; Ia knew they would clear on this gift-given day they had to. She went tentatively toward the western headland and stood looked down on the campsite and hoped nobody else had witnessed this apparition but as usual no folk were up the van doors shut the store by the pool still boarded; it was the same every morning. She went on toward the pathway steps and down on to the beach. Morning was her time since early days she had made it so; she cherished the calm the silent amity, thanked it each and every dawn and in return it gifted her with such delicate scent and colour she called it hers it was she alone who noticed.

She bent to the first orange and plucked it from the sand held it against her nose. An early childhood memory making juice she let the thought bathe her and become river. Oranges everywhere and each one picked and placed gently into the sack like precious stones. She found them floating in the rock pools and caught like crabs between the spurs of flint and barnacle, the skin tight the flesh firm she could feel the muscle of the thing between her fingers in her hands each one was a punch.

With the rocks and shingle combed through she sat with the

bounty between her legs and wondered where she might store the oranges to keep them from him. Two more days fishing two more days until his return Ia was determined to make the most of this freedom. Do what the fuck take flight let her imagination drift before the customary anchor drop and drag, no more fruit just fish and potatoes occasionally when he bothered to barter at the campsite.

She left the sack beneath the bench and walked the cliff to where the rock stabbed furthest into the ocean, a thin split of land barely wide enough for standing and yet every morning Ia did just this like a lighthouse it was her duty. Beneath her feet the shingle-rock plunged into the water no matter what tide it towered six hundred feet above sea level the closest she would ever get to knowing liberty. She lifted her arms and dared herself to push a little further forward step off, she heard her sister's voice call out to her a memory made old through remembering too much, she sat back and dug her heels into the turf.

As far as the eye could see a serpent wind raced across the sea coming in to spoil her day. It snapped low to the ground both tail and teeth looking for a way out a way into the caves the hollow trees the spaces that had yet to be claimed. Ia watched it follow the cliff path to her right and stop dead at the bite, saw it slip and crash into the sea be returned to the bay by the rip current; nothing could escape the place, if it had asked she could have told it this. Thirteen years ago she had asked the same question, now the distance between time and memory had fallen wayside, but sometimes it felt like the first year the first day the first fist-fight minute.

Thirteen years unlucky and still Ia did not fit or something about the north coast place did not fit her. When she arrived she had been twelve years of age and all for the show she did her best to please him. She'd learnt to gut and cure fish and clean and pet the caravan into how she supposed it should be and she was happy when she reached sixteen, a new bride. Despite no ceremony no ring she'd learnt to abide had made the van her home and she kept his dream of rebuilding the surrounding ruined cottage into a worthy house give him babies whatever he wanted she would do it. Ia had found her place in things: somebody desired her she was needed. She had told herself she could do this, be a wife a mother be her own woman.

Thirteen years and the caravan he had hoisted into the ruin was still their only home, though by the bind of ivy and bracken it had morphed into the ruin walls and like them it clung to that last remaining dream. And still no babies, no fruit grew from deadwood.

MARGARET CAVENDISH

'A Dialogue between an Oak and a Man
Cutting Him Down' (1653)

Oak

Why cut you off my boughs, which largely bend,

And from the scorching sun do you defend,

Which did refresh your fainting limbs from sweat,

And kept you free from thund'ring rains and wet,

When on my bark your weary head you'd lay,

Where quiet sleep did take all cares away,

The whilst my leaves a gentle noise did make,

And blew cool winds that you fresh air might take?

Besides, I did invite the birds to sing,

That their sweet voice might you some pleasure bring,

Where everyone did strive to do their best,

Oft changed their notes, and strained their tender breast.

In winter-time, my shoulders broad did hold

Off blust'ring storms, that wounded with sharp cold.

And on my head the flakes of snow did fall,

Whilst you under my boughs sat free from all.

And will you thus requite my love, good will,

To take away my life, and body kill?

For all my care and service I have passed,

Must I be cut and laid on fire at last?

See how true love you cruelly have slain,

Invent all ways to torture me with pain.

First you do peel my bark, and flay my skin,

Hew down my boughs, so chops off every limb.

With wedges you do pierce my sides to wound,

88

And with your hatchet knock me to the ground.
I minced shall be in chips and pieces small,
And thus doth man reward good deeds withal.

Man

Why grumble you, old Oak, when thou hast stood
This hundred years as king of all the wood?
Would you forever live, and not resign
Your place to one that is of your own line?
Your acorns young, when they grow big and tall,
Long for your crown, and wish to see your fall,
Think every minute lost whilst you do live,
And grumble at each office you do give.
Ambition doth fly high, and is above
All sorts of friendship and of nat'ral love.
Besides, all subjects do in change delight;
When kings grow old, their government they slight.
Although in ease, and peace, and wealth they live,
Yet all those happy times for change they'll give,
Grow discontent, and factions still do make,
What good so e'er he doth, as evil take.
Were he as wise as ever Nature made,
As pious, good, as ever Heav'n has saved,
Yet when they die such joy is in their face,
As if the Devil had gone from that place.
With shouts of joy they run a new to crown,
Although next day they strive to pull him down.

Oak

Why, said the Oak, because that they are mad,
Shall I rejoice, for my own death be glad?
Because my subjects all ungrateful are,
Shall I therefore my health and life impair?
Good kings govern justly at all times,
Examine not men's humours, but their crimes,
For when their crimes appear, 'tis time to strike,
Not to examine thoughts how they do like.
Though kings are never loved till they do die,
Nor wished to live till in the grave they lie,
Yet he that loves himself the less because
He cannot get every man's high applause
Shall by my judgment be condemned to wear
The asses ears, and burdens for to bear.
But let me live the life that Nature gave,
And not to please my subjects dig my grave.

Man

But here, poor Oak, you live in ignorance,
And never seek your knowledge to advance.
I'll cut you down, that knowledge you may gain,
And be a ship to traffic on the main.
There shall you swim, and cut the seas in two,
And trample down each wave as you do go.
Though they rise high, and big are swelled with pride,
You on their shoulders broad, and back, shall ride,
And bow their lofty heads, their pride to check,
Shall set your steady foot upon their neck.
They on their breast your stately ship shall bear

Till your sharp keel the wat'ry womb doth tear.
Thus shall you round the world, new land to find,
That from the rest is of another kind.

Oak

O! said the Oak, I am contented well
Without that knowledge in my wood to dwell.
For I had rather live and simple be
Than run in danger, some strange sight to see.
Perchance my ship against a rock may hit;
Then were I straight in sundry pieces split.
Besides, no rest, nor quiet shall I have:
The winds will toss me on each troubled wave;
The billows rough will beat on every side;
My breast will ache to swim against the tide.
And greedy merchants may me overfreight;
Then should I drownèd be with my own weight.
With sails and ropes men will my body tie,
And I, a prisoner, have no liberty.
And being always wet, shall take such colds,
My ship may get a pose, and leak through holes,
Which they to mend, will put me to great pain;
Besides, all patched and pieced I shall remain.
I care not for that wealth, wherein the pains
And troubles are far greater than the gains.
I am contented with what Nature gave;
I'd not repine, but one poor wish would have,
Which is, that you my agèd life would save.

Man

To build a stately house I'll cut you down,
Wherein shall princes live of great renown.
There shall you live with the best company;
All their delight and pastime you shall see.
Where plays, and masques, and beauties bright will shine,
Your wood all oiled with smoke of meat and wine.
There shall you hear both men and women sing,
Far pleasanter than nightingales in spring.
Like to a ball, their echoes shall rebound
Against the wall, yet can no voice be found.

Oak

Alas, what music shall I care to hear,
When on my shoulders I such burthens bear?
Both brick and tiles upon my head are laid –
Of this preferment I am sore afraid –
And many times with nails and hammers strong
They pierce my sides, to hang their pictures on.
My face is smutched with smoke of candle lights,
In danger to be burnt in winter nights.
No, let me here, a poor old oak, still grow;
I care not for these vain delights to know.
For fruitless promises I do not care;
More honour 'tis my own green leaves to bear.
More honour 'tis to be in Nature's dress
Than any shape that men by art express.
I am not like to man, would praises have,
And for opinion make myself a slave.

Man

Why do you wish to live and not to die,
Since you no pleasure have, but misery?
Here you the sun with scorching heat doth burn,
And all your leaves so green to dryness turn.
Also with winter's cold you quake and shake;
Thus in no time or season rest can take.

Oak

I'm happier far, said th'Oak, than you mankind,
For I content in my condition find;
Man nothing loves but what he cannot get,
And soon doth surfeit of one dish of meat,
Dislikes all company, displeased alone,
Makes grief himself if fortune gives him none.
And as his mind is restless, never pleased,
So is his body sick and oft diseased.
His gouts and pains do make him sigh and cry,
Yet in the midst of pains would live, not die.

Man

Alas, poor Oak, you do not know, nor can
Imagine half the misery of man.
All other creatures only in sense join,
But man hath something more, which is divine.
He hath a mind, doth to Heav'n aspire;
For curiosities he doth inquire;
A wit that nimble is, which runs about,
In every corner to seek Nature out.

For she doth hide herself, afraid to show
Man all her works, lest he too powerful grow,
Like as a king, his favourite waxing great,
May well suspect that he his pow'r will get.
And what creates desire in man's breast,
That nature is divine, which seeks the best,
And never can be satisfied, until
He, like a god, doth in perfection dwell.
If you, as man, desire like gods to be,
I'll spare your life, and not cut down your tree.

NICOLA CHESTER

'Desire Paths' (2021)[†]

It is bird nesting season and they're chainsawing the wood.

And not any old wood (if there were such a thing) but ours. Our wood. They are eating it up and spitting it out with enormous earth-churning machinery that looks apocalyptic: giant grabs, shears and winches on huge caterpillar tracks.

They came unannounced, the men. Without approach, consideration or enquiry, to the wood at the heart of our village, from sixty miles away in Somerset. What do they know of us and our wood? What it means, has meant and will mean? Our wood has many names: Post Office Woods, Greater Great Common, the Sticks Walk (our own name) and, perhaps more ominously, the Plantation or the Firs. In the distant past it was common land, but now the remnant heath and mixed, deciduous woodland has just two official footpaths running through it. Yet, over generations, the whole wood has been explored, 'desire paths' have been created, spots within it named and known, and wide, well-worn tracks with attendant meanders have long been established. The rich seam of bright ochre clay by the Ingle brook gave villagers the old name of 'yellowlegs'. It resurfaces still – the mud and the name – all over school socks and pram wheels, and rubbing off on brass band and rock band names, the Women's Book Club and the Dads' Drinking Club. Children, children's children and their children have grown up here, built dens, climbed trees, watched badgers, built bridges over the brook – and dammed the stream. Me and my own children included.

By the time anyone realised what was going on, the entrance to the wood had been clear-felled, the trees dangerous, apparently. All of them? A kite's nest in an ash tree had gone with it too. On the school run, I challenged the foresters, asking to speak to the foreman, notebook in hand, trench coat tied at the waist and a slick of postbox lipstick for confidence, channelling Lois Lane. 'And where is the ash tree, with the protected kite's nest in it?' 'No birds nesting here, love,' he said. 'And no ash trees. These are all old beech and some oak.' He bears down on me, looms. Legs planted deliberately, proprietorially. Hands in pockets, chest and groin thrust out, making himself as big as possible. I smile. 'That's an ash tree. And that.' I can tell ash from oak as well as I can hawk from chainsaw, even when I am mad with suppressed fury and it is lying on the ground, limbless and leafless.

There are dormice in this wood and adders. Protected species, undocumented. I can't produce papers or reports to show the foresters, like a magic trick or an inventory of rented land; a receipt for a place, its access and now its things, carelessly, particularly lost.

I feel small and silly, standing in front of the men with my daughter and these wild, bold claims of protected species. She, aged ten, stands tall and primed for action, incensed and righteous, a whippy sapling rooted in the place and confident in her conviction that this will not happen. And I have to turn away. I, who have brought her up with such stories. Of how I lay in front of cherry-pickers and breached police lines, stood in front of men wielding chainsaws inches from my face and wrists in another wood. But what can I do here?

The foreman is intimidating. He calls me back to say, with a cold, hard stare and an icy concern: 'Miss. You take very good care of yourself won't you?' He's been here before, I think. But then. So have I.

My son and older daughter spot the devastation from the school bus, take pictures, text urgently. 'The wood's been trashed!' says my son's text. They are deeply upset and incredulous. The beech trees formed a stained-glass, vaulted, cathedral-like aisle my son loved to cycle under. It was one of his favourite places. The beeches opposite remain, undangerously, breaking into leafy grief. The lane looks like the aisle of a bombed-out, broken half-of-a-church.

The footpaths are my teenagers' independent routes out of here –
and back home again: tracks worn by so many feet to the train station
in the next village, off the pavementless, unlit roads. Safe, scenic, secret.

The village and Parish Council get together, led by our steely,
indomitable Clerk. It seems hopeless. The wood is privately owned,
the forestry work legitimate. But the men have not reckoned on a
community shocked by austerity cuts and galvanised by a deep shared
history of childhood in the woods and love.

We venture into Sticks Walk. It is unrecognisable, broken. Paths
formed and followed for at least ninety years have been deliberately
targeted, as have favourite trees and dens. The scent of rising, leaking
sap, split greenwood and mashed foliage mingles potently with petrol.
I look mournfully at my feet for bird and dormice nests. For evidence.

We are angry. Angry at the way it's been done. The subterfuge, the
sudden arrival no one could prepare for. The complete disregard for
local people. The cynical tearing up of the oldest, most established
paths. The no-entry signs set there. The legal flouting of what we all
believe is law.

I hurt for the children and all our memories of this place and I
hurt because I can't stop it for them. The wood, and the way the paths
swing this way and that, over this fallen tree, past the one struck by
lightning; the way another is worn by so many hands swinging round
it – all this is in their blood, set down in their making like rings of
grain and rooted here. This wood grew them too.

I am angry at the timing.

Just when the tenderest leaves are unfurling. Everything is sacred.
Nothing is safe.

We meet, us women and children. Some men. Over cups of tea,
Victoria sponges and Pear Bellinis. Bottles of wine are drunk as
we warm to our task. While the men of the Yellow Legs Drinking

Club talk of us with fond patrony, and go back to comparing their lawnmowers and the best insurance deals, we work. We write, we enquire, we use social media. We connect. And in this way we gain confidence and leads. From 170 straight miles up the country, we get support and some interesting developments via tree protestors in Sheffield City.

The men urge caution. The foresters block our way. Hold up the bus. We move their things, remake paths; even the most conservative among us deface their signs with wit and a politic politeness. We make it look as if many of us came this way over the weekend. They take time off, but we live here.

We go off on tangents, diverging and coming back together on our own desire lines, with fresh news and revelations. I adopt a pseudonym, borrowed from long-gone, dispossessed commoners, and my mother's maiden name. I make calls to Somerset, I soften my voice as he raises his. I write. I find out. The cracks in the garden path mirror the lines we've been hand-drawing on maps.

And in the end, the power of our collective memory wins out. Our shared knowledge, our shared stories make for a partial victory. There is much work to be done. Paths to unblock, clear and remake, desire paths for generations to come, away from and back home.

FRANCES CORNFORD

'To a Fat Lady Seen from the Train' (1910)

O why do you walk through the fields in gloves,
Missing so much and so much?
O fat white woman whom nobody loves,
Why do you walk through the fields in gloves,
When the grass is soft as the breast of doves
And shivering-sweet to the touch?
O why do you walk through the fields in gloves,
Missing so much and so much?

LINDA CRACKNELL

'January Blues – The Call of the North' (2018)

I write this on 'Blue Monday', the day associated with winter doldrums, when holiday companies prey upon our sense of daylight deprivation, lack of exercise, divorce from life 'out there'. It's when I feel most like hibernating, so it was perhaps contrary to choose this time of year to travel 250 miles further north from my home in Perthshire's heartlands. In Orkney this is the season when empty frames stand on pavements as their swinging coffee signs are torn away by gales to announce a hiatus in hospitality. Days are defined by their extreme shortness.

The sky lightened before nine on my first morning in Stromness and as I took a pre-breakfast stroll through the crooked streets to Ness Point, fishing boats chugged out of the harbour escorted by noisy fleets of gulls. Chattering crowds of starlings hurled themselves into the low branches of garden trees. There was frost on the ground and a pink horizon. I was afraid to go back indoors; blink, and I might miss the day, the sense of life awakening.

Stepping out again an hour later to walk to the eastern shore of the bay, the wisdom of choosing this unseasonal journey clarified. The sun had risen low to the south and seemed to pierce deep behind my eyes as acres of clear blue domed above. Unobscured by high land, sunlight reflected from sheets of water. I walked and stopped. Walked and stopped. It was as if the place had been designed to capture light; I was inside a magical prism of glass worthy of a Philip Pullman novel.

The previous night I'd stood out on the ferry deck as we came through Hoy Sound and been thrilled by the inky waters, the flashing beacons suggesting fragmented peninsulas, points, and islands. Today's luminous contrast was exquisite. I suppose it's simple: If you're lucky enough to get sunlight here in winter, it will be magnified. And it's a particular quality of light which is made more precious by its brevity, and by its earthbound angle. The essence of North.

It soon became apparent that a charmed day was emerging, reflected in the wide-open eyes of all the people I met on foot and their generous greetings. Over the past three years, Orkney has seen a major increase in coach-based tourism partly resulting from large numbers of visiting cruise ships. Further growth is expected. How lucky was I now to feel like the only tourist in town! People responded kindly and with curiosity to my being there; later a remote shopkeeper made me a cup of coffee, a thumb stuck out on a lonely roadside elicited a lift (once there was any traffic). An urgent need for intense light levelled us as humans and we tipped our faces towards the sun and talked about weather and place and time, pulled into an acute intimacy with primal rhythms.

I've been to Orkney several times before, but always in summer when its many visitors marvel at its particular magic and long, light days. Having spent so much time in all seasons in Caithness across the Pentland Firth when writing a novel set there, many of the same features are recognisable here – the harshness and low-lying land, the phenomenal high-banked skies and scattered rural population, brochs, chambered cairns and the teasing manner of conversation. But perhaps here the convoluted jigsaw of land and water leads to something more concentrated. In this season it's more like a kaleidoscope than a jigsaw. Wherever I go I walk partly to internalise landscape, but on this day it seemed the topography, architecture, the people even, were built from light and it was this luminosity which characterised the sense of place.

Despite the long hours of darkness, or perhaps because of them, there was no sense of dormancy in nature. As I walked out of town redshanks waded the shallows, calling and running, awkward as long-legged schoolgirls. A group of wigeon slipped through the water in a chestnut glow. The air was so thrillingly still that birds seemed to have pirated the audio channels. Pausing at the point of the peninsula to note the walls that once outlined Copland's shipyard where a new pier now services the tidal and wave energy experiments, I heard screeching and watched two herons flap slowly across the mirror between me and the inner and outer holms. Curlews contributed a higher note to the rich orchestra. My brain censored out the hum of the MV *Hamnavoe* from the harbour in favour of the busy shoreline tinkle and click: turnstones doing as their name describes, making up a gang with purple sandpipers. Meanwhile cormorants lined a rock in such still silhouettes I thought them at first the upward spars of a wrecked jetty.

Even by midday the sun was only a little higher than the Hoy Hills as it made its passage west. I turned for the opposite shore and walked back through the town, not quite able to resist stopping off in 'Stromness Books and Prints', where beautifully curated shelves reflect the geographical location and its historical and archaeological significance. It also showcases the creativity of those who live in inescapable engagement with coast and tide and season – the better-known George Mackay Browns and Amy Liptrots alongside books and pamphlets published by Duncan McLean's Abersee Press, which brings new writing from the Northern Isles to wider attention. If I was to spend many dark hours here, there was still much of the local to experience in them.

There was still frost on the ground when I passed Ness Point again, the location of another historic shipyard. I took the path west along the southern shore, passing batteries which once defended Scapa Flow. Not long after 2.30 the sun dropped from sight behind Hoy's twin hills, but for a further two hours reflected light kept the place aglow. When I came just inland of Warebeth cemetery, which balances on a small cliff a mile or two out of town, the ornate nineteenth-century headstones stood like a cosmic chess game backlit by a roaring sky. With the temperature dropping fast, a hint of sea-smoke drifted under the dark Hoy cliffs. People were still arriving on the coast path to walk dogs, to watch the light change, making the most of it as the sea darkened, the Graemsay lighthouse pulsed more brightly and surf exploded white on nearby skerries.

People who come to Orkney fall in love with it for wildlife, the rich ongoing archaeological discoveries of 6,000 years, World War history tangible in the coastal batteries and the wrecks. And the light of course draws artists. I was principally there to explore the history of a couple of Stromness shipyards and their connection to seafarers in my own family, a history entangled with a couple of infamous pirates. It was this that took me to that cemetery and then indoors into the archives in Kirkwall for a day's detective work. And then, gloriously, I had another day to be outside.

I kept to the mainland for practical reasons of time and weather and winter timetables. I wanted to follow more coasts and drink in as much light as possible, so I chose a foray onto the St Magnus Way, a new long-distance pilgrimage route through Mainland, Orkney which follows the story of the saint in five stages. As well as route maps, the website and app offer related poetry and prompts for reflection on the journey, including an invitation to carry a pebble as memento or companion or something you wish to cast away. By the time I read this suggestion, a smooth, dull, red pebble was already treasure in my pocket.

I followed the first leg of the Way across the mainland's north coast from Evie to Birsay, the route on which the saint's body was carried after he was killed by an axe to the head on the nearby island of Egilsay. Although still bright and dry, the fickle weather now sent a brisk easterly to whisk up the sea and whip at me from behind. Despite these more 'normal' conditions, the thrill continued as my progress was monitored by seals, and I watched great slabs of sea sliding over stone pavements, waves crashing into deep geos, and passed stone relics, including that of eleventh-century St Peter's Kirk, gradually being dismantled by coastal erosion.

The path mostly skirts between fenced-in arable land and the low-tide mark, sometimes high, sometimes low, and can be rough underfoot as if it's not been much trodden yet; apparently the toughest section of the Way and still under development. Some stretches follow the A966, though I was pretty much the only traffic on it that day. Orkney's red-and-yellow sandstone glowed against blue sea and sky, and armies of greylag geese lurked in camouflage in low fields of stubble. Sometimes their waddling convoys betrayed their presence; long-necked and bandy-legged as cowboys. But more often my arrival lifted them into the sky to circle in a dark, squabbling squadron. With a growing resident population swelled by overwintering Icelandic cousins, they are not welcomed by farmers. The geese, and then the flocks of starlings who coiled as one body into complex knots befitting their maritime setting, took my eyes frequently skywards as much as to the land and to the sea and to the islands of Rousay and Eynhallow opposite. Later peewits, also known as 'teeick' in Orkney, jousted in the air above the Loch of Swannay.

Looking south in the early afternoon from the heathery high moorland of Costa, the Hoy Hills were turning misty and cloud had banked up in high columns. I knew storms were forecast. I'd been lucky, but I was up against imminent dusk. It was the wrong state of the tide to cross the causeway to the Brough this time. I hurried on, snatched the last light on the rich red stone of the earl's sixteenth-century palace, which surprises with its sense of past grandeur in a remote and windswept spot. And then with glowing cheeks I made it onto the only bus of the afternoon away from Birsay, as mist and dark swallowed the land.

'Blue Monday' is deduced from an 'equation' factoring the number of days since the excitement of Christmas, one's level of debt, the average temperature. It always points to the third Monday in January. I felt exhilarated to have resisted hibernation or a package holiday to the south. By going somewhere even darker, I'd somehow found more light; the right kind of 'January Blues'.

ANNE DACRE
'Untitled' (1595)

These words were written on the death of Anne's husband, Sir Philip Howard, Earl of Arundel, who was imprisoned for ten years in the Tower of London for charges relating to his conversion to Catholicism and where he died in 1595 of dysentery. His dying request to Elizabeth I, that he might see his wife and the daughter born after his arrest, was denied.

In sad and ashy weeds I sigh,
I groan, I pine, I mourn;
My oaten yellow reeds I all
To jet and ebon turn.
My wat'ry eyes like wintry skies
My furrowed cheeks o'erflow;
All heaven know why, men mourn as I,
And who can blame my woe?

In sable robes of night my days
Of joy consumed be;
My sorrow sees no light; my lights
Through sorrow nothing see;
For now my sun his course hath run,
And from his sphere doth go
To endless bed of folded lead,
And who can blame my woe?

My flock I now forsake that so
My sheep my grief may know;
The lilies loth to take, that since

His death presumed to grow;
I envy air because it dare
Still breathe, and he not so;
Hate earth that doth entomb his youth,
And who can blame my woe?

Not I, poor I alone – (alone
How can this sorrow be?)
Not only men make moan, but more
Than men make moan with me.
The gods of greens, the mountain queens
The fairy circled row,
The Muses nine, and powers divine,
Do all condone my woe.

MIRIAM DARLINGTON

From *Owl Sense* (2018)

At the age of fifty, when my life was showing some signs of falling apart and I should have been old enough to know better, I found myself in the grip of an obsession. A creature that is easy to love but hard to know flew into my dreams and would not let me be. Soon I became distracted, for instance, with the fact that an adult barn owl can swallow a whole field vole in one go.

Owls cannot chew, so within a few minutes their prey is crushed and dissolved in the bird's ventriculus, or stomach. Once the fluid and soft tissue in the vole's body have been liquefied, the fur and harder parts pass into the gizzard. This muscular stomach is an organ that birds have instead of teeth. It retains the indigestible bits – the bones, teeth, claws and fur – crushing them into a compact, gizzard-shaped pellet. The pellet will remain there for a period of hours until it is regurgitated and dropped to the ground. It is very tempting if you find one to take it home and try to identify what the mystery parts are. Fur and bone dissected with tweezers under a lamp through a hand lens become vole jaws with incisors and molars. There might be meadow pipit feathers, rat skulls, each pellet a map containing all the grizzled drama of the owl's nocturnal predation.

I began to store corpses in the freezer. My daughter, in a moment of wisdom, put signs on the freezer drawers that read: 'food' 'food' 'food' 'dead owls etc'.

Owls have an intense, complex attraction for humans. Their loose, soft feathers rather than the stiff, rigid plumage that other birds have can give an attractive, tubby effect. The gentle contours are not for cuteness however; they are solely evolved to insulate, and to cloak this predator in invisibility. Their patterning produces visually confusing camouflage that breaks up a silhouette beyond any hunter's wildest dreams. Their feathers are silencers, with baffles called fimbriae to mask themselves and not drown the subtle sound of their prey. While our ancestors may have been in awe of the owls' fearsome abilities as a nocturnal predator, these days we can have a tendency not to see beyond the fluffiness.

The hooked, sharp-edged bill, unlike that of the majority of other birds, which have a horizontal bill, is for ripping flesh. The acute hearing and the stealth-swoop are for murder by momentous, feathered eruption. The ferocious raptorial talons are for striking and gripping – these are zygodactyl talons: instead of three toes facing forward and one behind, the outer digit has a joint that enables it to swivel backwards so two toes can be placed at the front and two behind. The prodigious strength of its grip is vital. The Eurasian eagle owl's deceptively velvet-feathered feet act as boxing gloves. This giant owl deploys its thunderous punch to grasp, snap and puncture. Blakiston's fish owl, of a similar size and weight to the eagle owl, has spines called spicules on the underside of its toes to enable it to grip dicey aquatic prey.

Perhaps what also attracts us humans to owls is admiration, particularly that they have the skill to fly at night. This bird is feathered perfection; grace and beauty with talons. Just as a poem is the best words in the best order, this bird must be the best night-hunter in the best kit. Even without the glamour, we can't fail to envy the finely honed precision that is compressed here. The owl is made for one thing only: to survive, and to do so by stealth. For this reason, over time our suspicious minds have wondered whether it also has any supernatural qualities hidden under its cloak; was there the capacity for evil, for instance? For if *Homo sapiens*, the wise humans – who in general do not appear always to have entirely mastered their own baser instincts – possessed the same set of abilities, it would surely make a potent concoction. And so by projection this mysterious night creature has gained human meanings that meant nothing to it.

I was smitten, fascinated, in the grip of something that was beyond me.

Then one morning, one minute I was sipping my tea by the window, wondering how I was going to tell my husband I wanted to leave, and there was nothing but the palest edge of grey light and a wisp of steam from my cup – and then a shadow swooped out of the air. With the lightest of scratches, as if the dawn light was solidifying into life, there it was, perched like an exclamation mark on the balcony: a tawny owl, come to my home.

Its softly feathered feet and black talons were curled on the balustrade as if I had called it in, as if what I had been thinking had just made itself manifest. But there it was, right in front of me, and it turned its head and stared in at me as I stared out at it. It fixed its two dark eyes on mine. Its brown camouflage was exposed against the mist: the rust-tinged facial disc, the tree-bark beige and cream flourishes, the ambrosia-pale, flecked breast, the streaked back and the short, stubby tail. I was transfixed. The symmetry of its face seemed to reclaim all its unnerving, eerie mystery as it rotated and returned repeatedly to pierce me through with those huge eyes.

A little more steam rose from my morning mug of tea. My mind tumbled down the generations, struck by magical thinking. Thousand-year-old ancestors would have made this moment an omen. But this owl was just an owl, not a sign, and I was just lucky. But still. . .

Owls have been part of our landscape, psychological context and emotional ecology from the moment humans became self-aware. When the daily soundtrack of birdsong died down, we noticed the owl's voice in the dark and felt puzzled and unsettled. The human brain is primed for curiosity and story, so owls invited our myth-making. Now it is impossible to see these animals without clouding them with what anthropologist Franz Boas described as our *Kulturbrille*, a cultural lens that automatically colours the way we perceive everything. We observed owls' hunting skills, noted their powerful sensory capacities and coveted their silent mastery of the air. Owls have found their way into our mythology, art, literature and religion and so appear to be polarised. On one side, the imaginary owl of the mind, the human-created spirit bird, the familiar, the icon, the owl as commodity. Looking at any of these, we are really only looking at ourselves. On the other side, the real, live animals that breathe and fly and hunt, and this owl is so often beyond our reach. Until relatively recently, the more we have tried to understand them through the prism of our own experiences, the more we have obscured their true nature. And just as the 250 species of owl on the planet evolved as forest birds, we fail to see them disappear. We continue felling and burning and we are spelling not only their doom, but our own.

Once we lived much more consciously within the ecosystem. Our lives were sensitive to the wild, entirely embedded amongst predator–prey relationships, and animals were respected as part of our lives in ways which it is difficult for Western humans to remember or imagine. In December 1994 a group of three spelunkers, or cavers, were following an old mule path beside a cliff face along the Ardèche river in southern France, when they came face to face with an astonishing reminder of our connection to the animal world. They found a narrow slot in the rock of the cliff and climbing inside they felt a tiny current of air emanating from some rubble. The subtle breath from the rock could only mean one thing: there was an unexplored cave inside. They cleared the rubble and scrambled in. By the light of their lamps they found that the cave, larger than any they had seen before in the region, was scattered all over with the bones, scratch marks and wallows all from one extinct animal: the cave bear. Moving through the chambers of what came to be known as the Chauvet cave – named after one of the explorers, Jean-Marie Chauvet, who later wrote about it jointly with the other cavers – they found astonishing paintings. It began with red ochre dots and smudges made by the hands of Paleolithic artists, and as the chambers of the cave stretched out, for over 240 metres, they found each chamber contained new wonders. The red ochre was replaced by black, and these turned out to be the earliest paintings. In some places horses and bison had been engraved in the soft surfaces of the cave walls, perhaps scratched with a human finger. Small fragments of charcoal were lying about where they had been knocked from the artists' torches as if they were still fresh. A mammoth, a leopard, and soon a whole pantheon of animals danced across the walls, their forms vibrant enough to be recent. The artists had used the uneven surface of the rock as if the animals were emerging from it.

'Suddenly our lamps lit upon a monumental black frieze. It took our breath away. There were shouts of joy and bursts of tears. We felt gripped by madness and dizziness,' the cavers later wrote in their book *Dawn of Art: The Chauvet Cave*. They were staring at a panel that had been scraped clean and worked into a scene of a dozen hunting lions, their heads deftly shaded, their eyes alive and intelligent, their bone structure and musculature clearly delineated. These were familiar, intimate portraits. The expressions of the lions as they stalked were varied and well-observed. Carbon dating showed that the first of these paintings had been begun around 36,000 BC. They were far older than anything previously discovered. The bears, bison, reindeer, cave lions, rhinoceros, horses and mammoths had been depicted by artists who were skilled and attentive. The graceful depictions were accurately and lovingly rendered and showed that the artists must have worked calmly and reverently. Were these devotional images? Returning from the deepest part of the cave where the lions reside, and looking back into it, in a place where the floor had collapsed so that it was now unreachable, the cavers noticed that on the ceiling there was engraved a striking, solitary figure of a long-eared owl.

The Chauvet owl is the oldest known depiction of an owl in the world. It is forty-five centimetres tall − close to the size of a large long-eared owl, *Asio otus*. It has clearly etched ear tufts, and is perched on a downward-drooping rock pendant. Most interestingly, its back is shown facing outwards, wings folded, with fifteen streaks to demarcate the densely lined plumage. This closely observed owl is depicted as if swivelling its head 180 degrees backward to peer into the dark, its face turned to look out into the cave and meet the gaze of the people walking towards it. In view of the sophistication of the other drawings, the deliberate positioning of the bird suggests the artists understood something of the Janus nature of the owl, its troubling liminal status on the boundaries of light and dark. This owl captures a strange suggestion, its ability to face both ways, both out into the cave and back into the body of the rock and whatever that was thought to be concealing, as if the rock were merely a veil.

Our ancestors would have gazed into the anatomy of these animals and experienced resemblance. Peering into the entrails and skeletons of the birds, early humans saw the organs, the spine, the ribcage, the breastbone; the arm-like wings with fingery tips; the hips joined to the legs, the toes; all, at their core, reflecting our own human structure.

This kinship may have drawn us, or certain of us, more companionably into the dark, unknown recesses of the caves, as well as into the deepest recesses of our imaginations.

During the Renaissance Albrecht Dürer's melancholy portrait of a deep-eyed young tawny owl catches an elusive essence of owl-ness. The large eyes with fathom-dark pupils and the sharply hooked claws, the soft, brownish-grey camouflage, all show well-observed traits of this young, nocturnal predator. Fragile lines trace the long primary feathers and the softer down on the owl's breast. The fierce young bird is captured in a thoughtful moment, with its claws spread wide on a man-made surface, its wings furled, it poignantly suggests that this young owl has all his life ahead. The wild creature's isolation from nature in a captive environment suggests that Dürer cared for more than the simple appearance. In a poignant, vulnerable pose, its predatory power appears locked up, as if it cannot wait to be its simple self and fly free.

Since the phenomenon of Harry Potter, owls have been depicted as glamorous companions, and across the world an unintended effect of Harry Potter has spread with the books' fame. With its translation into many languages and vastly popular films, special-interest pet-owl groups have proliferated. In Java and Bali, where bird markets are widespread and owls are not protected, wild-caught owls are commonly sold as pets. The Pramuka market, the largest in Jakarta, may often have up to sixty owls for sale, with eight different species on show at a time. In Indonesia it is traditional to keep birds as domestic pets, but previously 'Burung hantu' or 'ghost birds' were feared and avoided. Now the ghost bird is called a 'Burung Harry Potter' and prices are rising for the rarer owls as more and more people wish to own one. The Javan owlet, the Bornean wood owl, the Buffy fish owl, the Australasian barn owl, and many scops owls are being sold as chicks or juveniles.

Framed in cages, in high resolution on our TV screens or in closely filmed nature documentaries, and in the world of consumerism, the owl has been reduced to an item to collect, sequestered for a companion, a fashion accessory. The owl has become an 'experience', a collectible, a postcard, and a pin-up. Where, amongst all this, is the real owl?

These raptors were on the planet long before us. Fossil remains of owls have been dated from 65 to 56 million years ago. In the Pleistocene, *Ornimegalonyx*, giant barn owls, ranged across the Mediterranean area. They stood over a metre in height, weighed twice the heft of today's eagle owl, and preyed on large rodents such as capybara.

In Britain the barn owl with its long, lightweight wings evolved for grassland hunting. As the ice sheets retreated from Northern Europe between ten and twenty thousand years ago and humans spread north in greater numbers, so followed this wraith-like owl. It was drawn by the pasture that small-scale farming created, and later found the protective nesting cavities that were offered by some of our cliff-like structures: farm buildings, attics and haylofts, churches and homesteads all mimicked the owl's native cliffscapes. For thousands of years our clearings, meadows and summer pastures have made a dense and diverse thatch – velvet grass, sweet vernal-grass, false oat-grass, red fescue, rough meadow-grass, smooth meadow-grass, Yorkshire fog, false-brome, wood false-brome, upright brome and cocksfoot – all useful species that when left un-mown or un-grazed decompose so slowly that they form a 'litter layer' providing protection for small mammals, and perfect foraging ground for predatory owls.

One softly raining afternoon I found myself in this landscape, looking at ejected pellets on an old barn floor. The barn was half-ruined. When I got inside, something alive was there, a presence beyond any mice or jackdaws. The quiet and the pattering rain were broken by a rattlesnake hiss. It bubbled up from nowhere in particular, making my skin prickle. Hunched in a corner, a small, downy face and two dark eyes stared at me.

A fallen owlet.

And higher up, the source of the hissing; a small snowdrift of siblings, calling from their high ledge. I had thought the owls might be nesting in a cavity in the huge old tree nearby, but apparently they preferred this rickety human-made space instead.

How quick we are to want to come to the aid of fallen things. This tumbled chick wouldn't last a night on the floor while the foxes had cubs to feed. I had heard news that the owls were in trouble that year.

But while we suffered our own weather patterns, they had survived well enough to produce young.

I scanned the wall for handholds. I could try to climb up and put it back. Then I'd quietly withdraw, hoping the parents would soon return. I placed my hands around its warm, tickly body. I checked the thinly muscled wings. Some of the adult feather shafts had begun to come through, encasing what might one day be flight feathers. It was way too small to fly yet. How old? Three weeks, perhaps four?

Its feet wriggled at first, but soon its feather-weight settled to my grip. I expected it to smell sweet, something like a kitten. Instead, its alien stink of rotting mouse, vole blood and acrid ammonia hurt my nose. There was something part-reptile there: I looked into its wincing face, felt its scaly feet, and at their tips, whetstone-grey talons, already gripping fiercely.

With one hand grasping it I started to climb, my fingers stretching for holds in the stone. I dropped back down; I needed two hands. The owlet fitted inside my shirt along with a suspicious, parasitical tickling. With both hands free I could get up there more easily. At the ledge, I undid the tangled claws from me, pushed the fallen owlet back with the others, and let go. I didn't know then, but know now, that this was the first of many lettings go. So many moments of trust have followed, of accepting the unfolding of the uncertain, of going into the dark, the unknown, the invisible future into which we each have to spread our wings in compassion and love and forgiveness.

KERRI NÍ DOCHARTAIGH

From *Thin Places* (2021)

There are places that dance around of us — like moths drawn to the light of a flame from a fire — just making ready to take its leave — or that may, in fact, have never even been lit at all.

There are places that may in fact be the moth itself — or maybe, perchance — a butterfly. There are places that are so ineffable that they do not take the shape inside our mouths that we will them to. We forget their names. We lose their locations on any map. Their co-ordinates shape-shift and turn themselves into a thing of invisible particles; into a thing not unlike the mist that lives on the frayed and jagged edges of the Atlantic Ocean. There are places that will not fit inside of us neatly. We try to shovel them down — like a thing that we must eat; for to steady the shake in us — that comes after too long with a belly full of emptiness. They will not stay down though, some places. There are places that — once we try to devour them hungrily — to fill the empty parts of our insides up with them — slither back up our coiled parts; eel-like and secret-heavy. We cannot carry these places in the way we would so very much like to. These places are not a dog that lets us throw their sticks. There are places that draw us into them — in a way that is both close, and all at once as distant as those other worlds — that exist in every single language, in every single era; in every single dream that haunts our waking.

There are places which I am beginning — only in this decade of my life — to understand, might even be the flame itself.

There are places that will not be pinned to any wall, no matter how exquisite their colourful, near-celestial markings.

There are places where space and time do not, can not, *will not* exist within the confines we have so keenly tried to erect here for ourselves

– on this here our solid ground – our carved out lands.

There are places that are so outside of what we claim to know is true – as to make them almost unreal – mythical in that way of labyrinths and nymphs, of unimaginable beasts; of stepping in the same body of water twice. Of curses and twisted things, of lost humans and found objects, of forgetting and forging, casting out and dragging down; of the power of naming and speaking it out loud on the highest hill to be found. Of holes and caves and caverns and nooks. Of crossing points and meeting mounds and halfway hillocks; of the in-between that maybe holds the still point. Places that sing of all that came – is here – that will come. Places that know of rivers flowing through lands that claim our dead without even knowing their name.

Places that speak in tongues, in stillness: in those delicate, moth-light ways; that cannot quite ever be silenced.

What does it mean to come from a hollowed-out place? From a place that is neck-deep in the saga of loss? What does it mean when your origins trace a line made of leaving – of going away to faraway lands – with the knowledge that *this* goodbye was to be the very last on any shoreline that you could touch? What becomes of a person, when the marks left by the highest spring tide, is still not a safe enough place to build?

To 'hollow out' is to remove the inside of something: to make an empty space in the place of something else. To leave a void in a spot – still warmed by the presence of something – heat and beat – shadow trace: left over by something which had, once; not yet gone.

> To build a cave,
> you'll have to *hollow out*
> the earth in the side of a hill.

During war, soldiers sometimes hollow out
trenches they can crouch in for protection
from gunfire. Animals, including woodpeckers
and several types of insects, also hollow out
protective areas for themselves, often from
dead wood in trees. And some kinds of drums
are also made by hollowing out a piece of wood.

> *Hollow* has an Old English root,
> *holh*: 'hole or hollow place'.

I am *across the border* – I have followed the gently carved
meanderings of Lough Foyle – from my hometown – past Culmore
Point at first, then Quigley's Point – to the body of water's western
banks at Moville; where the River Bredagh flows into the sea. Moville
has two possible Gaelic origins – Bun a' Phobail: 'Foot of the Parish'
and Magh Bhile: 'Plain of the Ancient Tree'. Cooley Stones and Skull
House are the most ancient sites – taken by Christian monastic settlers
and repurposed as a cross and a graveyard – when such things were
introduced to this northerly corner of the island, likely by St Finian
in this instance. I am camping on the ethereal banks of the Bredagh
River – at Glencrow, beneath the tallest trees I have ever known. I
have never seen so many crows in my life. They craekk and craw, and
they gather themselves into a murder – above the oldest bridge in
Ireland – built by the hands of Saint Patrick many midsummers ago.

I am at a staggeringly northern point, but I am in *the south*.

On my first day here alone, I take myself along the river – past
blackbirds that sing of the long-gone past – through a meadow that
catches the sun as it ebbs out of the June-pink sky. I am on my third
day away from a space that cannot quite be defined in its gossamer but
all at once silted and chalky texture. I take no images on my phone of

the elderflower and the butterflies, the dipper and the mating insects I cannot name; the folkloric copse and the cinematic coastline as it comes into view. I am off Instagram, Facebook and Twitter for a while. I will not be releasing these whispers of moments out into the ether as any post or Insta-story; no tweets will pin this moment to any wall. I want to see how it feels to just *be* in this place – free from the weight I have come to feel on my chest – free from the burden of clenching it all up into a living memory of light; or whatever it is I think that I am doing when I hold that small machine so close to me in my tight and tightening hands.

I walk alone along the shoreline and I think of all those who have stood on these sandy banks before me – in the shadows of coffin ships and grief.

From 1873 onwards emigrants leaving their starved, broken corner of the world through the port of Derry were carried down the Foyle to the spot on which I stand, to join the Allan and Anchor steamship lines. The liners could be seen by those they had left behind as they passed along this coastline en route to America or Canada. If there was a local person emigrating, it was customary to light a bonfire on O'Donnell's Hill, just above where I am rooted, so that it was visible to the passing ship; a farewell of light.

What does it mean to hallow a place?

When we hallow a place, we bless it and we make it holy. We sanctify and honour it; we consecrate and hold it as sacred. We keep its ways and we hold them close. We listen to the place and we feel its reverberations in our bones.

St John's Day is celebrated annually on 24 June – marking the birth of John the Baptist. The night before is linked to the summer solstice and is called 'bone fire night' in many parts of Ireland. Fires were originally lit as part of a Celtic celebration to honour the goddess

Áine, who was associated with the sun, fertility, and protecting crops and animals. However, as with many pagan festivals, the Catholic Church took over the event and linked it to the birth of St John.

On St John's Eve, the veil between the worlds is lifted entirely. White cats appear as women, folk dance themselves into different forms, and it is said that the fairies play sweet music and entice the people to come with them to their caves. The people that leave on this night never ever come back again.

This St John's Eve – my first night camping in this haunting place since I went sober – I slept in a crow-straight line – in the direct vision of an ancient fairy ring. My ancestors would have prayed by the fire for the land, and for good weather. If this did not happen, a bad harvest would surely come, and the white trout would not come back up the river as they were wont to with the midsummer floods. And so I knelt alone in prayer – a prayer to the mother of the land – a prayer to those that came before. A friend arrives and we tend the fire until the night has given way to the day. We talk of history, of borders, of women-hood, of ritual and of place; we talk of hope.

We awaken on St John's Day and we swim in the belly of the Atlantic – at Stroove Beach – beneath the lighthouse – under a sky full of oily-skinned cormorants in low flight. This is the day that swimming began for my ancestors, and as we swim we feel safe in the knowledge that the keeping of this ritual protects us two from drowning for the full year ahead.

We walk the shore path from Greencastle towards Moville, gathering driftwood for the fire; in the cove at the foot of the home of the great Brian Friel. We feel his presence with us as we gather – his hand steadying us as we think of what is ahead of us both in the coming months of Brexit – she in London, and I here – in this hollowed-out, hallowed place of echoing loss.

She leaves, and I am once more alone by the fire. I leave the ashes from last night where they are, and I build on top: crisscrossing the sticks; leaving space for the bones I will place into the hollow space later.

My ancestors were well aware of the effects of fire. Mastering this element had changed their lives, although fraught with danger. Homes then were temporary affairs and could be burned to the ground in the time it took to return from the well.

The sun was considered to bring great healing energy. Walking three times 'sun wise', or *cor deiseil*, around a fire represented the circling of the sun, and was a potent ritual invocation of the sun's healing power. I walk around the fire I have lit three times, and I think of the circles we all walk as women, over and over.

Bone fires have been being lit in this place for centuries, and the ashes and embers have been used to purify the space for just as long. Bones of our ancestors, keeping us safe; in the hollow of their hands.

A handful of weeks ago it was confirmed that bones washed up on a beach in Canada are those of Irish famine victims.

They are the human remains of twenty-one individuals, unearthed over a five-year period, from an 1847 Carricks shipwreck.

The ship left Sligo carrying 180 passengers fleeing the Famine, but it sank, killing at least 150 of those on board.

Fragile skeletal remains of three boys – two aged seven and one eleven-year-old – suggest rural Irish origins based on severe malnutrition held in the salt-wearied bones.

My St John's Fire can be seen from most points of Glencrow; a signal of a form. I think of beacons. Classically, beacons were fires lit at well-known locations on hills or high places, used either as lighthouses to lead folk to safety or for signalling over land that enemies were approaching.

Systems of this kind have existed for centuries over much of the world. Beacons have also allegedly been abused by ship-wreckers. A fire placed where it should not be placed would be used to direct a ship against shoals or beaches so that its cargo could be looted after the ship sank or ran aground.

The fall of Troy was signalled by a chain of eight beacons, burning on the shore to send the news across to Clytemnestra in Argos.

From where we stood today on the shore, Ballykelly – the village I spent my teens in – could be seen across the water. The fires we lit to fuel our nights of teenage angst would have been a beacon visible in the study Brian Friel wrote from.

The biggest fire I have ever seen was lit across the Foyle – on that opposite shoreline – the night our friend was murdered. The night his broken body was found in a hollowed-out part of the earth in the woods above our home.

This – the knowledge that our fire may have sent its light into the eyes of Brian Friel – moves me in a way I cannot quite find the words for.

Beacons, fires, lighthouses – what message – what signal – are our ancestors sending us across the waters between us and them, then and now? What signal are we sending to those in front of us, on the other shore?

The first time I became aware of fire as being something other than the warmth that filled our bodies, on midwinter nights in our impoverished Derry housing estate, I was battling my way through its inky thick smoke – a wee fragile eleven-year-old girl – whose home had just been petrol-bombed in a sectarian attack.

For decades the coal-black crow I met in that underworld of a childhood bedroom followed me around like the smell of smoke on young, not yet woken up skin.

I think about it all; I take every single shard of it and I hold it all in my shaky, sooty hands. I think of how that I learned – a handful of weeks before I began to write my first book – alone from my cold home – how to light my first fire.

How that even after enduring a history with fire painted as a bringer of terror and destruction – a flame-red thread that burned through my crimson-red blood line – I found the way back to the flames; across a different threshold.

I think about how that – even though my story is laced with a once paralysing fear – an inquietude that maybe only fire can instil – I found a way to jump the embers of the past; to teach my willing hands the way to tend to a hearth.

I think about the way that the first fire I ever lit outside was on St John's Eve – a night when the veil between worlds is lifted – in a delicate and echoing *thin place*. The first fire I lit outdoors – in that raw, boundless world – where I am both part of the scene yet not even a thought for the river and the tall trees – was tended by my own self alone.

There are places in this luminous, aching world that are glassy – like the lakes of a hundred years. They are both the mirror and they are the light that you seek; for which to find them with. Those places are more the wren than the eagle – although they are not winged things, at all, these places.

There are places that I know – in the exterior and hardened parts of my bones – and right down deep inside – in my very marrow – are in fact *the fire itself*. There are places that are both hollowed and hallowed all in one. They hold space for us. They watch as we lose our way – as we send away – as we are sent away; they wait in stillness for us to find our way back.

These places are like invisible snowfall – sensed without being seen – known without being heard; swimming through the veil like fireflies on Solstice.

They are not ours but we are theirs – we are *of*, not in them – we are – for the most celestial and ancient moment – those places themselves.

These thin and sacred places wait for us to *remember.*

I think about the bones of my ancestors, on whichever shore they may or may not wash up.

I think about my own bones – pieces of me – that still hold the imprint of generations before me – folk that saw such sorrow as to shape a century and a half's history in their wake.

I think about how that if one of those bones of mine was found on a shoreline, I would want it to be burned – on St John's. For my bones to become ash in the belly of a fire – to be placed back into the earth from which I had been formed – scattered over field and threshold – to bring protection, healing and nourishment; to be a beacon for all those still left on the shore.

GEORGE ELIOT

From *The Mill on the Floss*

A wide plain, where the broadening Floss hurries on between its green banks to the sea, and the loving tide, rushing to meet it, checks its passage with an impetuous embrace. On this mighty tide the black ships – laden with the fresh-scented fir-planks, with rounded sacks of oil-bearing seed, or with the dark glitter of coal – are borne along to the town of St Ogg's, which shows its aged, fluted red roofs and the broad gables of its wharves between the low wooded hill and the river-brink, tingeing the water with a soft purple hue under the transient glance of this February sun. Far away on each hand stretch the rich pastures, and the patches of dark earth made ready for the seed of broad-leaved green crops, or touched already with the tint of the tender-bladed autumn-sown corn. There is a remnant still of last year's golden clusters of beehive-ricks rising at intervals beyond the hedgerows; and everywhere the hedgerows are studded with trees; the distant ships seem to be lifting their masts and stretching their red-brown sails close among the branches of the spreading ash. Just by the red-roofed town the tributary Ripple flows with a lively current into the Floss. How lovely the little river is, with its dark changing wavelets! It seems to me like a living companion while I wander along the bank, and listen to its low, placid voice, as to the voice of one who is deaf and loving. I remember those large dipping willows. I remember the stone bridge.

And this is Dorlcote Mill. I must stand a minute or two here on the bridge and look at it, though the clouds are threatening, and it is far on in the afternoon. Even in this leafless time of departing February it is pleasant to look at, – perhaps the chill, damp season adds a charm to the trimly kept, comfortable dwelling-house, as old as the elms and chestnuts that shelter it from the northern blast. The stream is brimful now, and lies high in this little withy plantation, and half drowns the grassy fringe of the croft in front of the house. As I look at the full stream, the vivid grass, the delicate bright-green powder softening the outline of the great trunks and branches that gleam from under the bare purple boughs, I am in love with moistness, and envy the white ducks that are dipping their heads far into the water here among the withes, unmindful of the awkward appearance they make in the drier world above.

The rush of the water and the booming of the mill bring a dreamy deafness, which seems to heighten the peacefulness of the scene. They are like a great curtain of sound, shutting one out from the world beyond. And now there is the thunder of the huge covered wagon coming home with sacks of grain. That honest wagoner is thinking of his dinner, getting sadly dry in the oven at this late hour; but he will not touch it till he has fed his horses, – the strong, submissive, meek-eyed beasts, who, I fancy, are looking mild reproach at him from between their blinkers, that he should crack his whip at them in that awful manner as if they needed that hint! See how they stretch their shoulders up the slope toward the bridge, with all the more energy because they are so near home. Look at their grand shaggy feet that seem to grasp the firm earth, at the patient strength of their necks, bowed under the heavy collar, at the mighty muscles of their struggling haunches! I should like well to hear them neigh over their hardly-earned feed of corn, and see them, with their moist necks freed from the harness, dipping their eager nostrils into the muddy pond. Now they are on the bridge, and down they go again at a swifter pace, and the arch of the covered wagon disappears at the turning behind the trees.

Now I can turn my eyes toward the mill again, and watch the unresting wheel sending out its diamond jets of water. That little girl is watching it too; she has been standing on just the same spot at the edge of the water ever since I paused on the bridge. And that queer white cur with the brown ear seems to be leaping and barking in ineffectual remonstrance with the wheel; perhaps he is jealous because his playfellow in the beaver bonnet is so rapt in its movement. It is time the little playfellow went in, I think; and there is a very bright fire to tempt her: the red light shines out under the deepening gray of the sky. It is time, too, for me to leave off resting my arms on the cold stone of this bridge...

Ah, my arms are really benumbed. I have been pressing my elbows on the arms of my chair, and dreaming that I was standing on the bridge in front of Dorlcote Mill, as it looked one February afternoon many years ago. Before I dozed off, I was going to tell you what Mr and Mrs Tulliver were talking about, as they sat by the bright fire in the left-hand parlour, on that very afternoon I have been dreaming of.

CHRISTINE EVANS

'Bluebells in Nanhoron' (2007)

Y gwyllt atgofus persawr,
Yr hen lesmeiriol baent…

R. Williams Parry, *Clychau'r Gog*

Their rising unlatches the season.
Bright as flesh, as easy bruised, they gather
even in snow, shards of a mirror

where other selves drunk on wild honeys
harvest and grieve over armfuls,
or, dubbed with sap in their deep cool bed,

dizzy ringed with love and deep-vein blue
hug a slow way home as the hard faced moon
melts and lies down in the whispering aisles.

Like ours, their roots are naked. Bare as tubes,
not gripping or resisting, they suck
last year's sugar, feed this summer back.

Slowly the canopy closes.
In its caves, birdsong first echoes
then falls hushed. Curt with seed

the dry stalks rattle, ended. Yet this afternoon
a letter tells me *Driving Mother back*
to the Home in Wolverhampton

by Nant we stopped and opened all the windows
so she might smell the bluebells.
We could not tell if it was now she'd seen

or a wood long bulldozed under, but slow tears
rinsed her eyes and she cried out
of blue, like mist, and special sharp-edged green.

For an hour she talked with sense and without pain
of lives and places eighty years behind.
We never dreamed so much could have survived.

MARGIAD EVANS
Letter to her brother (1942)[†]

*Margiad's younger brother Lt Roger Whistler had been captured near
Dunkirk in May 1940, and remained a prisoner in Germany until the
end of the war. Margiad wrote to him every six weeks or so, to keep him
grounded in the landscapes of his youth and give him hope.*

June 9 1942

I must tell you about a day we had last week. Mike was shearing lambs,
I had been out hoeing. I was just clipping the grass border when a
boy came sweating up the path. It was burning wasting hot and I had
only a pair of shorts and a sun top on. 'Please Middis Williams, Middis
Scudamore's bees have swarmed and please she says if you like to come
you could help her take them. They're id the orchard. They're as big
as a bucket hanging in the plum tree Middis Scudamore says Middis
Williams.' 'Alright I'll come as soon as I've washed up' I say and off I
rush, clatter around, dress myself up like a diver and start for Panbrook.
Oh Roger it was stifling. The sun scorched the road, the grasses were
limp, the flowers flat open as if they gasped. In hat, veil, scarf, stockings,
trousers and overall fastened chokingly tight round the neck I staggered
into Margaret's presence with the smoker and all the rest. We had to have
a cup of tea and oh when one went into the orchard they were gone!
There was the skep, the white sheet spread, the beautiful clean scrubbed
hive all ready and us wandering wild and bee-less like Mary calling the
cattle home all over the fields. We searched the garden we went down
to the brook, we looked up the chestnut tree and down a fox's earth.
No bees. Oh the heat, the despair! Finally we thought that as we were
dressed up we'd carry out a delicate operation on our hive we'd been

planning – to cut a living cell out of her best hive and insert it in ours to strengthen stock and get a new Queen. It had to be done in ten minutes. With the precious fragment caulked up in a warm honey jar we fled uphill to Potacre. By this time our clothes were wet through with sweat and our eyes bulging with incipient apoplexy. Just as we flew to the hive Mrs Nelly Peg-Leg Saunders sticks her head out of the window 'three visitors for you. I've just sent them up to the field to look for you!' Horrors! We had to go on or the cell would have got cold. One honey box was full we must put the other on. In the thick of a cloud of bees the visitors arrived; Ruth, Hilda, David. Astounded they gazed at our wild unseeing faces – we looked as if they were not. And then Mike came home. 'Mrs Hill says have you got a swarm? There's one in her garden and it's gone into an empty tar barrel.' In the cool of the evening when we had all somehow had tea and bathed off the perspiration and put David to bed, a procession of us went to take the swarm. It seemed a huge party with a wheelbarrow, a wagon rope, a tribe of dogs, boys etc we went up the road, our veils streaming out on the thundery breeze. How we scrambled through bushes, listened with our ears against the rusting cask to the buzzing inside, how we bunged it, hauled it, roped it, pushed it, got it out from under that 'elum bough' (elder) and trundled it home I can't tell you. There's no room. Only by the time we'd done it all it was dark and a car had somehow tacked itself onto us at the rear, and people thought we were wheeling a sort of bomb. Oh how tired we were, how blown with laughter. It was a lovely night – hot, with the trees swishing and the wild parsley flowers swaying by the road – oh you would have enjoyed it. That was England, Roger, the country hubbub and Panbrook's lovely wild garden with the honeysuckle and the bee barrel being pushed up the path between the box and the dusk, and the two little boys 'staying up' to wait for their father who was coming home on leave. Yes and next morning when they opened the barrel for the swarm to go into the hive there was only about one bee in it.

SARA EVANS
'Under the Opium Spell' (2021)[†]

Poppy tea and opium pill
Are the fens' cures for many an ill

Local saying in the fens

The fragile blooms of the opium poppy (*Papaver somniferum*) don't look hardy enough to survive the vagaries of the British climate. Their soft-as-silk petals appear so delicate they could be blown away by the gentlest of winds. But opium poppies are tougher than they look. Although native to Turkey, and typically associated with the sun-baked lands of Afghanistan, China, India and Iran, opium poppies are no strangers to English soils. Perhaps one of Britain's most unusual cash crops, and quite likely its most beautiful, more than 6,000 acres of farmland now fill, in early summer, with the soft pinks and hazy mauves of flowering opium poppies. And the crops are doing well. Well enough to be yielding enough morphine to meet half of the NHS's medical pain-relief requirements. The rest is imported, mainly from Spain and Tasmania. Growing the exotic blooms is both straightforward and lucrative for farmers, who also find *Papaver somniferum* to be an excellent 'break crop', preparing the land for growing oil seed rape and cereals in the next season.

Although fields of opium poppies are becoming a more common sight in the south of England, this isn't the first time they have been commercially cultivated on home soil. Between the late 1790s and the mid-1820s, a brief period of horticultural experimentation focused on growing opium poppies commercially in Britain. This activity was spurred on by the Society of Arts, now known as the Royal Society of Arts. Their remit was to encourage and reward innovation and discovery in the arts, manufacture and commerce that brought wide-reaching benefits to humanity. During the 1700s, the Society had taken an interest in the benefits associated with introducing and cultivating non-native medicinal plants in Britain. Producing opium from home-grown poppies, making it more affordable and able to reach more people, was considered one such worthy endeavour.

One speculator was John Ball, a farmer from Williton in Somerset. In 1796, he wrote a letter to the Society informing them that his experiments in opium production had left him in 'no doubt it may be brought to the greatest perfection in this country, and rendered at one half of the price from which we have from the East, and without the least adulteration'. In an earlier letter, also to the Society, he noted that 'amazing quantities [of opium] are consumed every year' and that 'twenty times more opium [is] used now ... than there was fifteen to twenty years ago' and that opium was 'continually advancing in price'. Convinced by arguments like those of Ball, the Society decided to give incentives to agriculturalists to take on a possible new cash crop. As the eighteenth century drew to a close, the Society offered a gold medal or fifty guineas to anyone able to produce at least twenty pounds, considered a significant amount, of raw opium. Horticultural men of the time took up the challenge – mainly experimenting with white poppies, believed at the time to provide the highest yields of opium.

In 1800, after six years of experimentation, a Thomas Jones's crop of poppies growing on five acres of land near London yielded twenty-one pounds of opium, landing him the Society's fifty guineas. Efforts to increase opium yields continued at a pace. A decade after Jones's opium yield made news, he was trumped by a surgeon called John Young growing poppies in Edinburgh. Young produced fifty-six pounds of opium per single acre, and in a damper and colder climate to boot. He too received a gold medal for his work. Three years later in 1823, a Dr John Cowley and Mr Staines of Winslow in Buckinghamshire became England's most successful cultivators of opium, producing '143 pounds … of excellent quality, collected … from about eleven Acres of Land', earning thirty guineas from the Society for their achievement.

Although the first signs suggested that opium production in Britain could take off, there was a stumbling block – extraction. The method used by British opium growers was largely the same as that used in the countries from which opium was imported. Opium is extracted from poppies by making them 'cry'. When cut, unripe seed pods release a milky-white sap, known as opium tears. As it dries in the air, the sap turns brown and becomes tacky and malleable, and is known as crude or raw opium. The process takes a few days but can be speeded up by scraping the sap into a container and evaporating it. Opium can then be consumed in its raw form – usually by eating or smoking – or various liquids can be added, creating tinctures. This fiddly process was best suited to the small hands of children and deft fingers of lace makers. In *Opium and the People*, Virginia Berridge and Griffith Edwards noted that a Dr Alston, a professor of botany and medicinal plants at Edinburgh University who had been producing opium on a small scale since the 1730s, collected his poppy sap 'with a little Silver Spoon … and a "Finger" before dropping it into a China Tea-cup'. This 'exceedingly trifling' nature of opium harvesting means that it was time-consuming, and was where British opium producers came unstuck. Even though labour was cheap and workers' rights few, the cost in human hours was still prohibitive. This expense, combined with the 'precariousness of the weather' and 'marauding hares', meant that the wide-scale commercial production of homegrown opium never took off. It was just cheaper and simpler to concentrate on other cash crops that were more straightforward to harvest.

However, it wasn't just experimenting botanists and horticulturalists that cultivated opium poppies. They were also being grown in people's gardens, most notably in the low-lying marshy areas of the East Anglian fens. In Cambridgeshire, Huntingdonshire, Lincolnshire and Norfolk the poppies were considered a common sight; as noted by Charles Lucas, a fenland physician practising in the 1800s, who wrote in his memoir that a 'patch of white poppies was usually found in most of the Fen gardens'. These poppies weren't being grown for their blowsy, ethereal beauty. They were being grown for the contents of their stately urn-shaped seed heads to magic up medicine in the kitchen with. They were cultivated to make poppy-head tea.

Making the brew was simple, and generally concocted by the women of the house. First, dried poppy heads, the size and colour of walnuts, would be split open. From the torn seed head, the plant's little black seeds would be set aside for baking with or for sowing in the spring to guarantee a new patch of poppies come the summer. Next, the poppy heads were ripped and shredded until they resembled battered straw and then dropped into a pan of water on the stove and heated through until turning mushy. Once cooled, the mush was strained through muslin until dark, bitter-tasting liquid pooled out.

Although unpleasant tasting, poppy-head tea brought sweet rewards for the sick and those in need of a pick-me-up. This potent wonder-brew brought relief from a myriad of maladies including insomnia, toothache and diarrhoea. It also soothed coughs and sore throats, as well as neuralgia and rheumatics. Women drank poppy-head tea to dull menstrual cramps and ease pains associated with miscarriage and childbirth. It brought respite from the menopause, too. Made palatable with sugar, honey or camomile, poppy-head tea calmed teething babies, quietened screaming toddlers with tummy ache and soothed anxious children back to sleep after night terrors.

The tea wasn't just given to children who were ailing. It was also used to keep otherwise healthy children 'seen but not heard'. After the seventeenth century, when the draining of the fens began, more land became available to farm. But because the region was sparsely populated, there weren't enough people to work in the new fields. By the 1800s, many women found themselves recruited into 'public gangs', controlled by a gang master and required to travel and work around the fens, sometimes for weeks at a time. Unable to bring their babies and young children with them, many mothers had little choice but to leave their little ones at home. These left-behind infants, cared for by relatives or childminders, were often dosed with poppy-head tea. Any fractious or overwrought child missing its mother could be easily calmed with a sip or two of the narcotic brew. Reduced to sleepy little shadows, children drinking poppy-head tea lost their appetites, becoming easier to look after and cheaper to feed.

As the 1800s progressed, poppy-head tea fell out of use as the therapeutic tipple of choice. The traditional home-made cure-all was replaced by cheap and readily available commercial pain relief, and opium poppies gradually disappeared from fen gardens. Opiates were still the default painkillers, but opium in its crude form was the main ingredient in a variety of tinctures and potions. Laudanum, often referred to as 'ludman' in the fens, was a popular preparation, made by mixing opium with alcohol and distilled water. Like poppy-head tea, laudanum tasted bitter. In *How to Speak Fen*, Rouse comments that to make the preparation more palatable to fen children, it was common to add a few drops of laudanum to a lump of sugar. The doused sugar lump would be then wrapped in cloth and tied to a child's wrist so it could be sucked on like a dummy, enabling the child to self-medicate. Flavoured laudanum was also available. The off-putting taste was made palatable with all manner of culinary additions, including sugar, honey, cinnamon, cloves and liquorice, treacle, saffron and lemon. There were more than ten brands available just for children – including Street's Infant Quietness, Atkinson's Royal Infants Preservative and Mrs Winslow's Soothing Syrup. Adults took laudanum too. They drank it to numb pain and beat insomnia and to provide distraction from their harsh lives in the fens, imbibing it on those days when their 'souls needed rubbing down with silk'.

Opium pills, sticks, squares and lumps, as well as lozenges, salves and syrups were all available. In towns, opium goods could be bought cheaply from market stalls, general stores, grocers and chemists. In pubs, beer and spirits were laced with it. In his memoir, Dr Lucas noted that opium was so widely consumed in the fens, 'there was not a labourer's house ... without its penny stick or pill of opium, and not a child that did not have it in some form'.

At weekends, labourers left their farms for the towns, stocking up with opium. Not just for their own use but for their ailing animals too, because they 'fat better when they're not crying'. Those that stayed at home found their needs met by travelling hawkers selling opium wares in villages, visiting hamlets and isolated farms around the fens. Few would miss out on the opportunity to self-medicate.

Inevitably, the heavy use of opium in the fens began to be commented on. The small cathedral city of Ely in Cambridgeshire was widely referred to as the opium-eating capital of the fens, a place where 'the sale of laudanum was as common as butter or cheese'. In 1867, the British Medical Association estimated that half the opium imported into England was consumed in Norfolk and Lincolnshire. Such copious consumption took its toll. In *Opium and the People*, Berridge and Edwards note that death rates in the fens were unusually high. In 1840s Spalding in Lincolnshire, the rate was twenty-two per thousand − as high as in the industrial areas further north, like Huddersfield and Keighley. Death by opium poisoning in the region was also far higher than the national average. Fen populations, were, quite simply, coming undone.

In the towns, a rise in infant mortality rates also raised eyebrows. In north Cambridgeshire, in the market town of Wisbech, 206 children per 1,000 were dying, far more than in industrial Sheffield. Doctors noted that babies dosed on opiates, notably laudanum, were underdeveloped, 'wizened like little monkeys' and resembled 'little old men'. Typically, they died from malnutrition because of opium's effect of masking hunger and reducing appetite. However, the true scale of children dying this way could not be established because their cause of death was often recorded simply as starvation.

A newspaper report covering the inquest into the death of a little girl in the Lincolnshire fens in 1825 resonated with this description of opiated children. The report concerned Rebecca Eason from the village of Whaplode and was published in the *Stamford Mercury*. Rebecca was described as 'Diseased from birth', 'unable to walk or articulate' and despite being four years old 'did not appear to be more than a few weeks old'. The coroner investigating Rebecca's death, Samuel Edwards, concluded that although she 'Died by a visitation from God ... the great quantity of opium taken by [Rebecca's] mother during her pregnancy of the said child and of her suckling it ... greatly injured its health'. The newspaper report also noted that Rebecca's mother 'first began taking opium after the birth and weaning of her first child, which was and is remarkable healthy' but that all children born to her since 'lingered and died in the same emaciated state' as Rebecca.

Rebecca's mother, Mary, was an opium eater. A prolific one, consuming up to a quarter of an ounce of opium during the day, according to the *Stamford Mercury*. Of her six children, only two saw their first birthdays. According to the parish register, all of Mary and Thomas Eason's children were baptised and, apart from their first born, buried at St Mary's. There are no graves for them. As a labouring family, it's unlikely the Easons would have had the means to mark their little ones' last resting places. It was common practice for small poor children to be added to the coffins of adults buried the same day.

The sad destiny of Mary and Thomas's children was shaped by the time and place in which they lived and worked. Mary negotiated a difficult geography by sleepwalking through it in an opium haze, unintentionally killing her babies in the process. After Rebecca's burial, at St Mary's in 1825, there are no more references to the Easons in the Whaplode Parish Register. No more baptisms or burials. After so many related entries, Mary, Thomas and their children just disappear, like opium poppies vanishing from the fens.

CELIA FIENNES

From *Through England on a Side Saddle in the time of William and Mary, being the Diary of Celia Fiennes* (1888)

Celia Fiennes undertook her extensive journeys around England on horseback between 1684 and 1703. In 1702 she transformed her journals into a memoir for the enjoyment of her family. The first complete edition of her travel diaries was published in 1888, edited by Robert Southey.

Cumberlandshire

They reckon it but 8 mile from the place I was at the night before, but I was 3 or 4 hours at Least going it. Here I found a very good smith to shoe ye horses, for these stony hills and ways pulls off a shoe presently, and wears them as thin, that it was a Constant Charge to shoe my horses every 2 or 3 days; but this smith did shoe them so well and so good shoes y^et they held some of the shoes 6 weeks. Y^e stoniness of the ways all here about teaches them ye art of making good shoes and setting them on fast. Here I crossed one of ye stone bridges y^et was pretty Large wch Entered me into Cumberlandshire. This River together with ye additional springs Continually running into it all the way from those vast precipices Comes into a Low place and form a broad water wch is very Clear and Reaches 7 mile in Length, Uleswater it's Called, such another water as that of Wiandermer only that reaches 10 mile in Length, from Amblside to ye sea, and this is but 7 such miles Long. Its full of such sort of Stones and flats in the bottom as ye other, near the brim where its Shallow you see it Clear to ye bottom; this is secured on Each side by such formidable heights as those Rocky fells in same manner as the other was. I rode the whole Length of this water by its side, sometime a Little higher upon the side of the hill and sometime just by the shore, and for 3 or 4 miles I Rode through a fine forest or Park where was deer skipping about and hares, wch by means of a good Greyhound I had a Little Course, but we being strangers could not so fast pursue it in the grounds full of hillocks and furze and so she Escaped us. I observed the boundaries of all these great waters (which are a sort of deep Lakes or kind of standing waters) are those sort of Barren Rocky hills wch are so vastly high. I Call this a standing water because it's not like other great Rivers as ye Trent Severn, Hull or Thames &c. to appear to Run wth a stream or Current, but only as it Rolls from side to side Like waves as the wind moves it; it's true at the End of this being a Low fall of Ground it runs off in a Little stream. There is Exceeding good fish here and all sorts of provision at ye market towns. Their market town was Peroth 10 long miles. A mile or two beyond this Ullswater, – Tuesday is the market day wch was the Day I came thither. It's a Long way for ye market people to go but they and their horses are used to it and go wth much more facility than strangers. At ye end of this Ullswater is a fine round hill Look'd as green and full of wood very pleasant, wth grass and Corn very fruitful, and hereabout we Leave these Desert and Barren Rocky hills, not that they are Limited to Westmoreland only for had I gone farther to ye Left hand into Cumberland I should have found more such, and they tell me far worse for height and stony-ness about White haven side and Cockermouth, so y^et tho' both the Counties have very good land and fruitful, so they equally partake of ye bad, tho' Indeed Westmoreland takes its name from its abounding in springs which distilling itself on Lower ground, if of a spungy soil made it marshy or Lakes, and in many places very fruitful in summer grain and grass, but ye northerly winds blow Cold so long on them y^et they never attempt sowing their Land with wheat or Rye. Y^e stones and slate about Peroth Look'd so Red y^et at my Entrance into the town I thought its buildings were all of brick, but after found it to be the

Colour of the stone wch I saw in the Quarrys Look very Red, their slate is the same wch Cover their houses. It's a pretty Large town – a good Market for Cloth that they spin in the Country – hemp and also woollen. It's a great Market for all sorts of Cattle, meat, Corn &c &c. Here are two Rivers one Called ye Emount wch parts Cumberland and Westmoreland, wch bridge I should have passed over had I Come the direct Road from Kendall to Peroth, but striking off to Ambleside to Wiandermer I came another End of ye town. In this River are great falls of waters Call'd Cataracts, by Reason of the Rock and shelves in it wch makes a great noise wch is heard more against foul weathers into the town, tho' the bridge be half a mile out of ye town. The other River is Called Louder wch gives name to Lord Landsdown's house Call'd Louder hall wch is four mile from Peroth. I went to it through fine woods, the front is just facing the great road from Kendall and Looks very nobly, wth several Rows of trees wch Leads to Large iron gates, open barres, into the stable yard wch is a fine building on ye one side of ye house very uniform, and just against it is such another Row of buildings ye other side of ye house Like two wings wch is the offices. Its built Each Like a fine house jutting out at Each End and ye middle is wth Pillars, white, and Carvings Like the Entrance of a building. These are just Equal and alike and Encompass the two sides of the first Court wch Enters, with Large iron gates and iron Palasadoes in the breadth, and then there is an ascent of 15 stone steps turned round, very Large, and on the top Large iron gates pallisad of iron between stone pillars, wch runs the breadth of the front. This Court is with paved walks of broad stone, one broad one to the house, ye other of same breadth runs across to the stables and offices, and so there is 4 Large Squares of grass in wch there is a large Statue of Stone in the midst of Each, and 4 Little Cupids or Little Boys in Each Corner of the 4 squares. Then one ascends several more steps to another Little Court wth open Iron Rails, and this is divided Into several grass plots by paved walks of stone to the several doors, some of wch are straight, others slope: the grass plots being seven and in Each statue the middlemost is taller than the rest, this is just the front of ye house where you Enter a porch wth Pillars of Lime stone, but y^c house is ye Red sort of stone of ye Country. Below stairs you Enter a space that Leads several ways to all the offices, and on one side is a Large parlour wch Looks out on these green plots wth images. The staircase very well wainscoated and Carv'd, at ye top you are Landed into a noble hall very Lofty, the top and sides are exquisitely painted by ye best hand in England which did the painting at Windsor. The Top is the Gods and goddesses that are sitting at some great feast and a great tribunal before y^m; Each Corner is the seasons of the year wth the variety of weather Rains and rainbows, stormy winds, sun shine, snow and frost with multitudes of other fancys and varieties in painting and Looks very natural – it Cost 500$^£$ that room alone. Thence into a Dining room and drawing room well wainscoated of oak, Large panels plain, no fretwork nor Carvings or Glass work, only in Chimney pieces. 3 handsome Chambers, one scarlet Cloth strip'd and very fashionably made up, the hangings the same, another flower'd Damaske Lined with fine Indian Embroidery, the third Room had a blue satin bed Embroider'd. In this Room was very fine orris hangings in wch was much silk and gold and silver; a Little Room by in wch was a green and white Damaske Canopy bed wch was hung wth some of the same hangings being made for ye Duke of Lortherdale and had his arms in many places – by his Dying were sold to Lord Landsdon.

From 'Cumberlandshire', Celia travels through Durham and Darlington to Manchester, and thence to Cheshire, where stands a monument to her, and on into Shropshire.

There is another river Called the Shark wch runs into ye Uval. The market place is Large, it takes up two streets Length when the Market is kept for their Linen Cloth, Cotton tickings wch is the manufacture of ye town. Here is a very fine School for young Gentlewomen as good as any in London, and music and dancing and things are very plenty here – this is a thriving place. Hence I went a very pleasant road Much on ye downs mostly Campion ground, some few Enclosures, I went by Dunum the Earle of Warrington's house wch stands in a very fine park, it stands Low but appeared very well to sight, its old fashioned building wch apears more in ye Inside, and the furniture old, but good gardens walled in. I also passed by several Gentlemens seats, one was Mr Cholmonlys, another Mr Listers, surrounded wth good Walks and shady trees in rows, and several large pools of water some Containing several acres. I passed over two or three stone bridges Cross Little rivers, so to Norwitch wch is 14 mile. I Entered Cheshire 3 mile before I Came to ye town, its not very Large, its full of Salt works the brine pits being all here about, and so they make all things Convenient to follow ye making the salt so y^et ye town is full of smoke from ye salterns on all sides. They have within these few years found in their brine pits a hard Rocky salt that Looks Clear Like Sugar Candy and its taste shews it to be salt, they Call this Rock salt, it will make very good brine wth fresh water to use quickly. This they Carry to the water side into Wales and by those Rivers that are flow'd wth ye tide, and so they boil these pieces of Rock in some of the salt water when ye tide's in, wch produces as strong and good salt as the others. Thence I went to Sandy head 3 mile farther. There was 12 salterns together at Norwitch – all ye witches are places they make salt in – Nantwitch and Droctwitch they make salt, for at Each place they have the salt hills where the brine pits springs: this is not far from ye place whence they dig the mill stones.

From Sandy Lane head where I baited, to Whit Church is 16 long miles over a Long heath for 4 or 5 mile, then to Bestonwood and Came by Beston Castle on a very high hill, ye walls remaining round it, wch I Left a Little on my Right hand just at ye foot of ye hill, and so I Crossed ye great Road wch Comes from Nantwitch to Chester being then just ye mid-way to Either, being 7 mile to Each. There I think I may say was ye only time I had reason to suspect I was Engaged wth some highway men. 2 fellows all on a sudden from ye wood fell into ye Road, they Look'd truss'd up wth great Coates and as it were bundles about them wch I believe was pistols but they dogged me one before ye other behind and would often Look back to Each other, and frequently jostle my horse out of ye way to get between one of my servants' horses and mine, and when they first Came up to us did disown their knowledge of ye way and would often stay a little behind and talk together, then Come up again, but the providence of God so order'd it as there was men at work in ye fields hay making, and it being market day at WhitChurch as I drew near to y^et in 3 or 4 mile was Continually met wth some of ye market people, so they at Last Called Each other off and so Left us and turned back; but as they Rode wth us 3 or 4 miles at Last they described the places we should Come by, and a high pillar finely painted in ye Road about 3 mile off of Whitchurch (wch accordingly we saw as we pass'd on) wch showed them no strangers to ye Road as they at first pretended. I passed over a Little brook a mile before I Came to WhitChurch wch Entered me into Shropshire. This is a Large market town, here are two very fine gardens, one belongs to an apothecary, full of all fruits and greens; ye other was at ye Crown Inn where I stayed, it was exceeding neat wth orange and Lemon trees, Mirtle, striped and gilded hollytrees, box and filleroy finely Cut, and firrs and merumsuratum wch makes the fine snuff, and fine flowers all things almost in a little tract of Garden Ground. From thence its 14 mile to Shrewsbury and pretty Level way. Y^e miles were long and ye wind blew very Cold, I went on a Causey 2 or 3 miles to ye town, so y^et in ye winter the way is bad and deep but on the Causey.

Y^e town stands Low, ye spires of 2 of ye Churches stand high and appear Eminent above ye town, there is ye remains of a Castle, ye walls and battlements and some towers wch I walked round, from whence had ye whole view of ye town wch is walled round wth battlements and walks round, some of which I went on. It's here the fine river Severn Encompasses ye greatest part of ye town and twines and twists its self about, it's not very broad here but it's very deep and is Esteemed ye finest river in England to Carry such a depth of water for 80 or more miles together Ere it runs into ye sea wch is at Bristol. This Comes out of Wales, Ross and Monmouthshire, there it turns about and Comes to ye town. On Each side there are 3 bridges over it, in ye town one of them y^et I walked over had some few houses built on it, as London bridge, at one End of it. Its pleasant to walk by ye river; there is just by it the Council House, an old building. Here are three free schools together, built of free stone, 3 Large rooms to teach the Children, wth several masters. Y^e first has 150^£ a year ye second 100 ye third 50^£ a year and teach Children from reading English till fit for ye University, and its free for Children not only of ye town but for all over England if they Exceed not ye numbers. Here is a very fine Market Cross of stone Carv'd, in another place there is an Exchequer or hall for ye towns affaires, there is also a hall for ye Welsh manufacture. There is a water house wch supplies ye town through pipes wth water, but its drawn up wth horses and it seems not to be a good and Easy way, so they intend to make it with a water Engine in the town. There are many good houses but mostly old buildings, timber; there is some remains of a great abbey and just by it ye great Church, but nothing fine or worth notice save ye abbey Gardens wth gravel walks set full of all sorts of greens – orange and Lemon trees: I had a paper of their flowers – were very fine, – there was also firs, myrtles and hollies of all sorts and a green house full of all sorts of Curiosities of flowers and greens – there was ye aloes plant. Out of this went another Garden much Larger w^ith several fine grass walks kept Exactly Cut and rolled for

Company to walk in. Every Wednesday most of ye town ye Ladys and Gentlemen walk there as in St James' park, and there are abundance of people of Quality Lives in Shrewsbury, more than in any town Except Nottingham; its true there are no fine houses but there are many Large old houses that are Convenient and stately, and it's a pleasant town to Live in and great plenty wch makes it Cheap Living. This is very near bordering on Wales and was reckon'd formerly one of ye Welsh County's as was Herifordshire. Here is a very good school for young Gentlewomen for Learning work and behaviour and music.

ANNA FLEMING

'Dances with Hares' (2018)

Fresh snow lies thick on the ground. Heather, grass and rocks have disappeared under a deep Christmas-cake icing. A freeze-thaw cycle has yet to happen, condensing the crystals into a crusty snowpack, and so with each step my foot plunges into soft, slippery white. My legs are immersed to ankle, calf and, where the snow has drifted into small ridges, knee. There are no human prints to follow. I am the trail-breaker and wading through this sea is hard work. I shorten my steps and adjust my ambitions. Geal Chàrn (the White Hill) eludes me today.

Suddenly I have company. The track rounds a bend and lumps of snow lift and scatter across the hillside. Hares! – dressed in their winter camouflage of blue-grey-white. Some are timid and bolt from sight. Others are less concerned, lolloping across the slopes, front feet running, powerful hind legs following in paired leaps. They stop and sit up on their rear legs; ears pricked, dark eyes open in wide lenses. I am being observed. *What will the human do next?* I continue walking and the hares scamper again. The dance continues: with each twist in the track I disturb more hares.

Scatter, pause – scatter, pause. I am a child chasing pigeons.

The hares are better equipped than me to travel over the deep glittering powder. They distribute their weight across four paws and their wide, furry back feet act like snow shoes. Their energy seems boundless; I soon tire and long to rest. A Scots pine rises from the snow, sturdy russet trunk and luxurious green needles. I make for this island of colour and lunch beneath its boughs. The sun warms my cheeks and chin; my back cools against the pine. I pile on layers and settle for a while. The December sun is low in a sharp blue sky. The snow shines. Hills, hummocks, slopes and dips – the waves of the earth – are illuminated by shadows caressing the crystal carpet. Earth soars in shades of blue: not the grey-edged tints of the sea, but a clear radiance that cuts the air. I drink in the light. It is as clean and intoxicating as vodka.

Across the burn to my right, a hare sits on a low ridge. Like me, the creature also faces south into the sun, its left eye on the nearby predator. I stay seated and as time passes, the hare relaxes, slumping onto its front legs, rounding into a cat-like ball. Occasionally the hare twitches, nuzzling and fidgeting. Between these moments of restlessness, the hare is still, facing the sun.

We are sun worshipping.

I often meet hares on the hills around the Cairngorms. To ground myself in the vast, rolling landscape of this immense place, I wander into the remote moorlands where paths are scarce. Hours pass and I see no humans. Wading through swathes of thick heather, my feet stumble on rough ground – now sinking into mossy bog, now tripping through heather twigs, now lurching over a stony hump. On this terrain, an animal path is a blessing, a faint line of direction and purpose worn into the scrub.

Suddenly the ground explodes below my feet. My gut lurches, the reverberation speeds up through my lungs and lips and I shriek! My entire nervous system is set alight. I have disturbed a hare, hiding low in the heather, still and poised. The hare sprints away, vanishing into another refuge. As my heart settles, I examine the ground. Between twisted stems, a round mossy enclave opens in the heather: the hare's form. From the front door, a path tunnels through the heather, leading the hare out onto the moor. White fibres are snared on the edges of the form: soft wisps from the hare's winter coat.

There is something arresting about hares. I am by turns surprised, enchanted and confused by them. Science struggles. Knowledge of behaviour, life cycles, breeding and population remains fuzzy. Is the mountain hare population surging? Or are they declining? Recent research suggests that their population is cyclical, going through strong and weak periods over several years. The cycles can vary between four and eleven years with distinct regional differences. There is a lot to learn.

In the UK, mountain hares (*lepus timidus*) are now only found in Scotland and the Peak District, whereas the larger brown hare (*lepus europaeus*) is common through Britain. (Brown hares stay the same colour all year; mountain hares change their blue-brown coat for white each winter.) Mountain hares thrive on grouse moorland, where predators are reduced and heather is regularly burned to provide nutritious shoots for grouse. In these areas, some gamekeepers also manage the hare population. As images of culls (mounds of fluffy white bodies) are shared online, mountain hares become political. They are a challenging discussion point for Scottish estates, organisations and the government. Land-management strategies are hard pushed to find a middle ground between increasingly polarised perspectives.

The controversy and uncertainty around hares is perhaps a new iteration of an ancient troubled relationship between man and hare. A poem from the thirteenth century spells out some of the problems. 'The Names of the Hare' (translated by Seamus Heaney) provides a litany of nicknames that man must recite 'with devotion and sincerity' upon meeting a hare. There are few terms of endearment within the lengthy incantation. *The lambs-in-flight, the jumper, the racer:* some names describe the creature's swift movement. *The sit-tight, the fern sitter, the earth sitter:* other labels portray the hare at rest. The hare's stillness can be seen as sinister: *the lurker, the skiver, the skulker. The purblind, the wall-eyed, the starer* capture the hare's disconcerting stare. Other names gesture to the edginess of *the sudden-start* animal and the impact of its flighty movement upon the human: *the shake-the-heart, the scare-the-man.*

The hare is *the creature no one dares to name*. Perhaps such a wealth of nicknames exists because the hare's proper name was taboo. In the Cairngorms, Gaelic place names refer to many animals: Allt Bheadhair (Burn of the Adder), Creag a' Chait (Cliff of the Wildcat), Creag nan Sionnach (Rock of the Foxes); there are none for *geàrr* or *maigheach*, the hare. In the world of Harry Potter there is a similar linguistic avoidance. The powerful dark wizard, Lord Voldemort, is widely referred to as He Who Must Not Be Named. Direct naming can be dangerous.

Hares were considered powerful creatures. Across the globe, sinister folklore follows the animals. There are tales of fire, ghosts, hauntings and death. Some hares were thought to be witches' familiars. This culture of fearful respect may reach back through time to our ancient ancestors. In a soft limestone cave in south-west France, animals are etched into the dark walls. Among horses, bison, deer and humans, there is also a smaller mammal. A creature that sits, braced and attentive – poised, ready to spring across the dark walls. This animal has a large round belly, two delicate front legs, long ears and a huge staring eye. The hare etching is at least 11,000 years old.

George Ewart Evans, a writer who collected hare folk stories from around Britain, suggests that we have a troubled relationship with hares because the creatures are an archetype. For thousands of years, the hare has played the role of mythical symbol: a mirror that we use to understand ourselves; a reflection 'wherein [man] sees his own moods, his own virtues, his own vices'. My struggle to place the hare may not be so strange after all.

A few months later, I return to the track below Gael Chàrn with a friend who is keen to find mountain hares. Without snow the way is easy and we yomp along, taking bounding strides. Rounding a bend, we reach the stretch where the snowy hillsides crawled with white hares. Today, clouds race and heather flails. But there is no other movement. The hares have vanished.

Settling on a boulder, we pause for tea, looking out over a huge stretch of open moorland. Down in the glen a track leads up into the remote hills past a couple of ruined cottages. Dark holes in the roof and windows show where the birds get in.

Trickling water, grouse calls, a breeze in the heather. Bill is a composer, walking these lonely moors to listen to the world of the hares. Roaring burns, stag calls and wind loud as a jet engine: these are some of the sounds he will hear over the next seven days. From our rock, which rises out of an ocean of brown heather, we share stories of ghosts, magic and mystery. I point to the pine where I lunched with a hare.

We fall quiet. Then Bill asks an unusual question.

'How would you represent a mountain hare on the stage?'

I pause, turning the problem over in my mind. This is difficult. Hares have so many different aspects and behaviours. Running, hiding, watching, relaxing, frisking, quaking, yawning, bathing: one moment they are relaxed and calm; the next they have startled you out of your skin. They are movement and stillness. They are mystical and ridiculous. They are contradictory and strange. How could you possibly capture all of this on stage?

I picture the way that hares catch the eye in a dazzle of movement. In days gone by, these animals provided a mirror for our own shimmering complexity. They have been revered and feared. The hare's myriad nature is flashes of a thousand glittering faces. An image leaps to mind.

'A disco ball.'

We laugh and gaze across the dancing heather.

TIFFANY FRANCIS-BAKER

'Gone to Earth' (2021)[†]

I don't remember much from school science lessons. Physics was criminally dry, chemistry too difficult, and biology focused too much on the cell structure of a potato rather than tigers and rainforests and evolution. But I do remember something called the law of conservation of energy – the idea that energy can neither be created nor destroyed, only changed from one form to another. A stick of dynamite, for example, converts chemical energy to kinetic energy, heat and sound when it explodes, but none of that energy is lost. In the eighteenth century, the French natural philosopher Émilie du Châtelet became one of the first proponents of the law of conservation of energy, when she translated – and added to – Isaac Newton's book *Principia*, although, unsurprisingly, she has been largely forgotten by history, or remembered only for being the mistress of Voltaire. When I first heard the term, it was nothing but a factoid for me to regurgitate onto an exam paper, but it stayed with me nonetheless, slowly resurfacing over time until, within the last few years, it has changed the way I exist in this strange and wonderful world.

When I became a mother, the hormonal changes sent me into a depression. There was a chemical imbalance in my brain which the doctor treated with a selective serotonin reuptake inhibitor, a drug that is safe for breastfeeding but also gives me very vivid, mundane dreams, like the Tesco man delivering the wrong food. It took a few weeks for me to seek help because new mothers often experience 'the baby blues' after labour, a temporary sadness lasting a couple of weeks, and I was waiting to see if things would pass naturally. They didn't, and in my lowest moments I found I could not stop thinking about life and death – unsurprising, perhaps, when I had just grown a new life in my belly and brought her into the world. Motherhood is the closest I have felt to my mammal self, a mortal creature of blood and salt and bone.

Postnatal depression has been a lesson in accepting the things I cannot control. Medication allows me to feel myself again most of the time, but for those hours when my brain still refuses to right itself, I am learning to turn my back on the falsehood of depressive thought. At the lowest points, it feels like somebody has invaded my brain and planted ideas there that aren't mine, which means no amount of reason or reassurance can lift me out of the fog. I waste hours of energy trying to process anxieties that aren't designed to be processed. The battle is lost before it begins. Instead, I am now learning not to negotiate with terrorists. When these thoughts slip through the cracks and into my head, I acknowledge they are there, then turn away. Go for a walk. Make tiffins. Make tea. Watch *Poirot* and sing to my daughter until my little grey cells are reclaimed, and I can feel the sun, once again, pouring into my mind. Some days I can almost hear the battle raging, neurons firing, artillery crackling, and all I can do is sing a little louder.

In the second act of *Hamlet*, Shakespeare wrote that 'there is nothing either good or bad, but thinking makes it so'. It's a moral curiosity whether good or evil can be interpreted through perspective alone, but I have always loved the idea that you can choose if something will affect you in a certain way, whether to be angry or kind, whether the cup is half full or half empty. In the four months since my daughter was born, I have seen how powerful the mind can be, the self-saboteur convincing itself that life is grey and joyless. How different my postpartum walks felt, for example, in weeks five and fifteen. The former full of September sun, ripening fruit and birdsong, but everything I saw, heard, smelled – it all drew my mind back to darkness. Yet the latter, rain-soaked and grey-skied, the leaves rotten and winds fierce, were ablaze with the stirrings of life, gangs of long-tailed tits in the bare trees, mushrooms unfolding from the glistening earth. I felt the dichotomy of life and death to be an illusion. Energy cannot be created or destroyed, only changed from one form to another. I came from the soil and so did my daughter, and the energy that binds us – that which we tenderly call love or, perhaps, the soul – this energy is eternal, and will weave its way through the earth, the trees, moths, mountains and stars, for all time.

In the early 1970s, James E. Lovelock and Lynn Margulis had the idea that Earth and its biological systems behave as one entity, regulating conditions on the planet within boundaries that are favourable to living things. The luminosity of the sun, for example, has increased by 30% since life began almost four billion years ago, yet the Earth's living system has reacted as a whole to maintain temperatures at a level suitable for life. Their theory became known as the Gaia Hypothesis, named after the Greek goddess Gaia and the ancestral mother of all. Nature is often personified as female because women, like nature, are a source of life. Our bodies are regulated by cycles, giving many of us the ability to grow children in our wombs, give birth to them and nurture them. Wherever I look, I find the seasons ripe with feminine energy; frothing elder florets dripping with thunder flies, oak trees encased in a single bronzed shell, a waxing moon swelling the ocean tides, back and forth. In Wiccan traditions, a deity known as the Triple Goddess is formed by the Maiden, Mother and Crone, all aligned with the female body, the lunar cycle and the rhythms of life and death.

★

I am walking in the birch woodland near my home, sandy soil beneath my feet and a buzzard in the autumn sky. The dogs run in circles and my baby is asleep on my chest. The last leaves of the season are lingering like the embers of a spent fire. Turmeric, saffron, dusty red — each one, too, on my daughter's golden head. The air is cool but there is warmth, still, in the beating soil, and I think of Hazel Woodus in Mary Webb's *Gone to Earth*, a story about a young woman caught between the worlds of nature and men. She urges me, in her wild way, to keep seeking what she seeks — a craving for 'everything rich, vivid and vital.' We turn to the south, behold a lilac-veiled sky, and slip into the shadows of the burning silver trees.

ELIZABETH CLEGHORN GASKELL

From *Cranford* (1851–1853)

The mention of that gentleman's name recalls to my mind a conversation between Mr Peter and Miss Matty one evening in the summer after he returned to Cranford. The day had been very hot, and Miss Matty had been much oppressed by the weather, in the heat of which her brother revelled. I remember that she had been unable to nurse Martha's baby, which had become her favourite employment of late, and which was as much at home in her arms as in its mother's, as long as it remained a light-weight, portable by one so fragile as Miss Matty. This day to which I refer, Miss Matty had seemed more than usually feeble and languid, and only revived when the sun went down, and her sofa was wheeled to the open window, through which, although it looked into the principal street of Cranford, the fragrant smell of the neighbouring hayfields came in every now and then, borne by the soft breezes that stirred the dull air of the summer twilight, and then died away. The silence of the sultry atmosphere was lost in the murmuring noises which came in from many an open window and door; even the children were abroad in the street, late as it was (between ten and eleven), enjoying the game of play for which they had not had spirits during the heat of the day. It was a source of satisfaction to Miss Matty to see how few candles were lighted, even in the apartments of those houses from which issued the greatest signs of life. Mr Peter, Miss Matty, and I had all been quiet, each with a separate reverie, for some little time, when Mr Peter broke in—

'Do you know, little Matty, I could have sworn you were on the high road to matrimony when I left England that last time! If anybody had told me you would have lived and died an old maid then, I should have laughed in their faces.'

Miss Matty made no reply, and I tried in vain to think of some subject which should effectually turn the conversation; but I was very stupid; and before I spoke he went on—

'It was Holbrook, that fine manly fellow who lived at Woodley, that I used to think would carry off my little Matty. You would not think it now, I dare say, Mary; but this sister of mine was once a very pretty girl—at least, I thought so, and so I've a notion did poor Holbrook. What business had he to die before I came home to thank him for all his kindness to a good-for-nothing cub as I was? It was that that made me first think he cared for you; for in all our fishing expeditions it was Matty, Matty, we talked about. Poor Deborah! What a lecture she read me on having asked him home to lunch one day, when she had seen the Arley carriage in the town, and thought that my lady might call. Well, that's long years ago; more than half a life-time, and yet it seems like yesterday! I don't know a fellow I should have liked better as a brother-in-law. You must have played your cards badly, my little Matty, somehow or another—wanted your brother to be a good go-between, eh, little one?' said he, putting out his hand to take hold of hers as she lay on the sofa. 'Why, what's this? you're shivering and shaking, Matty, with that confounded open window. Shut it, Mary, this minute!'

I did so, and then stooped down to kiss Miss Matty, and see if she really were chilled. She caught at my hand, and gave it a hard squeeze— but unconsciously, I think—for in a minute or two she spoke to us quite in her usual voice, and smiled our uneasiness away, although she patiently submitted to the prescriptions we enforced of a warm bed and a glass of weak negus. I was to leave Cranford the next day, and before I went I saw that all the effects of the open window had quite vanished. I had superintended most of the alterations necessary in the house and household during the latter weeks of my stay. The shop was once more a parlour: the empty resounding rooms again furnished up to the very garrets.

JOSIE GEORGE

‘Forest’ (2021)[†]

Being in the forest in a wheelchair is different from being there on foot. It has been years since I have been able to walk freely under trees but I still remember it: the weight of my footfall meeting uneven ground, the bend and snap of stem, the give of leaf-litter, the crunch and sink. I remember the connection of it all.

I would touch things back then. I'd touch everything. Because I still got tired, I would sit on the ground and feel the damp reality of it rise through my jeans. I remember the outline of the treads of my boots in the mud – indentations like teeth. I remember looking for them behind me. I was *there*. I convinced myself that all this touching and marking meant that I belonged.

We finally found an accessible forest, on the island of Sjælland in Denmark, two and a half hours from my partner's house back on the mainland.

In my chair, I do not touch the floor. I do not make a sound. The sun is low, blinking in and out of distant gaps on the treeline. Elephant-grey trunks of beech carry the shadowed outline of the saplings that grow in their shade, all leaves turned yellow and bronze. My wheels glide over the raised walkway that threads between. It curves around the trunks or splits and opens to allow smaller trees to rise up through its middle, a gap carefully jigsawed around their edges to allow for growth, like a jumper knitted a size too big. The walkway is made up of sister trees, cut and smoothed flat, and around me are trees and above me are trees. I move slowly through them, not touching, not disturbing, the rhythmic thump of my wheels over the boards a soft, ghost-like heartbeat. Ka-thump, ka-thump, ka-thump. My hands are still on my lap; my feet unmoving in their footrests. I float, head and eye turning like an owl: silent, reverent.

I have been feeling squashed, lately. Squashed by other people's voices, their insistence, their identities and dysfunctions and lifestyles, their speed and their stories, their complaints and their busyness, their acerbic wit, everything dressed up in excuses and justifications. Everyone, it seems, is determined to be right and determined to be special: an exhausting cacophony of bodies trying to occupy the same space. It is a suffocating kind of squeeze. A frightening, claustrophobic trampling. I have been confused and lonely in it, because I know I do it too, this jostling for space and attention, and it feels like this terrible fog of a disease that we're all trapped in and I can't see the way out of it, as I battle to hear what is not said, who doesn't get to speak, what's shushed out to the edges.

I see it in our talk of nature and wilder spaces increasingly, too. Nature is being repackaged. To encourage us to love it better, to save it, we are told more and more that it will make us feel good, that it is something designed to heal us. I know it is true – that it can – but I don't know how I feel about that.

Do we secretly beg and wish as we move through nature now, even in places like this? Give me something. Give me something *more*, please?

I worry.

Often, when I read people's accounts of nature and our relationship with it, it conjures up an environment more artificial to me than the concrete industrial estate I'm used to back in England. I can't help but notice what has been carefully emphasised and wonder what, and who, has been left out. I wonder how the writer wishes to be perceived; what they wish to prove. I find I want to ask, to plead: tell me that you don't really know after all. Tell me that your stories, your perceptions, your truths, are all as unreliable as mine. That you're afraid and lonely too, that you're making up words and pouring out speeches because you're frightened that if you don't, you'll disappear. Maybe then I'll better believe what you have to say and be able to connect with it.

In the forest, everything is quiet and nothing is pretending. In this forest, there is even space for me, when I can't walk or swim or explore or conquer, or be the first to see or do anything. I can't be special here. It is a relief, I think.

I decide that I will not beg the trees to heal me. I believe they have enough to do. I think, instead, I will try to come and go and not demand a reward. I imagine that I hear the trees say in response, Yes, just see me clearly.

Not being able to access wild nature easily – only through the thoughtfulness of humans who lay down paths like this – reminds me that nature does not exist for me to enjoy it. It is wonderful when we can overlap peaceably in space and conversation like this, but the world has its own life and needs that do not need to always match or affirm my own. In the wheelchair, in the woods, my body disappears. It leaves no mark. I am surprised by how much courage it takes to let this happen; to let go of myself and my story, even for a moment.

I am afraid. I am afraid that if we don't find better ways of making each other feel loved, seen, valued, that we'll continue to mine all this around us in a hundred new ways. I'm afraid that our planet will die as we shovel things and people and nature itself into this great furnace of fear and unmet need.

Maybe what the world needs most is for us to simply take better care of ourselves and each other so that we don't always have to make such a noise and such a mess. There aren't many beliefs that I'm confident enough to put my name to, but a surety is growing in me that saving the planet is intrinsically tied up with learning to save ourselves, to save our own minds, and a willingness to not try and shape every story and every moment to serve us.

I am beginning to believe, too, that one of the gifts of accessible wild spaces is that it allows for gentler, quieter openings and partings like this one. A spaciousness and a freedom; a way for us to come and just be rather than come and claim, where we don't feel like we have to force or insert ourselves into the picture. Where we have to be humble. It means an easy coming and an easy going away again.

I leave the forest with the leaf light on my face. The hand of my partner behind me reaches to touch my shoulder as he pauses in his pushing. I think again what a gift it is to the world to know down to your bones that you are loved and safe; how it might be the one thing that stops us taking any more.

Sometimes I want to be right and special too. Other times I think I'd rather move in and out of life on silent wheels, confident of where I start and stop and where this complex, beautiful world overruns me, knowing that we belong together, that I've always belonged here, and that I don't need to prove a thing.

Sometimes I'd rather move just like this.

CHRISSIE GITTINS

'Otter' (2016)

I knew the river hid
behind the bank,
lying, like a length of silk,
stretched between the willows.

The surface ripped,
something dived –
gone too long to be a bird.

Weasel head above the water,
down he went again,
a flash of oily fur.

He swam up beside,
this time he stayed,
looking at me straight.
I walked to keep his pace.

I loved his length –
his tail his body,
his body his tail,
his tail the river's length.
We moved together
through the wind,
along the river's course.

Another dive,
I skimmed the current,
searching for his guise.

He'd gone on alone.
I felt him though,
gliding through
the river's strength.

SINÉAD GLEESON

'Islanded' (2021)[†]

June 2016

It was summer, and the days should have been sun-packed and heat-fuelled. Rain as distant as Christmas, or the red-leaf carpets of autumn, but I knew I couldn't count on that. Not in the remote place I was heading for. Getting to this place in Ireland – a country you can drive the length of in single-figure hours – took an entire day – and a taxi, train, walk, bus, ferry and a lift in a van. I was slowly trying to tilt my world, to transition into someone else. A writer, maybe. Going to a cut-off place seemed like the way to do it. Physically removing myself from family and work commitments. The chance to escape offered headspace, and I had waited months for this opportunity. Now that it was finally here I felt guilty – and if I'm honest – some dread. There would be nothing else to do but write. No hiding from the words, and no instant way back to the mainland.

I took the train west to Galway, across the waistline of the country, a belt of flatlands and flooded fields. Towns that bus routes now bypass, the motorway killing off newsagents and drapers in favour of Aldis and B&Qs on its edges. On the last stretch, light already dwindling, flashes of the Atlantic begin to appear. On this coast of Ireland the rain arrives with angular stealth, from Dingle to Donegal. Outside a café, awaiting the ferry, I sit under an awning listening to the rattle of raindrops, willing it to be summer.

The news has become unbearable. In Britain, a referendum on leaving the EU approaches and the discussion is shrill and combative. There are accusations and counter-attacks; everyone shouts. Lies and hyperbole drown out the debate. Facts are manipulated; hammered into the shape each side wants them to be. If the result is Leave, more than just one country will depart. It will be a disintegration of an (albeit troubled) economic bloc. Britain is Ireland's closest neighbour and biggest trading partner; there are centuries of shared history, many of them painful, and Ireland is the only EU country to share a physical border with the UK. The possible return of hard-border patrols would be traumatic for many in Northern Ireland. A residual trigger of past horror. Online polls speculate that the outcome will be Remain. Friends in England are nervous. Friends in Scotland, who voted Yes in the failed Independence referendum, even more so. I will be away. I will not watch the news. I will not look at Twitter.

The old bus to the ferry smells stronger of diesel inside than out. Leaving behind roundabouts and traffic lights, the rain rolls in and we crawl through coastal Connemara, places that make me think of the Famine or drowned sailors. At Ros a' Mhíl harbour the Aran Island ferries huddle, and the largest one is bound for Inis Mór, the biggest of the three islands. The Inis Oírr boat is smaller and less convincing. I eye it up, along with the rain-bulge of clouds and the night starting to fall. We pull out into the Atlantic and waves rear up instantly. Palominos of water gallop towards the boat, and people stay in their seats, green-cheeked. There are buoys along our path, one shaped like a bell. A klaxon against the swell. I fix on a specific spot, trying to keep my eyes on it as we dive forward. Eventually, the momentum forces me inside, where it's easier to ignore how vulnerable we are, out there on the ocean.

I've been offered an entire month of a residency which – for me – is not an option, so my stay will be less than a week. Accommodation is a small studio flat in an arts centre, the most westerly performance space in Europe. I drag my suitcase up to my room and make up the bed. The evening is darker than it should be for this time of year.

I lie down.

Unmoored.

Unsure.

The Aran Islands formed 350 million years ago and were first occupied in 3000 BC, and again in the late Bronze Age by people who built Megalithic tombs, which still survive. Its karst landscape of rugged limestone is shared with the Burren, across the water in County Clare. The soluble rock dissolves over time, and there are drainage systems and sometimes caves beneath, a land beneath the land. There's a sense, among all this stone, that this is the only place in the world. That it's everywhere else that is remote.

While here, I planned to finish a promised essay for a journal, and told the editor it was about ghosts. Ones I've felt – one in particular – and the mythology behind spirits and hauntings in Ireland. The more I wrote, with the deadline looming, the more the piece veered off in an uncomfortable direction. I tried to wrestle it back, to steer it another way, but it wouldn't listen, and insistently attempted to refocus my gaze. LOOK at me, it urged. Write about me, it said.

At the height of summer, Inis Oírr's year-round population of 250 swells. Just before the Great Famine in 1841, 3,500 people lived here, but the numbers have dropped, and many are seasonal dwellers. This is a Gaeltacht region and people speak Irish as their first language. From late May to September, tourists visit and children come to learn Gaeilge. I was here aged fifteen, sharing a house with ten girls and a Bean an Tí ('Woman of the House'). We took daily language classes, with punishments administered for speaking English. At night we gathered in a big hall for a ceilidh (Irish dancing), and afterwards drifted up the hill behind it to kiss someone. Bodies swayed in the road, mouths locked together. Droves of couples, an almost silence, save for the occasional whisper, and static in the air.

Islands are a place in the mind, a floating piece of grit on the retina, a shape seen in its entirety. Countries and continents expand into long lines of landscape, extend their tentacles into continents, but an island ends at its shores and cliffs. Lady Gregory, friend of Yeats, visited here in 1898 and craving solitude wrote: 'I felt quite angry when I passed another outsider ... I was jealous of not being alone on the island, among the fishers and seaweed gatherers.'

On the first morning, I wake to a wall of rain and go walking. The road to the harbour is blanketed in grass, mottled with white clover and daisies. Past an ancient rusted water pump, once yellow, now peeling, there's a curious brown horse. He pokes his head over a wall, and I feed him handfuls of wet grass. The island is so small it's possible to walk most of it in a day, and despite the season, I encounter few people.

Ireland is an island surrounded by islands, the crumbs of the mainland. There are 503 off our coast. During elections, voting takes place a day earlier in offshore constituencies. Ballot boxes are locked tight and given a police escort to ensure no one tampers with the democratic will of its remote citizens. I wonder how people transport cars here, or beds, or furniture. The small ferry only carries passengers.

The beach – a moon of white sand – is deserted, and the bay is calm. A sign warns of dangerous dolphins (bottlenose and short-beaked varieties are found off the coast) and another about local wildlife. Scouring the bay for minke whales and harbour porpoises, there is only a sole swimmer – a woman in flippers – scything through the waves, moving away from the shore.

In the summer of 1912 James Joyce visited here and wrote 'The Mirage of the Fisherman of Aran: England's Safety Valve in Case of War' for a newspaper. He wrote, idealistically, of plans to make Galway, not Liverpool, the new port of Europe, and of its potential usefulness for the United Kingdom in the event of war. In the context of Brexit, all of Europe's busiest ports now – Rotterdam, Antwerp, Hamburg, Valencia – are in continental Europe, not Britain. Joyce keenly felt a mysticism, Celtic or otherwise, that comes with the logistics, the location, the isolation of the people on these isles. He was enamoured of the locals who gave him tea and bread; with the old kings of Claddagh and the sunken Spanish Armada ships lying on the seabed. He wrote – as everyone who comes here does – of the rain, and the sea itself: 'We set out for Aranmor, the holy island that sleeps like a great shark on the grey waters of the Atlantic Ocean, which the islanders call the Old Sea.'

Every day I stare at the downpour, trying to gauge its mood. We sulk at each other, and it seems jittery, full of nervous energy. I briefly locate the horizon and imagine trying to scoop up a piece of this sea. Like picking up glitter with a fork.

The ferry is a lifeline for islanders. Only one service operates year round (the one I take) but there are more routes in summer. Aer Arran offer flights, and planes can be chartered, but for most, the boat is the main connection to the coast. Decades ago there was no reason to leave, except for work in Galway, Clare or Mayo. Going further afield meant not coming back, ensnared by cities and smoke and buildings of several storeys. Journeys, unlike today, that meant never coming back.

★

The first flight to the islands took place in 1970. There are stories of how, when the power went out – as it often did on a small group of islands – the locals with cars were summoned to the airstrip, their headlights straddling the runway, guiding the pilots' descent. Modern light-keepers with their engines humming.

I cave and look at the news. Brexit campaigning has peaked. The UK is an island, already physically cut off from Europe. It's not the empire it once was, and a century has passed since its policy of Splendid Isolation. Its islandness starts to feel ominous.

The ghost essay has slipped away from me. Writing it, digging back into the past has brought many difficult things to the surface. Outside, the rain, it taunts. I keep reminding myself that it is June. The sun is off in another part of the continent, deserting the people who want to swim and eat ice cream. I postpone yet another walk to the lighthouse, but have seen its black-and-white daymarks in the distance. I put one word in the front of the other. I make tea. I try not to turn on the broadband until I have a certain amount of sentences. The referendum looms and Europe feels very far away.

Summer is trying to assert itself, but at night it's impossible to ignore the wind. This is a lonely place, and the winters must be tough. Sleepless, I search Marine Traffic for passing ships, but at night, all the fishing boats are tied up. The ferries are silent until morning. Hundreds of miles out, there's a bulk carrier from Gibraltar, which left Murmansk eight days ago and won't arrive in Sardinia for another five.

One room in the apartment is an artist's studio with windows on all sides. A previous guest has stuck the words *'n eader'* ('I wonder') and

'It Could Be' onto the glass. Across belts of green and tessellated walls, I know the sea is out there. The rain persists as a steady drizzle, but occasionally it thins, and the Atlantic appears, a blurry version of itself. I glimpse the white curl of a breaker, and the rain clears for an hour. Finally, the bulk of the neighbouring island, Inis Meáin, looms into view. A storm moves in and it's gone again, reappearing later like a Fata Morgana.

Roderic O'Flaherty's *West or H-Iar Connaught* (1684) describes the layout of the three islands 'as in a sea parenthesis'. At one end of Inis Oírr lies the *Plassey*, a shipwreck from 1960, made famous in the opening credits of *Father Ted*. A rusted shell coughed up by a wave, now mottled orange in its resting place, it resembles the curve of a bracket. At the far end of the island, the lighthouse is an exclamation mark.

At night, the building quietens and I think of the island lying prone in the sea as the waves whip around it. Its grey mass like a whale at rest, never fully asleep. Islands must persist in their self-sufficiency, must maintain their connection to the mainland. Is this umbilicism reluctant, but necessary?

Having come so far to Aran, I am determined to visit Dún Aonghasa, an 1100 BC clifftop fortress on Inis Mór. It has been a lifelong obsession: its complex architecture and ancient circles, the commitment and dedication to its construction so long ago. There is no same-day ferry between the two islands, so making a pilgrimage requires staying over. Every hotel room on the island is booked, but I find a small room via Airbnb, near the harbour. The boat over is small, and I make the mistake of sitting outside, arriving in Kilronan wave-slapped and salt-sprayed.

★

Once, to deter a man who hassled me in a bar, I lied and said I was engaged. The lie widened like a truck of spilled milk and I declared that I was getting married the following month on top of Dún Aonghasa. I imagined myself as a Druidic bride, shouting my vows over the wind and stone.

The next morning I set off from Kilronan harbour, a seventeen-kilometre round trip to the fort on a hired bike. The last time I've cycled any distance was in my teens, when my unyielding bones struggled to rotate the pedals. The clouds are emptying themselves of all water, but I cycle the thin coastal road. There is a sole glitch, when momentum deserts me on a hill and I topple into a ditch, onto a recently deposited pat of cowshit. A French tourist stops to help, but I can't answer him through laughing. Rain-blind, I arrive in one piece at Dún Aonghasa.

Getting to the top involves a trek over uneven stones and narrow steps. Weather has made the rocks slippery and several elderly tourists turn back. The view is worth a hundred walks up. The half-circle fort is comprised of Chevaux de Frise, tiers of defensive stones. It is haunting and heart-stopping, and exceeds all expectations. Wind-whipped on the clifftop, with sea-salted hair, I watch American students stand on the edge taking selfies. An OPW (Office of Public Works) woman hovers, a warning on her lips. I lie on the ground and inch my eyes over the side, to the sea a hundred metres below. A boom like a cannon sounds, a gathering of noise in the air, from the waves rolling into the caves below the cliffs. This place is a spell. Magic and memory are hammered into the rocks.

Waiting for the ferry back to Inis Oírr, I get talking to an Englishwoman who is sorry to be missing her chance to vote to leave the European

Union in Thursday's referendum. What about your passport? I ask, your freedom to move around the EU?

What about it? she replies.

Back on my temporary island home, I open the ghost essay and try again. Night sounds are amplified: the bones of the building settling, the rattle of beams. Resurrecting ghosts on the page might just be summoning these sounds, the words infecting my hearing. I google the building. A former linen factory built in 1982: too young for hauntings, I think. But the land here is ancient. The spirit of any fisherman or jilted lover could wander up these steps.

On my last night, Ireland play Italy in the European Football Championships, and I watch the game with an Italian woman, the owner of the arts centre. We sip drinks and Marta is amused at men shouting bilingual encouragement. LEAN AR AGHAIDH! ('Go on!' or 'Keep moving!') and JESUS CHRIST! The room, us included, explodes when Ireland go ahead, and ultimately qualify for the next round. Tonight is my last night, and after solitary days, I'm glad of the company, of the beer, and Robbie Brady's goal.

I admit defeat on the ghost essay and email the editor to explain. The piece I eventually submit is about another place; somewhere that used to be an island but no longer is.

In the arts centre below, there is an exhibition of local stories, told through photos and text in the arts centre. One island woman talks of the red-flannel petticoats that married women used to wear here (navy for unmarried) that were handmade by locals. Another woman's tale – 'An Ribín Dearg' ('The Red Ribbon') – is about a local *seanachaí* or storyteller, who could cure headaches. He recited an *ortha* – a cure – over a sufferer, but the woman's grandmother was too ill to visit him. Instead, the *seanachaí* uttered the cure over the ribbon, dispatched it to her, and the woman wore it every time a headache came on, miles from his healing hands.

On my final day there is a wedding, and miraculously, abundant sunshine. An islander is marrying a girl from Dublin, and I'm brought to the house for tea. In the old cottage, the mother of the groom – a writer fabulously attired in an Iris Apfel way – holds forth. It is barely 11 a.m. but she offers to top up our coffees with Russian liquor, and talks about storytelling. Of how words are an ingrained way of life here; a means of survival, of entertainment, of cultural currency. Of the land, and how hard it is for the young to stay, of how they are pulled towards the magnetic strip of the mainland. Leaving an island is a complicated, timetabled experience. A reverse pilgrimage for many, who don't look back.

Instead of a month, I had only days to write here. Wintry weather and disorientating rain filled my head. It affected what I wrote, and what I didn't. Words receded into the mist, and I didn't follow them. But different words appeared; ones I didn't even know I was looking for. They accumulated and made sense. There is value in writing to figure things out, to put down words just to excise them. To learn something by subtraction.

In the tiny aerodrome, a woman instructs me to stand on a set of scales. She weighs my bag and makes calculations. The plane can hold eight people but there are only three of us, so we are distributed in seats according to our weight. Our English pilot is friendly and sits up front, making jokes. I think of asking him about today's Brexit referendum, but decide against it. We race along the tiny runway, and the craft feels more like a bus than a plane, until we lift up, and out over the rocks, across the navy sea to Connemara. Away from words I don't need and some I do, away from ghosts and ancient rock and the never-ending rain.

SALLY GOLDSMITH

'Caravan' (2021)[†]

It's late August and I'm laughing at myself for reading Thoreau's *Walden* in my old caravan. It's 1950s vintage, on a small basic site of around twenty vans in a narrow drystone-walled field and around twenty-five minutes from home on the edge of Sheffield. Midweek, and no one else is here – which is just how I like it.

My caravan is large and curvy with a bed, a small chubby wood stove, a gas cooker, a cantankerous fridge, some chairs and a table. Next door is a scrubby patch of brambles and fluorescent purple willowherb spires bending where an even older caravan sank into ruin and was removed. I come out maybe once a week to write. I tell myself that even Thoreau didn't live in his self-built hut next to Walden Pond all the time.

Most of the caravans are ancient, painted green to blend in, sort of. Some have been lovingly looked after for years, the oldest dating from 1953. Others are slowly sinking into a decrepit old age. Definitely not trendy retro though – no cutesy tarting with bunting. Shaun the Salford gravedigger, who comes every weekend, put some old patio doors in his, then made a good job of making the whole thing waterproof by roofing it with a huge plastic advertising sign from a motorway service station. His brother-in-law and workmate Paul painted his caravan black inside and gave it a cocktail bar. Once Paul had decked it out, they invited me in for the grand opening – just the three of us drinking some very cheap sweet alcohol and Shaun sharing macabre gravedigger stories. The oldest caravanner is old David who has been coming for over fifty years, every spring grumpily washing rook shit and old nest twigs off the roof. Always on his own, as his wife doesn't like it.

Today, late summer, the rowan berries are lipstick red and the grass is long and unmowed. Loud ticking from a robin, then it starts up a wistful song, different from the clarity of spring. Pigeons clump about on the roof. Though the rooks have long finished nesting in the beech tree above old David's caravan, I hear the croak of a lone one, though perhaps it's a crow. Strong breeze. It's already back-endish, as they say round here.

A breakfast of coffee, porridge and allotment blackcurrants with some local yoghurt from the village shop. I wash up with kettle water boiled on the stove, pour the waste water onto my little garden, surreptitiously tip last night's bucket of wee into the nettles.

I love the quiet – though it never is quite quiet as we're on a Manchester flight path and the strimmers will be busy later on. But the caravan is my unencumbered place, free from responsibilities. This is also my bit of frugal simple life and it's here that I've chosen to try to write a book about the lure of the countryside – why we yearn for it and whether it really is – and was – the romantic sort of place we believe it to be.

Not so long ago, most people lived and worked in the country, though some have sought even more solitude – like those ascetic saints on islands. I'm remembering St Cuthbert on Inner Farne with only the eider ducks for company. One duck obligingly dried his feet with its feathers.

Some, like my local hero – brave, gay, vegetarian, sandal-wearing, back-to-the-lander Edward Carpenter – believed the rural simple life was the way to go, part of what it was to be a socialist in the middle of the disastrous eco-emergency which was Victorian capitalism. Carpenter threw away his top hat and dress suit to get down with the locals, grow his own potatoes and campaign against the 'smoke nuisance'. Some of us 1970s hippies and feminists also thought it might be the way to go, and I lived in a rural commune for a while, back in the day.

Virtually all my ancestors, from grandparents and into the distant past, lived and worked on the land, toiling for others. No romance of the simple life for them. They were all poor. They had no choice until the agricultural depression drove them to the cities. At least the wages were better there. Others died as paupers, some in the workhouse. I find myself ignorant of their rural lives, the tasks they had to do, day in, day out and I vow to find out. I know that my maternal grandfather and his eleven siblings lived with their parents in a two-bedroomed cottage and a back-garden shed, which was built to house them as the family grew. Now my ancestors' cottages, made of local stone, cob and thatch, are lived in by people with money and reliable builders, and who drive to the city to work.

This village, beyond our caravan field, is far to the north of that place. It's a bit *Postman Pat* with a shop, a pub, a school, a church, a green, some stocks and a cross. It has a well-dressing in summer and a maypole in May, complete with dancing mobcapped and waistcoated children. A lot of walkers and cyclists pass through or stop for cake at the community-run shop, or a beer at the Red Lion. A deep, raven-haunted limestone dale carves itself into the landscape, hidden below the fields that thread the village. There are orchids and cowslips in spring. From the top field above the caravan you can see drystone walls strung across the land for miles, dividing it into strips that must be medieval or older. I've seen hares. Larks ladder their songs into the sky, swallows scoop out of the barns in summer and the lane verges are embroidered with scabious and meadow cranesbill.

Despite the swallows, hares, cranesbill, orchids, cowslips — biodiversity is low in the luminous green fields above the dale. It's all highly managed grassland, though this is the Peak District National Park. Every time a cottage comes up for sale, it invariably becomes a holiday cottage. I'm not sure how many of the inhabitants here are local. House prices are astronomical.

I read the *Peak Advertiser*'s property section in the caravan and yes, it's full of highly priced stone cottages suitable for holiday accommodation, with roses round the door and a view over fields – but the interior photos show cooker hoods, en-suite bathrooms, the ubiquitous wood stove. Outside there's usually a parasol on the patio and a barbeque. The locals must have moved away. Perhaps to the town. Perhaps, if they're lucky, to the few council houses still unpurchased under right-to-buy at the edge of the village.

When David Cameron writes his memoirs in a £25,000 shepherd's hut, painted by Samantha in Farrow & Ball colours – Clunch, Old White and Mouse's Back – you know the countryside has truly become a luxury item. I found an old shepherd's hut made in 1890 in a book of old farming tools and machines. It cost £11.10s.0d plus an extra £1.5s.0d if you wanted a wood stove in it. *The Archers'* Eddie Grundy said that the hut he is asked to build for Linda Snell mocks the working man's heritage. Good on yer, Eddie.

I suppose David Cameron and I have the lure of the countryside, if not the income or the outlook, in common. I'm trying, in this corner of Derbyshire, to critically study the longing for the rural many of us feel at a time when the UK has been identified as one of the most nature-depleted countries in the world, the earth never hotter, global politics never more unpredictable, inequality never wider. We crave David Attenborough, *Coast* and *Countryfile* on TV, holidays in fishing villages where no locals live. We read and read the newest crop of nature writers. We long for Arcadia, though it's surely a fiction.

But tonight, as I go out to the tap to fill my water container, a crescent moon is framed in the doorway and a frog jumps out of the drain. Up the field there are millions of stars and a planet over the toilet block. A hedgehog walks across the path on my way to the loo. Back inside, the old fridge hums, icing itself into inefficiency and the Manchester planes purr overhead as I sleep.

★

I'm thinking, next morning in bed in the caravan, about the five oak saplings on my allotment, saved from acorn caches that the jays forgot, and that I potted up. Via Twitter, I offered them up to anyone who could plant them. My mates Simon and Cecilia, who own and nurture a wood in the Peak District, say they'd like them. I'm to go in planting season and put them at its edge.

I'm thinking about last year, when I was out on Sheffield's streets every day – on the lookout for men with chainsaws coming to fell our street trees, 17,000 of them. Not much time for this caravan then, and even when I did make it, I'd invariably get called back to the city by a WhatsApp message warning of felling crews, chipper machines, cherry-pickers, barrier men, police, heavy-handed security personnel and arrests. It was guerrilla warfare the city over, trying to prevent the destruction of our urban forest, our little bit of country in the town.

I'm also thinking, having listened to the news on my tiny radio, about the Amazon on fire, about climate emergency and climate deniers – and about our government cosying up to them. I'm thinking about the black smoke choking the cities and wildlife. The man on the *Today* programme, introduced as an expert on the Amazon region, seems to make light of the fires, saying it's mostly subsistence farmers claiming a bit more land. How can we argue with subsistence farmers?

I'm thinking about how lovely landscapes have become a commodity, an aid in the urge to glorify the self. A couple of years ago the Isle of Skye was invaded by people who had travelled miles for selfies in front of iconic views, just to be shared on Instagram. A farmer who advertised for people to take selfies in his sunflower fields was invaded by thousands of people who trampled them and he had to close down access.

I think about the Neolithic, Anglo-Saxon, medieval farmers – the ancestors of my poor nineteenth-century farmworker ancestors – who assarted the land of trees, burning sometimes, grubbing out stumps with hand tools, in order to make more land on which to live and farm.

I think about Totley, the area on the edge of the city where I live. 'Tot' perhaps being someone's name, 'ley' an Anglo-Saxon word for clearing, the field names – Stubbins, Storth Ley – which mean this was once a wood. I think about how England wasn't much more wooded then than it is now, according to the Domesday Book. The Wildwood was a long time ago, if ever there was such a place.

I'm thinking about the contradictions inside the lure of the countryside, Englishness, manicured cottages, rural commuters, those poor long-ago labourers, the lack of black people, the bright-green fields here with no flowers, bleak moors with no trees, bereft of wildlife.

I'm thinking, early morning in bed in the caravan, about the seeming futility of planting five oak saplings.

ELUNED GRAMICH

'The Flowers of Wales' (2021)[†]

It begins at the Eisteddfod. We sit, my mother and I, in the audience, while an esteemed botanist holds forth about his book. We listen to his perfect, eloquent Welsh – the kind of Welsh I thought no longer existed. He speaks from another era, the learned late nineteenth century; after all, he is a naturalist, like those late-Victorian men who walked through the countryside with their specimen jars and magnifying glasses. The botanist says things like, *It occurred to me that we in Wales did not have a complete compendium of our flora, where those in other nations were fortunate enough to have several of such compendiums in their own language.* It was, he admits, an exhaustive undertaking. The heavy tome, *Blodau Cymru: Byd y Planhigion* (*Flowers of Wales: The World of Plants*), sits on a small plastic pedestal between him and the interviewer. The audience is rapt: women of a certain age, sharp, interested in every word.

He speaks of flowers that are native to Wales; flowers that grow in the high mountains, as though Snowdonia were comparable to the Himalayas or the Swiss Alps. He speaks of Anglesey and his native Flintshire – the plants there, special and separate from that ordinary fare from across the border, because of their names. The richness of metaphor. He gives examples: *Bysedd y cŵn* (dog's fingers), *llygad y dydd* (day's eye), *mwg-y-ddaear* (smoke of the earth). He speaks of the wild West, the plants raised on salt and limestone: rock samphire and glasswort, yellow horned-poppy and sea bind-wind, bright lilac blooms, growing out of the sand. He speaks of meadows and fields dotted with pyramidal orchid, horseradish and grass of parnassus, white flowers in wet earth.

And then I find myself at the farm again, a child, the climate temperate. Spring everywhere. The hedges full of pink and yellow petals, campions, fat foxgloves, red and taller than a man. I find myself walking along the road that leads to Mamgu, my mother's mother. There is room for one car at a time; a tractor ought to drive slow, but often doesn't. I reach the gate, and already the dogs are going wild. The land has long been rented out to other farmers who live in a caravan in front of the house, beside the barn and the road. They have multiple dogs, small and large, who leap over and under the gate. Mamgu, when she walks, carries a stick to keep them at bay, although she does not use it. The dogs know her.

They don't know me. I hurry past. They bark, follow on my heels; they're unsure about whether to stop me or let me pass until Sian comes out of the caravan and calls them back.

Shwt i chi? Iawn. Sut mae hi? Yn weddol.

The road curves into a muddy track, on the left, the field with the donkey Sian keeps for reasons my grandmother doesn't understand. He doesn't make money, but he is lovely, and that's enough. The donkey watches me navigate the deep ruts of mud. The washing line strung up; three tea towels, a red cardigan, for my grandmother's favourite colour is red. Bread crusts on the ground outside, for the birds, although it is Sian's dogs that eat them. A gooseberry bush grows outside the door, from which my Mamgu has often made a watery, sweet–bitter tart with a thick pastry lid.

Later, years later, the house will be packed up. I see it now, as I sit in the darkened audience chamber, listening, and then not listening. I see both how it was and how it is. The lino curling on the kitchen floor; a tin of biscuits, the tables covered with photographs, cards, the local paper, the *Tivyside, Y Gambo*. Tadcu's seat, which no one ever sits on apart from my mother. The sofa, also covered in old annuals, where her dogs used to sit: Rover and Prince, Jack Russells, both dead. Out of the cats, I only remember old Arthur, the black cat with one eye.

Mamgu sits in the front room. Another sofa, this time warm and covered in blankets, throws. A little tartan footstool. The fire in the Rayburn, where once she cooked pice ar y maen, welshcakes, on the griddle. On the wall, the old fathers and grandfathers look down; handlebar moustaches and long, serious faces. There are things here from all types of decades and fashions – leather bellows, paisley carpet, wooden dressers, plastic telephone; upstairs, the china collection – dogs and ladies, difficult to dust. Records but no record player. The floor is carpeted and uneven. The staircase is narrow and near vertical. The farmhouse is both full of things and empty of things, because there was a time when we went and put all of the things into black sacks and loaded them onto a cousin's trailer.

Dust in the air. My eyes watering. The double bed I shared with Mamgu when I was crying with earache. The sound of the vixens at night, screaming.

The botanist speaks his perfect Welsh, a Welsh my Mamgu and her neighbours never speak: *It is pleasing, of course, to finally see my life's work reach fruition. It is so solid a thing, don't you agree? This compendium. Although I don't doubt it is not as exhaustive as I would like it to be. There are sure to be flowers I have overlooked; flowers that have not yet been discovered.*

The flowers on the hedgerow are ordinary, discovered flowers. The red campions and buttercups. Quite ordinary. And yet I remember touching the thick, furry stems of the campions, ready to pluck them, and Mamgu instructing: leave them there for others to see. She walks slow with her stick, but she is strong. She is so strong that a neighbour has asked her to feed the Tamworth pigs in his absence. She takes me, a townie, with her; the spring sun is cool and bright. The sky is blue or, as we say in Welsh, green and blue at the same time.

The pigs are enormous. I take fright, step away from the sty where they push their long snouts against the wooden door. They are hungry, and so make terrifying grunting sounds. More like a roar than a grunt. Mamgu is slow to walk, has trouble standing for long periods of time.

I offer to get the heavy bucket with the dry feed and throw it in, but she sees my pale face, my skinny arms. *Paid â phoeni*, she says, and leans the stick against the wall while she heaves the bucket up and over the pigs' fleshy, saliva-spattered snouts. They bang their great white bodies against the flimsy wooden slats, and I move further back still, afraid they will break free.

The next day she does not ask me to go with her; she goes alone, afraid that the pigs might have broken free. It's best, she says, if you're not there if that happens.

I am relieved. I think: a sow once bit my mother's thigh.

When she washes the dishes, Mamgu has a habit of absentmindedly wiping the sink while looking out of the window at the gooseberry bushes. I don't know what she's thinking. Does she remember the days when this was a farmhouse, and she a farmer? Pigs of her own, and a barn full of dairy cows? At night, there are owls, here, in rural Ceredigion; their call is hollow and ghostly, a haunting from the other world.

Our world is a green world, maintains the botanist.

Then what colour is that other world – the world of the owl and the vixen who scream at night? I think of Arawn, the king of the underworld, and his white hounds with red-tipped ears. The car journeys at night where the headlights carve a corridor of light in the midst of countryside dark: the blackness of a moonless night; the hedges coming down like heavy, earthen waves. Beyond the hedges, a humanless, greenless place.

The book sits on the plastic pedestal. Its history a history of esteemed men with time and money. The botanist recounts them, his forefathers, the Welsh naturalists. But it is not through these men that I have discovered the flora of Wales, I think to myself, in a room full of women, sharp and listening to the botanist's supreme eloquence. A woman showed me the red campions and the foxgloves and the buttercups; the sticky creepers and the nettles; she taught me the difference between a vixen's cry and a woman's scream, warned me not to touch the nest of blue tits in the hedge in case they forget their mother.

Yet the world of plants is not eloquent; it is Cardi. It is my grandmother's Welsh – *scrammo* for scratch, *gweud* for say, cooker instead of *ffwrn*. It is sometimes putting in an English word if you don't know the Welsh; a Welsh word if you don't know the English, falling silent if you know neither.

Mamgu collects the gooseberries in a large willow-patterned bowl. The thorns are bigger this year, she says. I watch rather than help, for fear of scratching. My mother makes fun of me, but I prefer to be mocked than risk pain.

It is warm in the Eisteddfod tent, and safe of course. We applaud the botanist. The general light goes up and my mother says, What wonderful Welsh. The book sells out quickly, although I manage to get a copy. I wait to get it signed. The botanist does not need me to spell my name. I want to say something, tell him something about the nature of ordinary flowers, of what they make you think of, year after year; the way they hold the past inside their crown of petals. Their particular colour. His grey head is bowed over my book.

To Eluned, he writes.

Thank you, I say, taking the complete compendium for my bookshelf, where it is too quickly forgotten in the midst of my daily, town life.

JAY GRIFFITHS

From *Wild: An Elemental Journey* (2006)

Wild things have inherent grace, which is why all wild creatures are so bewitching – they are not just in, but they *are* a state of grace. They have that exquisite shimmer of sexual charisma that I knew in the jaguar in the Amazon. Life itself is a state of grace: at the heart of it all, there is this primaeval wild comedy, and the Earth is hot with, bursting with, fermenting with, dizzy with, hooting with, gasping with – *life*.

In the wastes of the cosmos, the black holes and implosions, the voids devoid of life, the blanks of darkness and the blanks of unliving light, the famishing emptiness, the dead stars shining light years away, light that has long ceased to be light, in the heart of the wasteland, there is this. The glad world gleaming in the dark, like the full moon in the flint.

Life. What are the chances? *Wildly improbable.* That in the wastes of space, there is this one wild and living planet, the complex, stonking grace of the thing: there is life here, now, and how it spins. Earth the feast in the famine of space, the festival in the desert. And even if Earth were home to just one iridescent dragonfly for just one morning, reeling one waltz over just one stream, it would still be enough, the flicker of grace. But life gives it more: another dragonfly, and other stream, another pitcher plant, another Mozart. Life gives it extra, just for fun. Generous, promiscuous, *have another one.*

Earth, self-created, born of self-will and stardust, made her self-willed way her own, the aboriginal I Am. Wilful and subversive planet that she is, grinning into the dark, roaring out her rebel yell, Earth is the rebel against the whole damn (solar) system; Earth, protesting against vacuum, in riot and revolt, throws her knickers at the space police. Wildness is subversive and Comedy's a rebel angel: Earth itself the ultimate wild comedian.

It is Earth that makes the eternal precession of the stars a harlequinade, primordial carnival in the puritan black. Earth the maenad, drunk on her own juices in the sober cosmos. Earth the vagrant, the flagrant minstrel, singing out her songlines to the universe. Earth the revelry, Earth the circus, doing a turn every day, with the stars for footlights and the sun the spot. Earth, clowning around the heavens, the joker in the pack of planets, the wild card. Earth in levity and gravity, rises and falls (and so holds her sway), jester to the stars. Earth with her (ice) cap and (hare) bells, the drum of the sun, penniless holder of the horn of plenty: Earth the shaman, Earth the fool, Earth the most entire and sublime joker in the ultimate subversion, subverted deadness, made life out of laughing gas and quickened creatures from slow rain, made puns of the galaxies on the spiral of a snail. She was the original anarchist wit who cracked the first joke, which split the sides of the moon and roaring with a dirty laugh fit to soil herself with good brown muck, said the first word – FUCK! – again and again. Earth the nomad, Earth the maenad, Earth the shaman, Earth the clown in boots too big, walks the wild way, the curly way, curling the stars, on, on, in fecund riot and feral grace.

MELISSA HARRISON

From *All Among the Barley* (2019)

My name is Edith June Mather and I was born not long after the end of the Great War. My father, George Mather, had sixty acres of arable land known as Wych Farm; it is somewhere not far from here, I believe. Before him my grandfather Albert farmed the same fields, and his father before him, who ploughed with a team of oxen and sowed by hand. I would like to think that my brother Frank, or perhaps one of his sons, has the living of it now; but a lifetime has passed since I was last on its acres, and because of everything that happened I have been prevented from finding out.

I was an odd child, I can see now – certainly by the phlegmatic, practical standards of the farming families thereabouts. I preferred the company of books to other children, and was frequently chided by my parents after leaving my tasks half-done, distracted by the richer, more vivid world within my head. And sometimes I talked to myself out loud without meaning to, usually as a way of drowning out a thought or a memory I didn't want to have. Father would sometimes tap his head and call me 'touched' – only in fun, I'm sure – but perhaps, looking back, he was right.

I was thirteen in 1933, the year our district began to endure its famous – or infamous – drought. It crept up on us: the hay came in well, and when the rick was thatched Father was pleased, because he knew it was dry and wouldn't spoil; this meant that the horses would have enough fodder to last the winter, and he would not have to buy any in. But without any rain the field drains ran dry and by August even the horse-pond by the house had shrunk to a thick green scum. I remember John Hurlock, our horseman, taking buckets of well-water to Moses and Malachi when they came in from the fields at three o'clock; I can see as though it were yesterday how greedily and noisily the great horses drank, how at last he would fill the buckets again and fling the water over their twitching flanks, washing away the white rime of sweat from their chestnut coats. Oh, my beloved creatures, how they must have missed walking into the cool horse-pond, as they always had, and drinking their fill.

Frank was sixteen by then, and doing a man's work on the farm; Father was starting to rely on him almost as much as he did on John. My sister Mary, who had married Clive that spring, already had a baby boy, and although Mother harnessed our little pony Meg to the trap and drove over to Monks Tye once a week with a loaf or a suet pudding, we saw little of her at Wych Farm. With Mary gone I felt strangely suspended, as though awaiting what would come next – although I couldn't have told you what that was. It was like hide-and-seek, when you're waiting for someone to find you; but the game had gone on for too long.

Of course, the drought meant that the cornfields suffered, and that year the harvest was down, our wheat barely sixteen bushels to the acre.

'Seven Acres will lie fallow next year,' Father said as John and Doble, our yardman, came in for their supper after the last of the corn was in. It wasn't what you might call a harvest home, but there was ale, and a ham, and boiled batter pudding, and mother had twisted a few ears of barley into a rough figure and set it on the kitchen table. Opposite me Frank glanced up, alert, at Father's words. The men took their places, and John remarked that Seven Acres had lain fallow only the year before.

'Do you think to tell me how to farm?' asked Father; but John did not reply. Mother sat down, I mumbled grace, and we began to eat.

The autumn of that year was the most beautiful I can remember. For weeks after harvest-tide the weather stayed fine, and only slowly that year did summer's warmth leave the earth.

In October, Wych Farm's trees turned quickly and all at once, blazing into oranges and reds and burnished golds; with little wind to strip them, the woods and spinneys lay on our land like treasure, the massy hedgerows filigreed with old-man's-beard and enamelled with rosehips and black sloes. Along the winding course of the River Stound the alder carrs were studded with earthstars and chanterelles and dense with the rich, autumnal stink of rot; but crossing Long Piece towards the Lottens the sky opened into austere, equinoctial blue, where flocks of peewits wheeled and turned, flashing their broad wings black and white.

At dawn, dew silvered the spiders' silk strung between the grass blades in our pastures so that the horses left trails where they walked, like the wakes of slow vessels in still water. At last, wintering fieldfares and thrushes stripped the berries from the lanes, and at night the four tall elms for which the farm was named welcomed their cold-weather congregations of rooks.

The dew dampened the stubble in the parched cornfields, drawing from it a mocking green aftermath that had grandfather recalling the flock of purebred ewes that once were overwintered on the land.

'It's not worth the shearing of them these days,' Father said. 'I've told you that.'

'I wholly mislike good fodder going to waste,' the old man replied, banging his stick upon the floor, 'and that's a fact.'

The year wore on, the leaves torn from our elms by autumn gales until the branches were stark. I read *The Midnight Folk* and spent my days pretending to be Kay Harker and embarking on imaginary adventures involving knights, smugglers and highwaymen, Rollicum Bitem Lightfoot the fox and a coven of witches so terrifying I eventually wrapped the book in a feed-sack and buried it under the dung-heap in case they should burst from its pages and carry me away, so consuming had my enthusiasm become.

Father sent Doble out with a billhook to brash the hedges of their summer growth, and as he worked his way around the farm, his bonfires sent columns of smoke into the winter sky. Stenham Park, a few miles away, held a pheasant shoot, and Father and John were beaters; they returned with two couples each and a brace of hares John shot near Hulver Wood on the way back.

We threshed in late November. Woken at dawn by the roar of an engine, I watched from my bedroom window as the huge and curious contraption processed along the lane towards the farm, helmed by the machinist and trailing its ragtag crew. Its wheels seemed nearly to top the hedges, and I was glad that we had not had rain; one year it had become stuck in the lane's deep mud and was only dug out in the afternoon. There had been rough words between Father and the engine driver over who would pay for the lost time.

Downstairs, mother was making tea and frying bacon.

'I expected you down half an hour ago, child. Cut some bread, enough for the threshers; the men have already eaten. And wash your face.'

I fetched two loaves from the pantry. They were round and dense and wrapped in white cloths; mother could never get the bake as light as she wanted and blamed the range, but I loved the way her bread always stuck to your back teeth and made you feel fed. Father often told her that she should use the brick bread oven in the hearth, but she said it was old-fashioned and dirty and took up too much of her time.

When breakfast was ready she went to the back door, wiping her hands on the blue apron that was always tied around her waist, and called to the machinist and his crew; they took off their caps as they came in, and sat awkwardly at the kitchen table. Shy of their strangeness and the deep accents of their speech, I made myself some bread and jam and took it outside.

Doble was in the barn making it ready for the grain, the terrier that travelled with the threshing crew busy about his feet after rats. In the rick-yard the thatch had already been stripped from the ricks; Father and John were by the engine, helping to check that the drum was level. Frank was up on the first rick, pitching the first sheaves down to the platform, his breath pluming white in the morning air; I wished that I could be up there with him, pitching sheaves, but although I helped with haymaking and weeding and standing the cut corn into stooks to dry in the fields, threshing was men's work.

All day, while I was bent over my schoolwork and breathing the odour of damp books and ink and chalk, the ricks diminished steadily. When I returned at four they were nearly gone, the engine still clanking and roaring, the men serving it as though it were some kind of heathen god. In the barn the new yellow straw was beginning to stack up, and there were sacks of chaff and seed corn and two piles of the precious grain, ready for the merchant's lorry that would soon come to take it away.

'What a mess, what a mess,' Doble muttered to himself, stooping to collect the stakes and wooden spars that he called 'springles', which had helped hold the sheltering thatch on the ricks. He hated the barn to be in disorder, as though the storing of grain were an imposition and not its true purpose.

I went to find the cats, for I felt I should be useful, and surely they would be needed to keep the mice out of the barn until the lorry came. Nibbins, the matriarch, was sleeping in the stable, but her grown-up kittens, feral and unpredictable, were nowhere to be found. I clapped my cold hands in their rough wool gloves and she raised her head and regarded me, but wouldn't stir. She knew the little terrier was at the farm, no doubt.

'Another day of it,' mother said, inside. She looked weary; even more so than usual. 'That's what your father says.'

'Just two days?' I asked, taking my satchel from my shoulder and hanging it on the back of a kitchen chair. 'Are we keeping some over? John says wheat often fetches a better price come summertime.'

'No, your father means to thresh it all now. It's just – there isn't much. It saves the wages, I suppose.'

HANNAH HAUXWELL

From *A Winter Too Many* (1989)

*Hannah Hauxwell was a Pennine hill farmer who farmed for sixty years,
much of that time alone and without running water or electricity, and
whose grace and candour won the hearts of millions through a series of
ITV documentaries about her life.*

'One's had a few winters over the years, bad winters and there's
something in my very bones that rebels when the bitterness comes
– the snow, and the cold, and the bitterness. No! I hate it! That's the
only expression for it. I know there's a certain beauty, which is very
nice, but it doesn't … it doesn't appeal to me because I detest it so.'

JACQUETTA HAWKES

From *A Land* (1951)

Perhaps I am particularly conscious of the power of Lyme Regis because I was taken there when a very small child, and, much awed by my surroundings and the strangeness of the whole affair, was left to pick out Gryphaea (or Devil's Toe Nails, the shells that had roused John Strange) while my elders used their hammers to extricate belemnites. It was, I think, my first encounter with fossils in situ, and it made a very deep impression on my imagination.

But if any recent memory haunts those mouldering cliffs, it is the spirit of Miss Anning. Mary Anning was the daughter of a carpenter at Lyme whose one claim to fame was a small transaction with Jane Austen, an encounter which took place when Mary was only five years old. Jane Austen, an honest child-hater, probably looked with a cold eye on the future 'most eminent female fossilist' whose limited fame would have seemed even more improbable than her own triumph. Now both women are part of Lyme, an element in the place as real as the Cobb itself. Like Hugh Miller, Mary Anning is a proof that even the simplest kind of creative force is irresistible, that its possessors will always thrust themselves up through the mass of their fellows. Hers, if tradition may be believed, was strangely come by. During a Lyme horse-show a storm developed, and after a terrific flash of lightning three people and a baby were seen lying on the ground under an elm tree. The three adults were dead, but the baby, Mary Anning, 'upon being put into warm water, revived. She had been a dull child before, but after this accident became lively and intelligent and grew up so.' Lyme was already conscious of its proximity to the past; a local fishmonger displayed million-year-old fishes on the slab among the day's catch, while Mr Anning himself was an established fossil hunter, often no doubt bringing back to his shop the fragments of reptilian spines which were familiar enough to have acquired the local name of 'Verterberries'. From very early years Mary went with him to the cliffs, and when he died, she carried on the trade because she and her family needed the money. In 1811, nineteen years before the young Hugh Miller saw his first Devonian fish, this twelve-year-old girl found the first complete ichthyosaur. In 1824 she made the earliest discovery of a plesiosaur; writing to Dean Buckland she commented with pleasure on the presence of its coprolite still resting on the pelvis and added that 'the neck has a most graceful curve'.

Mary Anning's extraordinary record of discovery helped to attract many of the great pioneers of geology to the little resort. She was a lifelong friend of de la Beche; Lord Enniskillen and Sir Richard Owen used to scramble over the cliffs with her, while Dean Buckland himself in his younger days was often seen in her company 'wading up to his knees in search of fossils in the Blue Lias'. During a visit from Roderick Murchison, it is recorded that Mary Anning and his wife trudged along the beach with pattens on their feet. Perhaps her greatest social triumph was a visit from the King of Saxony; she wrote her name in his pocket book and assured him that she 'was well known throughout the whole of Europe'. As is clear from her portrait, Mary Anning was quite unaffected by such triumphs; she remained secure in her own citadel, the simple woman who had made great discoveries, who had recalled much from oblivion.

EDITH HOLDEN

From *The Country Diary of an Edwardian Lady* (1906)

The Erd Shrew or Shrew-Mouse, inhabits subterranean tunnels, which it excavates in the soil. It feeds upon insects and worms; and its long flexible nose is a great aid to it in its search after food. The Shrew is very impatient of hunger and cannot endure a protracted fast; it is suggested that the many dead shrews which are found in the autumn on the country roads and footpaths, owe their deaths to starvation, the worms having descended too deeply into the ground for them to follow, and the insects having concealed themselves in their winter hiding places. The reason that their dead bodies are not carried off for food by Weasels, Owls etc. probably exists in the strong odour which exhales from the Shrew. In country districts a superstitious fear and hatred was formerly entertained against this pretty and harmless, little animal.

KATIE HOLTEN

Irish Tree Alphabet (2020)

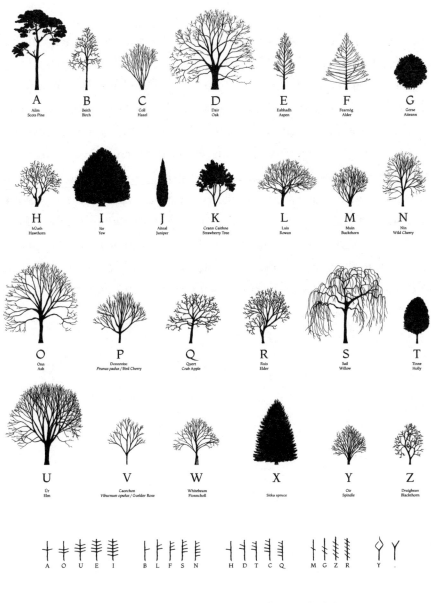

IRISH TREE ALPHABET

OLGA JACOBY

From *Words in Pain* (1910)

When during these last months of my life I admire a starry night, a calm or boisterous sea, a fine sunset, no voice whispers in my ear, 'It is beautiful, I grant, but as nothing compared to the splendours of Heaven.' To me nothing can surpass in beauty the marvels of this world; I love and admire without reserve, and thus is created in me even now the joie de vivre, which in its turn creates unselfishness better than any creed, for it appeals to our logical reasoning power, to our sense of justice as well as to the heart. I dare not spoil for anyone the beauty of the world; smile I must to give to others some of the joy I have found. No one has the right to absorb sun and happiness without being willing to radiate it again; and radiate we do, even if unconsciously, just like the moon brightens the dark night.

KATHLEEN JAMIE

'Migratory III' (2015)

Those swans out there at the centre of the loch
a dozen or thirteen
moored close together, none adrift –
they've only just arrived
an arrow-true, close-flocked, ocean-crossing skein,

and bone-weary, sleep now
heads under wings,
so darkness can restore them,
though darkness is what they've just flown.

None today is the Watcher, none the Vigilant One,
scanning the rushes of the shore
for a few notes of movement,
a fox, say, or a lad they recall
thousands of years ago
skulking in a skin boat with his broken flute
and pockets filled with sling-stones.

JULITH JEDAMUS

'The Cull' (2012)

Last night I heard gunshots in Richmond Park,
but my November mind, thick with smoke
    and fear of wars
and phantom men mistook the reason:
the cull of bucks and stags after the rutting season,
    when mast is scarce.

At dawn I walked through Bog Gate, and found
nothing: no drag mark, no blood on the ground,
    no trace of violence.
Mist threaded red bracken, and the broken ridge
of pollard oaks that march towards Holly Lodge
    and its sharp defence.

By the track they call Deane's Lane I saw him:
a twelve-point stag, his scraped horns trimmed
    with moss and bracken,
his hindquarters lean, one shin gored and clotted.
I watched him browse for chestnuts, and waited
    for a quickening, an unseen sign –
    his, the day's, mine.

'The Lucombe Oak' (2012)

It was an accident, this cross-bred tree,
this evergreen error that stands its ground
improbably, having survived two centuries
of wind and lightning. Its singular parent, found
by chance in a garden in Devon, is dead now –
killed by the man who loved its gnarled
limbs and bronze-cast crown.
A hundred feet tall it stood, his frail
colossus, until he felled it – and saved the boards
for his coffin. By the time he died they'd rotted.
Does this tree recall that vanity? Listen: the wood's
creaking. They're falling, love: the knotted
arms, snapped knees and elbows. It is no lesson,
this tree. But still, love, listen… Listen.

JULIAN OF NORWICH

From *Revelations of Divine Love* (14th century)
trans. Elizabeth Spearing (1998)

Julian of Norwich eschewed the open sky for an anchoress's cell. The doorway though which she entered would have been bricked up behind her and she would have remained in this 'room of one's own', at her own expense, indefinitely. Food was passed in and waste out through a window, another window would have given onto the street, and a third into the church of which she was the 'anchor'. The servant whom she describes recalls the vision of Mary Magdalene who mistook the risen Christ for a gardener, which in turn recalls the gardener of Eden, Adam. We are reminded that the gardener is a magician, a figure of immense power, the alchemist who brings forth 'treasure' in the form of 'noble and plentiful fruits' by their labour.

There was a treasure in the earth which the lord loved. I marvelled and wondered what it could be. And I was answered in my understanding. 'It is a food which is sweet and pleasing to the lord.' For I saw the lord sit like a man, and I saw neither food nor drink to serve him; this was one marvel. Another marvel was that this dignified lord had only the one servant, and him he sent out. I watched, wondering what kind of labour it could be that the servant should do. And then I understood that he would do the greatest and hardest toil of all – he would be a gardener, digging and ditching, toiling and sweating, and turning the earth upside down, and delving deeply and watering the plants at the right time. And this would continue to be his work, and he would make fresh water flow, and noble and plentiful fruits spring up, which he would bring before the lord and serve him as he wished. And he should never turn back until he had prepared this food all ready as he knew it pleased the lord, and then he should take this food, with the drink as part of it, and carry it very reverently to the lord. And all this time the lord would sit in the same place, waiting for the servant whom he had sent out.

And yet I wondered where the servant came from; for I saw that the lord has within himself eternal life and every kind of goodness, except for the treasure which was in the earth − and that had its origin in the lord in wonderful depths of endless love − but it was not entirely to his glory until this servant had prepared it nobly in this way, and brought it to him, into his own presence; and without the lord there was nothing but a wilderness. And I did not understand all that this parable meant, and that was why I wondered where the servant came from.

JACKIE KAY

'The Kindness of Trees' (2012)

Deep in the forest there stood
A tree whose heart beat in the winter wood
Who understood everything that was bad
And everything that was good.

It extended long arms to woo you
As the winter wind blew and blew
And every thing a child could think,
The tree already knew.

And every time a boy was sad,
The tree dropped a pine.
And every time a girl got mad,
The tree roared in the wind.

In the dead mid-winter night,
The tree blew a hello, goodbye;
When every child was asleep in bed,
The tree sang a lullaby.

And when Christmas time came round
The tree's song soared and soared.
And when gifts adorned the ground,
The tree blushed, made a sssh sound.

And people gathered round the tree:
To sing the winter song, in harmony;

One to keep the bright light glowing,
A song of what we know without knowing.

It had a sad and piercing melody –
A worry for the ash, sparrow, bee.
The polar bear, the ice melting.
A worry for you, me, dear tree.

In the depths of the winter wood,
The friendly tree stood, kind and good,
And breathed a word that caught the mood:
A pledge, a promise, a plea for good.

MARGERY KEMPE

From *The Book of Margery Kempe* (1436)

Margery Kempe is probably the first memoirist writing, or rather dictating, in English. Margery, referred to in the text as 'the creature', was endeavouring in 1433, at the age of sixty, to sail from Ipswich to visit her daughter-in-law in Danzig, but was blown off course. What follows, therefore, is possibly the first autobiographical account in English of a storm at sea.

The said creature and her companions entered their ship on the Thursday in Passion Week, and God sent them fair wind and weather that day and on the Friday. But on the Saturday, and Palm Sunday also, our Lord – turning his hand as he liked, trying their faith and their patience – sent them on those two nights such storms and tempests that they all thought they would perish. The storms were so severe and terrible that they could not control their ship. They knew no better expedient than to commend themselves and their ship to the guidance of our Lord; they abandoned their skill and their cunning, and let our Lord drive them where he would. The said creature had sorrow and care enough; she thought she had never had so much before. She cried to our Lord for mercy and for the preserving of her and all her company. And she thought in her mind, 'Ah, Lord, for your love I came here, and you have often promised me that I should not perish on land or on water or through storms. People have many times cursed me for the grace that you have worked in me, desiring that I should die in misfortune and great distress; and now, Lord, it is likely that their cursing is coming into effect, and I, unworthy wretch, am deceived and cheated of the promise that you have many times made to me, who have always trusted in your mercy and your goodness, unless you soon withdraw these storms and show us mercy. Now may my enemies rejoice and I may sorrow, if they have the intent and I be deceived. Now, blissful Jesus, remember your manifold mercy, and fulfil your promises that you have promised me. Show that you are truly God, and no evil spirit, that has brought me here into the perils of the sea, whose counsel I have trusted and followed for many years, and shall do, through your mercy, if you deliver us from out of these grievous perils. Help us and succour us, Lord before we perish or despair, for we may not long endure this sorrow that we are in without your mercy and succour.'

Our merciful Lord, speaking in her mind, blamed her for her fear, saying, 'Why do you fear? Why are you so afraid? I am as mighty here on the sea as on the land. Why will you mistrust me? All that I have promised you I shall truly fulfil, and I shall never deceive you. Suffer patiently for a while, and trust in my mercy. Do not waver in your faith, for without faith you may not please me. If you would truly trust me and doubt nothing, you may have great comfort within yourself, and might comfort all your companions, whereas you are all now in great fear and grief.'

With such manner of converse, and much more high and holy than I could ever write, our Lord comforted his creature, blessed may he be. Holy saints that she prayed to conversed with her soul with our Lord's permission, giving her words of great comfort. At last our Lady came and said, 'Daughter, be comforted. You have always found true what I have told you, and therefore don't be afraid any longer, for I tell you truly, these winds and storms shall soon cease, and you will have fair weather.'

And so, blessed may God be, a short time afterwards her ship was driven towards the Norwegian coast, and there they landed on Good Friday, and remained there Easter Eve, Easter Day and the Monday after Easter. And on that Monday all who belonged to the ship received communion on the ship.

On Easter Day, the master of the ship and the said creature, and the most part of the company, went on land and heard the service at the church. After the custom of the country, the cross was raised at about noon, and she had her meditation and her devotion with weeping and sobbing as well as if she had been at home. God did not withdraw his grace from her either in church, on the ship, on the sea, or in any other place that she went to, for she always had him in her soul.

When they had received the sacrament on Easter Monday, as is written before, our Lord sent them a fair wind that brought them away from that country and blew them home to Germany as they desired. The said creature found such grace in the master of the ship that he provided her with food and drink and everything that she needed as long as she was on the ship, and he was as gentle with her as if she had been his mother. He covered her while on board ship with his own clothes, for otherwise she might have died of cold, as she was not prepared like the others were. She went at the bidding of our Lord, and therefore her Master, who bade her go, provided for her so that she managed as well as any of her company – worship and praise be to our Lord for it.

LOUISE KENWARD

'Searching for Seahorses' (2021)[†]

I kneel down in the damp sand. My jeans soak the salty water up from my feet. I unscrew the lid and offer up the jar to the incoming tide.

Not land, and not sea, the intertidal zone is a space of rock pools: of green crabs and beadlet anemones, barnacles and mussel beds. It's rich with life, adapted to living on land and underwater. It's a place that tracks time: across hours, months and millennia. Dog whelks race, their movement faster than mine. Crabs scuttle and lugworms burrow, traces and casts leave echoes of their trails. Limpets fix themselves so tightly to rocks they make circular indents, home scars a place to return to each day. As fossils are immortalised in stone, so ghosts haunt these edges of land and sea, life and death echoes, and shadows of what was, hold firm.

This is a place I know well – the seashore at Bexhill, and these in-between spaces. The coast, the very edge, is somewhere that for a long time I became estranged from during a period of illness. Unable to walk to the beach at the end of the street, I was more than a year adrift from the sea. Establishing an understanding of what went wrong in my body has been as vague as the experience of it – profound fatigue, brain fog, concentration waxing and waning – a life suspended. As soon as I could I returned to the sea, gathering evidence as I went – photographs at first and then, attempting to conjure my recovery, to make visible the intangible, I went each day with a jar and knelt at the edge. Each day I caught a wave and took it back to keep it safe, storing the energy of the ocean for myself. A hope I might make 'real' the unreality of the illness. A hope I might recover.

Recovered in part, I am now neither well nor ill. No longer bed-bound, this is not a life I recognise, either. So I search out a landscape that reflects this, and find myself at the beach. Turn up at high tide and you only see water. Arrive at low tide and it is shingle and sand. Living with an energy-limiting illness, I am neither sick with obvious symptoms, nor well with a life I would recognise from 'before'. Sometimes it feels like I am a half person. Or, like the beach, I am twice the person, with twice the experience and twice the life. I have access to both, though only temporary residence.

I remember what it is like to be at depth under water, diving in the Mediterranean, searching for seahorses. Difficult to find, seahorses are therefore difficult to study. They are 'data deficient' – not enough have been found to establish they are at risk, not enough have been found to list them as endangered. And yet they need protection. As the global trade of dried seahorses sees an annual 20 million sold for traditional Chinese medicine, some people are clearly better at finding them than others. Thought to cure everything from asthma to impotence, and highly sought after, they have been symbols of strength and power since the Greeks and the Romans.

Five years ago I was diving twice a day at multiple dive sites collecting data from seahorse sightings – a month-long citizen science project. Even knowing where they were likely to be, even swimming directly above them, I couldn't always see them. I had to swim slowly, look closely, stare at blades of seagrass and patches of sand for a long time before gradually my eyes adjusted and there they were, tails wrapped around blades of seagrass.

It was to be our last dive of the month, and we clambered over rocks to a dive site we hadn't visited before. It was a data-gathering exercise recording sea urchins, one of the 'indicator species', the presence or absence of which helps to monitor the water quality. The sea at the surface was rough, spitting us back out as my dive buddy, Sarah, and I tried to climb in. Eventually below the waves, we descend and set out the fifty-metre transect line. I recorded each sea urchin with a short graphite line on a slate (a rectangular piece of hard plastic fastened to my kit with a carabiner clip and long cord) – four short lines and the one to cross them through marked five urchins, a separate row for each species – black, rock and violet. My concentration was so intense I had reached the end of the line before realising how much time had passed. I looked around for Sarah, who was still some way off. I hovered and stared at the rocks around me, looking down and around at where I had been. I began to draw on the back of the slate, attempting to capture something of the seascape. Staring at a tiny piece of seagrass, I thought I must be hallucinating, my eyes imagining her into being from staring at small patches of ocean for hours each day. I put up my arm for Sarah to see and continued in my focus. There she was, a seahorse that shouldn't be there, a new one previously unrecorded by the project – *hippocampus hippocampus*, a short-snouted seahorse never before seen. A tiny, plated, 'S'-shaped dinosaur, no bigger than my middle finger, with frilly green tendrils across the top of her head and a narrow snout. I had mixed feelings about uncovering her hiding place. Each new find is recorded and given a name back at the office; she was registered and I got to lend her my name for finding her. A seahorse called Louise lives just off the coast of Spain, in the Bay of Roses. Sea monster, horse caterpillar: a fish, not with scales, but an armoury of plates. This fragile, mighty creature has inhabited the oceans for 25 million years. I hope no one finds her again.

Here on the beach at Bexhill, I look out across the Channel. This is now a protected area of the sea, a recently approved Marine Conservation Zone. Since being protected, seahorses have been found here, too. I hope one day to put on my wetsuit again, to go and look for them – my dive boots are still by the kitchen door, a hopeful reminder of what was. For now, I am content to know they are there.

Each day for a hundred days I have walked to the water's edge and greeted it: 'Hello sea!' I have offered my jar up to the wave and caught one. Perhaps this will help, I think, taking the sea home with me. A magical place might be able to cast magical spells. I take each jar home and store it carefully on the shelves of my glass-fronted bookcase. Shelves fill as I number each jar with a luggage tag – noting the day and time of the wave's capture. How many to replace the water in my body? Another 300? A transfusion, not of blood, but of saline – from freshwater to ocean.

Looking up, and staring out, the horizon barely discernible through mist and drizzle, I remember what it's like to be twenty, thirty metres deep, diving as I fly through the ocean. A place of transformation, at depth, where rocks become octopus, sand becomes fish. And maybe that's where I am now, another space of transformation, of needing a stillness to notice as I change from rock to octopus, sand to fish, ill to well.

When nothing else exists, and I am all but disappeared, these shelves of tiny oceans remind me I can be both – I am the sea, I can fly, I am fish.

The tide is coming in, reclaiming the land. A place that exists twice each day, ruled by the moon, is a space where possibility lives. Perhaps, in time, I will learn to live half my life underwater and half on solid ground. I will learn to adapt, adapt and evolve, like Louise the seahorse, somewhere in the Bay of Roses.

LINDA LEAR

From *Beatrix Potter: A Life in Nature* (2007)

Among the drawings [of fungi] that Beatrix showed McIntosh that October afternoon were the two she had drawn at Lingholm. 'I happened by lucky intuition,' Beatrix explained, 'to have drawn several rare species.' One of them McIntosh had also discovered for the first time that summer in a wood at Murthly, and 'another, like a spluttered candle', was similar 'to one he had found just once in the grass at the road-side near Inver tunnel'. 'He was certainly pleased with my drawings,' she reported happily, 'and his judgement speaking to their accuracy in minute botanical points gave me infinitely more pleasure than that of critics who assume more, and know less than poor Charlie.' Deeply impressed with his knowledge, and grateful for his evaluation, Beatrix concluded, 'He is a perfect dragon of erudition, and not gardener's Latin, either.'

During their hour-and-a-half visit, Beatrix and McIntosh discussed a variety of points about fungi: how they grew, their habitat, classification and proper nomenclature. McIntosh 'became quite excited and spoke with poetical feeling about their exquisite colours'. They also discussed techniques for drawing under the microscope, agreeing to an exchange of talent: he to send her fresh specimens in the post and she to return a drawing of them. After he had shown her his remarkable one-handed drawings, Beatrix gave him her sketchbook with fungi drawings that he had so admired.

A box of specimens arrived from Birnam quite soon after she returned to London. She sent her first fungi drawings to McIntosh in early December, telling him, 'it is a real pleasure to copy them, they are such lovely colours', but she had become more curious about their taxonomy and wanted to learn the proper botanical techniques of illustration. Sensing a willing student, McIntosh supplied each specimen with its scientific name and Beatrix worked at becoming more proficient at nomenclature and classification.

In December Beatrix described an unidentified fungus that had sprouted on the same piece of broom where an *Agaricus velutipes* had previously grown. 'Miss Potter wonders,' she wrote with unusual formality, 'whether it grows out of doors at this season or whether it is brought out by the heat of the room?' She included a microscope sketch of the finger-like *primordia* of the new fungus, showing where it had appeared on the broom, its scale and its characteristics. McIntosh had also sent some mosses. They were harder to draw because they had to be done under magnification. She would not return drawings of those, though she made some excellent ones for herself. But she took exception to the 'horrid plant like a white stick with a loose cap which smells exactly like a dead sheep!', and also suggested that McIntosh mark the rarest plant in each box so that she could draw it before it got damaged or too mouldy.

In London, Beatrix's study of fungi was limited to what was available at the Natural History Museum. She spent a great deal of time looking at the portfolios of drawings and printed plates in an effort to learn the taxonomy, but it was not easy. The most important reference book available was James Sowerby's monumental work, *Coloured figures of English fungi or mushrooms* (1793–1803), a work of over 400 hand-coloured plates. Otherwise she had only the museum's limited collection of fungi preserved in alcohol, or a sort of pickling brine in small glass bottles, and a few dried specimens. She found these so badly labelled as to be all but useless.

Beatrix was already frustrated that there was no one at the museum 'to give any information'. They did not have the reference books she wanted, and they 'take no interest whatever in funguses at large'. 'Some day', she promised McIntosh, she would 'ask at Kew Gardens whether there is anyone who knows more about the names'. In the meantime she made do with what was accessible, and by the time the Potters returned to Dunkeld the following summer, she had become familiar with the basic literature on fungi classification and was prepared to take issue with the Kensington museum staff over the identification of some of their *Boletus* and *Hygrophorus* specimens.

JESSICA J. LEE
'Tree' (2021)[†]

It was late October when the storm wound its way inland, blasting trees from the ground with the force of a hurricane. Younger trees were bent parallel to the ground, roots forced from the clay by the pressure. Older growths were toppled quickly, knocked down rigid like boxers taking blows. At a higher altitude than so much of London, the Northern Heights were vulnerable to extreme weather. That storm took down over a hundred trees on Hampstead Heath. I hoped and prayed and wished from a distance that mine wasn't among them.

My tree – not mine, per se, but mine all the same. A small-leafed British lime. A linden. A *Tilia cordata*. My tree, surrounded by other, smaller oak trees and skirted by blackberry bushes and the mixed seed grasses that cover Parliament Hill Fields. My tree with a southern exposure and, being much taller than the other trees nearby, a vulnerability to strong gusts of wind. My old tree – so old that I'd been worried for a few years now about how much time was left. For all these reasons, I knew in my heart that mine was likely among the hundred. But I didn't want to believe it.

I was 3,500 miles away. It was already near winter in Toronto. I'd unearthed my parka and begun wearing it for half the year; having left my adopted home in London to pursue a Ph.D. back in Canada, where I was born, I was still readapting to the cold. I would never adapt to the distance.

From Toronto I scoured photographs on Instagram, looking for evidence of my tree in the weeks after the storm, fingers crossed. I found a way to call it work: I was researching an environmental-history dissertation about Hampstead Heath, longing – perhaps obsessively –

to stay with the place I loved so much. Though work had flung me back to Canada, where I least wanted to be, my mind inhabited the Heath's fields.

But I was frustrated, my writing stunted, as I was incapable of conjuring from a distance the exact scent of the place – a mingling of clay soil, grass, and pond water – or the silent sound the Heath made when I stood amidst the woodland towards Kenwood. I lingered instead over past moments on the Heath, hopes and happinesses and grievances. I lingered over lost things.

A year earlier, I'd taken a graduate seminar on environment, culture, and the myriad ways in which the two overlap, entangle, and co-constitute one another. The methods in the class ranged from theoretical to personal to mystical. In the second week, I gave a presentation on loss, mourning and the environment. I spoke openly about my tree – about the steadying force the tree had in my life – and about my fears and struggles in accepting that, like all things, my tree wasn't going to be there for ever. I spoke of the year my tree turned a lurid, sickly yellow instead of the usual bright green. I spoke of my tree as a child speaks of a parent whose mortality has suddenly become a reality. Perhaps I should have stayed quiet.

Because so much of my relationship to the tree was in those small, unspoken fears, rituals and beliefs I constructed while standing underneath, gazing at the fields. I first found the tree when I was twenty-two. I had just moved across from the Heath in Dartmouth Park and I'd begun walking the hills daily. At weekends I had taken to lounging in the long grass under a tree whose rustling leaves sounded like rushing water. I told people they could find me on the Heath by listening for the one tree which sounded nothing like the others. And there I lay, newspaper in hand, gazing at branches and sky as London rolled on around me. The years I spent living by the Heath were some of the best but, for a variety of reasons, most difficult years. I had found the tree at just the right time.

On the day I handed in my master's dissertation, I had walked out onto the Heath and stood under my tree. I stood, hoping that all would be well. Touching my hand against the crumpled bark, I felt steady – I felt I was in the right place, doing the right things.

On the morning we got married, my husband and I walked under my tree and spoke about what we hoped for, wishing silently together that it would all be all right. I stood in the same spot two years later, after we had separated. Our marriage hadn't worked out, but everything was all right.

On the morning I left London for Toronto, I woke up early to walk on the Heath. I was alone, divorcing, and moving somewhere both new and old to me – though the move to Canada brought new possibilities, I felt in some way that I had failed. I was terrified to leave the Heath, but it was only under the tree that I could really let myself feel the full volume of that fear. I felt safe under the tree.

How much of these feelings can be boiled down to superstition doesn't worry me all that much. My tree appeared in my life at the time I needed stability most. I kept a picture of the tree on my phone so that when I was across the Atlantic, riding the subway, I could remember how it felt to feel so steady. I had a botanical drawing of its leaf tattooed to my forearm, and I often traced my fingers along its lines when I felt out of place. In the years that followed, I made the spot under the tree my first and last stop every time I went back to London. And so it was when I stopped on the Heath, three months after that destructive autumn storm.

In their book on trees and tree places, *Tree Cultures*, Paul Cloke and Owain Jones write that 'trees gather places around themselves' (p. 87). This has been my experience. Under my tree I built and dismantled a life, and under my tree many others gathered – for picnics, lazy afternoons in the long grass, for a bit of shade on a rare sunny London day. The tree was a focal point in the hedgerow, pulling the long, grassy field inward. As Cloke and Jones write, 'The presence of trees in a place contributes to and adapts the physical character of that place' (p. 88). To see this tree was to be drawn in. The tree gathered the Heath and its people into a place. It was in moving towards the tree that I felt my own heart grow to its fullest.

Michael Pollan once wrote that our metaphors about trees by and large determine their fates. I can't help but feel that this falls short in some way, because the power of my own metaphors is far exceeded by so many other, greater forces or agencies – that of 99 mph gusts of wind, battering rain, or indeed, of time itself. And to take these into account is to understand as best as I can the full complexity of a place – this tree, which had withstood the hurricane-force winds of 1987, had an entire life beyond the tiny moment shared with me. And indeed, after the storm, this place would find new life.

I walked towards Parliament Hill Fields from the north, approaching the tree's overgrown hedgerow from behind. There was no peak in the row of trees, no spray of branches cresting above the others. Rounding the field's edge, a dense pile stretched across the ground where I used to lie. Land-management policies on the Heath meant that my tree would remain there, prostrate and broken, working its way into the ground. Within months this place would no longer seem like a scar on the landscape I knew – indeed there would be new life, new places, large and small, in, on and around this fallen tree. Limes are trees that send up new shoots, spreading new life beneath the soil. They create, as Roger Deakin once said, a kind of Birnam Wood, new trees springing to life in their advance across a landscape.

★

I began writing that week, something I had failed to do for months. The whole of the Heath — sand, clay, grass, gorse, water and hedgerow — gathered my attention. I fell freely into work, swallowed by the full force of the place, which extended so far beyond me and the stories I told myself about a tree.

RACHEL LICHTENSTEIN

'Neither Land nor Sea' from *Estuary: Out from London to the Sea* (2016)

The Essex littoral: a shoreline which, though historically embattled and often aesthetically derided, is today a place of great ecological and cultural importance ... the tidal shoreline as a unique setting – an 'edge condition', if you like – where the ecological, the ethical and matters of the spiritual and the numinous, meet in a fruitful and prescient way.

Time and Tide: The Moral Theatre of the Essex Shoreline, Professor Ken Worpole, Burrows Lecture, University of Essex, 2011

Between the railway track and the Benfleet Downs sits a sparsely beautiful agrarian landscape of part-flooded salt marsh inhabited by grazing cattle and wild horses, with the ruinous remains of Hadleigh Castle on a hill behind. Beside it runs Benfleet Creek, a narrow inlet of water that ebbs and flows with the tidal Estuary. In the mid-nineteenth century, during the construction of the London to Southend railway line, the charred remains of human skeletons and ship's timbers were uncovered there: probable remnants of a battle between the Saxons and the Vikings over a thousand years ago. Traces of earlier marshes and submerged forests can sometimes be seen on the foreshore at low tide, along with bones and shells from the prehistoric era.

One bright but crisp February morning I met the author and cultural historian Ken Worpole outside Benfleet station, which overlooks the creek. As we began walking eastwards, Ken pointed towards the container ships drifting past in the deep-water channel beyond the flat terrain of mud, water and sky ahead. Canvey Island lay on our right. 'For me,' he said, 'Essex is special because it fails to conform to conventional ideas about what is beautiful in the English landscape.' Ken has written extensively about Essex as a place of significant cultural importance and as a laboratory of environmental, cultural and social change in the twentieth century. For *350 Miles: An Essex Journey*, a collaboration with photographer Jason Orton, he walked the entire coastline of the county over the period of a year. Much of it was familiar to him already, as his family had moved to Canvey after the war, 'as part of that great exodus of people from the East End looking for a better life'. Ken spent his early years on Canvey living in a wooden bungalow on stilts near the sea wall, exploring ditches full of dragonflies and reed beds between the unmade roads. Every week he would read in the *Southend Standard* the list of ships and their cargoes that would be passing by. 'People were interested. Shipping was part of the landscape of our lives, along with the visual world of the refineries and the flat Thames.'

The family moved to the island the year before the Great Flood in 1953, then lived for a while in nearby Thundersley, opposite a chapel belonging to the Peculiar People – a group unique to Essex. 'It was a revivalist Christian sect started in the 1830s in Rochford by a drunken farmer who had an epiphany. They had quite a lot of affinities with the Plymouth Brethren, which meant they refused blood transfusions, which made them unpopular.'

We started walking towards Benfleet Marina, where a variety of boats were moored up on the muddy banks of the creek, next to a quirky pub on a former barge called the *Gladys*. 'Most of the boats here are very old,' said Ken, 'and some of them are still used for fishing, unlike the leisure craft at lots of very expensive marinas around the coast of Britain.' Benfleet Marina is also one of the only places along the Estuary foreshore where people still live on the water, and quite a few houseboats can still be found there, from narrow boats to converted barges to beached hulls and ex-army landing craft. An earlier, much larger colony of houseboats once stretched from the creek right up towards the footpath of the castle in Leigh. These ramshackle floating homes were built from timbers rescued from bombed-out buildings and wrecked boats, and housed a range of people, from travellers to those who had been made homeless by the Blitz.

'There is a culture in Essex of setting up DIY independent communities,' said Ken, 'from self-built homes in places like Jaywick and Canvey, to the plot lands in Laindon and Basildon. Land colonies were also a big feature of the late-nineteenth-century Essex landscape, partly because of its proximity to London and also because land was relatively cheap. This part of Essex has always been a place where social reformers in the East End established experimental communities.' Ken told me about some of these settlers: the suffragette on Canvey Island who set up a boarding house in which young seamstresses could recuperate from their work; and the Salvation Army colony established by William Booth at Hadleigh Farm, next to the castle, as a settlement for alcoholics and homeless men from London's East End. Booth's project is still going and is now the longest-surviving land colony in Britain. Today, they run a café there that employs young people with learning disabilities.

We moved on to a high, grassy embankment, which runs through the marsh from Benfleet to Leigh. On one side, the tidal estuarine landscape stretched out before us, with the North Sea beyond. On the other side were the Benfleet Downs, dotted with sheep, cattle and other wildlife, and historic Hadleigh Castle up on the hill – the best place along this coastline to see fantastic panoramic views across the Estuary.

Hadleigh Castle is popular in the English imagination: it was painted by John Constable in 1828 soon after his wife died. The artist's earlier works are full of life and images of serenity –working landscapes with lush vegetation – but his painting of Hadleigh Castle depicts a ruin: all emptiness, with bleak skies beyond. At the time of Henry III's reign, when the castle was built, the sea would have reached the base of the hill and the marsh would have been completely flooded. The embankment we were walking on was a relatively recent construction, built to protect the land from the incoming tide.

As we walked through the intertidal zone of salt marsh and mudflats, Ken spoke about the beauty of the landscape. 'Some people would call it desolate, but the fact that you have got the sea and the sky in a dynamic relationship to each other makes it pretty magical – at least to me.' It was low tide, and the muddy banks of the creek were covered in the footprints of all kinds of wading birds, creating a beautiful kind of Cyrillic writing made by ducks, turnstones and curlews. We looked across the Estuary waters to the farmland in the far distance on the Isle of Grain, and the post-industrial wilderness of the power stations and silos, which we both agreed had a certain melancholy beauty of its own.

An article in *Country Life* once awarded Essex zero points out of ten for landscape quality. Irritation with this article, along with the 'continual drip-feed of nonsense about Essex being a wild, barbarian county and the knowing jokes about Essex girls or Essex man', inspired Ken to start writing a counter-narrative of his own. In his superb essay 'East of Eden' (in the anthology *Towards Re-enchantment: Place and Its Meanings*, 2010), Ken focused on the particular qualities of East Mersea, one of several inhabited Essex islands, with its dusty roads and little cottages, where people still in the summer put out boxes of apples or plums on tables to sell or give away.

Towards Re-enchantment, a collection of specially commissioned pieces by writers with a shared interest in the meanings and interpretation of place, was first published by Artevents in 2010. I had listened to Ken read from the book during the launch at the *London Review of Books* shop. Iain Sinclair spoke about Hackney and Springfield Park, and Jay Griffiths brought wildness into the room with her sensuous and passionate recitation of her essay 'The Grave of

Dafydd'. The lively discussion that ensued afterwards, chaired by co-editor and maverick curator Gareth Evans, was a catalyst for me for a new way of thinking about the Essex coast.

The book was part of the wider re-enchantment project, which focused around W. G. Sebald's *The Rings of Saturn*, which tracks a long walk around the East Anglian coastline and explores some of the lesser -known histories of Suffolk. Ken and I had both been asked by Gareth to speak at the writers' symposium taking place in Snape Maltings as part of an extraordinary weekend put together by Artevents, which included the launch of *Patience (After Sebald)*, Grant Gee's translation of Sebald's work into celluloid, which features the book itself as artefact, as landscape. During the film, Iain Sinclair gave a warning to would-be psychogeographers planning to walk the route mapped out in *The Rings of Saturn*: it was a pointless exercise, as Robert Macfarlane found on his attempt.

As Ken and I walked across the marsh that day and spoke about the re-enchantment project and its impact on our work, I told Ken how I had met Jo Catling after the screening of Gee's film during that winter arts festival in Suffolk. Jo is an academic from the University of East Anglia who worked closely with Max Sebald* for decades. She compiled an anthology of essays, academic writings and newly translated works by and about Sebald after his death. For the front cover, she chose a photograph of Max standing outside a hotel in Aldeburgh, holding a couple of books in his hand. She was curious to find out what the titles of the books were, and when she looked closely with a magnifying glass she discovered the small volume was one of mine: a slim, limited-edition, alternative walking tour called *Rodinsky's Whitechapel*. I was overwhelmed to hear this. I had felt nervous about doing a presentation the following day at the symposium dedicated

---

*   W. G. 'Max' Sebald, the German writer and academic, author of *The Emigrants* and *The Rings of Saturn*.

to Sebald, the person whose writing has had a deeper impact on me than any other artist, and it felt as if he had given me a blessing from beyond the grave that night. It was after that weekend that I decided I would write a book focusing on Essex, and after my trip on *Ideeal** that the idea for this book on the Estuary really came into being.

Ken enjoyed this story, with all its Sebaldian coincidences and recurring themes. As we walked through the sparse terrain of the Benfleet marsh, he gestured around us and said, 'Sebald helped revive interest in the agricultural interiors and bleak maritime landscapes of Essex and East Anglia.' Ken has continued to explore these places in his work. In his most recent book, with Jason Orton, *The New English Landscape* (2013), he discusses the need to reinterpret contemporary landscapes anew, particularly hitherto neglected areas such as the Thames Estuary. 'Landscape is still the largest visual component of our lives,' he said as we strode across the wetland, 'reflecting where we are today, emotionally and psychologically.'

We walked in silence for some time then began to talk about Liverpool Street station, another recurring theme in Sebald's work. Ken remembered the place when steam trains were still operating. He

---

* *Ideeal* is a fifty-ton Dutch barge, which had originally been built in the 1920s as a working barge to carry freight and has since been converted into a live/work studio by owner Ben Eastop although it remains a seaworthy vessel. Ben had asked if I would be willing to be writer-in-residence for a multidisciplinary arts project he was organizing, the focus of which was responding to place. The idea was to take a five-day experiential cruise on *Ideeal* along the Thames Estuary with a mixed crew of visual artists, an archaeologist of the recent past, a musician, a filmmaker, a writer and an ornithologist. the journey would be deliberately slow-paced, a direct and immersive experience of the ancient waterway. We would amble downriver, drift on the tides, meditate on the unique seascape of that place. I signed up as the writer-in-residence, the idea appealed to me immediately, as the Estuary and the mud-flats of the Thames were the landscapes of my childhood. I grew up in Southend-on-Sea and spent my school holidays paddling, swimming and playing in the Estuary waters. When the tide went out I walked on the mud for miles, catching crabs and shrimp in the little pools of water left behind by the receding sea. I knew the dangers of the incoming tide and also something of the military history of the place, having visited the remnants of crumbling forts along the coastline. I had heard the stories of the ship filled with bombs sitting on the riverbed, but before my trip on *Ideeal* I had never spent any time on the water itself. Most Estuary dwellers haven't either. For the majority of people who live in the many towns and communities dotted along the Essex and Kent coastlines, the Estuary is little more than a much-loved scenic backdrop to their lives. It remains, for most, an unknown landscape, as it once had been for me. When Ben approached me that evening, I accepted his offer without hesitation, intrigued to see what would happen to my perspective on and understanding of this landscape by physically being on the water. It was after my trip on *Ideeal* that the idea of writing a book about the Estuary started to take shape.

recalled that coming into the station was like arriving at a vast, smoke-filled cavern – and, for a child, rather scary. In his guide to Essex, originally published in 1954, Nikolaus Pevsner suggested that people were put off visiting the county because Liverpool Street station had once been so unbearably grim. Sebald, too, felt discomfited by the associations of the station, and connected the history of East Anglia with the history of Europe, especially the Kindertransport: 'Liverpool Street was the main starting point for people going to Europe and coming from Europe at the outbreak of the war, as well as for Jewish refugee children arriving.' He notes that the station is physically populated by these ghosts: there is a sculpture of Jewish children with suitcases, and a marble memorial to the Great Eastern Railway employees who died during the First World War.

We talked for a while about Jewish settlement from East London to Essex. Ken's wife, Larraine, came from the Jewish East End, as had my family, and likewise settled in Westcliff. Then, as we continued our walk towards the edges of Two-tree Island, Ken spoke about the volatile relationship between the coast and the sea, about that landscape being both a place under constant threat from climate change and flooding and a place of constant shape-shifting and evocation of past lives. 'The physical landscape is continually evolving here,' he said, 'and shaped daily by tides, resulting in a unique environment for particular plants, flowers, birds and insects, which thrive in these rich intertidal habitats.'

We reached the tip of Two-tree Island, one of many former landfill sites along this part of the Thames Estuary now turned into wildlife-conservation areas. When Ken was growing up here, Two-tree Island was still the main rubbish tip for Southend Corporation, and he remembers seeing endless convoys of dustcarts trundling past Leigh station, tipping rubbish. After it reached capacity, the tip was seeded, and successional overgrowth reclaimed the land. Subsequently, artificial lagoons – non-tidal and independent – have been constructed to the west of the island and have become one of the principal UK breeding grounds for avocets. The marsh sands around the island are covered in rough saltings and clumps of eel grass, which from a distance make the mud look green when the tide goes out. Thousands of dark-bellied Arctic geese arrive at these salt marshes every winter to feed, before returning to the tundra to breed.

I often walk my dog on Two-tree and visit the bird hides scattered around the perimeter of the island. I had recently also visited the Lower Thames Rowing Club there, the headquarters of which (two shipping containers) overlooks the Canvey Yacht Club, on the other side of the creek. I spoke with Vanessa Bradford, a local woman from Leigh who has been rowing competitively on the women's racing team with this club for the last couple of years.

They race in Norwich, Brightlingsea and Richmond, amongst other places, but most of their training takes place on the Estuary, which she describes as an exhilarating environment. 'There are all these hidden dangers in the Estuary you've got to be really aware of. Every time we go out it's different, and so much more challenging than being on a gentle river. You're dealing with waves and traffic and the whipping currents out in the channel.' She said the mud had changed since the dredging began, especially since the big container ships started coming downriver. Some sandbanks had shifted; others had appeared. 'It's a bit like sand dunes – it looks different every week, and when the tide's in you lose perspective of where the channels are – but learning in these conditions means that we win all the races.'

'It doesn't matter how many times I have done this walk,' Ken said as we reached the end of the embankment and started heading towards Leigh station, 'it's always different. The big skies and long vistas allow your mind to wander.' I waved goodbye and stood and watched three big ships out in the deep shipping channel queuing up, waiting for the tide to come in.

ANN LINGARD

From *The Embalmer's Book of Recipes* (2009)

March 18th 2001. Madeleine receives the phone call from Ministry that she has been expecting and dreading. Whitefoot's flock is to be culled, a contiguous cull because it lies within three kilometres of a farm where foot-and-mouth disease has been confirmed. For each infected farm, there are three or four others that must be culled out.

The lad who speaks to her on the telephone is dispassionate; he doesn't know her, he's merely doing his job. Mrs Tregwithen owns the farm next to Low End, so her animals must be killed. His office is in Carlisle, he's probably not long out of school and is looking forward to the end of the week to go drinking with his mates. The valuer and the vet will visit her farm this evening, he says, to estimate the value of her sheep – the hoggs, the ewes in lamb, the tups, all her flock. The slaughterers will come tomorrow.

She has to fetch the sheep in, to collect them together in the in-bye land. She calls George on his mobile.

'I can't come, boss,' he says. 'I'm "dirty". I was wanted over at Sowerbys' yesterday and I've got to wait forty-eight hours before I'm officially clean.'

'But my sheep will be killed anyway,' she says. 'You can't infect them now. What does a few hours matter?'

'It's bloody stupid, aye. A month ago we had to wait seven days, then they said five'd do. Now they're that short of help they need us all the time.'

'George.' She cannot bring herself to plead but she needs his companionship, she needs a familiar face.

'Aye,' George says softly, and she senses that he's nodding. 'I'll come.'

★

Ruth is staying away, despite the mats and footbaths of disinfectant, because she doesn't want to risk carrying the virus onto Whitefoot land. She and Madeleine have discussed this, and although it is the safest solution, it is also inconvenient because she has had to set up a temporary workshop in her kitchen. She never seems to have the right materials to hand. But it surely cannot be for much longer, surely the disease will soon be contained.

George and Madeleine stand in the yard and listen to the roaring of the sheep as they mill around in indignation and fright.

'Will you stay?' Madeleine asks, knowing she is being unreasonable.

But when the valuer walks into the yard, she recognises him as David, an auctioneer from the mart, a man she trusts and likes.

She touches George's shoulder, an unusual gesture for her. 'No, go along home, lad. You need a break.' In fact, she longs to throw her arms around him, and hug him, to weep against his shoulder.

David looks grey and drawn. 'Madeleine. George.'

George nods, then lifts a hand in farewell. 'Aye, I'll be off then. See you, Madeleine.'

What more is there to say?

As they move amongst the sheep, Madeleine tells David what he needs to know about their background, and he takes notes as he goes, filling in columns, counting. The Herdwick hoggs, still black-fleeced, are in particularly good condition, fine sturdy little animals, and he compliments her and gives them a good price. She'll receive financial compensation, money to help her restock; that is why David is here.

'But where will I get more Herdwicks, David? Will there be any left to buy?' She feels empty, completely devoid of hope.

David, normally a robust, smiling man, known for his wit and persuasiveness in coaxing higher prices out of buyers at the mart, is flat-voiced with tiredness.

'Robinsons down in Borrowdale have got it now. If it's in the fell flocks, that's the end. You can't contain it. They're setting up a Herdwick sperm bank – but how do you replace a hefted flock? How do you ever replace the generations that know their home heaf?'

'Robinsons!' She is shocked that the disease has crept so far amongst the fells, to strike at the best and most-prized flocks.

'Aye, and Mark and. . .' He stops writing and looks away, swallowing hard. 'Mark and Dorrie Platt. They were culled out as dangerous contacts. Three hundred and forty sheep. And when the results of the test came back, not a single sheep had tested positive. They lost stock that had been in that family for two generations. Dorrie brought some of her dad's ewes over from the old farm when they moved across. She said those animals were like family themselves.'

Madeleine is silent: there's nothing to say. She knows and admires Dorrie, a small blonde woman who is tough and uncompromising, daughter and grand-daughter of hill-sheep farmers.

David refuses the offer of a cup of tea. 'Thanks, no, Madeleine. I've scarcely seen my wife and children for four nights in a row.'

'You look like you could do with a good night's sleep.'

'That too. I wish.'

He grips her hand with both of his, and she can see that he is on the verge of tears again as he turns and walks away.

March 19th. The vet comes early next morning and she sets to work taking samples from the sheep. The slaughter team arrives soon after and takes control, herding the sheep into the pens. They move through with their bolt guns, laughing and joking amongst themselves, shouting to each other as they work. Thud. A ewe falls to her knees. Thud.

Another keels over, legs twitching. Every one of the breeding ewes, each with one or two lambs inside her.

Madeleine picks out some of the sheep she knows: a good mother; a bad influence; an old ewe with a uterus as cavernous as an aircraft hangar, inside which a third lamb has been known to hide – an old ewe with a kind white face.

'Treat her with respect. Why don't they treat her with respect?' Tears trickle down her cheeks.

The vet is a young woman who speaks with a Welsh accent. 'It's the only way they are able to cope, Mrs Tregwithen,' she says. 'Jeff – he's the team leader – told me he's already had to kill twelve thousand healthy sheep.'

She takes Madeleine's hand and holds it tightly, and they watch as the bodies are carried out and piled in neat, straight lines. Later, when the team has left, she comes and sits in the kitchen, exhausted and traumatised. She cannot speak in sentences.

'At the old motel,' she says. 'Drafted us in from all over the country. Can't sleep. Vets are supposed to save lives, not take them.'

She tells of a milking parlour. 'Empty. Except for an old armchair covered with a blanket. Robbie Stebbings and his pedigree Holsteins. No one came to collect the cows' corpses for nine days. Virus everywhere. When the wagons came Robbie had to move them himself. Bodies falling apart as he scooped them with the tractor. Legs and guts falling out of rotted skin. His little boy's stopped talking.' She cannot stop. 'And ewes down by the river, further west. Some had lambed. Dead lambs. A ewe with feet and head hanging out of her backside. No one would go near to help. No farmer with cows'll go near, Mrs Tregwithen. Will no one listen? Why doesn't Blair come and see?'

She cannot stop; her speech is slurring, but she has to keep talking.

'And on the salt marshes we had to chase the sheep ourselves, and two stuck in the mud and we couldn't reach them before the tide came in. No fences. No dog.'

'Why don't you stay and have something to eat?' Madeleine breaks in, even though she would now rather be on her own. 'Go upstairs and have a hot bath, Bron, before you set off again. Get the smell of sheep off your skin. You need a break.'

'Have to get your tests sent off. Too much paperwork.' Bron's mobile rings. 'I'll be there in half an hour,' is all she says, and she is already picking up her bag.

Madeleine goes out to the field to look: a long dyke of grey and white bodies already stiffening, like stones.

She is quite alone.

The three Suffolks are incongruously large, their size exaggerated by the corpses of the lambs that lie beside them. Danny keeps Suffolks and he persuaded her to try them; he sold her the ewes for a good price. She liked their haughty black faces and their floppy black ears, and the way they strode around stiff-legged, looking down with queenly disdain at the shorter-legged fell sheep.

'You should rear pure-breds,' Danny said. 'Bring them over to me, Maddie lass, and we'll put them to my tup.' Had he winked at her? No, that had been in her imagination as had, surely, so much else. Danny would not have winked.

She kneels down next to their stocky black-faced lambs, their eyes glazed and dull, and she strokes a soft ear and a gentle muzzle that only a few hours ago was tugging its mother's teat for milk. She thinks of them as Danny's lambs. The small dead Suffolk lies on her lap. It is cold and stiff, but she cannot bear to let it go. She goes to sit by the little dog's grave, which is marked by a rough lump of sandstone and set amongst the bare trunks of the birches, and she is numbed and her mind is empty.

In the distance, two lorries grind up a hill with loud gear changes, but here in the afternoon there is nothing but silence.

The wagons come, and George returns with his tractor and the scoop. Madeleine hides in the office, with the local radio station turned up loud, and she jumps when Ruth shouts her name from the kitchen.

'I couldn't let you be here alone. I saw the wagons, I had to reverse all the way back along the track to let one by. I've got my sleeping bag, I'll stay in the studio, I don't—'

'Oh Ruth.'

And then she is clutching at Ruth and she cannot stop the grief that wails out from deep within her. 'Oh Ruth. What am I to do? They're all dead. My lovely sheep.'

The words gasp and judder out of her, and Ruth puts her arms around her, and rocks her wordlessly, like a child, until she has quietened and can breathe again.

Ruth brings mugs of tea, and the brandy from the sideboard, and Madeleine turns off the radio because the local news is now too personal.

'What am I going to do, how will I fill the days?' She eventually asks, picking at her sleeve that is damp with tears.

'Knitting? Take up watercolours?' Ruth tries to lighten the mood.

'I hear that felting's all the rage,' Madeleine attempts to smile and takes a gulp of tea. 'Perhaps you'd better teach me to stuff animals, instead.'

March 20th. Just after seven in the morning Danny telephones; Ruth is asleep in one of the guest rooms but Madeleine, out of habit, is up. She assumes he has called to find out how she is faring after the cull.

'Six of the Lims have got it,' he says straightaway. 'And the old cow, old Jayne. She can't stand any more, her feet hurt so much. You should see her, Maddie – she looks to me to help her, she calls to me when she sees me. And I've let her down.'

He goes quiet, she can hear him breathing deeply, and she knows he's struggling.

'When's the vet coming?' she asks, to give him time.

'There's stuff coming out of her nose, her gums are bleeding. I'd put her out of her misery right now if I had the means. Soon. "Soon", that's what they said. "As soon as he can get there". Maddie, it breaks my heart.'

Jayne. Daniel had named the young heifer after Jayne Mansfield, 'because she had a big tit'. When he told Madeleine the reason, she had been disconcerted. But that had been many years ago. And now old Jayne is in distress, and Danny's beasts are ill and suffering. All of his 150-strong herd of dairy cows will soon be dead.

'The army are coming, so at least they'll take them away quick. After.'

'Yes.' She cannot tell him about Robbie Stebbings. 'And the ewes'll go too?'

'They have to. The Suffolks and the mules.'

Neither of them speak for a while. Words are no use.

'I'm sorry, Danny. I don't know what else to say.' She wants to say, 'I love you,' but that would be inappropriate.

'No, Maddie lass. There's nothing left to say, and you've been through it too. But it's the end, Maddie.'

March 21st. The samples taken from Whitefoot's sheep show that two had been infected with foot-and-mouth disease. Whitefoot must be treated as an infected farm, and its name is posted on the website and listed amongst the lengthening tally on the local radio. Daniel and Elaine Nicholson's farm too. All over Cumbria, farmers are hearing how the disease is creeping closer to them.

★

Friday April 13th, Good Friday. All through the north-west of the county, uninfected sheep are herded into lorries and taken away to be slaughtered. None will rise again.

June 21st, Midsummer. Daniel Nicholson owns neither a bolt gun nor a shotgun, but he finally finds a way to take a life. He hangs himself from a beam in the milking parlour.

AMY LIPTROT

'Daylight and Multiplication' (2021)

This year, on the spring equinox, I left the baby in bed with his dad and went for a sunrise swim. In the lake, the water only just above freezing, but I didn't hesitate as I waded in. After the last year, I felt indestructible.

What I most remember of last summer, the summer of my pregnancy, is lying in bed watching the swallows. I was nauseous, weeks of 'morning sickness' with lethargic afternoons napping while the summer happened outside. But there were swallows nesting in the eaves above my bedroom window and I watched them circle the treetops then approach the house at high speed, at the last moment slowing and shooting into the tiny opening. They were making their nest and laying their eggs. We were both gestating.

Smells began to be unpleasant. I was aware of car fumes and ripe bins. Coffee tasted dirty, bananas made me gag. The supermarket was an onslaught of detergent and plastic and artificial fragrances. The only smell I found pleasant was the woods after rain: the fresh, earthy petrichor scent of rain on dry soil and grass.

Often I would rouse myself by evening and walk in the woods at the edge of town, along the river, up the old packhorse trails up the side of the valley, onto the moor tops. Outside and walking, I was calmed. There were swifts overhead and wagtails, dippers and herons on the river. I think I heard a nightingale. The ferns were bright and lush and I watched the sky change.

Sometimes I just went into the woods and cried. They were not tears of sorrow, but of the pain of change and of adjustment to the new ride I was on. In the lonely weeks of early pregnancy before we told people – when I didn't look pregnant and found my sickness and preoccupation hard to explain – the natural world was where I could let it out.

I lie in the grass and watch bees visiting flowers and cobwebs in the sun. I make eye contact with deer. I pee in the undergrowth. I enjoy being an animal. Thinking can be overwhelming – this unexpected baby changes everything and the mysteries of life are happening inside my body – and I just need to be a wild beast, a physical being using my senses.

I amble in the woods and eat hungrily when I get home. I sleep in the afternoon and rub oil on my growing belly. I walk to relax my tense limbs and sluggish digestive system. I walk up out of the valley and try to catch some sunlight. I swim in the reservoir, laughing to myself at the idea of 'taking the baby for a swim'.

I feel seasick but the ocean is inside my body. There are swells and tides and currents and I am a barometer. My body is a measuring instrument. I am alert to changes in air pressure and the pull of the moon. I monitor the meteorology of my health. My blood pressure is a little lower than before. I have heartburn, vertigo and muscular twinges. I imagine the shipping forecast of my pregnancy: 'Fragile, increasing to tearful, occasionally horny.'

By August I began to feel my baby move: strange flickers, internal rolls. My sickness subsided. I continued to walk in the woods as summer passed its peak, increasingly encumbered and steadier on my feet. I turned slowly in bed like a cargo ship while, just above me, the swallows were still there, chicks hatched, noisy and shitting.

By winter I stopped swimming outdoors but kept walking. My pedometer told me my steps decreased with each month of my pregnancy. The baby's movements get stronger: what was flutters and pops is now wriggles and thuds. My sleep is disturbed. In the mornings I'm fizzing with health but later in the day I want to cry with bone-deep weariness. I delete all the social media apps from my phone. I am quietening and turning inwards. The outside world – international politics, the next town, friends online – are increasingly distant and muffled. I talk less; I look down at my own body. I am a whale shark, a deep-sea fish.

In the weeks leading up to my due date, everything felt heightened. At this time, boundaries between worlds are thinned and I think about your past and future and the generations. For those prone to madness, this time is thrilling and dangerous. I tried to stay calm and look after myself. I was excited but must stay sane. I walked gently along woodland paths in crisp air. The baby had hiccups inside me and I saw my tummy pulse. Everything was symbolic: the world wasn't just counting down to Christmas but to the birth of my child; the storms and stars and lights and birds were all portents. The first snow comes when I am heavily pregnant and on a cold, bright day I walk uphill across fields and feel on top of the world, a strange energy. I see a robin.

My son was born – early and astoundingly alive – on Christmas morning. We spent four days in hospital with an infection scare, adrenalised and wakeful and under fluorescent lights. We brought our baby home in the darkest, deepest days of winter. Opening the curtains after surviving the night in those first days, the brief hours of daylight were incredibly healing.

The days after the birth were hard. I had hormonal surges, which, combined with sleep deprivation, made me fear I was losing my mind: paranoid, out-of-control thoughts, adrenaline and fear. On the eighth day of his life, we managed to take him out for a walk to the end of the road. On the ninth, around the block. A few days later I took him out alone. I was still an open wound, shocked and surviving, feeding at 4 a.m. through cracked nipples, crying with exhaustion and pure liquid emotion.

At five weeks old, carrying him on my front, he threw his head back and opened his eyes wide, looking at the sky and not minding the cold rain. My baby likes the sky, I thought and my heart lifted. There are moments of light when I can see that things are going to be OK.

'If in doubt, get out,' said my friend Nell, also a new mum. I am finding ways to cope. When he is grouchy in the late afternoons, I strap him to my chest and go walking in the woods and around town, the same places I walked when pregnant. I discover new footpaths and my phone counts my steps. The baby and I both calm down, moving in the cold air. I walk along the canal with him in the sling, and the birds, the hills, the trees seem shining with beauty and emotion. I see seven robins. I think he likes the sound of the river, rushing after days of rain and melted snow. He often falls asleep. I love to carry him, calm and alert, just watching the trees, listening to the birdsong. The birth, although relatively fast and straightforward, was still brutal and I repeated the events of that Christmas night over and over in my mind. As I walk, I gradually move from shock and indigence at its violence, to pride and wonder at my own strength.

There was a cold wave across Europe. It was below freezing for a week. Icicles grew from windowsills and it was bright white each morning when I opened the curtains, but I put my wellies on and wrap the baby in layers, hold him close to my heart, and go outside.

The days get longer as motherhood begins to seem more manageable. At first the nights are feats of endurance, and so long, but we begin to find a routine. I am almost recovered from the birth, although it took longer than I had anticipated. Then my healing falters; an infection in stitches is a setback. The winter keeps coming back, a bitter east wind and another covering of snow after Easter. It's been winter for the baby's whole life. There are still snowdrifts on the moor when I see the first lapwings in their courtship dance.

By the beginning of spring, he is no longer a newborn. He's moved out of the 'fourth trimester', when I needed to keep him close like he was in the womb, and become more interested in the outside world, turning away from my body in the sling. He can smile and laugh and babble. He hears a robin sing. The world is opening up as the light is returning.

When we go out walking now, instead of always falling asleep, he looks up at me and around at passing surroundings. In his eyes, which keep changing colour, I see the reflection of my silhouette, and the winter trees, bare branches against the bright sky. It is high contrast like the black-and-white books we have been given for him. The sound of the river is like the 'white noise' we play at night to help him sleep. We are mimicking the natural world when sometimes it's better to just go to the source.

As we walk, I am adjusting to this sudden-onset family. I'm taken aback by the love and its burden. Last night I woke at 4, 5, 6 a.m. and checked on my sleeping baby. Their woes and triumphs are mine too. I have reproduced. I am multiplied. My feelings and nerves are now in other people. On my chest, the baby is calm and alert, raindrops on his face. He sticks his tongue out, attempting to drink the sky.

KAREN LLOYD

From *The Blackbird Diaries* (2017)

August 1

'Any chance you can come over this afternoon? The last few fledglings will be leaving any day now.'

I'd been waiting for a visit to Tanya and Edmund Hoare's house and their colony of swifts. The Hoares are national experts, advising local communities and authorities on swift nesting sites and speaking at the British Trust for Ornithology (BTO) Conference. I set off for Lowgill.

The Grayrigg road rises out of Kendal, winding and twisting, passing the eastern end of the Whinfell Ridge where a panoramic view of the western mountains opens up. Through Grayrigg itself and on, along the narrow lane leading past meadows bounded by dry-stone walls, down the steep hill passing under the M6 and the West Coast Main Line, then taking the turnoff to a row of sandstone ex-railway-workers' cottages.

On the TV in the sitting room, four sets of images – all from nest cameras. Two of the nests were empty, the young already flown, but the third had a single pulli cupped by the shallow circular nest, and it was performing swift press-ups. The fourth camera showed two youngsters, one occupying the nest itself and also doing press-ups. Up and down the swifts went, pressing down on their outstretched wings to build muscle and strength for that maiden flight. The second swift had manoeuvred itself to the edge of the nest and was perching on the lip beneath the eaves of the house.

'They stay like that for days,' Tanya said, 'then off they go and we've no way of knowing if they ever come back.'

Edmund said, 'Come outside – you never know – you may see that one leaving.'

Down a flight of stone steps into the garden, the Howgill Fells were close in, just across the woodland and the River Lune gorge below the houses. These are the smoother, more rounded hills of Lakeland's far eastern terrain. There were garden sheds, washing lines, painted garden furniture, trees, flower beds and lawns.

Edmund brought me back to the job at hand. 'If you look up there,' he said, pointing to the black-painted eaves, 'count three stanchions along and you'll see a gap – that's the nest with the two young ones in.'

There was no movement, no adult birds winging in and out – they had already set out for Africa, leaving the young to make that momentous flight alone.

'We have twenty-two potential swift nest sites – in the eaves, nest boxes or swift bricks. Fourteen have been occupied this year, and we expect more will be over time,' Edmund said.

'There's been a forty per cent decline in UK swifts over the last twenty years,' Tanya said. 'The problem is mainly people doing up old houses. They fill in all the gaps, all the crevices where swifts make their nests. These birds are faithful to their nest sites, and they're not adaptable to change, so if they return to find their entrance blocked up, that's probably one more season without breeding. You can see them trying to get in, flying up to the entrance and coming away again. It's so unnecessary. Swifts are very clean too – they don't make a mess like swallows or martins.'

I looked up at the eaves, imagining the youngsters inside, the impetus to leave pulsing through their bloodstream.

I told them of the big old house on Kendal Green that had been put on the market after twenty years or more of standing empty and quietly crumbling, the garden increasingly impenetrable. Inevitably, the new owners had the builders in, and I'd seen screaming parties of swifts zooming between the chimney stacks and the narrow passage between that house and the next.

'That's exactly the kind of place they could be using, and if they were, it's highly likely they've been displaced,' she said.

I thought of the scaffolding, the roofers, the constant jab and bang of nail guns, the drilling out of crumbling mortar and the systematic, hermetic resealing, of the chimney stacks being repointed, of the swifts, night after night careering around the chimneys once the builders had left for the day. Next year, our house will have swift nest boxes.

My closest encounter with a swift came early one morning years back, when I rented a studio space in an ailing Georgian building on the main street in town. In winter, gaps in the roof and the ceilings rendered the place as cold – colder, I think – than Siberia. But in the summer, it was a cool place to work, and I favoured getting there early. I went into the small kitchen to put the kettle on. Lifting the washing-up bowl, something – a treacle-brown creature – struggled uselessly in the bottom of the sink. I am ashamed to admit it: I shrieked. Instantly, I felt an idiot. I'd behaved stupidly, though to be fair, I had not previously encountered a brown, shuffling creature underneath a washing-up bowl. The poor thing must already have been scared half to death, even before I came along. The swift attempted to manoeuvre itself hopelessly around the sink.

After what could have been hours of being stuck there, it was clearly exhausted. My friend Lara arrived. Gently, she wrapped the swift in a tea towel and together we took it down into the yard at the back of the building where, with great good fortune, the local RSPCA office was located.

'I don't hold out much hope,' the man said. 'Birds in acute shock rarely survive.'

Later, we called in, but of course the swift had died. It must have found its way through cavities in the stonework and somehow into the kitchen, where a high window offered the enticement of daylight.

What an ignominious end for one of an avian tribe that, in a lifetime, will clock up an average of over 2 million kilometres.

'Come and see the bathroom,' Tanya said, and we went back inside, climbed the stairs and turned into the bathroom at the back of the house. Set into the white-painted wall were six neat, white-painted cupboard doors, each about twenty square centimetres, finished with a small brass handle. Edmund opened one of the doors. Inside, protected by a double-glazed panel, was a nest box, complete with a circular wooden nest cup lined with white feathers. More white feathers were strewn across the plywood floor.

'They seem to be attracted to white feathers,' Tanya said.

More doors were opened, revealing similar deserted nests and more white down. This would, for me, be heaven – soaking in a bath with that view of the Howgill Fells and occasionally looking across to watch swifts winging in and out. Suddenly, I had a severe case of swift-nest-box-cupboard envy.

'We put all the infrastructure in whilst we were being re-roofed. It was all ready to go when the swifts came back in the spring.'

We went into a bedroom at the front of the house. Two more cupboards were set into the outside wall. Edmund opened a door, and inside was the single chick from 'Swift TV'. We peered in, talked in whispers.

'Sometimes the young need to lose weight to be able to fly. The bodyweight-to-wing ratio is critical. If this were a human, the wingspan would be eighteen feet.'

The youngster began its press-ups, and again I saw those crumpled feet and legs, the pale edges to the primary wing feathers.

'They'll leave here,' Tanya said, 'and head down to the Congo where they'll stay maybe until Christmas time, then some go on even further south to Malawi. We think that the further north they breed, the further south they fly in winter. In April, they begin to move to West Africa, and then north to Europe. One tagged bird took only six days to travel from Liberia to Cambridge.'

'That's some speed of travel,' I said.

'They're too small to carry satellite tags, but geolocators are beginning to be used. The BTO have asked if we could tag some of our swifts with them.'

Downstairs again, Edmund asked if I'd ever seen a swift parasite.

I wasn't sure that I wanted to, but he disappeared into the room next door, returning with a plastic jar, the lid mercifully fixed tightly in place.

'*Crataerina pallida* – the flat fly,' Edmund announced, handing the jar to me. 'Collected from the nests after the swifts have gone.'

With the slightest movement, the dead parasites rattled together like voodoo charms. I held the jar, at once repelled and horribly enthralled. The parasites were black with three pairs of legs that looked specifically designed to grab on – and not let go. Seeing them, it was impossible not to think about scale: were swifts the size of humans, *Crataerina pallida* would be like a medium-sized crab. Thanking the heavens for small mercies, I handed the jar back.

On the television screen, the swift on the lip of the nest peered out from beneath the eaves. I wondered about the magnetic allure of the outside, about how exactly the bird might sense the world, or the idea of scything through the sky for four years, over a continent as different and distant as Africa, when its current experience is little more than the view of a flight of steps, a grassy path, a shed – not that the swift knows them as such, of course.

The fledgling shuffled around on its hopeless feet and came to rest facing the camera. Close to, the face is surprisingly pale compared to the rest of its peat-brown feathers. The eyes are large, bright, very round and very dark, rimmed with the same pale colouration that spreads around the face and down to the throat. Face on, the beak is a Cupid's bow, almost cartoon-like, sweet and perfect. It is hard to reconcile this with the sky-farming machine that is a swift, collecting several hundred tiny insects at a time, compressing them into a ball, or bolus, and storing them in their crop ready for disgorging at the nest.

The sweet face turned away, the feet shuffled and the swift perched again on the very edge of its knowledge and experience. The bow-shaped body rocked slightly, its scythe-like wings crossed at their tips. What must that be like, to be on the edge of such a momentous journey?

We talked some more, drank mugs of tea and watched 'Swift TV'. I found that I was simultaneously willing the young swift to leave – and to stay. I wanted to bear witness to the moment of departure, but I wanted it to stay, too. For when would I be in such intimate proximity to a swift again? This was television like none I'd seen before.

August 3

We gather in small groups and loiter on corners, watching the skies. We meet mid-evening and stay out late – or until darkness falls. Oh yes, we know how to live. God alone knows, though, what people make of us.

Wednesday night is swift night. Our group, one of a growing network across the country, gathers to record the places where swifts nest. Once you've got your eye in, it's an addictive pastime. Kendal is great swift territory, given the number of old stone buildings replete with cracks and cavities, though our sub-Saharan visitors also take well to swift bricks and boxes installed on newer houses. The trick is to plan ahead, install the infrastructure ahead of their arrival back from Africa in May, and even play recordings of swifts screaming from tiny speakers set next to or inside the boxes. Then stand well back and wait for young breeders to investigate. With a bit of luck, they'll turn it into a home.

JANE LOVELL

'Aigrettes, Spring 1893' (2019)

my tiny skull
you will remember
is as delicate as jingle shell

those strange blue
ligaments below my wings
slick with blood
you won't

they have not been
mentioned

my hinged spine
collapsing to a clef
in water-lap
   the pitch-shift
as the tide of carcasses
lifts and settles
all along the shoreline,
you would not have
noticed

you wanted the 'Valkyrie effect'
Mercury wings, the elegance
of Mephisto aigrettes

such elegance
this side of the Atlantic!
You say
watch me take flight!

your gown of black duchesse
adorned with tiny swallows
swishes as you turn

your companion is iridescent:
whole skins of kingfishers
and paroquets
a humming bird stripped
and fixed upon the brim
still struggling in panic
from its bones

their young below the nest
bellies twisted rind,
you'll never even
contemplate

I have become light
I scatter across the room
alight upon the plumes
that once were mine

see me everywhere you turn

remember as you lift
your glass, my tiny skull

'Vixen' (2020)

and there
through this Japanese ghost garden
this monochrome dreamscape
slips a half-dreamt wraith

born from the last shades of dusk
she is tip tip toeing on footfall so soft
it uncurls snails
dizzies galaxies in dew

her vagabond heart
beats with the tremors of the earth
balances on owl call
and the breeze rushing the trees

behind her swim timorous worlds
we can never enter

so slight and swift she moves
that without the moon billowing through
the cherry and all the fallen blossom
luminous as snow
I would not see her

HELEN MACDONALD

From *Falcon* (2006)

What is it like to be a falcon?

Claiming to understand the life-world of another person is philosophically suspect; for a different animal, the attempt is perhaps absurd – but undeniably fascinating. Our common-sense anthropomorphism suggests that the world the falcon experiences is probably rather like ours, only more acutely perceived. But from the available evidence it seems that the falcon's sensory world is as different from ours as is that of a bat or a bumblebee. Their high-speed sensory and nervous systems give them extremely fast reactions. Their world moves about ten times faster than ours, so events in time that we perceive as a blur, like a dragonfly zipping past our eyes, are much *slower* to them. Our brains cannot see more than twenty events per second – falcons see seventy to eighty; they are unable to recognise the 25-pictures-per-second moving image on a television screen. Seeing things closer together in time than we do allows them to stretch out a foot at full speed to grab a bird or a dragonfly from the air.

When fixing their eyes on an object, falcons characteristically bob their head up and down several times. In so doing they are triangulating the object, using motion parallax to ascertain distance. Their visual acuity is astonishing. A kestrel can resolve a two-millimetre insect at eighteen metres away. How is this possible? Partly through the size of the eyes: these are so huge that the back of each orb presses into the other in the middle of the skull. The retina is avascularised to prevent shadows or light-scattering; instead of blood vessels, nutrients are supplied to the retinal cells from a projecting, pleated structure called the pectin. Falcons' visual sensory cells, the rods and cones, are far more densely packed than ours, particularly the colour-sensitive cones. While we have around 30,000 cones in the most sensitive part of the retina, the fovea, raptors have around 1 million. Moreover, each of their photoreceptive cells has individual representation in the brain. Associated with the cone cells are coloured oil droplets that are thought to sharpen contrast and pierce haze, or may protect those cells from ultraviolet radiation. While humans have one fovea, falcons have two – thus, two images of a single object focused on these foveae may fuse in the brain and produce a true stereoscopic image. Furthermore, between these two foveae, there is a horizontal streak of increased sensitivity, a kind of 'smeared fovea' running between them. This allows falcons to scan the horizon without moving their heads. But not only do falcons see more clearly than humans, they also see things *differently*. They are believed to see polarised light, useful for navigating in cloudy skies. They also see ultraviolet. Overall, falcons have a radically different phenomenal world. Humans have three different receptor-sensitivities – red, green and blue; everything we see is built from these three colours. Falcons, like other birds, have *four*. We have three-dimensional colour vision; they have four. It is hard to comprehend. Dr Andy Bennett, researcher in the field of avian vision, considers the difference between human and bird vision as being of the same order as that between black-and-white and colour television. In the barest of functional terms, a falcon is a pair of eyes set in a well-armed, perfectly engineered airframe.

The beak is extremely powerful; anyone who has been bitten by a falcon will vigorously attest to this. A sharp projection on the upper mandible fits neatly into a notch in the bottom mandible. This 'tomial tooth' is used to sever the vertebrae of prey, an efficient method of administering the *coup de grâce* to avoid a tussle on the ground and broken feathers. Beak dimensions vary between species and sexes. Southern-latitude peregrines have proportionately more massive beaks than northern birds. Once thought to be an adaptation for killing dangerous prey such as parrots, the reasons for this gradient are obscure. There is, however, a strong correlation between foot shape and prey type. Bird-killing species such as the peregrine and lanner have relatively short legs to withstand the impact of hitting prey at speed; their toes are long and thin. On the underside of each toe are warty pads of skin that fit closely against the curve of the talon when the foot is clenched, giving the bird secure purchase on feathers. Sakers and gyrs have proportionately thicker, shorter toes and longer legs, a better arrangement for catching mammalian prey in snow, grass or steppe scrub. The toes have a 'ratchet' tendon mechanism: after the initial effort of clenching the foot, falcons can hold them locked shut with no muscular effort, an invaluable strategy for carrying prey in flight or sleeping on a branch in high winds. At rest, falcons habitually tuck one foot up underneath their feathers. Here, it is often invisible. Visitors to falconry centres often ask staff why they have so many one-footed falcons.

The skeleton is light, strong and highly adapted for the demands of flight. Some bones are fused. Major bones are hollow, air-filled and reinforced by bone struts. These pneumatised bones are connected to the bird's respiratory system. *Really* connected: a bird suffering a compound fracture of a wing or leg can breathe through the exposed end of the bone. The massive flight muscles, making up around 20 per cent of the weight of a peregrine, are attached to the sternum, or 'keel', and are served by oxygen from a highly efficient respiratory system. Rather than an in–out lung system like ours, air is drawn continuously and in one direction through the lungs via a series of nine thin-walled air sacs throughout the body; these also have a thermo-regulatory function. Overall, falcons' respiratory and circulatory systems are far more efficient than ours; despite the far greater metabolic rate of falcons, they breathe at about the same rate we do.

Compared with other birds, a falcon's digestive system is short, for flesh is easily digested. Falcons cannot digest feathers and fur; these are stored in the crop and ejected from the mouth in the form of a tightly packed 'casting' some hours later. They drink infrequently, for most of the moisture they require is derived from their prey and their water economy is impressive; falcon faeces – 'mutes' or 'hawk chalk' in falconers' parlance – are composed of faecal matter and a chalky suspension of uric-acid crystals. Falcons can excrete uric acid 3,000 times more concentrated than their blood levels. That's acidic enough to etch steel.

SARA MAITLAND

From *A Book of Silence* (2009)

Then, that winter, I got snowed in.

This was not the usual sort of getting snowed in. Early in 2001 there was a major outbreak of foot-and-mouth disease. It was horrible. The horror was exacerbated by a feeling that the government was being totally incompetent – the rules and regulations made no sense; the contiguous cull was probably illegal and widely held to be useless; and the disposal of the slaughtered livestock was both unsanitary and insensitive. In many rural areas people felt frightened and powerless, and in isolated places like the Durham moors, social life was completely disrupted. The markets were closed, people did not want to visit other farms or have people on theirs. More immediate to my personal comfort, the moors, like the rest of the countryside, were closed to walkers, so that I could not take my usual exercise and had a sense of being 'cabin'd, cribbed, confined'.

In late March there was a period of severe snow and blizzards. The rural roads of County Durham are normally snowploughed by subcontracted local farmers using their own tractors – but they were confined to their farms by the outbreak, so the road to and from my house was unploughed and soon became unpassable as the snow drifted across it. Without any choice, and without much preparation, I was alone and locked into an involuntary period of silence. Since the telephone lines were down, I had no source of information as to what was going on in the 'real world'. I knew, for example, that my brother's farm was under special measures – a legally binding series of restrictions on movement in and out of the farm – and that he was anticipating the slaughter of his stock, but I did not know if this had or had not happened (his sheep were eventually culled, but his dairy herd was not, which was in itself rather frustrating and confusing), or how the epidemic was progressing throughout the country, including my own moor, so it was not a comfortable time or place to be confined. Part of me regressed – I built a splendid snowlady in the garden, daily expanding the magnificence of her bosom and the glamour of her costumes, but another part of me became increasingly scared. Some anxiety was 'realistic' – would I eventually run out of food (or in my case more seriously, of cigarettes)? What would happen if the weather did not improve? Was my family all right? But more of it was emotional – despite the fact that I was supposedly longing for quiet. I increasingly felt invaded. The silence was hollowing me out and leaving me empty and naked.

The cold intensified that sense of being exposed, and sometimes when the weather was particularly wild just getting the coal in from the coal shed was exhausting and even frightening. When the weather was calmer, however, I realised that snow produces a peculiar acoustic effect: it mutes nearby noises (presumably because the softer ground surface absorbs them) but causes distant sounds to carry further and with a startling clarity. In addition the snow itself flattens everything visually. These effects disorientated me and made me increasingly nervy and jumpy. One day, walking to my gate, the collar of my jacket blew up against the back of my head and I screamed aloud, viscerally convinced I had been attacked from behind.

One afternoon I needed to break out and I took a walk up the undriveable road, despite the fact that there were flurries of 'snail' (a mixture of snow and hail) which, driven by a harsh wind, cut into my face. Then, about half a mile from the house, I started to hear the most agonised wailing noises – the wailing, it seemed to me then, of the damned. I was completely terrified. I would be on this hill in this wind for ever howling and desolate. I would never see another human being again. I would freeze in hell. It turned out that this strange and deeply disturbing noise was in fact no manifestation of my inner torment, but caused by a strange and fascinating phenomenon. The unfenced roads in that part of the north-east have snow poles – tall posts, marked in black-and-white foot-wide stripes that show you both where the road is and how deep the snow is. Older snow poles are made of iron and, to make it harder for them to be blown over, they have holes drilled in them for the wind to pass through. Essentially they were Aeolian harps or organ pipes and they were responding to the wind with these extraordinary sounds. But I know I was lucky that I identified the source of the noise fairly quickly, because otherwise it would have driven me insane. I can only too easily understand how this sort of silence can drive one beyond panic and into true madness.

MARY MALYON

From The School Run Instagram Project (2021)[†]

January 6, 2017 (St Mary Bourne,
North Wessex Downs, Hampshire)

Back on the school run and it is Arctic. Overhead a pair of ducks race: wings butterfly-beating, pudding bellies drenched in morning sun. Then we spot it: still, eerie, crouched in the bare-bone stubble, eyes half alert, ears folded, frost sprinkling the black, tawny pelt. We edge closer, no movement. How strange to see a hare so close, so relaxed; it must be dead. We potter on, playing guess-the-birdsong as a distraction.

January 18, 2017 (St Mary Bourne,
North Wessex Downs, Hampshire)

It is finger-splitting steel cold: deep January. But on the school run we spot catkins floating on bare winter twigs and a buzzard swoops under shafts of sunset.

January 20, 2017
(Hurstbourne Priors, Hampshire)

We race helter-skelter through the day at toddler speed. Then here, on this bridge, a chink of calm – of river water clattering pebbles, winter sun and bulrushes.

January 22, 2017 (St Mary Bourne,
North Wessex Downs, Hampshire)

We are trundling, pushchair and all, along farmland tracks; starlings float like dandelion seeds above us whilst partridges race ahead, blades gliding over stubble.

January 23, 2017 (St Mary Bourne,
North Wessex Downs, Hampshire)

We edge through fog, the calcified hedgerows echoing spring's hawthorn blossom. As I take these images, a squat muntjac deer rustles into half-sight, nosing the floor like a tiny tapir.

PIPPA MARLAND

'Enlli: The Living Island' (2021)†

Islands come trailing clouds of myth and legend, refracted through the eyes of others like distant land through a sea mist. Some small islands have been imagined and written into existence so powerfully and so many times that their materiality and the lived experience of their inhabitants – human and non-human – are overshadowed. Ynys Enlli (Bardsey Island), lying around 3 km off the Llŷn peninsula in North Wales, and roughly 1.6 km long and 1 km wide, is such an island. This tiny patch of land in the Irish Sea is more pre-troped than any other place I can think of: it is the romanticised 'Island in the Currents'; the final resting place of 20,000 medieval saints; King Arthur's Avalon and the location of Merlin's crystal palace and the Thirteen Treasures of the Island of Britain. And like any small island with its own individual heritage, it is also susceptible to the broader legacy of literary works that have, over the centuries, shaped our vision of islands, so that its shore is stalked by the figures of Odysseus, Crusoe, Prospero, Caliban, and Gulliver, and haunted by dreams of Edenic perfection or their converse – nightmares of dystopian hell.

Along with its impressive raft of myths, legends and half-truths, Enlli has a rich social history that belies its small physical stature. It was the site of a medieval abbey, the ruins of which lie in the northern part of the island, and has a chapel, a working farm, a lighthouse, and ten sturdy farmhouses built in the 1870s. From the late eighteenth century until the 1920s the island had its own king. Enlli's human population has fluctuated over the last 150 years. Over 130 people were living there in the 1880s, but the octogenarian last king of the island, Love Pritchard, led an exodus of the older islanders in 1925, after which the population gradually diminished to its current level of single figures in the winter months. Most of the farmhouses are now let as holiday homes in the summer, a scheme administered by the Bardsey Island Trust, which bought the island in 1979. Enlli also has an immensely rich natural history, geologically composed of metamorphic rocks dating back over 600 million years to the Pre-Cambrian era, and renowned for its puffins, dolphins, porpoises, choughs, Manx shearwaters and grey seals, as well as its rare plants, lichens and unique variety of apple. The Bardsey Bird and Field Observatory, founded in 1953, monitors the bird life and complex ecology of the island.

Given such fame, is almost impossible to visit Enlli untouched by the stories that precede it. How does one begin to write about such a multilayered place? How does one find an original means of encounter with such a predefined, pre-imagined landscape? And, given the masculinity of the touchstone characters of literary islands, how might a woman write herself into an island setting? I visited Enlli in the early summer of 2014, on the trail of two extraordinarily talented female authors – Brenda Chamberlain and Christine Evans. Chamberlain lived on the island between 1947 and 1961, and Evans, who made her first trip to Enlli in 1968, is still a resident. In 1962, Chamberlain published *Tide-race*, a semi-fictionalised account of her time on Enlli. The book is a genre-defying mix of memoir, nature writing, mythological fantasy and poetry, interspersed with Chamberlain's own distinctive illustrations. 1995 saw the publication of Evans' *Island of Dark Horses*, a poetry collection focused entirely on Enlli, and in 2008, her prose work *Bardsey* came out, lavishly illustrated with photographs by Wolf Marloh. Both writers display a strong emotional attachment to the island. 'Listen:' *Tide-race* begins, 'I have found the home of my heart.' Evans, who initially visited the island somewhat sceptically at the invitation of a teaching colleague, also found the home of her heart, confessing, 'Reader, I married the boatman.'

What makes reading these works so fascinating is not just their individual brilliance but the way in which they exist in a kind of dialogue with each other. Evans arrived on the island at the end of the decade in which *Tide-race* appeared, and a number of the islanders Chamberlain included in her book still lived on Enlli, with the real incidents she recounts still fresh in their memory. Evans' husband Ernest's parents, Wil and Nellie, feature in *Tide-race* thinly disguised as the characters Jacob and Rhiannon Lloyd. In turn, Evans writes about Chamberlain in both *Bardsey*, and in a beautiful elegiac poem entitled 'Brenda and the Golden Snake'. She remembers being asked during her first visit to the island if she had read *Tide-race*, and finding a copy of Chamberlain's poetry collection *A Green Heart* in one of the houses. Both writers refer to the rocks, the seals, the farmhouses, the ruined abbey, the association of the island with Avalon, and the 20,000 saints, and their lives are punctuated by the nocturnal cries of the shearwaters and the beam of the lighthouse. There is a tension for both writers between the attractions of the myths and legends of the island and their need to resist these in order to meet Enlli on its own terms. Both also write in a conscious awareness of their gender and their female embodiment. But this is not to say that their experience is uniform. Chamberlain and Evans' accounts of Enlli are, in the end, like different faces of a coin, expressing profoundly divergent ways of knowing, and being in, their island world.

From the start of *Tide-race*, Chamberlain demonstrates her knowledge of Enlli's cultural legacy. Looking across to the island from the mainland, she frames it in terms of its religious history and its Arthurian claims. It is 'the sea–crag to which three pilgrimages equal one to Rome', where the 'treasures of Britain are to be found [...] for Merlin buried or planted here in some secret place certain mystical properties'. She is also alert to the broader literary tropes of island adventure, seeing herself as beginning, with some trepidation, a 'Robinson Crusoe-type of existence'. But while revelling in these elements, she also satirises the expectations of others, mocking a fellow visitor who dreams of sinking into the past, led along a Celtic shore 'by long-footed maidens with anaemic faces'. At times she clearly tries to fight off her own attraction to the mythic, and there are passages of fine nature writing in *Tide-race* – for example, her closely woven description of gulls hatching on the island's cliff ledges on a hot day in early summer. There is also an anthropological dimension to the book. Chamberlain writes about the day-to-day activities of the island's 'fisherman-farmers' and their families, and though some of the islanders felt wounded by their portrayal in *Tide-race,* the book's dedication reads, 'TO My Neighbours On The Island'.

Nevertheless, Chamberlain is almost inexorably drawn back to the mythic, in search of some kind of symbolic personal or universal truth. Encounters with seals on the island prompt forays into the selkie story: she dreams of stealing a seal cow's pup to be her own child, and having a selkie bull-seal husband who abandons her. A rock face, initially seen in a positive light as the 'ivory-bright bird-bone perfection' of the remains of our ancestors, leads her to think of death, and the idea of bodies entrapped in stone through more cruel, enforced metamorphoses. As these mythologising tendencies come to the fore, the material Enlli begins to blur. At the same time, *Tide-race* is increasingly dominated by a generalised theme of death and decay. Chamberlain describes a rusting anchor chain as 'salt-bitten, repulsive as an unearthed corpse', and when she has her own encounter with human remains she is filled with revulsion and guilt: 'Feverishly, we washed and washed our hands, to deny having touched the bones.' The book ends with a vision of the islanders performing the *danse macabre*, with the shadow of death falling upon them all.

If the fear of death overshadows Chamberlain's island, the promise of new life animates Evans' Enlli, which emerges as a vibrant world constantly remaking itself, surrounded by the living, breathing presence of the sea. Her approach is characterised by a sustained attentiveness to its landscape and its human and non-human voices. Like Chamberlain, while fully versed in the island's myths, Evans resists them, sometimes quite fiercely. 'Bardsey is fertile ground for legend,' she warns us, 'but it is too real for Camelot, too anchored in rock and full of squelch and slither and stench of rotting seaweed.' Enlli continually 'brings us back/to our senses', and Evans relishes the ways in which the physical realities of life on the island keep breaking through the mists of legend. The rotting seaweed, which speaks of the kind of entropy Chamberlain feared, does not trouble Evans. When I asked her whether the legend of the 20,000 saints and the physical presence of human bones in the island earth had had an impact on her, she replied, 'Not so much [...] yes, there are bones in the ground, but then if you think about it, we all live where there must be bones.' For Evans, our ultimate materiality – our death and bodily decay – is merely one aspect of the regenerative round in which all life is involved, and is a phenomenon to be welcomed rather than feared. In the same interview she told me: 'I find that immensely comforting, to think that you're going to be remade.'

While always aware of the presence of mortality, Evans is much more fascinated by the life of the island, and part of her resistance to romanticised notions of Enlli comes from her desire to emphasise its ongoing role as a place where people live and work: 'I did not want to write about Bardsey in a misty Celtic-twilight sort of way; for me, it was a place to live (to *make a living*, that lovely phrase implying hard-won satisfactions): practical, pragmatic.' While her writing celebrates the natural world of the island, she does not see this as separate from its human life. In *Bardsey*, she traces the way in which the island has supported human habitation almost continuously from the Bronze Age to the present. 'It has remained,' she writes, 'the only permanently occupied offshore Welsh island, the only one that can still be called a home.'

I was only on Enlli for a handful of days, and yet the visit stays with me as one of the most vivid experiences of my life. Like Prospero's island, it was full of noises, with the aural backdrop of seals singing through the day in gloriously mournful tones, and the raucous sounds of the shearwaters as they woke me, streaming over the roof shortly after midnight to roost. Less than half an hour after arriving for my 'solitary' stay, a knock on the door heralded a friendly Canadian woman who took me swimming and later provided wine while we watched the sunset with the island's resident artist. I visited the ruins of the abbey and then, on entering the chapel, found myself inadvertently part of a Taizé service to which I lent my agnostic voice. With the permission of the warden, I went into the house in which Chamberlain lived to see the murals she painted on the walls sixty years ago. I met with Christine Evans, and we sat in her garden, and then walked to the island's well. The family who farm on Enlli were busy in the fields as we passed, and the Observatory generator reminded me of the work going on there. It was as if time had telescoped, or the past was filling out a present that was already brimming with activity.

Islands are often written about in tones of elegy and lament – for the ruined, empty houses turning their blank faces to the sky; for centuries of human ways of being in the world shattered by the onset of modernity. Places such as the Blasket Islands, St Kilda and North Rona spring to mind. In the thinning of non-human life and the ongoing horror of the Anthropocene, it's perhaps right that there should be places like this, gradually reclaimed by the birds and the seals. And yet in these islands humans lived sustainably for centuries, side by side with the non-human. So it is with Enlli even now. It is still a home, still cared for passionately by islanders with a vision for its future. It has a new ferry, built by Evans' son Colin, a new orchard, and flourishing populations of seals, puffins and shearwaters. Carrying all of its culture and nature together in a dizzying richness, Enlli is a living island, future-facing, still in the current of life.

BLÁTHNAID McANULTY
'Climb trees to another world' (2017)[†]

When I was really little, I wanted to be up high, to be up with the birds and the sky. I wanted to make a daisy crown and be Queen of the Trees, and I did. I felt like I was in a wonderland of dreams and it felt amazing.

As I grew I climbed higher and higher.

I climb up a giant snake when I'm in a tree. I fight dragons when I'm in a tree. I ride a unicorn when I'm in a tree. I climb mountains when I'm in a tree. I'm an adventurous explorer when I'm in a tree. I've actually discovered new species in a tree, but shush don't tell anyone. I'm saving them for when I'm older and a real life insect expert.

I travel through the jungle when I'm in a tree. My best friends join me when I'm in a tree.

I dream when I'm in a tree. I dream of talking ladybirds, dancing kestrels and raindrops that taste like chocolate.

I like to make things from bits of trees, branches that the ground has left for me to use. They were all shouting. Pick me. Pick me!

To feel moss, lichen and the bark is like feeling my own heart beat. If I could melt into the tree to find out its secrets, I would. Oh, but wait. I do know!!

ZAKIYA MCKENZIE

'Memories Live in the Forest' (2021)[†]

Nov 5, 2019

My mother died before I knew myself as British. When my only recollections were still those of Jamaica, my tangible ties (in my mind) to the country of my birth were the friends and family who flew to the island to stay at my home in Kingston. England was the richly lilted Guyanese accent of Auntie Greer against that of her London-born daughters – phrases, call and responses that my sister and I still evoke to this day. England was Uncle Liam (thick Yorkshire twang) asking for 'a cuppa tae', sitting with the sun, sweating and sipping from a steaming mug. My England was my unreasonable obsession with the Spice Girls, Emma in particular, learning all her part and dressing like her, thanks to platform shoes, baby-doll dresses, 'matey bags' given to me by Michelle, my older cousin in Port Antonio, who is always ahead of the style curve. Removed from the place itself, this is how my England was constructed. England was little Nile declaring, 'Oim noh foive, Oim foive an'a hawf', as he climbed the outside grille with ease and ran barefoot among Julie mango, East Indian mango and a special pongonut tree. No matter who came, we would always go to the countryside because that is where my mother's family, my family, live.

I didn't know it, but my mother's England was much richer. She left rural Jamaica, Swift River, to a strange country in the pit of winter. She came to know more about South London than she did about the island of her birth. It was Tulse Hill, Brixton, working at Sabbar Bookshop. She was lovers rock, and rocksteady, rocking crested at Twelve Tribes reggae sessions. This time, more South London than Global South. I feel such a sense of longing when I am in these places now, wanting her to show me the landscape, the places that still remained. I am wanting that part of my mother that I do not know and never cared for until I myself became an adult and mother and know how much of me there is that my child will not see with children's eyes.

And what is my England now? Places where I am sure she never saw, yet still stood in her time. Leigh Woods is the kind of place to get lost in and think of these things. The slow rustling of bush and birds above bring me ease, fresh inhale. There is so much that is special to see here. Come see Bristol whitebeam trees – *Sorbus bristoliensis* – it only grows wild here in the Avon Gorge, in my Leigh Woods. These glorious trees take precedence here. In fact, it's the best place in the world to see a variety of whitebeam, trees that you'd be hard-pressed to find anywhere else altogether like this. They are old and I like old, because old means it stood when my mother stood and so I hold on to it for it holds the memory. Another namesake, Bristol rock cress – the furthest back in time you'll find this plant is here in the Gorge. The peregrine falcon nests around the jagged ridge. And cliff hooks, apparatus show that climbers brave the precipice for another kind of thrill. The strawberry tree, strong and sprouting high over the old quarry, a wonder for a tree hunter to find. There is a treacherous trail to see this beauty but it is certainly rewarding. With careful shuffling. When I do see it, it is shedding its 'skin' to expose a smooth brown underneath. Yet the 'skin' crunches away, and I feel the crispy outer layer fall off. It is gone from the living tree, dust to dust, ashes to ashes. Still, the steadfast trunk holds the branches reaching out to me. It sheds skin and drops to dirt, but the tree still stands.

I feel tied to the old dirt. I am tethered to the movement of living things here, for I walk with them and think how close my mother was many decades ago, when this same place was under the sky. This wood holds a surety for me. It was here to witness lives untold and still holds the memory.

JEAN McNEIL

'Arboreal' (2021)[†]

In the winter of 2005–6 I lived for four and a half months without seeing a tree. It's difficult to avoid trees – not that I was doing so deliberately – but there are definitely no trees in Antarctica, where I was stationed as writer-in-residence with the British Antarctic Survey (BAS). We did have an artificial Christmas tree on base, which had possibly been pressed into service first in 1953, if its frayed plastic fingers were anything to go by. It lived in our dining room (technically called 'mess hall' – most Antarctic terminology, even of terrestrial life, is militaristic in origin) for a few days over Christmas, bleaching in the forever sun of the Antarctic summer.

The way in and out of the British Antarctic is studded with two other relatively treeless waystations: the Falkland Islands and Ascension Island. The Falklands is one of the windiest places on the planet, which definitely discourages trees from growing – they tend to trawl along the ground, bonsai-like. As for Ascension, it came to life ten minutes ago, geologically speaking, and coconuts have to travel 1,300 kilometres at a minimum to reach its shores, so the tree life of the island is still relatively juvenile.

I left Antarctica that year via those barren islands. Our flight on the ricketiest 747 left on the planet, a relic 200 series from the early 1970s, landed at RAF Brize Norton in mid-April. The leaves on the trees in England were just getting going. Still, the eyes of our motley group, consisting of me, several ship's officers, an engineer and three scientists, all of us still dressed in BAS faded tangerine regulation fleeces, drank in the filigreed splendour of bud-studded branches. Some of my colleagues had been in Antarctica far longer than I had – a year or a year and a half – and they were doubly stunned. On the bus to Oxford we tried to describe what we were seeing. 'What are those puffy things?' Mike, the engineer, joked. 'Aren't they surplus to requirements? They take up so much space!' We were weakened by jetlag and culture shock and so roared with laughter.

In my months on base, I'd noticed that several long-term inmates had calendars tacked up on their walls. These were always of scenic places in the British Isles ('Wild Wales'), of birds or, in one case, 'Trees of England'. In the Antarctic I was not conscious of missing trees. The duochrome glamour of the continent seduced me, along with its reduced visual field; they seemed to me to clarify things, on all levels. In the Antarctic it was easier to think, to separate self from society and to simultaneously meld with the natural world. We were in the most complete wilderness on the planet, we were all fortunate to be there, and sacrifices had to be made. Not smelling grass or trees or drinking water that had not been desalinated or eating cheese that had not been frozen and so crumpled in your hands or not eating an avocado for perhaps years were part of the menu of logical relinquishings.

When I looked at the Trees of England calendars in the jerry-built offices we inhabited on base, I noticed I felt calmer. If the doctor hadn't been cutting someone's hair at that moment – doctors doubled as hairdressers on base – I would have asked her to take my blood pressure to see if it dropped, just by looking at the photo of a mulberry tree photographed somewhere in Gloucestershire. The tree appeared to me as a giant brooding sentinel, thick with grape-hued knowledge, an envoy from deep time.

I had to go all the way to Antarctica to realise I didn't know very much about English, or British, trees, despite having lived in the UK for sixteen years at that point. I grew up in Nova Scotia and New Brunswick, eastern Canadian provinces. One of the few things I knew about my father was that he was a forester. I think my mother met him while she was doing a teacher-training master's and he was completing a master's in forestry at the University of New Brunswick, one of the best forestry degrees in North America.

I could identify far more Canadian trees than I could British, despite never having paid much attention to them. It occurred to me that trees were part of the grammar of one's life, as much as any spoken language. We absorb their presence in part through street names, furniture made from their limbs, from song and cinema and folklore and anecdote. There was no way I would confuse a larch for a birch or a tamarack for a spruce, yet I wasn't at all able to distinguish an ash from a silver birch. The neighbourhood in Halifax, Nova Scotia, where I spent six years of my childhood, was organised on a grid of trees: chestnut, walnut, larch, cedar, all helpfully planted with examples that bore their name. But in Britain, I realised that day on our spaced-out journey from RAF Brize Norton to Oxford, I had neglected to learn the language of the trees that surrounded me. My period of abstinence from trees in the Antarctic had sharpened my respect for them, my hunger for their balm.

In the early autumn the year I returned from Antarctica, I went to the National Arboretum at Westonbirt, near Bristol. Even after all these years in Britain, every time I visit a park, RSPB reserve or National Trust site in England I am still struck at how un-wild they are. In Canada, when you go to a national park your first task is to avoid being eaten (simultaneously – what fun) by mosquitoes, grizzly bears or wolves. In England, it's whether to have a cup of Earl Grey first or afterwards and which tea towel to buy.

After I'd navigated the play areas and Gruffalo sculptures, to walk into the Arboretum itself was to enter a serene lair of commanding, towering giants. Who knew there were so many walnuts? Black walnut, cut-leaved walnut, Texas walnut, Manchurian walnut. Or the stiff poetry of the junipers: flaky juniper, temple juniper, savin juniper? I slinked under gargantuan Scots pines, so large I thought they were

California red cedar. The Arboretum hosts native species alongside trees from around the world, some of them very rare.

The air rearranged itself around me. It felt like entering a force field, not too different from spending time among a herd of elephants, who communicate largely on a frequency too low for the human ear to hear, but our brainwaves pick it up. That trees are sentient is now widely accepted. They emit a force field – of what, though? Memories and events encoded in the trees' pheromones, perhaps. I sometimes think they have eyes; a recent visit to the Sachsenhausen concentration camp memorial north of Berlin solidified this. The trees that ring the perimeter of the camp are unlike any I have seen in my life. They have an alert sentience that spooked me. They watched me as I rotated around that blood-soaked ground in a dank early November, like solemn spectators in an arena.

My grammar of trees is now a widening lexicon of home, or multiple homes. I know how to identify by sight thirty-two species of African savannah tree, and now that I live part of the year on the Indian Ocean of East Africa, I have learned a new language: maembe (Kiswahili for mango), mbambakofi (pod mahogany), neem, casuarina, msufi (cotton tree), mvunge (mangrove). They are now my trees, and I am theirs. My flat in Stoke Newington, where I write this now, looks out on a small common and its cargo of London planes. They are my interlocutors as I write my books, modest guardians of the estuary sky. To see trees every day and to be seen by them is a privilege. I wonder what they think of me now, in these early days of 2020, a winter which is for me soaked in anguish and concern over the future of the country whose tree grammar I have learned by rote, and which I may need to relinquish, thanks to a turn of political direction. The London planes outside my window are my allies, with their emancipatory name that combines the name of the city I still love and that of a machine which will some day soon lever me into the sky.

I never thought I would leave Britain. I thought this was my home for ever. I still feel a kind of succour, flying back to Britain from having been away for a while, at the dark verdant patchwork beneath me, the seething, almost fluorescent green. If Britain – and England – has been such a reassuring place for me, at least until recently, it has been in part because of these simple but protective elements: green, trees, moisture. I have felt less exposed to the world's ravages here, sheltered by the suppliant, parental limbs of the London planes outside my window. It is possible to draw a link between the trees of a country and its essential political character. Perhaps the historic tolerance, openness and dynamism of Britain is encoded in its cloistered, accommodating verdancy.

I wonder what attracted my father to trees, about his arboreal life. I can't ask him, as he was killed some twenty years ago in a freak accident while piloting a glider. I do know that after I was born he went on to be a forester in Canada's Yukon province, in the Arctic. I wonder if his zeal for trees has somehow been bequeathed to me.

I have only one picture of him. He is young – perhaps twenty-four or so – his face, in which I see my own buried like a blueprint, is upturned, looking at the sky. Behind him is a wall of russet New Brunswick maples. It is early autumn and he wears a cloth cap with a peak, shoved back on his head. In the reflection of his eyes the veins of the tree branches he regards are visible, like giant retina, reaching out to all the world.

CHARLOTTE MEW

'The Farmer's Bride' (1916)

Three summers since I chose a maid,
  Too young maybe—but more's to do
  At harvest-time than bide and woo.
     When us was wed she turned afraid
  Of love and me and all things human;
  Like the shut of a winter's day
  Her smile went out, and 'twadn't a woman—
    More like a little frightened fay.
      One night, in the Fall, she runned away.

"Out 'mong the sheep, her be," they said,
  'Should properly have been abed;
  But sure enough she wadn't there
  Lying awake with her wide brown stare.
So over seven-acre field and up-along across the down
  We chased her, flying like a hare
  Before out lanterns. To Church-Town
    All in a shiver and a scare
  We caught her, fetched her home at last
    And turned the key upon her, fast.

She does the work about the house
  As well as most, but like a mouse:
    Happy enough to chat and play
    With birds and rabbits and such as they,
    So long as men-folk keep away.
  "Not near, not near!" her eyes beseech

When one of us comes within reach.
      The women say that beasts in stall
      Look round like children at her call.
      I've hardly heard her speak at all.

Shy as a leveret, swift as he,
Straight and slight as a young larch tree,
Sweet as the first wild violets, she,
To her wild self. But what to me?

The short days shorten and the oaks are brown,
      The blue smoke rises to the low grey sky,
One leaf in the still air falls slowly down,
      A magpie's spotted feathers lie
On the black earth spread white with rime,
The berries redden up to Christmas-time.
      What's Christmas-time without there be
      Some other in the house than we!

      She sleeps up in the attic there
      Alone, poor maid. 'Tis but a stair.
Betwixt us. Oh! my God! the down,
The soft young down of her, the brown,
The brown of her—her eyes, her hair, her hair!

ALICE MEYNELL

'A Dead Harvest in Kensington Gardens' (1921)

Along the graceless grass of town
They rake the rows of red and brown,–
Dead leaves, unlike the rows of hay
Delicate, touched with gold and grey,
Raked long ago and far away.

A narrow silence in the park,
Between the lights in a narrow dark.
One street rolls on the north; and one,
Muffled, upon the soul doth run;
Amid the mist the work is done.

A futile crop! – for it the fire
Smoulders, and, for a stack, a pyre.
So go the town's lives on the breeze,
Even as the sheddings of the trees;
Bosom nor barn is filled with these.

EMMA MITCHELL

'The Muntjac' (2021)[†]

Autumn arrives and my brain feels spent, empty. A summer of intensive writing, deadlines and no time for a holiday has left my neurons feeling fused. There's a leaden grey emptiness to my thoughts that comes with mental exhaustion. The undertow of depression is threatening to drag my mind downward. This sluggish, depleted state of mind brings with it an urge to stay still, to swaddle myself in the warmth of the cottage and in the soft reassurance of blankets. Motivation evaporates and I find it difficult to move, but I know that if I venture into the woodland behind our house I can remain afloat. I can disperse the pall of neuronal cloud that is lurking in my mind if I am in a green place.

I reach for the lead. Annie our lurcher sees me do so and begins to leap in the air like a gleeful fish. Before I can clip it to her collar she pulls the lead from my hand, scampers from room to room with it trailing from her mouth and performs a low, extravagant play bow. Her words are clear: 'Are we going to the wood? Are we? Because if we are I am very much on board with this plan, in fact let's go now, this instant, there should be no more delay.' Her hopeful enthusiasm is so intense and endearing that it cuts through the dingy shroud in my mind and we make our way from the cottage.

The signs of early autumn are beginning to shift the palette in the wood. One in every twenty or so hazel leaves has a yellow hem and along the mown pathways there are flashes of claret and aubergine as the chlorophyll's trademark green is withdrawn from this year's cow-parsley leaves, and anthocyanins display their warmer colours in its place; the euonymus leaves have turned a Barbie pink so vivid that they leave an imprint on my retina that remains when I move my eyes away from them; the hawthorns are thickly garlanded with berries, like sylvan strings of garnets, and the last of the wild carrot flowers are in bloom; the sun is low in the sky and casts a veil of hazy gentle light tinged with gold.

My urge to gather small finds as I walk is strong: a bright leaf, a hedge-parsley seedhead, a feather. I am certain that this urge stems from our foraging past. Several thousand years ago our ancestors would have spent a significant amount of their time searching the landscape for berries, edible and medicinal foliage, nuts and honey, and stems they could transform into textiles. Each discovery had a direct impact on their survival, and the Darwinian pressures on humans to become skilled and thorough foragers would have been strong. A successful foraging trip would not only have resulted in food, medicine or useful materials for their social group, increasing their chances of remaining nourished or able to hunt or keep warm for another day, but would also have resulted in mental rewards. Seeking out and discovering such resources in a landscape causes the release of a neurotransmitter called dopamine in our brains, leading to a feeling of elation: a natural high. Our ancestors would have wished to trigger a replay of this pleasurable feeling and in doing so find more food for their family and community. The natural high I feel as I stoop to pick up the empty shell of a grove snail is a legacy from my ancestors. I am grateful for it today.

One of the paths winds through a patch of land that has a different microclimate from the rest of the wood. The way dips into a hollow planted with beeches and in places it is thickly bordered on each side with waist-high nettles and hogweed. There is always a patch of cool air trapped here. When the rest of the wood is bathed in sunlight and its warmth can penetrate layers of clothes, the shadowiness in this dip and the damp chill that hangs about the trees brings relief on scorching days. I suspect that there may be a source of water beneath the soil here creating this sort of oasis in a temperate but dryish woodland and I relish the transition from foliage parched by a protracted recent dry spell to sudden lush vegetation as I descend into the hollow. I dawdle in this cool, cave-like place and there is an intense smell of green things, of crushed leaves and of leaf mould. I inhale deeply and the dragging fog of exhaustion and melancholy lifts a little more.

This further upward shift in the timbre of my thoughts is not simply due to the pleasing shadow patterns made by beech leaves in the hollow.

Research shows that when we enter a green landscape, several elements of our biochemistry respond within fifteen minutes. Our pulse rate and blood pressure drop; numbers of natural killer cells, a type of immune lymphocyte that seeks out and destroys virally infected cells, are boosted; the levels of the stress hormone cortisol in our bloodstream fall away and we feel less anxious. Cortisol is a substance whose levels increase during times of chronic stress. When its daily levels are raised for long periods, symptoms can develop, such as low energy levels, sleep disruption, high blood pressure and low mood. Prolonged elevated cortisol levels are associated with the development of anxiety and depression, and patients with persistently high levels are less responsive to psychotherapeutic treatments. A brief walk on a recreation ground, in a park, field, or wood just two or three times a week can help to keep cortisol levels down, which potentially diminishes the chances of depression developing or worsening.

One of the factors that elicits these biochemical changes is the inhalation of phytoncides. These are oils, blends of volatile compounds such as terpenes that are produced by plants as part of a chemical defence against the viruses and bacteria that could infect them. Phytoncides have been shown to cause the measurable changes in our circulatory, immune, endocrine and neuronal systems that are elicited when we walk in a green space. The green smells of crushed grass and hogweed, the slightly ferric tang of nettles and the fungal smell of deep leaf litter I inhaled in the hollow are made up of a cocktail of phytoncides. I breathed in the very compounds used by these plants to defend themselves from infection, I took this volatile botanical apothecary chest into my nose and my body responded. The rapid and multifaceted cascade of effects triggered in our systems by these plant compounds speaks of an ancient connection between humans and plants. All that is required for us to turn on these medicinal pathways is to walk into a garden or wood.

I emerge from the hollow and with each step the air becomes warmer. I've moved into a part of the wood where the trees are sparser and the leaf mould is drier; the rich green smell in the hollow is replaced by something closer to the smell of parched soil and pebbles overlaid with the mineral scent of chalk. The beeches have begun to shed their leaves and they lie in caramel-coloured drifts beneath the branches; the golden tint of the autumn sunlight combines with the beech leaf litter to cast an amber filter over this place. Suddenly I hear the sound of dried leaves crunching. Blackbirds often forage beneath these beeches, periodically turning leaves over with their beaks to find beetles and worms, but this sound is more percussive, sudden and regular, as though someone is stamping on the ground. I squat down to peer under the beech branches; there is a scuffle and the movement of a dark shape. A muntjac buck is there, perhaps ten metres away, and peering at me from a gap between the tree trunks, his small antlers visible above large eyes. He seems unperturbed and doesn't make to run away; instead he stands his ground and continues to stare at me. Then he begins to stamp every few seconds with one of his front hooves, explaining the sharp rhythmic crunching sound that I'd heard. Later I read that this is an alarm signal, but he is not so alarmed that he leaves the scene. It is then that he emits a startlingly piercing cry, sounding at once triumphant and despairing.

The sight of the muntjac causes a burst of elation in me. This feeling of giddiness and joy at the sight of him, this nature-spotters' high, might be linked to ancient hunting instincts. It's likely that our ancestors would have seen the muntjac as a potential meal for their community. I have no urge to eat him, so these mood-enhancing pathways are now triggered by simply catching sight of an animal or bird. Witnessing this muntjac's display – his stamping and his calling – make this encounter even more intense. Most of my brushes with wildlife last just a few seconds: a glimpse of a sparrowhawk as it slips between trees or the sight of a common lizard's tail as it scampers away, but this sighting is prolonged: the muntjac and I have been gazing at one another for several minutes. There is a connection between us. After seeing him I left feeling exhilarated. The time spent with the muntjac has lifted the dismal cloud of low mood yet further and my energy levels rise. Interacting with this wild mammal has added to the relief I began to feel as I spent time in the hollow and picked up the shell. This walk has altered the way I feel and the effect lasts for several hours.

Walking in green spaces: parks, recreation grounds, moors, woodland or even in a garden centre or florist is like walking into a natural medicine cabinet for both our bodies and brains. When we inhale phytoncides from the plants we walk upon and among, there are several interconnected responses in our biochemistry that make us feel uplifted, calmer and alter our blood and immune system in such a way that regular walks really can have a positive impact on our long-term mental and physical health. If we take time to notice the shapes of leaves, the exact colour of berries and the petals of a primrose, and perhaps make a small seasonal collection of finds to bring home, there is an additional positive effect. By immersing ourselves in the careful attention to the small details of the landscape we are in, we can trigger the responses our ancestors may have had to seeking out medicinal or food plants, adding to the effects of inhaling plant oils. Finally, if we see birds, mammals or insects while we're in that same green space, there may be a change in our neurotransmitters linked to ancient hunting pathways. Together these three sources of change in our neuronal and somatic systems resulting from our interaction from the landscapes we walk in can explain much of the relief we feel, that tangible lift in mood that can occur when we step from our homes or offices into a tree-lined place.

The number of annual diagnoses of mental illness is increasing worldwide and the most serious cases pose a threat to life. I suffered a bout of severe suicidal depression in the spring of 2018. The NHS treated me, but along with antidepressants, the sight of some saplings on the A11 and watching the small visitors to a bird-feeding station in our garden moved my mind away from that dark place and kept me going each day during those mental-storm-filled weeks.

Humans evolved in wild landscapes; they will have gained mental rewards when foraging, hunting, seeking medicinal plants and resources with which to build shelters, make tools and textiles. All those activities, each taking place among and involving trees and plants, will have had a direct and tangible impact on the survival of those individuals and their communities. There is increasing evidence that these pathways remain intact in twenty-first-century human brains and that we can now tap into them, harness their effects and use them to alleviate mental illness and perhaps begin to allay its severity and the number of yearly cases. During my recovery from severe depression last year, I took several walks of fifteen minutes or so each week and this helped to prevent the difficult days from becoming steep-walled wells of dark thoughts. Instead they were hollows, dips in my mood like the dip in the wood, and the time spent among trees helped me walk out of them again. This highly effective wild remedy is starting to become mainstream; indeed, in October 2018 Scottish GPs began to 'prescribe' nature walks alongside pharmaceuticals and talking cures for diagnoses of depression and anxiety. To the woods, to mend.

JAN MORRIS

From Wales: Epic Views of a Small Country (1986)

In the waters of Wales, around the rocks, life has probably existed as long as it has anywhere on earth. Certainly it was here, in 1964, that the oldest surviving life form was identified – the organism *Kakabekia barghoorniana*, which was found near Harlech in Gwynedd, which looks like a microscopic orange slice, and which Harvard scientists declared to have been in existence for 2,000 million years.

The trees feel quite old enough. Much of the country is bare of them, but much is richly wooded, and several kinds of tree always had special meanings for the Welsh. The oak was the symbol of divinity, the rowan and the gorse would protect you against demons, the birch was the image of love, the alder the badge of kingship, the ivy stood for permanence, the honeysuckle for fidelity. In some parts a walnut tree was considered a prerequisite of domestic bliss, which is why, if you look hard enough around any old Gwent cottage, you are likely to find one somewhere.

They say that Wales was once covered all over with stout oaks, denuded down the generations first by house-builders, then by contractors for the British navy's warships. When Lord Nelson visited Gwent in 1802, he came to inspect the state of the fleet's raw materials, and as a result the famous oak tree at the village of Basaleg, said to be the biggest tree in Britain, was converted into 2,446 cubic feet of timber for the shipyards, then the most ever recorded from a single tree. Today the battleship oaks have almost disappeared. The wild oaks that remain, in small twisted thickets all over the country, are the stunted sessile oaks, with crinkled leaves and cracked-looking barks, and these are the most Welsh of Welsh trees now: they have a dogged but mysterious air, crouching there in the lee of the hills, or standing in contorted sentinel up farm lanes, their shapes are often cranky or goblinesque, and they have a look of wizened age that makes them proper partners to the caves and boulders.

The yews of Wales are suggestive too, and rich in allusion, like the twelve lugubrious yews of Llanelli in Gwent, which form a supposedly magic circle around the village church, or the bleeding yew of Nevern, Nyfer in Pembrokeshire, which oozes a sticky sap immemorially supposed to be blood, or the old yew in the churchyard of Guilsfield, Cegidfa, in Powys, under which Richard Jones, Gent., when he died in 1707, caused to be placed this epitaph:

> Under this yew tree
> Buried would he bee
> For his father and hee
> Planted this yew tree.

In parts of the south there are forests of beech, and piquantly isolated here and there all over the country remain the stands of ornamental trees, redwoods and Japanese willows, hornbeams and exotic limes, planted by proud squires long ago, now all too often strangled by creepers, tangled undergrowth and rhododendron uncontrolled.

And marching inexorably upon them all, or so it often seems, come the armies of conifer forests, whose geometrical splodges we saw from our high vantage point in the Desert of Wales. In half a century, hardly more, they have transformed the look of Wales, for they have sprung up suddenly, massed rows of larch, spruce and fir, wherever land can be acquired by the foresters – high on moorlands or in valley pockets, appearing abruptly, growing so fast that in a few years huge areas can be made all but unrecognisable to the returning native. They are like invaders from some alien sensibility, for generally their woodlands take no account of the contour of the land or the style of the setting, but are planted in stern, disciplined ranks of profit – the very opposite of the wrinkled coppices of little oaks whose place they have often usurped, or the lonely magic rowans of the Welsh memory.

HELEN MORT

'Barn Owl' (2021)†

Smaller than I thought and cloud-coloured, silent
through the daylight sky by Bamford Edge,
sweeping from leaf-tip to fencepost.

I cannot see the texture of her feathers, bark
of her talons, only that she must be starved
to hunt so early, dart into the corrugated barn.

I do not know why I say 'she' any more than I know
how to slake her hunger. Soon my son
cries from the car like a baby bird

and my breasts prickle and milk comes,
ghostly barn-owl pale. He is dressed in down,
nested in his blue coat. I feed him

hunched in the driver's seat, the owl rests
far in the landscape of her want. The news
reports a three year old from New York State

has just been saved from weeks lost in the woods.
He told his mother how a winged creature watched over him
by night, built him a rustling bed of leaves.

Truth is a milky thing, a thinness through the trees.
I cannot follow it because I hold my son.
I only hope this world will feed him.

ELIZABETH ROSE MURRAY

'An Affinity with Bees' (2021)[†]

I.

There is a hilly strip of grassy boreen near my West Cork home that I call the bee highway. Bees criss-cross the open area between ditches, edged with fuchsia and gorse, feasting on pollen. Sometimes, a bee or wasp will land on you and hitch a ride further up the bank; other times, drunk on the abundance of food, they smash into you, head first. Rebounding, confused, they fly helter-skelter before following their instincts for another feed. Most of the year, this laneway is a delight to climb. It rewards with views over the islands of Roaring Water Bay: Cape Clear, Sherkin, the Carthys, the Calves, Long Island, Horse Island, Goat Island, Castle Island and Heir are all visible from this spot. But in the closing weeks of August, it's a spot to approach with caution. The bees are dying and they're angry.

My mother was always angry and once she threatened, 'Remember, I'm the queen bee.' I was a curious kid, a bookish child in a house with no books, and always too eager to please. So I sought out my beloved encyclopaedias at the local library and did my research. Raised in a peanut-shaped queen cell or queen cup, queen bees are the lifeblood of the hive. Selected by the worker bees, she is the only sexually active female and, therefore, fiercely protected for her offspring. The queen bee is fed exclusively on royal jelly, and this is how she develops differently into her royal status. Only my mother wasn't talking about the honey-making queen when she made her claim; she was referring to the Aussie soap opera *Prisoner Cell Block H*. Buried in her queen cell, she gorged on junk TV, nicotine and cheap lager. Not quite royal jelly, but the difference between her and other mothers quickly grew apparent.

2.

Like a celebrity, the queen bee is surrounded by a flock of attendants. These attendants are vital because the queen is incapable of tending to her own basic needs – feeding, grooming, leaving the hive. My mother yearned for attention, but also feared it. She rarely went outside except to buy smokes and booze from the corner shop, and even then she usually sent us with a note to get her messages on tick. It was a far cry from the life she talked about with my father, running amusement arcades and driving a Jaguar. My father used to 'catch wasps by their ears' – snatching them out of the air between thumb and forefinger – but he was always kind to bees. He wasn't kind to my mother and so she left him after nineteen years, four children in tow. He clearly didn't understand her status: their relationship was over a long time before *Prisoner Cell Block H* ever graced the screen.

But having an absent father was not the torturous part of my childhood that people often expect. It did, in fact, instil hope. It meant that I could dream about something other. I could believe in possibility. I could believe in change. I was always an outsider; time in foster care had shown me other worlds, some good and some not so. My father being out there somewhere, an unknown entity, meant there was yet another world to explore that might be a better fit. I used to fantasise about him appearing one day to rescue me. While I was waiting, I'd write long, lyrical stories that ended in hangings and beheadings, where there were good men but women were always cruel. In my mythical landscapes, people who acted badly towards others received rightful condemnation and those who were brave escaped their pitiful circumstances and found where they truly belonged.

3.

Beekeepers need to check their brood regularly; the queen is the heart and soul of the hive and the key to how the others behave.

A good queen means a strong and gentle hive – but what happens when a queen goes rogue? Aggressive queens increase tension in the hive, leading to battles, revolts and attacks. I cannot remember a single day without aggression or violence at home as a child. Yet we learned early on to keep silent. As my mother's young attendants, we would shift allegiances, lie and cheat, trying to please her. Always to no avail. I recently came across someone who had met my mother; he could not remember any physical details. What he remembered was coldness. 'There was no love in that room,' he said. The self-confessed queen bee may have been at the centre, but she was not concerned with the good of the hive.

And what about your father? you may ask, just like I questioned many times alone in the dark. The truth was, he had sold everything he owned and moved into a mobile home with a partner forty years his junior. I discovered this aged thirteen after he suddenly got in contact with social services; I remember thinking, he's finally here, all that wishing was worth it. Meeting my father was like staring into a mirror; I realised how much we all looked like him. A daily reminder for our mother of what she had lost; of the lifetime ahead with kids she didn't want. When I roamed the bluebell woods near his home, walked the nine dogs that I couldn't control, gathered eggs or made dashes past the geese to put the rubbish in the dustbins – my father always watching, laughing as I dodged beaks and wings – I was truly home. But holidays lasted a week at most, and the hive always called me back, where my mother would never say anything so kind as 'sit down, I'll do it, you stay warm'.

4.

Despite being much bigger, the queen can be difficult to spot in a hive, so keepers may choose to clip her wings and daub paint on her thorax. These processes are not harmful but make it easier for her to be found. However, the queen's nature is programmed to escape detection in one of two ways: a running queen will use speed and stealth to avoid light, while a hiding queen will remain motionless in comb depressions and spaces between the comb, sidebars and bottom bars. My mother was a hiding queen; when family, friends or neighbours called, she would pretend not to be home and hide behind the sofa. She rarely sustained a friendship. I have never figured out whether she was lonely or she preferred things this way. I don't think she knew, either. She was clipped and daubed and yet no one could find her.

Much of my childhood was spent hiding. From the various debt collectors – the 'leccy man', the Provident loans man, the gas man, the TV man. Everything was rented and nothing was paid. The estate had a communal key for each meter; kids would run from house to house, following the trail like a treasure hunt. It meant you could never answer the door to anyone in a shirt because it wasn't easy to explain why you had enough electricity to last the next month but not a single fifty-pence piece inside the meter. Often my brother and I would hide in the privet outside our home. We would tip ourselves into the foliage, balancing on the metal pole running through its centre. Mother would come out and yell for us, but we knew from the tone whether to reveal ourselves and she wouldn't persevere for long. Once we decided to hide for good and run away. We packed a carrier bag each, spent the day walking along 'the black path' – a local disused railway line – to some unconsidered destination. But as hunger struck, guilt set in; we'd both seen the prepared pans of veg (carrots, turnips, potatoes) for a cooked dinner. It was rare for her to make such effort, so we turned back, steeling ourselves for her fury. But the house was dark, she was still in bed, the veg cold in the pans and the house reeking of piss and whisky. She hadn't noticed a thing.

5.

I am not angry today, but I am angry often. I do not get angry when bees sting me. Usually, I apologise. After all, I'm in the bee's space and bees will only attack if feeling seriously threatened. My mother must have felt threatened all the time. As a child, I used to apologise for my mother every day. For the missing uniform or unwashed clothes, the lost reply slips for trips, the torn report card, the bruises, the tiredness after another night of her blasting 'Ernie the Fastest Milkman in the West' by Benny Hill at 3 a.m. to annoy the neighbours. Later, when I cut ties, I apologised for daring to be independent and to forgive enough to not care any more – to let her live without contact or judgement if I was allowed the same liberty. In my mother's eyes, it was a relief. But when I began to talk of my mother to others, it made people so uncomfortable, I quickly relearned the silence that was so natural in childhood. I have struggled even to let my pen talk.

My 'bee highway' is actually called Coffin Hill because it was once the road for funeral processions. The coffin would be carried by horse and cart, or on foot. My dog likes to walk up here, but he sometimes gets spooked on his way back down. He tucks into me, tail lowered, ears flattened, the whites of his eyes showing as he looks to me for help. I wonder what it is that he senses and sees, but without words, he cannot tell me. Halfway up the boreen there is a boulder, and this is where the coffin would be rested while a break was taken. I often sit on that rock to write, but first, I press my palm to its coolness. I look out to sea, my hand resting on the imprints of people, corpses, ghosts; hundreds of years' worth of lives and stories. Last August, I was so transfixed by the waves, I didn't see the dying bee turning circles, its stinger wriggling, seeking out my flesh. I was too busy wondering who else had paused there, what they had been waiting for, what life they had expected and whether it had delivered.

6.

My mother kept her sting to the end. On her deathbed, there was no sudden revelation or recompense. She still displayed no love, and was visibly annoyed that four of her five children came to see her at all. I don't think any of us was shocked by her negative response, but I think one of us was sad. Was that because they still hoped that anything other was possible; that she would finally say something kind? As a writer, I think a lot about words or the lack of them, and why humans find them so difficult. I often wonder, if my mother had ever held a pen, could have written her desires and darkest moments without fear of them being seen, what would she have said? If I could hold the pen for her, guide her hand, these are her words I would offer: the world never once held up a mirror for me. Life did not deliver.

How to treat a bee sting: Treat with sodium bicarbonate made into a paste. When you remove the stinger, resist the urge to grab the end and pull. The venom sac is at the end and you'll just squeeze more out. Use your nail (a credit card works well too) and scrape the stinger free. If you're near a hive, calmly move away. Do not swat, or run, or wave your arms about. Don't freak out, as the more stressed you are, the more likely you are to upset the bees. Quickly remove the stinger, as it releases pheromones that signal to other bees that you are a threat. But even if you do everything right, you can expect the pain to linger; when you incur the wrath of a bee, especially a queen, you will never forget the sting.

STEPHANIE NORGATE

'Jackdaws' (2008)

Some days we try to close our ears
like this morning when we wake to hear
jackdaws squawking in the disused chimney
where the hand of the gale has thrown them,
their cries unnerved and unnerving,
a scuffling amplified in our skulls,
as though we can hear the heart of the house
beating against brick.

We leave for work telling ourselves
the birds will find their own way out,
that we're late already. In any case,
we're only renting, can change nothing.

In the car, the crying yammers in our heads
so, halfway down the flooded lane,
we reverse, and home again, fetch the hammer,
claw off the board that blocks the flue,
let fall the sooty mess of nests
and wind washed gravel, force up
the glossed-in sash, then wait.

The wary birds stay hidden,
quiet as our held breath.

Eventually three jackdaws squinny out,
a slow flap of feathers scattering ash,
brightening again into their own blackness,
as each bird senses the open sash, the upthrust
of light and wind welcoming their wings.

This time it's easy, wiping away droppings,
knocking hardboard tight in the chimney gap.

But there are other days when we close our ears
look away, don't drive back.

Then through the window crack, we'll hear
a squabble of jackdaws cawing –
What have you done? What have you left undone?

ANNIE O'GARRA WORSLEY

'An ancient royal fernery, August 2019' (2021)[†]

The afternoon is warm and bright, the air heavy with sap and salt. I am following a trail through a thin stretch of dunes at Hightown in Merseyside, down to the mouth of the River Alt. As the path broadens and vanishes into a broad beach, my feet crunch loudly on shells and crisps of seaweed. A dark rope studded with detritus forms a curving high-water strandline until it too thins and vanishes in the nearby mudflats, salt marsh and reed beds of Altmouth. This is a small place, hidden and ripe with a variety of rich habitats, and in the quiet calmness it feels old, a place abstracted from the hustle and bustle of modern life. The sensation passes; I can hear a distant train and the chinking of metal from three yachts moored in the deep mid-river channel.

I am visiting the site with a research colleague. Along one section of dune-edged riverbank a large area of sand has vanished in the turbulence of high tides and powerful gales, revealing a thick, solid gloop of peaty material. We have come to examine this recently exposed bed of sediment, take photographs, record outline dimensions and collect material samples for laboratory study as part of a wider research project on Holocene environmental change.

The river here curves in a large loop through the village of Hightown; on an OS map it is a knobbly shepherd's crook. It is thought the loop may have begun to form over a thousand years ago but over the last four centuries great linear sand dunes grew and expanded, slowly swallowing and burying the estuarine landscape of the ancient River Alt. A map drawn in 1577 describes the Alt flowing almost true west into the Irish Sea, but by the late 1700s a survey conducted by William Yates showed it had veered south. Where it had once flowed north-west, the river responded to extensive dune building by doubling back on itself to pour out into Liverpool Bay.

Altmouth is the only major natural aperture in twenty-one kilometres of 'barrier' sand dunes that run from the mouth of the River Mersey at Crosby to that of the Ribble near Preston. The 'Sefton Dunes' are fronted by great swathes of gently sloping sand flats while behind them low-lying peatlands are carved into fields by old, in some cases early medieval, systems of drainage ditching and banking. Internationally recognised for their flora and fauna, they are one component of an enormous soft-sediment coast comprised of dunes, salt marshes, mud- and sand flats, and estuaries stretching from North Wales to Cumbria, known to coastal geomorphologists as 'Cell 11'.

Sedimentary coastal environments are highly mobile; they are governed by unique partnerships between geomorphological processes and living organisms. Grain size variations, wave and wind action and the mechanics of movement couple with the types, natural abundance and density of living organisms and with their life forms and functions, all ebbing and flowing in response to changing climate and sea level, and to human activities. One of the great joys for environmental geographers is that the spatial and temporal histories of various components of these inherently natural partnerships are measurable on human timescales.

Biotic (living) and abiotic (non-living) processes in combination drive the complex beauty and character of myriad habitats. In North-West England there is a wealth of scientific evidence and historical documentation as well as oral histories attesting to changing local conditions over thousands of years, with some specific events such as sand storms or flooding that had profound impacts on people living by the sea. And there is compelling evidence of the adaptation of both natural and human communities to rapid environmental change. Periodic erosion of the dunes in Sefton during severe weather has revealed deposits that tell of quite different natural environments existing in situ millennia ago and it has also uncovered remnants of past human lives. Underneath large expanses of sand dune and beach are remnants of rich organic soils, forests, salt marshes, rivers, creeks and peatlands, part of the many drowned lands found all around the coast of Britain. From time to they emerge, their hidden mysteries revealed by wind, wave and science.

Underfoot the exposure of peat is quite solid. It has been compressed over millennia, buried under sand. I slip as my wellies meet the slick, shiny, wet surface. Sunlight glances off the wetness. There are tree stumps and branches blackened by the acidic conditions of the entombing peat, beautifully preserved bark and the imprints of leaves. Birch, oak, alder and hazel lie where they died, part of an extensive forest that succumbed to dramatic and rapidly changing environmental conditions. I notice an area where the peat's surface appears to be glass-smooth and I carefully slither across to have a closer look. It is harder to walk here because there are no roots or branches to help slow my sliding and provide helpful grip. Even in the bright sun it is possible to discern patterns in the peat. Its surface looks like a William Morris wallpaper, all curves and complicated scrolls, finely intertwining and with intricate repeating motifs. I kneel down to have a closer look and find myself on a carpet of preserved ferns. The fronds are long and broad. They are staggeringly beautiful and as clearly defined as the finest Chantilly lace. Carefully I ease one frond up from the stickiness and hold it up to the light. The morphology of the leaf is clear,: this is *Osmunda regalis*, the 'Royal Fern'.

Some of the fronds are over a metre in length, splayed and spread as if pressed between paper by diligent and experienced hands. I can see a startling number of enormous fronds. There are more leaves than peat matrix. I have only ever seen *Osmunda* growing in wetlands as smallish plants dotted among and cowed by the dense growth of alder and hazel or in recently felled woodlands whose soil is rich and damp. Each individual plant usually stands upright, tall and proud, their shape reminiscent of the scrolled stonework atop the columns of many classical buildings in our major cities. Once on a journey home I spotted a newly felled railway embankment covered in young *Osmunda*, as if the removal of trees alongside the line had released some long-held store of seeds. Later the ferns were accompanied by herbs and grasses springing up from the debris and wood shavings, but it was *Osmunda* that had first claimed the new space and best light.

Leaning closer to the peat surface, I wonder if the enormous ferns in the peat beds of Altmouth grew in a similar woodland clearance or whether they were part of a pristine ancient wetland. An image of a jungle-like landscape, of complicated channels, pools and small raised areas springs to mind and I remember fieldwork in the tropics, in patches of dense undergrowth with occasional open glades, quiet apart from insect-drone and birdsong, flickering with light.

Cutting down through the peat reveals multiple layers of fern fronds, some incredibly long, all beautifully preserved. The peat and forest beds at Hightown and Altmouth have been extensively studied by palaeoecologists and archaeologists and in the main dated to between five and six thousand years ago. Studies have also revealed that the ancient places were not untouched by human hands. A trackway and stone artefacts such as scrapers and arrowheads have been recovered and a general interpretation of the ancient landscapes proposed, one of coastal and estuarine mudflats, reed beds, barrier sand dunes and raised islands covered with shrub and woodland standing within wetlands of alder carr. Pollen (and spore) diagrams from the region contain alder pollen in superabundance, reflecting the dominance of fen-reed swamp for thousands of years and in some, *Osmunda* spores are also plentiful, suggesting a distinctive relationship between fern and fen here.

The peat bed is a small ephemeral feature already eroding at its western edge. Clumps of peat and several tree stumps have collapsed into the sands and mud by the river. As I walk back up to the dunes, water is slowly sluicing over the site. High white clouds have been pulled in from the north by the brisking breeze. A powerful low-pressure system is forecast to blow in from the Atlantic overnight and it will be hard for the peat to resist the waves such weather will bring. Within a few days the enigma that is a prehistoric *Osmunda* carpet will be washed away, its magnificent lacy leaves, and its secrets, for ever lost.

IRENOSEN OKOJIE

From *Nudibranch* (2020)

The way Gill told the story, the boys had gone into the secret caves at Lydstep Cliffs on a dare. Ziggy had bet him two *Beano* comics and his mountain bike on loan for a day he wouldn't see it through. And Gill, never one to back down from a challenge, had agreed. The boys were similar in athletic ability but Ziggy had the edge as a better swimmer, while Gill was agile, light on his feet. They'd gone in, egging each other on. It was late afternoon; the caves seemed cavernous, dark and deceptive. Like the further you went in the more dimensions you'd find. Forty feet below, a crystal blue lake beckoned, a watery eye leaking slowly into the cracks. They'd left their bikes at the cave's opening, which looked like two hands in prayer; their wheels spun against its ceremonies of feet sinking into sand. Ziggy had been in a strange mood all day, reckless, more so than usual. The cold hit them first, as if the caves hadn't let a past winter out of their clutches. There was evidence of vagrants passing through: a soiled sleeping bag in a corner, a few heroin needles, an old wind jacket, empty beer cans. Damp fossils between the rocks gleamed as the boys climbed down slowly, Gill ahead. Ziggy cracked a joke about their supplementary science teacher, Mrs Gaskill. Distracted, Gill slipped, hurtling down. Sheer terror gripped him. His throat constricted so tightly he couldn't scream. It happened in split seconds. His bomber jacket billowing, the flutter of a *Beano* comic falling out, coins spilling from his pocket, Ziggy leaping off the rocks in pursuit, the breaking of water, the discovery that falling into water from a great height was painful. Gill hit the water hard, went down. He tried to swim up but couldn't, arms flailing. His trainer laces were caught on a rock. He attempted to free himself. He couldn't reach properly. His chest was filling with water.

Pain shot through his left leg. He couldn't hold his breath much longer. Through the panic underwater, he saw Ziggy swimming towards him. He untangled him, removing the offending black Nike trainer, which began to tumble down towards the murky bottom. They each broke the surface gasping, heaved their bodies onto the edge, coughing. Gill's teeth chattered; his body shook so much he thought the chill would never leave him. Ziggy turned to him, holding his contentious black footwear like a flag. 'I told you the drop was crazy. The old crow's dying – cancer,' he said, throwing the trainer at Gill. Above them, one heroin needle pierced the trapped winter. The other cried blue water.

DEBORAH ORR

From *Motherwell* (2020)

In 1966, when I was almost four years old, my parents were dragged into a vast social experiment, and we moved into a high-rise housing scheme, Muirhouse, on the edge of the erstwhile steel town, Motherwell, in Lanarkshire, Scotland. Remedial interventions to salvage the place have been poked in its direction ever since. The usual fixes, like cladding, and less cosmetic ones, like sports fields, much needed and much used. However, the marshland that was drained to make those sports fields would be protected now as a valuable natural habitat, I think. I hope.

The marshland, for a time, was my kingdom. I had many of those during my childhood. Whatever its shortcomings, the truly wonderful thing about Muirhouse was that it was on the edge of lush, rich and varied countryside. I gathered my territories slowly, moving further away from our flat as I got to know this copse, that stream, a hedgerow, a field, a river, a wood. The marsh was an early passion, because it was right by the scheme, only about eighty yards from our building. I was probably about eight or nine when I got serious about it, went truly marsh-crazy.

I spent hours on those few acres, fascinated by something I understood as a world apart, but didn't know then was an ecosystem: Caddis grubs, who made little tubular homes for themselves, from their own silk and the water's detritus; water boatmen, the long-legged insects that skittered across the surface of the water like a six-armed man rowing a scull; dragonflies and damselflies; diving beetles and whirligig beetles; frogs and newts, sometimes even a great crested. I got all the names from my Ladybird book, *Pond Life*. Those illustrations are printed on my mind.

There were always lots of meadow brown butterflies – masses of them. Bulrushes grew in the marsh, and great reedmace – which people generally call bulrushes by mistake. Once I took some reedmace home for Win to put in a vase, instead of the artificial ones I didn't like, because they were hard, not soft, plastic covered in nylon flock, in garish reds, oranges and blues. But the rushes made a mess. The big, brown velvety sausages of flower were teeming with meadow brown caterpillars, which wriggled about, spilling seeds (200,000 seeds can be produced from a single inflorescence!). Today, I have Win's green and brown vase that the reedmace stood in. It's fashionable again, that vase – as all those vintage German ceramics from the 1970s are.

The marsh, in time, became a stopping-off place, where I would check that all was still as it should be before I entered the wood. I was wood-crazy by this time, enthralled. The wood was so much bigger and, in terms of plant life, so much more complex. Obviously, I liked the trees, which were a real mixture: pine, yew, oak, chestnut, sycamore, beech, hazel, ash, rowan... So many shapes to identify! So many names to learn! Sometimes, there would be a tree that was hard to name, that would turn out to be mulberry or an araucaria. I didn't know then that the families who owned the estate, the Dalziels and the Hamiltons, had been keen horticulturalists, devoted to bringing home exotic trees from around the world to plant on the estate. Multi-horticulturalism.

I didn't know that this land had first become a royal hunting forest before the mediaeval period, in 843. I didn't know that 'forest' was a word for a place where deer lived, nothing to do with trees at all. But it was obvious that some of the trees were very old, one of them, an oak, so old that it had spread wider than many of the trees were tall. As an adult, I learned that this tree was called the Covenanter's Oak, because a group of John Knox's followers had met here to hold services in the seventeenth century, when Presbyterian Protestantism was banned in Scotland's churches. There's a sign by the tree now, telling people this stuff. There are also wooden stanchions, holding up its weary old boughs, offering the ancient tree some life support. But none of this was there when Motherwell was a place with a future. The heritage industry moves in when people don't know who they are any more and have to focus on who they were instead.

I saw the trees as a community, a more calmly interdependent community than the one at my school, where I felt bullied and isolated, one that would host me and let me be. I understood that the trees and plants were all in some sort of complex symbiotic relationship, even though I wouldn't have been able to put it into words, let alone into scientific parlance.

Scientists only found out in 2019 that the apples that don't fall far from the tree are bad apples. The seeds of a parent tree do better the further from that tree they fall. I didn't know either that trees trade, via a fungal internet that connects them underground, allowing one tree species to store excess nutrients and swap them with nutrients that other tree species have a different superfluity of. No wonder similar species don't like to grow too near to each other. Too incestuous. Too little opportunity for trade in times of hardship.

But I liked what I saw. I liked the various ways in which the plant life under the trees had adapted to the environment, rich in the nutrients provided by the deciduous trees and their leaf mould, yet limited in terms of sunlight. These woods were called the Dalziel Estate and, like many places in Scotland, were perfect for rhododendrons and azaleas. They thrive in soil that has coal in it, soil that has conifers on it, soil that has weathered the sulphur dioxide that heavy industry pumps out. Acid soil. The landowners who had lived there, before nationalisation prompted a move to Surrey, had made their fortunes and planted the estate from the wealth created by their investments in coal and steel in the first place, so there was a pleasing circularity in the

way that the plants carried on without them. In late spring I'd comb
the margins of the woods, keen to spot the rhododendrons that were
out of the ordinary, not bog-standard purple – lovely as those were –
but crimson, peach, pale pink, pale lemon, the ochre colour of honey.
Each new find made me feel I was like local boy David Livingstone,
charting a jungle unseen by a single soul, apart from all the souls who
had seen these things before…

Bluebells are the most obvious among plants adapted for woodland
survival. They bloom in that brief period when the weather is warm
but the trees haven't come into leaf. But the wood anemones do that
too, covering the woodland floor in midnight starlight weeks before
the bluebells cover it in bright spring sky. The ramsons are around at
this time too, their white globes of flowers and garlicky smell declaring
that they are wild alliums. Alliums were not fashionable plants in the
scant gardens of Motherwell. We'd only see those purple flowers when
onions grown for their bulbs were 'shot' – had been left too long after
they should have been harvested. I wouldn't have dreamed of bringing
some home for Mum to cook with and she wouldn't have dreamed of
taking me seriously if I had. Wood sorrel? So pretty, its leaves so light
and effulgent, its little white flowers so delicately traced with their lacy
network of purple veins. I still don't know if eating it would delight or
poison. Delight. I think.

The ramsons, though. Now these plants are more widely called
wild garlic and are seasonal staples among foodies. I daresay you can
actually buy it. Lots of restaurants fall over themselves to serve it in
spring. As for actual garlic, we did have a little jar of garlic salt, in
among the other grungy jars on the pair of Schwartz spice racks. But
garlic in a bulb? That was a Continental thing that made European
breath stink, especially the breath of the French, who also ate horses,
frogs and snails. We knew what real garlic looked like. It looked like a
beige powder.

★

I also, from the age of about nine or ten, knew what a semi-erect penis looked like, as it was being stroked and fondled in the hand of the man attached to it. There was a particular yew tree that my friend Gillian and I liked to climb – we hadn't been the first, because there was a smooth, varnished plank nailed up there already. The great thing about this tree was that up at the top all the branches stretched out, so you could sit inside this piney, fragrant cone of sunshine, and no one would know you were there. Or so we imagined.

One day, we were lounging in the tree when a young man's voice shouted up to us.

'You two need to be a bit more careful. You could break your necks. That's right. I can see you. Come down from there.'

We stuck our heads out from the branches and looked down.

He was young, a skinhead, dressed in denim jacket and jeans, double-denim not being the fashion crime then that it would become. He continued to berate us – for our own safety – and tell us to get out of the tree. Except that all the time he was gently wanking and not – to his small credit, I suppose – getting very far. We stalwartly refused to get down. Eventually, saying that (by some miracle of investigation) he'd tell our mums if he saw us up the tree again, he left.

'Did you see what I saw,' asked Gillian, once we were sure he was gone.

'Yes,' I replied, rapt.

Gillian: 'It looked just like a big sausage.'

Later, in Gillian's kitchen, which was exactly like mine, we sat at the table, unable to stop giggling because on the sideboard there was a large Cumberland sausage on a plate, covered by an upturned glass bowl. We couldn't tell our parents what had happened though, because they were always going on about 'bad men' and wouldn't let us down the woods any more if we did. And I loved those woods. To me, they were Arcadia. Not being able to go to them? That would have been the worst thing possible.

Lurking people – lurking men – made the woods dangerous, despite their bucolic pleasures. The wanking skinhead incident hadn't even been my first encounter with a bad man in the woods. And it wasn't at all the scariest. I'd gone to play and explore there with a new friend, Marilyn, a year or so before, when we were eight or nine. The woods had an abandoned Scots baronial mansion in the centre, Dalziel House. (It was sold by the council in 1985, for a penny. It's luxury apartments now.) The River Clyde provided a boundary to the woods, and a water meadow stretched from the river to the house. The two of us had been picking wild flowers – red campions, foxgloves. (I'd wondered hard about these gloves for foxes, and why foxes would need or want them. Why would foxes need gloves? Decades on, I learned that 'fox' had emerged from an oral tradition, and that the flowers had been known as folks' gloves – mittens for fairies.) This was before you were told that you shouldn't pick wild flowers.

We'd reached the meadow, Marilyn and I, and we were trying to get up a tree to get some horse-chestnut blossoms. As Marilyn punted me up the tree, I saw a man, smartly dressed in a brown suit, walking quickly and purposefully along the fringe of the woods at the top of the meadow, away from us. I pointed him out to Marilyn and said: 'That might be a bad man.' She dismissed my worries, and got on with the task of thrusting me into the chestnut boughs. Suddenly, like a pheasant breaking cover, the man came rushing towards us. By now I was up the tree, and I saw his pale face with its black eyes that were fixed on me, his Brylcreemed dark hair falling in a lock over his forehead, his white shirt and dark tie so incongruous in this suddenly perilous situation. I glanced in panic towards Marilyn. She was already a tiny, running figure at the far end of the meadow.

As I scrambled down the tree to escape, he grabbed me round the waist with his strong arms, holding me fast. I kicked and flailed so hard that he lost his grip for a second, and I skittered out of his arms. Bizarrely, I remember calculating whether I had time to pick up my bunch of flowers and decided that I did. Grabbing them, I ran too, like I've never run again, before or since. I felt so strong that it was almost like flying. When I ran towards a barbed wire fence, there was no hesitation. I'd be too scared to attempt this at any other time, but on this occasion, I sailed over it. Adrenaline. I caught up with Marilyn, who was cowering in the trees, waiting for me, shaking with fear. She relaxed as she saw me: 'Didn't you pick up *my* flowers?'

That was the worst of many weird encounters in those woods, though it didn't stop me going back, again and again. Marilyn and I had agreed not to tell our parents, but she never played with me again. I think I just reminded her too much of how close we'd come to something unspeakably awful. Girls in the woods, when they are unlucky, learn about the darkness of human nature, just as unlucky women sometimes do too.

ALICE OSWALD

'birdwatcher' (2009)

The Birdwatcher moves quietly,
Seeing his way in the dark.

White-throated, splay-footed,
Sways with the reeds,
Watching the swans in their kitchens.

All night the piercing police whistle curlews
Are searching the marshes,
Keeping the river on red alert, but he kneels
Non-descript in his hide,
From headland to headland
His blue eyes glide not blinking.

He sees everything:
The grebe's nest under the weed,
The waders resting on fold-up stools along the tideline.

Everything down to the lowest least whisper
Of ducks tucked in self-pillow
And meals wriggling under stones,

Even the shiver of an owl's wing
Moving through stars
          he perfectly hears...
At last at low water he stands up,
Remembering his heavy feet.

Now he splashes away through the heavenly reed fields
And the numberless pools of the Dawn...

Behind his back there are twenty tiny goddesses
Washing their dresses in the waves.

And the doves in the woods
Clap awake when he walks.

RUTH PADEL

'Nursing Wing' (2018)

Where have you escaped to
    still air of the nursing wing
    last room on the corridor
we shared in those long   hushed   hours

air breathed by a dying mother
with all her children round her
as she goes
    labouring
        towards the light
climbing new Himalayas at every breath
    resolute   as always
    glasses off but unafraid.

Forgive me   little-wing   for opening a window
    when we filled her hands
    with snowdrops and myrtle
to let her spirit out
    losing you in compound shiftings of the breeze
      ruffling the blackbird   standing guard
    over February buds
    on the bare cherry tree outside.

I have heard your molecules   stir
somewhere else since
some place I cannot remember
and when I stepped out into the cold of March
you had gone

gentle
dust-filled
exact

your particles of time
        your frost damage
        and mystery pentangles
        of family relationships
lifting

into the smoke of ordinary life
like starlings spiralling to roost
in the Avalon Marshes

where last November
a white egret waited
        hunched   alone
in half-ignited sunset
angling for eels
in the bountiful waters of Ham Wall
        until the first mist
of incomers danced across the heavens

and a million birds
    which close up   we knew   would be shimmering
        with metallic oils
    sapphire   emerald   violet
        pointilliste on charcoal feathers

spun
    into a shape-shifter silhouette
balled up tight as a balloon
    then loosening
        to soot chiffon
            stretching across white sky

a nursing wing
with the helical twist of DNA
and folded swirl of a tornado.
First time in all her ninety-seven years
    she witnessed
        a murmuration.

THOMASINE PENDARVES

From a letter to the Ranter Abiezer Coppe,[*] recounted
in *Some Sweet Sips, of Some Spirituall Wine Sweetly and
Freely Dropping from One Cluster of Grapes, Brought Between
Two Upon a Staffe from Spiritual Canaan (the Land of
the Living, the Living Lord) to Late Egyptian* (1649)

I was in a place where I saw all kind of Beasts of the field, wild and
tame together, and all kinds of creeping Worms and all kinds of Fishes
– in a pleasant river, where the water was exceeding clear – not very
deep – but very pure – and no mud or settling at the bottom, as
ordinarily is found in ponds or rivers. And all these Beasts, Worms,
and Fishes, living and recreating themselves together, and me with
them. Yea, we had so free a correspondence together as I oft-times
would take the wildest of them and put them in my bosom, especially
such (which afore) I had exceedingly feared, such as I would not
have touched or come nigh, as the Snake and the Toad, etc. – and the
wildest kind as ever I saw, and the strangest appearances as ever I saw
in my life.

At last I took one of the wildest, as a tiger or such like, and brought
it in my bosom away from all the rest, and put a collar about him for
mine own. And when I had thus done, it grew wild again, and strove
to get from me. And I had great trouble about it. At first because I had
it so near me, yet it should strive to get from me. But notwithstanding
all my care, it ran away. If you could tell me the interpretation of it, it
might be of great use to the whole body.

Now I must acquaint you I am not altogether without teaching in

---

[*] The letter is signed T. P. Todd A. Borlik identifies the author as Thomasine Pendarves (*Literature and Nature in the English Renaissance: An Eco-Critical Anthology*, CUP, 2019)

it. For when I awoke, the vision still remained with me. And I looked up to the Father to know what it should be. And it was shown me that my having so free a commerce with all sorts of appearances was my spiritual liberty ... There is another scripture which hath much followed me. And that is, 'God beheld all things that he made, and lo, they were very good.' Now concerning my taking one of them from all the rest (as distinct) and setting a collar about it – this was my weakness. And here comes in all our bondage and death, by appropriating of things to ourselves and for ourselves. For could I have been contented to have enjoyed this little, this one thing in the liberty of the Spirit – I had never been brought to that tedious care in keeping, not that exceeding grief in losing.

KATHERINE PHILIPS

'Upon the graving of her Name upon a
Tree in Barn Elms' Walks' (1669)

Alas, how barbarous are we,
Thus to reward the courteous Tree,
Who its broad shade affording us,
Deserves not to be wounded thus!
See how the yielding bark complies
With our ungrateful injuries!
And seeing this, say how much then
Trees are more generous than men,
Who by a nobleness so pure,
Can first oblige, and then endure.

DOROTHY PILLEY

From *Climbing Days* (1935)

Initiation (Tryfan)

As we rounded the bend of the road above Capel Curig and first caught sight of it, I remember trembling with delight and fear. The two summit rocks (ten feet high) were to me, as to so many others before and after me, two humans spell-bound in eternal conversation. I was told that they were called Adam and Eve and that a climber's duty was to spring lightly from one to the other. I asked naively (I have since blushed to recall) why one should not be content with ascending the mountain by the easiest route. The question to the non-climber or 'mere walker' seems natural and proper enough; but I was soon to learn the climber's answer. In fact, from that day on, 'climbing' was to become a word with a specialised meaning not to be used just for walking up steep slopes. The climber speaks generally of 'going up Snowdon' when he follows the zig-zags of the path, and 'climbs' only when he uses his hands as well as his feet.

When I got out of the car by the tenth milestone from Bangor on the Ogwen lakeside – for the first of how many times? – the mountain seemed to hang over our heads. We wound up the boulder-strewn slope to the foot of the climb and then I made my first acquaintance with the scree. Harmless substance enough, but singularly terrifying to the uninitiated. The mountaineer knows that if he jumps onto that rock scrap-heap it will slide with him about a foot and then settle down till he jumps again. But the beginner feels sure that he will start sliding and never stop till he lies a mangled body at the bottom. So the heroes of Crockett and Rider Haggard novels have their most ghastly escapes on scree slopes. And years later I recall that an American friend, after coming gallantly and recklessly up an east-face climb on Tryfan, halted at this very scree funnel, to declare that it 'sure was a mighty mean slope to fall down'.

This danger past, the climb that followed showed no terrors. It was a journey full of discoveries as to how well the body fits the rocks, how perfectly hand- and foot-hold are apportioned to the climber's needs. I was later to find out that this was a peculiarity of Tryfan rather than of climbing as practised by modern experts. In the exhilaration of these discoveries, the climb seemed over before it had properly started. I felt like a child when the curtain goes down at the end of the pantomime. Why hadn't I enjoyed it ten times more while it was on? Every moment was glorious and as quickly gone. The cold wind was whistling round Adam and Eve by the time we reached the summit. It persuaded half the party to walk down to the car. Herbert Carr and I descended the South Gully and, undamped, rushed off in the dusk to scramble up the windswept Bristly Ridge, that comes down Glyder Fach to Bwlch Tryfan, and make our way over to Pen-y-Gwryd. If we had conquered the hardest climb in the district we could not have rejoiced more. 'Mountain madness' had me now forever in its grasp.

Followed four days of ecstatic climbing in perfect weather. Bluebells were in the woods and ranunculus in the swamps as we passed on our way up to the cliffs. They were lovely beyond belief; but my thoughts were mainly on the *footholds* and *handholds*. Each *pitch* or passage of the climb seemed as important as the Battle of Waterloo. The Horseshoe of Snowdon for the first time, the Parson's Nose, the Crazy Pinnacle Gully on Crib Goch, and a day on the Nantle Y Garn were each, as a member of the party was fond of repeating, 'a day which will live'. Y Garn gave a lesson which was to prove useful. It is a mountain with a bad reputation for large, loose, treacherous blocks. In 1910 Anton Stoop, the brilliant young Swiss climber, was killed there. He was lowering himself over a huge block that two heavier men had first descended without its showing signs of danger. It heeled out with him and carried him down, helpless. Knowing this story, we treated everything with our utmost care. Nevertheless, just as the party left a terrace of poised blocks, one of them, like a slice of cheese, slid away without warning. The crash and the sulphurous smell shook us violently and reaffirmed our need for caution.

After this I was alone in the hills for some weeks. It was now impossible for me to keep away from the high ridges. I wandered round the Horseshoe of Snowdon alone and with any party that would follow me. Greatly venturing, I went up 'Lockwood's Chimney', a dark chasm under Pen-y-Gwyrd, alone. With what wild glory in my heart did I wriggle out of the hole and find myself in the sunlight on the giddy upper wall. I induced a large, not-too-willing party of novices to come up the Great Gully of Clogwyn-y-Garnedd after me. By this time I had become the proud possessor of an Alpine rope (from Beale's, with a red strand though it!). How I had studied all the particulars about its strength in George Abraham's *The Complete Moutaineer*. How ashamed I was of its brilliant newness; it had to be muddied at all costs. A first pair of climbing boots shine like twin stars in memory, too. They were large, much too heavy, and too high in the leg, but the whole village used to come to see them. I still did not dare to go about Beddgelert without a skirt, and was rather balloony in a thick, full pair of tweed knickerbockers under a billowy tweed skirt, which I put in the sack at the foot of the climb. I was particularly careful never to hide it under a rock, having read of Mrs Aubrey Le Blond's adventure on the Rothorn. How I admired that great woman climber's exploit. To traverse Rothorn from Zermatt nearly down to Zinal and then – discovering that her skirt had been left on the summit – to go all the way back again and down to Zermatt to round the day off! What an exemplar to contemplate when the ridge of Crib-y-Ddysgl seemed long and narrow in the windy morning.

June came and a week's leave for Herbert Carr. We were both more full of enthusiasm and energy than ever. Our joint ambition, we hardly dared to whisper it, was the conquest of Lliwedd. It is impossible, now that Lliwedd climbs have become such well-known ground, to recapture all the awe and fascination that hung about them then. Though from the shores of Llydaw on any cloudy day the gloom of those black precipices can still daunt the heart. The water laps against the boulders in an inhuman, endless song. The wind streaks the surface with thin lines of foam. Across Llydaw, a loose strip of corrugated-iron roof bangs drearily in the gusts and a sheep baas as though in anguish. There in the hollow of the Cwm the dark smooth walls of Lliwedd tower up. The men who made those steeps their playground seemed to me a race of giants – mysterious beings hardly of this world, undauntable, diamond-nerved and steel-sinewed. Many a time I had peered down from the sharp crest, to shudder at the curve of its terrific slabs. To the lay eye there seems no room for a human foot upon it. That men could have worked their way up by scores of routes was incredible. Most of all when clouds swept down from Y Wyddfa and the gulf under the crags seemed bottomless. The precipice of Lliwedd then might be ten instead of merely 1,000 feet high.

But there were no clouds about when we set out. It was hot walking in my thick tweeds across the green slopes above the lake. The long swamp grass rustled dry underfoot; the sunlight cut out the ribs of the cliff above the Horned Crag, showing the Terminal Arete in sharp definition against the blackness of the shadowed gullies. We came into the shade on the litter of scree at the foot as though into a cave of secluded mysteries. Lliwedd from here heels over – like a *Titanic* just about to take its plunge. The immense parallel sweeping lines of its buttresses, echoed by every one of their scores of minor ridges, tilt over together. This heel does not disguise the steepness of the cliff; it gives it indeed an extra touch of loftiness (as of a ship's spars) from the scree and is one of the secrets of the mountain's hold on the imagination. Climbing on it, you can never for a moment forget where you are. We put on the rope and set to work somewhere on the West Peak. I doubt if I could find the exact point today.

It was the first time we had been on ground which felt really *steep*. Or rather, it altered our conception of steepness for us. On Tryfan you halt on ample ledges – places where you can walk about and sit down with a choice of comfortable positions. On Lliwedd, for long stretches at a time, when you halt you have to stand where your feet are, for there is nowhere else to put them. Or this at least is the novice's impression – on the harder routes of the East Peak an exact one. As we mounted, the sense of the scale of Lliwedd gained on us. We felt like tiny insects creeping from ledge to ledge, from scoop to scoop, insects lost among the vertical immensities about us. All went well, the excitement of achievement blended with the radiance of the day. Crib Goch across Llydaw swam in a haze of sunlight; and when we came, after hours that had seemed like minutes, to a pleasant grassy nook that invited us to pause for rest and lunch, there could have been few happier beings in the world than we. The main difficulties were overcome. Above was easier climbing at a gentle angle. We seemed to have done what we had set out to do.

When we had eaten and smoked we went on. I had become an avid reader of the famous Climbers' Club Pocket Guide-books to the Welsh Crags, and phrases from that master of terse description, Archer Thompson, were always echoing in my memory. One of them about 'belaying the rope around a stook of bollards' wandered from nowhere into my mind just then. It was well that it did so. Herbert was cautiously mounting a steep rib built of massive blocks. A tempting bollard adorned my ledge and, acting more in the spirit of Thompson's phrase than from any particular apprehension, I had cast a turn of the rope around it. Herbert was to my right and about fifteen feet above me.

Just as he clasped the crest of a block with both arms – somewhat in the monkey-up-a-stick position – the block yielded and heaved out with him clinging to it. How he managed to disengage himself from it I hardly saw. The physical sensation of horror, a quick but heavy pulse of sickness, flashes through one almost before one sees what is happening. Then, as though all the feeling had been plucked away, a clear mental calmness follows. I had time to cry, 'My God! Look out!' before the block thundered down the cliff with Herbert after it. He hit my ledge and rebounded outwards, disappearing backwards from my view over the edge. Though I held him, the rope ran a little through my hands, leaving a white burn scar that lingered on my palms for weeks. Quickly though these things happen, they seem in passing to be almost leisurely. One has time to take in the rope, time to think whether there is anything more one should do, time to decide that there is nothing, time to reflect that if the *belay* holds all will be well, and that if not... time to perceive with complete and vivid particularity the whole scene – the greenness of the grass ledge, the shape of the lurching boulder and the movement of the falling man, the play and course of the rope cutting into the turfy edge. Time for all this and for a pause of anguished expectancy in which to wonder just how bad what had just happened will turn out to be. The pause was broken by a small voice that seemed to come from very far away saying, 'I'm all right!'

He was not all right by any means. Somehow with some pulling he managed to get up to my ledge, white and shaking but composed and self-possessed. Then we could see what the damage was. One leg was broken, the shin-bone being exposed for five inches. Fortunately the bleeding was slight. What proved worse was a bad sprain to the ankle. For a while he rested on the ledge. We had no brandy flask and an orange was the best I could provide as a restorative. The sleeves of the white blouse I used to sport in those early days came in usefully as bandages.

But the time came when our further movements had to be planned and undertaken. With great courage and resolution, Herbert insisted on leading up the remaining 400 feet. He thought my climbing experience still too little to deal with such loose terrain. We were more than halfway up the cliff where it could be dragged than on the way down the endless slopes into Cwm-y-Llan. I can recall all the struggle, the coming out into the sunlight at the summit – Snowdon in a dreamy distance above us – the agonising progress down into the Cwm, Herbert using me as a crutch. After a long while we reached a stream where we bathed the leg and I went on to telephone a doctor and fetch a car. I recall all this and going up again at dusk to fetch him in, and then a blank of falls.

In the eyes of those not infected with mountain madness this episode should have put a proper and summary end to my climbing aspirations. And, in fact, strong parental and other influences were marshalled to prohibit them. I was forbidden to climb again. Beddgelert shook its head. The lack of all proper perspective shown in such climbing enthusiasm was pointed out to me. But in vain! After his six weeks in splints, my climbing partner and I, with keenness unabated, were at it again. Even before Herbert was on his crutches, I was out on the rocks with his father. And each evening I would look in to cheer the invalid with stories of the day's doings and he, in imagination, would be sharing the climbs. The instant he was well enough, such was his ardour, he would come out to shout ribald comments to us from the Ogwen Road, as we struggled with the Milestone Buttress.

SYLVIA PLATH

'Poppies in July' (1962)

Little poppies, little hell flames,
Do you do no harm?

You flicker. I cannot touch you.
I put my hands among the flames. Nothing burns

And it exhausts me to watch you
Flickering like that, wrinkly and clear red, like the skin of a mouth.

A mouth just bloodied.
Little bloody skirts!

There are fumes I cannot touch.
Where are your opiates, your nauseous capsules?

If I could bleed, or sleep! –
If my mouth could marry a hurt like that!

Or your liquors seep to me, in this glass capsule,
Dulling and stilling.

But colorless. Colorless.

KATRINA PORTEOUS

'The Marks T' Gan By' (1996)

I asked Charlie what a fisherman must know.
'Aal bloody things!' he answered me. 'How so?'
'A fisherman hetti hev brains, y' kna, one time;'
His fingers twisted round the slippery twine
In the stove's faint firelight. It was getting dark.
'Them days,' he said, 'w' hetti gan b' marks.

'Staggart, the Fairen Hoose; Hebron, Beadlin Trees...'
Thus he began the ancient litany
Of names, half-vanished, beautiful to hear:
'Ga'n roond the Point, keep Bamburgh Castle clear
The Black Rock, mind. Off Newton, steer until
Ye've Staggart level the Nick a the Broad Mill.'

Novice, I listened. In the gloom I saw
The rolled-up sail by the long-unopened door,
A traveller,* stiff with rust, a woodwormed mast –
All the accumulation of the distant past.
'Now, keep the Chorch on Alexandra Hoose,
An' yon's the road...' 'Oh, Charlie, what's the use?'

I said. 'These memories! I know they're true,
And certainly they're beautiful. But how can you
Compete with all the science of these modern days?
The echosounder's finished your outdated ways.
Efficiency. That's what they want; not lore.
Why should the past concern us any more?'

I could not see his face. The stove had died.
'There's naen crabs noo,' said Charlie sadly, and he sighed,
And seeming not to hear me, sealed the knot.
'When ye see lippers** comin', when t' stop
An' when t' gan – that's what ye need t' kna.
The sea's the boss. Me fatther telled me so.

'Them marks,' he said; 'he handed aal them doon
Like right an' wrang. Them buggers for' the toons,' –
He sliced the twine he sewed with, savagely –
'Th' divvin't kna what's right. Th' gan t' sea –
Their only mind's for profit. They'll no give
Naen thowt t' hoo their sons'll hetti live.'

I saw, then. 'So,' I said, 'as we embark,
The past is map and measure, certain mark
To steer by in the cold, uncertain sea?
We leave it, like the land. But all we know –
What to hang on to and when to let go –
Leads from it...' 'Aye,' said Charlie. 'Sic an' so.'

---

*   *Traveller*: iron ring for hoisting lug-sail on mast.
**   *Lippers*: breaking waves.

JINI REDDY

From *Wild Times* (2016)

The night sky is inky black and luminescent with a veil of glowing pinpricks, stars brighter than any I've ever seen in Britain. I have a crick in my neck and the North Sea is blowing a chill wind, but I am rooted to the spot.

While we gaze at seascapes, climb mountains, hike through our forests or lose ourselves in Van Gogh's swirling canvases, rarely do we dedicate meaningful time to the stellar vista above our heads. How often do we contemplate the cosmos? How many of us meander down celestial trails with our eyes and our imagination? We can't all be astronauts or astronomers but we can, in our earthbound way, immerse ourselves in the heavens.

Mariners, desert explorers, farmers, gardeners, storytellers, soothsayers and even common folk: all were once guided by the alignment of the stars alone. Alas, in modern times, though we may rhapsodise about the Milky Way, rarely do we see it with the naked eye the way our ancestors did. This is hardly surprising with the advent of street lamps, and the haze over our cities.

Fortunately, crossing over to the dark side is still possible. Several areas in Britain that are blessedly free of light pollution have been designated Dark Sky Parks and International Dark Sky Reserves – the latter awarded where light pollution is managed to enhance the existing brilliance of the skies.

Parks and reserves are a human construct, of course: the night sky is the night sky. It doesn't have a beginning or an end. From an earthly perspective, it transcends time and place and the vastness of the universe eludes us. But to connect with the darkest of skies, we need to immerse ourselves in wild, tranquil landscapes – such as those found in Northumberland.

This ravishingly beautiful county is home to some of Britain's blackest skies. The zone around Northumberland National Park and Kielder Water and Forest Park, close to the Cumbrian border, is an International Dark Sky Park. The telescopes at Kielder and the observatory and their event nights are popular with visitors.

But me? I want *wild* dark skies. I want to stargaze away from people and bricks and mortar (or, in this case, the Douglas fir cladding of the pier-like building). I also want to be somewhere accessible by train. So instead, I head to the Northumberland coast. My mission? To 'tour' the dark skies on Lindisfarne, otherwise known as Holy Island, the pilgrimage site and wildlife haven, a mile off the coast.

My guide is Martin Kitching, a wildlife expert, birdwatcher, scientist, photographer and astronomy guide who runs Northern Experiences. Along with wildlife expeditions, he offers stargazing trips. One wintry, sunny December afternoon he meets me at the train station in Morpeth, a county town. The plan is to drive up the coast before crossing the causeway to the island as dusk falls. 'The tide will be out, and you'll still get to see the island in daylight,' he says.

The Northumberland coast is special: wild, unspoilt and beautiful, its tranquillity is a force field to which you willingly succumb. Dolphins, seals and even whales have been spotted in the waters and the shoreline is rich in birdlife. Today the skies are blue and clear, flecked with seabirds and the promise of a show-stopping twilight. Breakers crash on a shoreline that extends for miles from Coquet Estuary north to Berwick-upon-Tweed, on the Scottish border.

Martin is a man of few words and not given to small talk, but he has a finely tuned radar where nature is concerned. On the roadside near Druridge Bay we pause by a gnarly old oak shorn of its leaves. 'A little owl often perches in that branch,' he says, as we peer at it hopefully. There's no sign of it, but he tells me that the yellow-eyed, chocolatey-brown spotted owl is fairly common in the North-East.

Otters are also often seen in these parts. 'They've even been spotted in here,' he says pointing to the River Aln, as we cross it at Lesbury. We drive past farmland, gaze up at Bamburgh Castle, lofty on its rocky plateau, and wind our way through the seaside town of Seahouses. The light is fading, the sky streaked with lavender and orange, as we approach the causeway and the promise of a star-peppered sky beckons.

To kill time before it's safe to cross onto Holy Island, we detour down a narrow lane which deposits us at the Fenham Flats, part of Lindisfarne National Nature Reserve. A dune bay, it's the winter home for huge flocks of wading birds, escaping the cold in Iceland and Scandinavia. 'The pale-bellied brent geese come here from Svalbard,' explains Martin, pointing to the birds barely visible out on the mudflats.

It's serene and windswept and a little melancholic here. We scan with our binoculars across the water. In the half-light, the castle and priory ruins of Lindisfarne, once the heart of Christianity, resemble a pair of castaways.

Back in the car, we carry on down the winding road to the causeway. The tide has only just receded, water sploshes the car windows and the mudflats, filled with birds delicately high-stepping and pecking at food, including the elegant curlew with its long curved bill, are starkly beautiful.

Over on the island, by the time we sling on our warm, windproof over-layers, walk through the village and out towards the dunes, it is so dark I am briefly disoriented. We can make out the outlines of the priory and the castle, both even ghostlier now. But all the action is in the sky.

Magically, the little gold speckles appear, lanterns lit millions, trillions of light years away. A beam of light, I learn, travels 300,000 km per second. 'It would take about a second and a half at light speed to reach the moon,' says Martin. 'A light year is the distance light can travel in one year.'

With the naked eye it's easy to spot the Plough, its ladle shape reassuringly familiar, and the North Star. A constellation, Martin explains, is entirely made up: a human attempt to make sense of the skies and break them up into bits. 'Different constellations are visible at different times of the year,' he says. 'In ancient times farmers used to use them to tell them what month it was.'

Martin has now set up his telescope. He points out the cluster known as the Pleiades, and the startlingly bright, yellow Capella. Cassiopeia is a sort of flat W-shaped constellation. 'In Greek mythology Cassiopeia was the Queen of Aethiopia and wife of King Cepheus,' my guide explains. 'She was placed in the sky as punishment for boasting that her daughter Andromeda was more beautiful than the Nereids, the sea nymphs who accompany Poseidon.'

I love the way the stars appear to multiply the longer I look, almost by stealth. You see one, then another and then in the blink of an eye, boom! Suddenly, the sky is a radiant tapestry. 'See that?' says Martin, pointing through the telescope to a luminous and mesmerisingly orange dot. 'That's Aldebaran. It's huge, many times the size of our sun.'

Up in the skies, it's all go: a shooting star whooshes past and then a satellite. 'It's pulled into the earth's orbit by gravity,' explains Martin. 'Just like the moon.' I spend long minutes trying to make out Pegasus, its four stars shaped like a square. Sadly none of the three planets – Jupiter, Venus and Saturn – is visible tonight. 'In December they all rise just a few hours before sunrise,' he says. No matter: the Milky Way, made up of billions of stars, is the highlight of the night. Here it dazzles, a hazy belt of light, spiralling through the sky. Through it runs a long band of black. 'It's the Great Rift,' says Martin. 'Space dust that has obscured the stars. They're still there; we just can't see them.'

If this is hard to grasp, then harder still is the humble place we occupy in the universe. 'The earth and the rest of our solar system, made up of everything that's orbiting our star, the sun, are all part of the Milky Way. And the Milky Way is just one galaxy among the billions that make up the known universe,' explains Martin.

Exploring the heavens invites the biggest questions of them all. Is there intelligent life elsewhere in the cosmos? Given the size of it, it seems we'd be colossally vain to imagine otherwise. And what exactly does it all mean? Perhaps the Incas, the ancient civilisation of Peru, had an inkling. They revered the stars. They not only identified them, they also ascribed meanings to them. They believed everything in and around our world was connected. Maybe they grasped what we, on our planet Earth, have yet to.

RACHEL ROONEY

'Fishing' (2011)

I feel it, first as a stir,

turning deep in the murky water.

Surfaces up for air, a twitch

on the lake in my head.

A flip, and it disappears.

Wait for it. Let myself settle

close to the edge, my reflection and me.

Next ripple, a gentle skim and a dip

holds the weight of a thought

in the drag of my net.

Raising the pole, bent heavy,

my catch thrashes hard. Through the reeds

I can glimpse a glitter of skin.

Won't let it go now.

I have this idea.

Hauled out and tipped in a tub,

I'm watching it flap; its mouthing pout,

that eye that stares defiantly back.

A sizeable fish. How big?

As big as a poem. See!

LYNNE ROPER

From *Wild Woman Swimming*, ed. Tanya Shadrick (2018)

Paramedic Lynne Roper began swimming outdoors in 2011 while recovering from a double mastectomy. She was soon at the heart of the Outdoor Swimming Society. For five years, until a brain tumour made swimming and writing impossible, Lynne kept a diary. Wild Woman Swimming *is a celebration of Dartmoor, the Devon coast and the community that grows from shared adventure.*

Quarry

Mist is descending and the wind picking up as Honey and I walk along the bleak track to Foggintor Quarry. The approach looks like something from a post-apocalyptic movie in this grey November light. Most people imagine Dartmoor to be a wilderness, but it's a man-made landscape. The earth has been quarried and mined for millennia; Foggintor and neighbouring Swell Tor were hollowed out in the eighteenth and nineteenth centuries. Their granite now lives in the walls of Dartmoor prison and some other famous landmarks, including Nelson's Column.

As we draw alongside the quarry entrance we see a little vista opening up through the passageway to the centre of the tor. Juicy green turf, ivy-green mosses, and little ponds of lettuce-green weed entice us through to the pool. Sheer cliffs rise around fifty feet from the slaty water, which is being whipped into wavelets. From time to time, I watch the progress of a gust of wind as it agitates the surface causing a swirling, transient opacity. The smell of sheep wee fades.

I change in the chill wind, and swim towards the tiny islands. The water is cold and satiny. I pass over tumbled heaps of granite and

343

occasionally scrape my hand or my knee; sometimes I notice them in time and bank like a low-flying jet-fighter negotiating a canyon. When I look up I see the cliffs begin to fade like ghosts into the mist.

I love being in the womb of what was once a tor; I think of how the heart was ripped from her, and how nature has mended her wounds with a skin of turf and moss. The spring has bled into her exposed core and filled it, making a place for animals and birds to drink and wash, and for me and Honey-dog to swim.

River

Honey and I popped over to Spitchwick this morning. It's a warmish autumn day, with a slightly chill breeze. There's still some heat in the sun which pops out occasionally from behind puffy, greying clouds illuminating the ponies grazing on the common by the river. We can smell their gorgeous, horsey scent and, in Honey's case, the mouth-watering whiff of tottering heaps of steaming dung.

It's 11 degrees in the water today, so I decide on a wetsuit because I want to swim for at least thirty minutes. As I enter the river down the stone 'steps', I notice a dipper, who performs his jerky little dance from a rock by the island before bobbing under the water, then zipping away downstream. His cream bib makes his low-level flight visible for a little while. Honey potters around in the shallows, then swims across and back. I can hear her breathing in little puffs as she passes.

The water today is mirror-black on the far side. The leaves on the trees behind are turning and their full height is reflected as though soaked into the water. On the near side I can see coppery patches here and there, but for the most part the gravelly bottom has been obliterated by huge drifts of autumn leaves and twiggy debris from last month's stormy weather. The leaves blacken as they decompose, and the newer ones – orange, greeny-yellow and tan – glow randomly through the peaty water like jewels, flashing in the current. When I step in, I sink to my ankles in the spongy layer then slide to the side as my foot hits a hidden rock. It's safer to just swim, so I leap forwards and plunge straight under before turning to head upstream against the current on the far side, where it's deep.

The water of the Double Dart smells and tastes of the moors: chill, fresh, pure and peaty. I swim in front crawl to warm up, and the water beneath me is black as night. Silver bubbles arc from my hands, which glow disembodied through the water in an eerie, copper light. Icy rivulets push through the neck of my suit and down my back like shivers from a ghost story. And then it hits: full-on ice-cream head for the first time since the spring. I try to swim through but have to stop, so I float on my back, arms outstretched, in a cross. The pain in my forehead subsides and I can hear only my amplified breathing in my submerged ears. Blue sky, clouds, oak trees, and the edge of a backlit cloud. I begin to turn in the current and stay there for a while, before swimming again. After the third go, the ice-cream head is no more, so I carry on upstream, then back down at four times the pace, then float around until I start to feel cold again.

I can hear Honey growling and barking from the bank and stand up to watch her. Her hair is soaked and curling, and she's charging around the common in a zig-zag pattern with a stick in her mouth. Occasionally she tosses and catches the stick, arse and loopy tail waving, having a big, doggy laugh. I love that a wild swim affects my dog in the same way that it affects me, or maybe we're both just crazy bitches?

On the walk back, I notice that a crone of a crab apple tree, bearded with lichens, has shed her load of pale yellow fruit. We stop, and I pick them up in my towel, leaving the ones that lie in horseshit for Honey, who is partial to a windfall apple or ten. She tries one but declines the rest, possibly because they're a little sour, or because the horse poo is not fresh enough, like sour cream.

Gazing up at the tree, I see a sprinkling of crab apples still clinging to the branches and looking, against the greeny-grey lichen, like a fruity tiara on a tipsy granny at a barn dance. The music of the river fades as we walk away.

Pool

High on Dartmoor, the Double Dart slows briefly between two sets of rapids to form Sharrah Pool. There are plenty of breathtakingly beautiful places on this stretch of river, but Sharrah is special. It's enchanting, entrancing, and it never fails to throw buckets of Dartmoor pixie-dust at anyone who sees it.

Today there is a sprinkling of snow and it's still falling as we arrive in the glade by the pool. The temperature hasn't gone above freezing for days; it's 3 degrees in the river. The water is much paler than usual and has lost its deep coppery gleam and black depths. By the rapids, it's almost turquoise, and there's a gelid, greeny tint that I've never seen here before.

Wearing wetsuits, boots, gloves and hats, we slide into the river and swim up the eddy towards the top falls. Ice creeps through the neck of my suit. I dip my face under and taste pure chill; my lips freeze almost immediately. We reach the rapid and throw ourselves off the rock. It's like jumping into a beautiful cocktail made with crème de menthe and the most effervescent volcanic water. The bubbles burst fast on the surface in a shower of sparks like fireworks, and I can hear the fizz above the roar of the waterfall. Then I shoot along as though in the tail of a comet.

Snowflakes drift past. Icicles coat the rocks at the falls, and it's hard to tell them from the gushing spumes of water. The boulders in the glade are iced with snow. Honey jumps between them, following us upstream.

My fingers slowly freeze from the tips down, and after fifteen minutes or so I'm forced to leave this magical water world. We change, eat shortbread and drink hot chocolate. We dip our fingers in warm water from a flask. Mine are blue and the intense pain whirls me back to my childhood of wet wool socks in wellingtons and winter chilblains.

Stream

I intended to dip by Leather Tor Bridge, an elderly and very narrow granite crossing of the Meavy above Burrator. There has never been a road here, only a hardcore track. It's a beautiful, gentle valley where the rocks and trees are softened by mosses and ferns, and where potato caves, their walls luminous with troglodyte lichens, hide beneath banks and rocks. The local farmers were evicted in 1917 to allow for a purer catchment and the eventual deepening of Burrator reservoir. Then the Forestry Commission littered this productive valley area of tiny newtakes, Devon banks, and fungus-clad beeches and oaks, with fast-growing non-native pines. Somehow in places the indigenous lushness breaks through the forestry, like green satin knickers from beneath a witch's black cloak.

Honey and I climb over a stile downstream and pick and tunnel our way through the undergrowth and trees to a long and darkly mysterious pool. I find it littered with hidden black rocks and mostly not deep enough to swim in. I navigate and propel myself upstream with my arms to the little waterfall and lie back to let the river pass over me. The sound in this bongo-shaped haven is deep and resonant, and we're cocooned by trees.

We scrabble out and walk down to Newleycombe Lake (in this part of Devon, a 'lake' is a stream). Here in the lower clearing, wild yellow flag irises are coming into flower. Wending down the narrow falls, I perch on a comfortably mossy rock and listen to the bubbling tinkles, plinks and plops of the water as it worms around roots and rocks. Hemlock sprouts everywhere.

Reservoir

Our numerous attempts at Moon Gazey swims tend to be scuppered by the Devon weather. This evening, however, we were somewhat optimistic, this being the Imbolc moon that heralds the start of spring, the spawning of frogs and the lactation of ewes. The Met Office online map even showed a sliver of moon peeking from behind a white, fluffy cloud at precisely the time of our swim.

And so it was that Honey and I stood in the car park near Venford in the dark. As our eyes adjusted, the pewter almost-glow of the water silhouetted the forestry evergreens that for some reason always clutter the shores of Dartmoor reservoirs – it's as though someone decides that if there's one man-made thing, no matter how beautiful, a few hundred thousand foreign trees sucking the life from the ground and upsetting the ecosystem won't hurt.

Sophie, Matt and Queenie arrived, and we toddled through the trees to the shore, where we changed in the frigid air and wondered what the water temperature might be. Sophie told us it had been just over one degree in the Dart on the previous day. A brief glow on the eastern horizon elicited a Moon Gazey frisson that swiftly morphed into the headlights from an approaching car.

In the end, the moon was provided by Queenie, who with her wild swimmer's twisted logic had decided that it would be less hassle to skinny-dip. Honey paddled, snorting softly, while the rest of us sidled in. The cold was almost indescribable, and we all struggled and howled. In the absence of the Moon Goddess there was nothing to distract us from the pain of icy werewolf talons of water shredding our thighs.

CHRISTINA ROSSETTI
'A Frog's Fate' (1885)

Contemptuous of his home beyond
The village and the village-pond,
A large-souled Frog who spurned each byeway
Hopped along the imperial highway.

Nor grunting pig nor barking dog
Could disconcert so great a Frog.
The morning dew was lingering yet,
His sides to cool, his tongue to wet:
The night-dew, when the night should come,
A travelled Frog would send him home.

Not so, alas! The wayside grass
Sees him no more: not so, alas!

A broad-wheeled waggon unawares
Ran him down, his joys, his cares.
From dying choke one feeble croak
The Frog's perpetual silence broke: –
'Ye buoyant Frogs, ye great and small,
Even I am mortal after all!
My road to fame turns out a wry way;
I perish on the hideous highway;
Oh for my old familiar byeway!'

The choking Frog sobbed and was gone;
The Waggoner strode whistling on.

Unconscious of the carnage done,
Whistling that Waggoner strode on –
Whistling (it may have happened so)
'A froggy would a-wooing go.'
A hypothetic frog trolled he,
Obtuse to a reality.

O rich and poor, O great and small,
Such oversights beset us all.
The mangled Frog abides incog,
The uninteresting actual frog:
The hypothetic frog alone
Is the one frog we dwell upon.

VITA SACKVILLE-WEST

From 'Spring' (1926)

The spring was late that year, I well remember,
The year when I first came on the field of fritillaries;
So late, the cottars meeting in the lanes
Would stop to marvel mildly, with that old
Unplumbed capacity for wonderment
At Nature's whim. The calendar told spring,
But spring was heedless: April into May
Passed, and the trees still wore their livery
Of lean black winter's servants: very strange
Most lovely Easter played three days at summer,
A heavy summer over winter's fields,
Three days, and then was vanished, like a queen
Dropping the lifted flap of her pavilion.

Nightly I leant me at the window-sill,
Telling this chaplet of the slipping days,
But still the lamp streamed wet on polished stones,
And still the nights were empty silences
Robbed of the nightingale: they only held
The slanting strings of rain: Orion marched
Invisible down the hours from dusk to dawn,
Till morning pallor lost him, but the clouds
Hid all his gradual latening; that year
He shot his midnight javelins unseen
And dipped the horizon into other skies,
Lost to the North, till autumn should renew

His captaincy, with Rigel, Betelgeuse,
Aldebaran, and brightest Sirius.

Have we so many springs allotted us,
And who would rob a pauper of his pence?

Then broke the spring. The hedges in a day
Burgeoned to green; the drawing of the trees,
Incomparably pencilled line by line,
Thickened to heaviness, and men forgot
The intellectual austerity
Of winter, in the rich warm-blooded rush
Of growth, and mating beasts, and rising sap.
How swift and sudden strode that tardy spring,
Between a sunrise and a sunset come!
The shadow of a swallow crossed the wall;
Nightingales sang by day. The pushing blade
Parted the soil. The morning roofs and oasts
There, down the lane, beside the brook and willows,
Cast their long shadows. Pasture, ankle-wet,
Steamed to the sun. The tulips dyed their green
To red in cottage gardens. Bees astir,
Fussing from flower to flower, made war on time.
Body and blood were princes; the cold mind
Sank with Orion from the midnight sky;
The stars of spring rose visible: The Virgin;
Al Fard the solitary; Regulus
The kingly star, the handle of the Sickle;
And Venus, lonely splendour in the west,
Roamed over the rapt meadows; shone in gold

Beneath the cottage eaves where nesting birds
Obeyed love's law; shone through the cottage panes
Where youth lay sleeping on the breast of youth,
Where love was life, and not a brief desire;
Shone on the heifer blaring for the bull
Over the hedgerow, deep in dewy grass:
And glinted through the dark and open door
Where the proud stallion neighing to his mares
Stamped on the cobbles of the stable floor.
For all were equal in the sight of spring,
Man and his cattle; corn; and greening trees,
Ignorant of the soul's perplexity,
Ignorant of the wherefore and the end,
Bewildered by no transient ecstasy,
But following the old and natural law,
Nor marred nor blazing with a royal excess;
The law of life and life's continuance.

That was a spring of storms. They prowled the night;
Low level lightning flickered in the east
Continuous. The white pear-blossom gleamed
Motionless in the flashes; birds were still;
Darkness and silence knotted to suspense,
Riven by the premonitory glint
Of sulking storm, a giant that whirled a sword
Over the horizon, and with tread
Earth-shaking ever threatened his approach,
But to delay his terror kept afar,
And held earth stayed in waiting like a beast
Bowed to receive a blow. But when he strode
Down from his throne of hills upon the plain,

And broke his anger to a thousand shards
Over the prostrate fields, then leapt the earth
Proud to accept his challenge; drank his rain;
Under his sudden wind tossed wild her trees;
Opened her secret bosom to his shafts;
The great drops splattered; then above the house
Crashed thunder, and the little wainscot shook
And the green garden in the lightning lay.

POLLY SAMSON

From *The Kindness* (2015)

Lucifer flew well for her in the fading light, falling through the sky when she summoned him and away again towards a great bruising sunset. She was alone on the ridge at first: just her, the bird and the wide-open view. It was one of those nervy summer days of sudden strong winds that fretted the hawk's feathers as he stared at her from his perch on her gauntlet.

She was wearing a long red shirt over jeans and sandals, her hair was breaking free of its band. A leather pouch hung from her belt and a whistle from a cord around her neck. The hawk braced his feet on her wrist, making a leather tassel swing from the gauntlet. She felt the breath of his feathers on her face as he departed and she watched him go with the wind right under his wings, scattering crows like drops shaken from an umbrella.

Julia was trying her best to get it right for the bird, the morsels were small to keep him active. A shaming twenty-six ounces he'd weighed on the scales that morning. She called him with the whistle, two sharp bursts and there he was: a dark Cupid's bow firing straight at her from the heavens.

She continued along the ridge, Lucifer steady on her arm, his manic eyes never leaving her face until she gave the signal. She sent him reeling to and fro and neither of them knew that this was to be their last dance. The evening started to chill. She'd almost forgotten that Julian was supposed to be meeting her there or perhaps she'd just given up hope. He was panting when he arrived, still red in the face from the run up the hill, his bike and its useless tyre abandoned. He had the air of a boy who'd crossed three continents to see her, his sweatshirt knotted round his waist. Impossibly young, with hair falling over his eyes and an uncertain lope, one leg of his jeans still tucked into a sock. He didn't dare kiss her, he said, with the hawk glaring at him like that from the end of her wrist.

The hawk shrugged his shoulders and she sent him flying. They kissed and when Julian stopped to glance nervously at the sky she took off her gauntlet and pushed his hand inside. She urged the hawk with her whistle, moving Julian's arm up and down, the gauntlet's tassel dancing, but Lucifer only soared higher, the wind whispering murder into his ear and deafening him to her call. Julia ran cursing, Julian lolloping beside her. She grabbed back the gauntlet as the hawk fell to his kill. Julian's hands were warm on her waist and it seemed to them both that the scream of the rabbit went on for ever.

ANITA SETHI

'Perspective on nature in the city' (2021)[†]

Flight 1

A ladybird spread its wings wide and then vanished against the concrete of the school playground in Rusholme, Manchester. I had been peering intently at the tiny patch of beauty on the grey earth and felt a fluttering within at the sudden emptiness. Then I inspected the grey concrete for another little spot of redness. I would find another ladybird, I knew, for they clung to the bush at the edge of the playground beyond which the great beast of a city roared all day long. The ladybirds crawled out into the greyness every now and then and the children put their palms onto the ground so that the ladybirds tickled their heart lines. I liked looking at ladybirds, their intricacies. It helped, in this great blur of a crowded city into which I had been born, to focus.

A ladybird was fluttering through my mind at 8.30 one morning as I sat nibbling the soggy edges of the Weetabix. They were the most beautiful thing about my new school. The first time I saw one opening its wings I thought it was dying, the way its body seemed to be splitting open. But then it flew, flapped about in the air, dived back down and became again a small oval solid thing, so still, unmoving, that the first time I ever saw one I didn't know it was a living creature and thought it might have been some kind of colourful pebble.

Mum didn't know anything about the ladybird that had found its way into my head. She hung clothes out to dry all around the house, laying faded white sheets over the doors, the radiators, the chairs, crumpled wings covering the surfaces, sighing as she did so as if there was something heavy like a stone in her heart weighing it down, making breathing tricky.

When she came to collect me, for it was time to leave for school, she saw the bowl still full of food and forced my mouth into the bowl until there was a chinking sound of teeth against porcelain and the ladybird vanished into a sudden blackness. Mum held my head back and forced the silver spoon down into my mouth – *just get it down will you* – and screamed into my face words that were banned from the school playground. I swallowed and swallowed and swallowed but when Mum went out of the room, I ran outside and sicked up all the Weetabix into the soil.

My split lip hardened as the day passed at school, my whole self seemed to shrink to become the hurt on the face. During the day, my lip swelled up on the right-hand side, making my whole mouth feel lopsided. It felt like a rock sitting on my face. 'How do you spell FAMILY?' the teacher asked. And it was my turn to spell, but when I opened my mouth to speak, the lump laired up and the pain awoke so that the letters that tumbled out of my mouth were all askew and clattered to the floor like arrows which have missed the mark, so that the whole class erupted in laughter.

I tried to conjure the ladybird back into my head but its wings were frayed and faltering then and couldn't seem to fly past the great lump of pain.

There seemed to be a rock growing up in my stomach too as the days passed, planting itself there so that whenever any food touched it, it hurled it back out. Every day was the same rigmarole at meal times. I hid the food in plastic bags and stuffed it in the bins around the house. I flushed it down the loo. I pushed it into my coat pocket, and when I went to the corner shop to buy sweets, I threw it in an outside bin or near a tree in the park. I fed it to the birds and watched them flock towards me with huge and loving wing beats.

And all the while, the hunger grew, insatiable.

Ladybird, ladybird fly away home, your house is on fire, your children are gone.

It was a ritual to kiss Mum on the cheek every day as she dropped us off for school, and we'd say, 'Love you,' and she'd say, 'Love you too.' And then we'd race each other to the gate, bobbing along the road in our yellow school uniforms and joining the children in the playground, who looked from the distance like a sea of daffodils sliding along the grey concrete.

But after a time, the kisses stopped and I would even avoid looking at her eyes for fear of the daggers that lived inside them, the crazed glint that swam in them, surfacing unpredictably. When the time came to say goodbye and get out of the car, my eyes instead hooked themselves onto her cheek, the space above her shoulder, some image inside the head, but never those eyes.

It was the first word to go. I opened my mouth to speak the usual words and nothing came out. They'd got stuck somewhere in my throat, deeper even, buried like bullets in my gut, tunnelling in deeper and deeper.

And so – without touch or language – I fixed my gaze on the school gates and raced away from the car, desperate to dissolve the terrible sense of this new, confused self in the mass of children.

Thereafter opened up a gulf between us, as slight as the distance between a mouth and cheek; as light as the weight of words. Carrying all the distance between being and nothingness.

I liked being in the classroom when the teacher was speaking and I myself did not have to speak, when the white chalk was being stroked across the blackboard. My mind was clear and calm as I held the paintbrush.

The day is sheeted with rain outside and the class stay in and can paint whatever we want. I move the paintbrush over the page and retrieve the ladybird then, each stroke of the paint on the paper, I bring it back to life until it is flying again, inside my head.

I carry the painted ladybird back home with me, and leave it where

I know Mum will find it, a little piece of inarticulate love. I wonder if I will find it crumpled and thrown away, but the next day it is stuck on the wall, in all its inky glory.

When Mum drops me off at school the next week, I ask to her to come and see the real ladybirds and we walk to the playground, and watch for a while, and there is one. I put my palm down and it crawls on to it, I feel it on my skin and laugh, and then it spreads its wings wide and we watch together as it soars into the sky.

Flight 2

I sat on the top shelf of a row of shelves against the far wall in my grandmother's corner shop, Mama Shop, delivered there by Dad's shoulders, nearby the display window and nestled between boxes of Kellogg's Cornflakes no bigger than myself. There I was, hidden between breakfast supplies, human and food together. While Mum was at work we sometimes stayed at Mama Shop, which curved around a corner of Stretford, Manchester nearby the Lancashire Cricket Ground. From this vantage point I saw for the first time the tops of the houses, the sloping tiled roofs, the chimneys puffing out smoke. I could see much further than I had ever seen before in this city. I could see the clouds, if not their silver linings, the birds sometimes level with my own new height, while the people below seemed much smaller from up here. I could see the tops of their heads instead of gazing up at them. Before, I had had no idea what lay beyond our city, but now, after a family trip to the Lake District, I peered towards the horizon. Perhaps I could catch a glimpse of the Lakes if I looked closely enough, and although I could never see them, I could think of them lying out there, beyond sight, but still there. I was above it all.

If I moved too much or wriggled around I would surely fall. So, I held in my breath and watched and waited to be retrieved again and brought back down to earth. Dad's shoulders would return and I'd slip back on and put my arms around my father's neck and he'd lower me back down onto the floor. After that, even when I was back on ground level, I knew that life and the world looked different depending on how high up you could get.

All that day I had been sitting on the top shelf, telling Dad I didn't want to be taken down. I had been gazing out into the sky and had noticed swirls of birds there, swooping and diving in a pattern in the rich red sunset over the chimneys. They would swoop towards each other so that they were in a tight dark mass of wings, and then dive outwards, separating, and again repeat it, making great glorious arches and a symmetrical pattern in the sky. I could see how, above all the chaos of the football traffic jammed below, and the shouting drunken fans, above them in the sky the birds were making a beautiful symmetrical pattern with their flight.

'The birds are getting ready to migrate to Africa,' said Dad when he caught me looking at the birds. 'The opposite journey to the one I did from Africa to get here,' he said, 'and before that, from India.'

The autumn leaves had fallen fast that year, layering the park across the road with a thick coating of burnished copper which shone resplendently before being turned into grey mush by the rain. The birds each year flee from the cold and fly to warmer places, explained Dad. Except for the pigeons, who don't migrate; the pigeons stay put in their home town and are made of thicker skins. We humans would have to remain behind too and instead wear more thick layers of clothing to survive the winter when it came. I had already started wearing my duffle-coat inside if I sat on the top shelf, as the warmth from the gas heater didn't reach so far.

When I wasn't sitting on the top shelf, when I was level with the ground, I helped to stamp the sell-by dates and prices onto the boxes and tins and packets – bright luminous orange stickers with wonky numbers. The blank labels shot out from the machine and then were printed with whatever letters or numbers you chose. I enjoyed the stamping of the numbers onto the blank stickers and through helping out in Mama Shop, through turning the handle of the machine which made the numbers and letters, and watching the correct ones shoot out in black ink, I practised counting and reading. At lunch time, Dad came back to the shop from work and Mama had steaming aloo gobi and roti ready for him. Mama looked after the shop on her own all day and although she was old and walked with a slight stoop, she had, in her time looking after the shop, fended off gangs of violent lads, armed robbers, thieving thugs.

Mama polished the front shop window so vigorously that it became lethal to birds. Each morning she was awake at the crack of dawn with a mop and a bucket of soapy water, scrubbing the windows until they gleamed. One day, as I was sat on my perch on the top shelf, amongst the cereals, delivered there by Dad's shoulders, legs dangling above the tins of food, watching the birds swoop about in the air, somersaulting, and then suddenly one flew right at me. It flew towards the glass window, which was so clean it looked invisible, and the bird's body smashed against the window and flopped on to the floor. I started wailing and the customers turned in shock in the direction of the crying coming out of the cereal boxes to see a small child nestling between the cornflakes. Another bird flew through the open shop door, and round and round the shop, wings beating furiously as Mama chased after it, her white sari fluttering madly like a bird itself.

It turned out that the bird who had smashed against the window and fallen to the floor wasn't dead, but injured, and so Mama gathered up the bird and made a makeshift nest for it in an empty cardboard box layered with newspaper and put some water and food nearby before searching a number for a vet in the big Yellow Pages. I thought how beautiful the bird was, noticed how its wing that still worked twitched, the strange wounded noises it let out like the saddest sounds from my recorder. I wondered if it had any children or family that would miss it during its time in our shop.

Soon the days passed and the birds stopped swooping, they seemed to have vanished except for the little bird with a broken wing who still lived inside the cardboard box in the shop. It seemed as if the vet had forgotten to come for him.

One Saturday morning there was a flurry of sound, like a heart beating in my ears, a loud beating and then a great piercing cry and it was the bird with the broken wing soaring through the shop! Mama dashed to open the door and, after circling the shop a few times, frantically, the bird flew out of the door, away, and soared high up into the sky. It was a cloudy day and thick grey monsters of clouds filled up the air, so thick that even sitting on the top shelf I couldn't see the chimneys any longer. Soon the bird had vanished amidst the grey clouds. Would she find the way back home? Did she have a home any longer if her family had already migrated to Africa? And how would she survive through the winter when other birds like her had to flee to sunnier climes to survive? Mama didn't comment on the bird's departure but let out a great laugh and seemed happy that the creature's wing had healed, and had flown the nest, alive and well.

That night as I lay in bed – back in my own bedroom with the boiler whispering beside me – that night as I lay in bed I became a bird, not a bird plummeting to its death, but a bird soaring high above the houses, a bird looking down upon these houses, their chimney tops and slate roofs, able to see the whole picture. I looked down on my own bedroom from on high and saw myself in there, saw my family and saw the street in which I lived and saw the great beyond. Looking down upon my life in this way, I felt all the bad emotions drain away. I felt a great peace flood me. That night I flew in my dreams, somersaulted through the sky, felt all the soreness drain out of my limbs and I flew all the way to the Lakes and watched the moon gleaming on the black expanses of water. That night I sensed that whenever I felt trapped in the house, I would be able to escape; that night in my dreams I soared and soared and soared.

HILARY SHEPHERD

'Beloved Cow' (2021)[†]

It's six in the morning, it's dark and it's cold and I battle the old Land Rover with tears running down my face, because I'm taking my dear friend to the slaughterhouse. I feel the weight of her in the stock box behind me, pulling on every bend. My friend of ten summers, lying in the sun and pausing in her cudding to talk to me as I work in the garden. My friend of eleven winters, when I've warmed my cold hands in the fold between her leg and her udder before I start milking. The giver of abundant milk, purling rhythmically into the bucket, the pure white froth rising to the brim, and sometimes – being a cussed old sod as well as a dear friend – choosing the very last minute to suddenly lift her big white back foot and bring it very deliberately down in the bucket and spoiling the lot, because that's the sort of friend she is. We're on shouting terms, as well as groaning-in-the-sun friendliness. And today we are going to the slaughterhouse, because what else do you do when a cow goes seriously arthritic, even if she is the best of friends?

Her name is Bracken. She's been with us since our second summer farming and her first calving. A plush, smooth-coated red-and-white cow with giveaway stripes on her haunches that tell any expert that she has Jersey blood in her, as well as Hereford. She is square and stocky for all that. She reminds me, now, of my grandmother. It's somehow appropriate. The country woman came out in Grandma when she went back to live in Wales in 1967, along with the Welsh accent she'd kept through all those years in London. *Your heyfer got out, did she?* she said, tickled pink, when she learned of the latest exploit of my brindled cow. Before she left Wales as a young woman, Grandma had no doubt done her fair share of chasing recalcitrant *heyfers*. But now it is 1992. Grandma is dead and my *heyfer* is an old lady with noisy hips and a limping gait and her time has come.

The slaughterhouse is a small place behind a butcher's shop in a village fifteen miles away, so I take her there, and then we put her in the freezer, and we eat her.

Is this shocking? I wonder now, having two vegetarian daughters-in-law and two young Californian grandchildren who gaze into my eyes with a kind of horrified awe as they say, 'You eat meat, don't you Grandma?' Their father became a vegetarian twenty-five years ago, at the age of sixteen ('It's just a phase, Mum!'), on account of the pigs. Gudrun and Ursula. From *Women in Love*, of course. Appropriately. Gudrun, my other great friend, once made love to me in the shed for the hour it took to wheedle her into the stock-box to go to visit the boar. A sow on heat is hot, and peppery too, and all she wanted was to lean her chest on mine and murmur sweet piggy nothings into my face and be done with this stupid stock-box business.

So yes, I do know how many people will find the juxtaposition of life and killing very shocking.

But.

Life is about death. Everything we eat involves destruction. And three-score years and ten – or twenty, or thirty – is nothing in the scale of time. We return into the earth, we are a part of the cycle. But because we are complex social beings we lose sight of this, we feel we should take responsibility, somehow, and in so doing we lose our connection with the earth.

It's a huge privilege to own a parcel of land. We owe it to that land to make the best use of it we can in our brief relationship with it. To harvest and reinvest, be part of the network of production involved in our own inevitable consumption. In our crowded Britain to own land simply to control space and make it ours alone is particularly dubious. Vegetarianism is an emotional choice but not defensible if you eat eggs and dairy products. Vegans wouldn't get far living off these ancient upland fields, too high and wet to grow more than swedes and oats but ideal for producing grass-fed meat. What is the nature of the contract we make with the land, in this overpopulated age? Build on it, if we're not willing to eat off it? Increasingly export our food production elsewhere and let others make the moral decisions, leaving the empty countryside to turn back into woods? This is a very complex place to tread.

Years after I took my beloved cow to be butchered, the darkly handsome Hereford bull with the astrakhan curls faced the same fate. Whenever I unrolled the big straw bale round the cattle shed the elderly Chester forgot his creaking hips to paw the ground and butt the bale playfully, but he was no longer mounting the cows. We couldn't keep him; he had to go. One summer afternoon the kennel man came out with his humane killer. We held Chester on a rope in the corner of the field by the gate and it was swift and clean and quiet. Most of us, if we knew what was coming to us, would happily swap.

This time there was no question of the freezer. By 2001 modern farming methods had caused BSE and the thirty-month rule brought in to control it meant the meat was condemned, so Chester fed the hounds in the hunt kennels. A better end? I don't think so.

NAN SHEPHERD

From *The Living Mountain* (1977)*

Being

Here then may be lived a life of the sense so pure, so untouched by any mode of apprehension but their own, that the body may be said to think. Each sense heightened to its own most exquisite awareness is in itself total experience. This is the innocence we have lost, living in one sense at a time to live all the way through.

So there I lie on the plateau, under me the central core of fire from which was thrust this grumbling grinding mass of plutonic rock, over me blue air, and between the fire of the rock and the fire of the sun, scree, soil and water, moss, grass, flower and tree, insect bird and beast, wind rain and snow – the total mountain. Slowly I have found my way in. If I had other senses, there are other things I should know. It is nonsense to suppose, when I have perceived the exquisite division of running water, or a flower, that my separate senses can make, that there would be nothing more to perceive were we but endowed with other modes of perception. How could we imagine flavour, or perfume, without the sense of taste and smell? They are completely unimaginable. There must be many exciting properties of matter that we cannot know because we have no way to know them. Yet, with what we have, what wealth! I add to it each time I go to the mountain – the eye sees what it didn't see before, or sees in a new way what it had already seen. So the ear, the other senses. It is an experience that grows; undistinguished days add to their part, and now and then, unpredictable and unforgettable, come the hours when heaven and earth fall away and one sees a new creation. The many details – a

---

* A draft of *The Living Mountain* existed in 1945.

stroke here, a stroke there – come for a moment into perfect focus, and one can read at last the word that has been from the beginning.

These moments come unpredictably, yet governed, it would seem, by a law whose working is dimly understood. They come to me most often, as I have indicated, waking out of outdoor sleep, gazing tranced at the running of water and listening to its song, and most of all after hours of steady walking, with the long rhythm of motion sustained until motion is felt, not merely known by the brain, as the 'still centre' of being. In some such way I suppose the controlled breathing of the Yogi must operate. Walking thus, hour after hour, the senses keyed, one walks the flesh transparent. But no metaphor, *transparent*, or *light as air*, is adequate. The body is not made negligible, but paramount. Flesh is not annihilated but fulfilled. One is not bodiless, but essential body.

It is therefore when the body is keyed to its highest potential and controlled to a profound harmony deepening into something that resembles trance, that I discover most nearly what it is *to be*. I have walked out of the body and into the mountain. I am a manifestation of its total life, as is the starry saxifrage or the white-winged ptarmigan.

So I have found out what I set out to find. I set out on my journey in pure love. It began in childhood, when the stormy violet of a gully on the back of Sgoran Dubh, at which I used to gaze from a shoulder of the Monadhliaths, haunted my dreams. That gully, with its floating, its almost tangible ultramarine, *thirled* me for life to the mountain. Climbing Cairngorms was then for me a legendary task, which heroes, not men, accomplished. Certainly not children. It was still legendary on the October day, blue, cold and brilliant after heavy snow, when I climbed Creag Dhubh above Loch an Eilein, alone and expectant. I climbed like a child stealing apples, with a fearful look behind. The Cairngorms were forbidden country – this was the nearest I had come to them; I was delectably excited. But how near to them I was coming I could not guess, as I toiled up the last slope and came out above Glen

Einich. Then I gulped the frosty air – and I could not contain myself, I jumped up and down, I laughed and shouted. There was the whole plateau, glittering white, within reach of my fingers, an immaculate vision, sun-struck, lifting against a sky of dazzling blue. I drank and drank. I have not yet done drinking that draught. From that hour I belonged to the Cairngorms, though – for several reasons – it was a number of years before I climbed them.

MARY SIDNEY

From *Psalm 139* (1599)

O sun, whom light nor flight can match,
Suppose thy lightful flightful wings
Thou lend to me,
And I could flee
As far as thee the evening brings:
Even led to west he would me catch,
Nor should I lurk with western things.

Do thou thy best, O secret night,
In sable veil to cover me:
Thy sable veil
Shall vainly fail;
With day unmasked my night shall be,
For night is day, and darkness light,
O father of all lights, to thee.

DANIELA F. SIEFF

'Persephone's Tor' (2021)[†]

It is late afternoon and overcast when I bolt. The rough and messy moorland of Devon opens before me, and my lungs expand to breathe in the widening expanse of space and air.

I am on a retreat in the middle of Dartmoor with two dozen other women. It is the heart-child of three crones: Marion Woodman, a Jungian analyst, teacher and author, Ann Skinner, a voice and mask coach, and Mary Hamilton, a dance and movement educator. The week offers an opportunity to drop into the shadowlands of our unconscious minds and bodies, and to explore this inner terrain. Our work is guided by the myth of Persephone's descent into the kingdom of Hades.

One day, Persephone — goddess of the Spring — is picking flowers in a meadow when the surface of the earth splits open and Hades, Lord of the Underworld, emerges in his golden chariot. Seizing Persephone, he urges his horses to leap across the river Styx — the threshold that divides the land of light from the realm of darkness — and drags the terrified maiden down into his kingdom.

When Persephone's mother Demeter discovers the abduction, she beseeches Zeus to intervene. There can be no Spring without Persephone and Hades is ordered to return her to the light. But no sooner have her feet touched the ground than Persephone reveals that she has eaten pomegranate seeds from Hades' orchard, and so is bound for ever to his realm.

A compromise is reached: for nine months of each year Persephone will dwell on the surface of the earth, and for three months she will reside in its dark interior as the wife of Hades and Queen of the Underworld.

On this particular afternoon we are to use Persephone's time in the underworld as inspiration. If we hold this image in mind while allowing our bodies to dance, what might we discover in our own inner darkness? Are there unlived parts of ourselves which are ready to take shape? When we stop moving, we are encouraged to write or paint; the hope is that what began to take form in our bodies might find more definition on paper. I do not want to paint or write. I am feeling hemmed in and claustrophobic from journeying into my underworld. I want to be away from the retreat and out in the light. I want to feel living earth under my feet, and wind on my skin.

It is at this point that I bolt.

A dull light wraps the moors in a shadowless veil. Wild ponies and sheep are dotted across patches of grass, triggering timeless memories of prehistory, when humans were just another creature inhabiting the wilderness. I start to run, and with each stride my foot finds a velvety cushion of ancient turf. A sense of freedom, joy and wonder fill my being.

After a while, I come to a stream. A couple of miles beyond, a rugged tor rises dramatically towards the sky. I had followed this path on previous days, and turned back at this point rather than cross the water. This afternoon, however, something feels quite different. The tor calls to me.

I am torn: a part of me is keen to answer the call and explore new terrain, but an inner demon has taken up his customary perch on my left shoulder, and he counsels me to remain safely on familiar ground. *'You don't really want to cross the stream,'* he purrs in a seductive whisper, *'There's no bridge and no stepping stones, let alone a chariot of gold.'* And he goes on: *'You won't get across without wading through the water. Your shoes will get soaked. Your socks will become soggy. If you run with wet feet you'll get blisters. Anyhow, it's nearly time for the evening meal. If you keep going you'll miss dinner and go to bed hungry. You've run far enough now. Be sensible. Turn back.'*

I ignore my demon's whispered warnings and pick my way cautiously through the cold water.

On the other side of the stream the ground begins to rise, whereupon the demon moves inside my body and starts bombarding me with a new list of objections: '*Your lungs are burning. Your legs feel like lead. You are jarring your back, which is just starting to recover from a whiplash injury. Really… be sensible. STOP. NOW. TURN BACK.*'

I ignore his objections and run on.

At the base of the tor the path steepens and I slow to a walk. As I start to climb, I become aware of massive boulders poised around the rim of the summit. Their leaden surface sucks light from the overcast sky and leaches colour from the grass. The murmurings of the wind are muted by their bulk. It is as though the world is turning towards darkness and death.

Carved and fractured by millennia of frost, rain and wind, three groups of boulders stand apart from the rest. Taking on the form of mythical sentries, they appear as Dartmoor's answer to Cerberus, the ferocious triple-headed hound belonging to Hades. To the left of the path are what appear to be a Razor-Beaked Turtle and a Fire-Breathing Vulture. To the right, a Sabre-Toothed Bear. They stare down at me, daring me to approach, warning me to keep away.

Surrendering to my trepidation, I begin to perceive these creatures as my fears. Frozen to the spot and trembling, I wonder what to do. Should I heed their warnings and turn back? Or should I accept their challenge and walk onward? As the debate gathers momentum inside my head, I become aware that my feet have taken their own decision, and I am walking nervously forward.

On reaching the summit, light, colour and the murmurings of the wind flow back into the world. Much to my surprise, I am standing in a grassy hollow which is crowned by an irregular garland of boulders. The granite has weathered differently on this side – rather than being jagged and fractured, it is rounded and smoothed. Life, in the form of lime-green lichens, flourishes on its surface. Gazing out through the gaps between the rocks, I see bracken moorland and autumnal woodland, tufted meadows and furrowed fields, unruly hedges and roughly hewn walls. Browns and purples, greys and greens spread across the land in a mess of shapes, textures and experiences. Taking in this expanding view, I sense that when I enter willingly into the kingdom of my fear, its shape shifts and I glimpse the world with new understanding.

After spending some moments marvelling at the transformation, I detect the chattering of voices. A group of hikers is approaching the summit by a different path. I am not yet ready to re-enter the everyday world, so I walk a small circle of reverence around the crown of the tor and quietly head back the way I came. As I descend between the sentries, I turn and bow to the Razor-Beaked Turtle, the Fire-Breathing Vulture and the Sabre-Toothed Bear and, silently, thank each of them for their gift.

On my way home, I hear the swirling flow of the stream before I see it. Halfway across its chilly waters, I reach below the surface to pick up a stone that is speckled with seeds of pomegranate red. Then, alighting on dry land with soaked shoes and soggy socks, I relax, relieved to be back on more familiar ground. However, just as I start to wonder whether I might find some leftover supper, the setting sun discovers a gap in the golden pink clouds of dusk, and there, on a bank of grass ahead of me, stretching away from my left shoulder, is my shadow.

ALI SMITH

From *Winter* (2017)

Charlotte is demeaning him and simultaneously making it look like
he is demeaning his own followers. It is galling in so many ways. She
knows it is. She is tweeting about snow specifically to be galling to
him. She knows he has had everything planned, that he's been planning
for quite some time for when it *does* properly snow, if it ever does
again, for a piece about it in *Art in Nature*. He is – was – going to be
riffing on the theme of footprints and alphabetical print. *Every written
letter making its mark, digital or ink on paper, is a form of track, an animal
spoor,* a line that's been in his notebook for well over a year and a half.
She knows full well he's been waiting because of the warm winter
last year. He has such good words now, great words to conjure with
– trail, stamp, impress. He has also been collecting unusual words for
snow conditions. Blenky. Sposh. Penitents. He is – was – going to get
a bit political actually and talk about natural unity in seeming disunity,
about how unity can be revealed against the odds by the random grace
of snow's relationship with wind direction, the way that snow lands
with an emphasis on one direction even though a tree's branches go in
so many directions. (Charlotte thought this was a really lame idea and
gave him a lecture about how he was missing the point, that all but
the very best and most politically aware nature writers were habitually
self-satisfied and self-blinding and comforting themselves about their
own identities in troubling times, and that the word snowflake now
had a whole new meaning and he should be writing about *that*.)
He's been making notes on the give and take of water molecules; he
was going to subhead it Generous Water. He's been noting why, on a
cold day when there's very little breeze, something turning to ice will
produce what looks like smoke, like a fire, and making notes about the

combination of snow and ice called snice, with which buildings can be built because it's so strong, and about the feathery fern-leaf shapes ice makes when it forms on some surfaces and doesn't on others, and how it's actually *true* that no two snow crystals are ever alike, on the difference between flake and crystal and the communal nature of the snowflake – that's also quite a political thing to write about – as well as how flakes falling from the sky are their own natural alphabet, forming their own unique grammar every time.

Charlotte tore the pages out of the snow notebook and threw them out of the window of the flat.

He'd looked out and seen what was left of them in the treetops and the bushes, on the windscreens and roofs of the cars parked underneath, blowing about on the pavement.

CHARLOTTE SMITH

'Huge Vapours Brood above the Clifted Shore' (1783)

Huge vapours brood above the clifted shore,

Night o'er the ocean settles, dark and mute,

Save where is heard the repercussive roar

Of drowsy billows, on the rugged foot

Of rocks remote; or still more distant tone

Of seamen, in the anchored bark, that tell

The watch relieved; or one deep voice alone,

Singing the hour, and bidding 'strike the bell'.

All is black shadow, but the lucid line

Marked by the light surf on the level sand,

Or where afar, the ship-lights faintly shine

Like wandering fairy fires, that oft on land

Mislead the pilgrim; such the dubious ray

That wavering reason lends, in life's long darkling way.

STEVIE SMITH

'Alone in the Woods' (1930)

Alone in the woods I felt
The bitter hostility of the sky and the trees
Nature has taught her creatures to hate
Man that fusses and fumes
Unquiet man
As the sap rises in the trees
As the sap paints the trees a violent green
So rises the wrath of Nature's creatures
At man
So paints the face of Nature a violent green.
Nature is sick at man
Sick at his fuss and fume
Sick at his agonies
Sick at his gaudy mind
That drives his body
Ever more quickly
More and more
In the wrong direction.

JEAN SPRACKLAND

'The Birkdale Nightingale' (2007)
(Bufo calamito — the natterjack toad)

On Spring nights you can hear them
two miles away, calling their mates
to the breeding place, a wet slack in the dunes.
Lovers hiding nearby are surprised
by desperate music. One man searched all night
for a crashed spaceship.

For amphibians, they are terrible swimmers:
where it's tricky to get ashore, they drown.
By day they sleep in crevices under the boardwalk,
run like lizards from cover to cover
without the sense to leap when a gull snaps.
Yes, he can make himself fearsome,
inflating his lungs to double his size.
But cars on the coast road are not deterred.

She will lay a necklace of pearls in the reeds.
Next morning, a dog will run into the water and scatter them.
Or she'll spawn in a footprint filled with salt rain
that will dry to a crust in two days.

Still, when he calls her and climbs her
they are well designed. The nuptial pads on his thighs
velcro him to her back. She steadies beneath him.
The puddle brims with moonlight.
Everything leads to this.

ALETHEIA TALBOT

From *Natura Exenterata* (1655)

An ointment for an Ache, Rheum, or swelling in the
Joints, made with Swallows. By Mrs Kempe.

Take twenty Swallows and put them quick into a mortar of stone
(*Memorandum* the Swallows may not touch the ground) and put
therein Lavender-cotton, Spike, Knottgrasse, Ribwort, Balm, Valerian,
Rosemary tops, Woodbine tops, Strings of Vines, French mallows, the
tops of Aloes, Strawberry strings, Tutsan, Plantain, Walnut leaves, tops
of young Bayes, Violets, Sage of Vertue, fine Roman Wermwood, of
each a handful, two handful of Roses, as much Chamomile, beat all
these together and put thereto a quart of neatsfoot oyl, or May butter,
and grind all these together, and beat with them an ounce or two of
Cloves, put them all together in an earthern pot, and stop it very
close with a piece of dow round about, so that no air come out, and
set them nine dayes in a Cellar; and then take them out and seeth
them six or eight hours upon the fire, or else in a panne of water, but
first open your pot, and put in halfe a pound of wax, white or yellow,
whether you will, and a pint of oyl or butter.

SARAH THOMAS

'An Island Ecology' (2016)

A saloon car pulls up beside us and its spotless body perfectly reflects our anoraked forms. A greying man with a youthful smile hops out.

His greeting: 'You can get in if you don't have whale blood on your shoes.'

It is a fair request. His car is much smarter than one I'd expect to pick up a hitchhiker – especially *three* hitchhikers, with luggage. But this is the Faroe Islands and it has already been a day of surprises.

'All three of us?'

'Ja ja, get in.'

He shifts some boxes from the back seat into the boot.

It is an early June evening and the sun is showing no sign of descent. I am in the village of Miðvágur on the western island of Vágar, one in an archipelago of eighteen. I am attempting to reach the capital Tórshavn. On the rocky hillsides cradling the bay, the light coaxes dazzling green growth through last year's dead grasses; a fragile skin regenerating. A shoal of small clouds, white with grey underbellies, hovers still in the thin blue sky as if waiting for wind. I am laden with a backpack and flanked by a Polish couple I met last night in a spartan and gloomy hostel during a cataclysmic rain storm. How our fortunes have changed in the past twenty-four hours.

We were the only guests. Unusually, an international gymnastics competition had filled the limited accommodation in Tórshavn and I found myself in the out-of-town barracks out of necessity. Last night, as the fog licked the mountains and the rain nailed at the windows, we had all wondered what we were doing there.

This morning at breakfast our question was answered. Gazing out at the grey-white threshold of sea and sky a flotilla of small fishing boats moved at speed across the bay. Jakob the Pole noticed it first and began clicking his camera on rapid fire. He leant over to me and zoomed in on the LCD. I looked more closely and saw that the boats were chasing a cluster of dark fins. 'It's... a *whale hunt!*' I exclaimed, my emotions an unreconcilable commingling of anticipation and dread.

We quickly gathered our things and strode along the asphalt road to the harbour, through the drizzling fringes of last night's storm. As we rounded into the bay, the salt smell of shoreline danced in my nostrils with the fresh scent of damp soil, and something else quite new to my senses. It struck us from some distance: the sea was steeped an opaque coral red. The kill had been quick. The whale pod had been driven by that flotilla of boats from the open sea into this, the nearest bay.

We reached the beach at the innermost part of the bay and lay down our backpacks, joining a crowd of onlookers. There was a buzz of urgent purpose and co-operation. Perhaps 200 men, most of them in trousers and woollen jumpers, were heaving their roped bounty to the towboats, waist-deep in seawater and blood. It was as if they had dropped whatever they were doing and waded straight in. A few hundred villagers lined the shore, their delight tangible. It had been fifteen years since the last hunt on this island, they told me.

A bearded man, his arms folded, leaned towards me and asked if we were from Greenpeace. I responded in Icelandic, which seemed to eradicate the need for further questioning. An unspoken kinship emerged in the place of fear. 'Many people judge us for this,' his companion said.

'Hi Sarah!' A voice came from behind me.

I turned, surprised that anyone here should know my name. It was Andreas, the man from the airport tourist-information desk. I had spent more than an hour picking his brains when I had landed, whilst I decided in which direction to travel first. Tourism is still embryonic here, the airport no more than a small former British Army air base.

I had asked him about luggage storage. There was none, so he had let me keep a bag in his office for a few days.

'We'll all get lots of meat in our freezers from this, so everyone is happy,' he said, smiling shyly.

The day was waking up and the news was spreading. More onlookers arrived. I noticed the hunters, still wet, lining up at the window of a police car.

'What are they doing?' I asked Andreas.

'Each hunter has to give his name to the police, so they can calculate his share of the meat. The people who spotted the whales get one whale plus their share; the hunters and the boat owners who helped get a larger share than the villagers. And the rest is shared equally among the village, and then the island. There might even be enough this time to share with other islands!'

I was glad to have a perspective on this scene from a villager; one who had, as many Faroese do, lived and studied abroad but not resisted the umbilical tug back to his homeland and its traditions. His quiet politeness sat interestingly with his obvious thrill at the morning's events and the red sea behind him.

'They'll spend the next few hours getting the whales up to the pier and calculating shares,' he continued. 'Good time for a walk if you feel like it? It's not raining. You can leave your backpacks at my house, just up that hill.'

This personal relationship and lack of protocol resonated. We stood there as humans finding direct ways to meet needs, which can happen when people speak and listen to one another; when ecologies and economies remain aware of their connectedness, and the currency is trust and common sense. It reminded me of Iceland when I first started going there in 2008. That was before Iceland entered its touristic zeitgeist, the sheer number of visitors making personal gestures to outsiders less tenable, even though they had been sold the ideas of 'friendly locals' in 'unspoilt landscapes'. The powers that be in the Faroes wished to follow Iceland's lead and I wondered how they would fare. For years the Faroese have been under international pressure to cease this whaling tradition, left aghast that their critics are nations who engage in industrial farming. Tourism puts Faroese values under increased scrutiny.

But the whale hunt is a tradition that may have to cease for other alarming reasons, for which we are all responsible – least of all the Faroese, who have lived in close connection with their land and sea for centuries. The pilot whales that they hunt are not considered endangered, but they are now toxic. These 'pristine' seas swim with pollutants, which accumulate up the food chain and torture sea life from the inside. Whales, almost at the top, accumulate dangerous levels of mercury and PCBs, which are passed on to those that eat their meat and blubber. Developmental problems in children, cancers, immune-system dysfunction and a host of other illnesses are among the effects we are only beginning to understand. Seabirds too are dying en masse, their food supplies dwindling and their insides a tangle of plastic. Their bodies and their guano are toxic, polluting the very places they depend upon to breed.

We returned some hours later to wander with the villagers among the ranks of black rubbery bodies lined up along the pier, straight and stiffening, their fluid motion forever suspended. One hundred and fifty-four pilot whales, most the length of a bus. Five young ones perhaps three metres long. Their bodies flanked the pier and the harbour front, whale after whale after whale. A membranous tangle of pink and grey innards spilled onto the concrete from squares cut out of their bellies; small doors into this toxic truth. Each whale had a number and its volume incised into the blubber. 124, 123, 122: pink slit in black.

We walked the length of this upside-down world from the end to the beginning: the subaquatic brought onto land, their swimming stilled, their insides out. Thick blood pooled beneath the bodies, coagulating with the day's progress. I touched number 87. It had the properties of skin, an inflated dinghy and a sandbag all at once, my fingers leaving a gentle impression where I had pressed. Around the burnished curves of its jaw was a constellation of rings, each formed of light grey dots. The marks were as delicate as a hand-applied pattern on *raku*-fired porcelain. A lady in orange rubber dungarees looked official holding a clipboard. I asked her what caused the marks.

'These whales *love* squid,' she said fondly. 'It's the marks left by the squid's suckers as they struggle to escape death.'

59, 58, 57. Around the corner, along the long harbour front. Villagers posed for photos next to the bodies, beaming with co-existence and pride, despite the unfortunate fact that one was dead and the other was not.

6, 5, 4. Together, we rounded the last corner into a courtyard lined with baiting sheds. A woman washed blood from her hands in a small waterfall tumbling from a cliff. A young boy stood on a fluke as his father cut out the teeth with a saw.

Seeing our curiosity, the father proudly informed us how well regulated this practice is. How the police only give the go-ahead for the hunt to proceed if sufficient time has passed since the last one, if it's felt that the meat is needed. How those who kill must be qualified in humane slaughter and must use the correct tools. How the police calculate how the catch will be divided. How each whale is documented and has been since the sixteenth century.

He pulled out the detached block of jaw and teeth.

'It's like tree rings,' he explained. 'You can see their age from the teeth, and from the ovaries how many young they've had.'

I stepped closer to look at them, blood pooling beside my boots.

'Everyone in the village gets a share,' the woman added, wandering over to join us, 'whether they are ninety or newborn.'

A sheepdog circled another specimen as its owner wheeled a barrow along the pier. It was filled with knives and beer, ready to cut out his share and celebrate once the police announced what it would be.

We all squeeze into the back seat. In the front there is a passenger already. The car is as full as it can be.

The driver grins in the rear-view mirror, pulling away. 'I'm Marni and this is Jeff. You are *very* lucky to see this hunt.'

'I know,' I reply, wondering if there is a more appropriate word than 'luck'.

'Jeff here is a top chef from London, who thinks he knows everything, and I'm here to show him that he doesn't.' Marni gestures at his companion who turns to greet us.

Jeff is full-bellied with a dark sculpted beard and from his accent, clearly hails from New Zealand.

'Yeah, I can't believe what I've eaten in the past twenty-four hours... guillemot eggs, gannet chicks. And now we'll be trying the whale.'

Marni has evidently seized the opportunity to impress his client and driven here to partake of this most Faroese of food events.

'Well, we have to run an errand on the way to Tórshavn. I can drop you at the bridge or you can come with us,' Marni offers.

We hitchhikers are united in our curiosity: 'We'll come with you.'

'You are open and curious. In the Faroes this is a good thing!' he enthuses.

We pull up to an unmarked warehouse on the seafront. Following them inside through a door-length fringe of rubber, it becomes clear that this is Marni's empire. Seawater flows gently through a system of plastic tanks housing a small ecology of creatures. Aubergine-coloured sea cucumbers sway gently in the current. Sea urchins, mint green and dusky pink, perch brittle and unwelcoming. The brown whorls of sea snails lurk amongst dancing dulse.

'Marni,' says Jeff, 'supplies me with the best and freshest seafood I've *ever* known.'

A white-coated teenage boy appears to be the only employee in this bizarre laboratory. Marni issues a brief instruction. The boy returns with several polystyrene boxes. Marni opens one which is partitioned inside and starts filling it with living langoustines.

'Tonight Jeff will be experimenting,' Marni smiles. 'Will you be joining us for dinner? We'll start with the whale.'

JESSICA TRAYNOR

'Apple Seed' (2020)

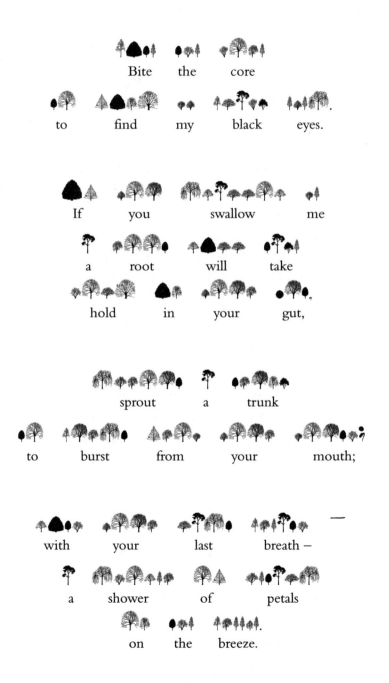

Bite   the   core

to   find   my   black   eyes.

If   you   swallow   me

a   root   will   take

hold   in   your   gut,

sprout   a   trunk

to   burst   from   your   mouth;

with   your   last   breath –

a   shower   of   petals

on   the   breeze.

TRILEIGH TUCKER

'Arthur's Magic Birds: Once in Shadow,
Future Bright' (2021)[†]

I was standing at Tintagel in Cornwall, where a bronze statue of a hooded man – *Gallos* – Cornish for 'Power' – evokes both the stories of King Arthur and the deep history of this place. This was the farthest point of my journey from the United States to understand how my English and Welsh ancestors may have connected with the birds of their land since Arthur's time. My beloved father, now ninety-five, had always treasured his connections to this region once called 'Dumnonia'. On his Luttrell mother's side, our ancestors could be traced back to Dunster Castle in Somerset, and Glamorgan, Wales. His Tucker father's lineage was from Tavistock in Devon and, in Cornwall, Lamerton and Henland (now Helland), just a few miles from where I was standing in Tintagel. My Tucker family name may be derived from *Tuatha car* – Gaelic for 'beloved people' – and I've always loved the motto emblazoned on our family's crest, *Nil desperandum:* never despair.

Arthur's association with this headland was tentative. Geoffrey of Monmouth, who first made the link, wasn't known for his historical self-discipline. But in soils older than the thirteenth-century Tintagel castle, newly discovered sixth-century artefacts suggest that Dumnonian royalty may have lived here. So it was at least conceivable that those people of legend had trod the same paths as my ancestors, walked the very steps I'd taken in this mystical place.

Gulls wheeled over *Gallos*, their loud calls piercing the stiff breeze. As I walked, little dunnocks and stonechats poked busily through the dust for seeds kicked up by visitors' sensible shoes. I listened for the onomatopoetic call of the red-billed chough: the black bird so long associated with the bronze-bearded king.

For as long as we've been human, birds have been our companions in person, place, myth, and symbol. During our journey with our winged neighbours, we have used birds for food and decoration, imagined ourselves as birds, given birds human characteristics, and been inspired by birds as we create art, symbolism and meaning. We've buried our forebears with birds. We even identify not only ourselves, but also our homes, by bird terms: hundreds of places in Britain are known by ancient names of birds, usually with an associated landscape; for instance, Cranborne or Caer Bran, meaning 'crane-stream' and 'raven's fort'.

Birds' omnipresence, their ability through flight to enter realms inaccessible to humans, their music, and their intelligence made them natural key characters in the stories people created to help provide meaning in their lives:

When Arthur sent his knights on a quest to find the maiden Olwen, beloved of Culhwch, he chose those with special gifts. One was Gwrhyr Gwastad Ieithoedd, who could speak and understand any language. Along the way, the knights sought to release the prisoner Mabon, held so deeply and so long that few knew of him. Their search brought them to the Blackbird of Cilgwri, and Gwrhyr asked in the bird's language if he knew where Mabon was. The blackbird explained that, as old as he was, he didn't know of Mabon — but knew someone else yet older who might. In turn, a stag, an owl, and an eagle each told Gwrhyr of their vast age without hearing of Mabon, and with humility sent the adventurers to the next animal who might know. Finally, a salmon was able to take them to free the prisoner. (Adapted from the *Mabinogi,* translated by Patrick Ford.)

The *cyfarwyddiad,* early medieval Welsh storytellers whose tales make up the *Mabinogi,* were deeply familiar with the habits of birds. To the *cyfarwyddiad's* spellbound audience, the supernatural flowed smoothly through the natural; Cartesian divisions between nature and spirit were off in the misty future. Birds' soaring might be *auspicious*: literally, allowing 'divination by observing the flight of birds'. Birds and their behaviour were rife with significance for human meaning: not only as parables for human behaviour, but as messengers from the supernatural realm to humans.

More than any other animals, birds were the subjects of the tiny, detailed paintings created by gifted illuminators of bestiaries, psalters, and books of hours – including the stunning Luttrell Psalter commissioned in the early fourteenth century by my ancestor Sir Geoffrey Luttrell. Birds served as symbols, decorations in initials, actors in biblical stories, and characters in marginalia. During this period when nature was being observed with new care and accuracy, scribes rendered in fine script the sacred texts that were then illustrated by artists trained in careful observation. Small everyday birds fill the margins of illuminated volumes, giving us a glimpse of how medieval artists saw the birds of daily life in fields and farms.

But it is the dramatic and symbolic wild birds who most prominently populate the medieval imagination in speech, script and symbol: crane, owl, blackbird. Cranes with their feminine shapes evoked the wisdom of the crone, serving as guardian and sentinel; in legend, Fionn MacCumhail's grandmother transformed herself into a crane to rescue him. Clever and cunning corvids – crows, jackdaws, magpies, choughs, and especially ravens – are the primary symbol in many heraldic settings. These black birds, such as 'theef chough' in Chaucer's *Parlement of Foules,* were burglars and brilliant and bringers of fire: *incendaria avis.* The voices of ravens were interpreted by Roman soothsayers to foretell the future through augury, a term potentially derived from the Latin for birds' chatter.

King Arthur in particular has, for at least half a millennium, been associated with such black birds. In 1605, Cervantes' Don Quixote asks his friend if he has not read of 'an old tradition, and a common one, all over that kingdom of Great Britain, that this king [Artus, or Arthur] did not die, but that, by magic art, he was turned into a raven; and that, in process of time, he shall reign again … for which reason it cannot be proved that, from that time to this, any Englishman has killed a raven?' Noted nineteenth-century antiquarian Robert Hunt refines Cervantes' characterisation: 'The tradition relative to King Arthur and his transformation into a raven is fixed very decidedly on the Cornish Chough, from the colour of its beak and talons. The "talons and beak all red with blood" are said to mark the violent end to which this celebrated chieftain came'. Now on Cornwall's official coat of arms, choughs were considered so important to Cornish identity that until the sixteenth century, no non-Cornish coat of arms was allowed to display them.

When in *Culwych and Olwen* the three birds advised Gwrhyr of their venerable ages, blackbird and eagle, the symbols of [masculine] kings, told of hammering an anvil and erosion of stone. But the Owl of Cwm Cawlwyd, feminine queen of the night, spoke of living woodlands and their cycles of death and rebirth:

When first I came here this great valley you see was a wooded glen and a race of men came and laid it waste. A second forest grew in it, and this is the third… (From the *Mabinogi*, translated by Patrick Ford.)

Remembering the Owl's words, geographer I. G. Simmons calls *Culwych and Olwen* 'a chronicle of woodland demise and regrowth'. Such is the story of the forest and fen and field that were home to Britain's earliest magic birds: harvest and replanting, valleys filled with villages, wood becoming byway and highway.

Modifying the landscape, as we always have, we shift its birdscape. Widespread woodlands remained at the beginning of Anglo-Saxon times; woods-associated place names, such as Cotswolds, Birkenshaw and

Chislehurst, predate the Norman Conquest. But by 1086 the Blackbird of Cilgwri and Arthur's Cornish choughs knew different lands than their predecessors. Roman settlers and the Briton people before them had cleared many of the island's vast woodlands for farming and grazing of cows, sheep, and pigs. By 1200 most of England's wildwoods were gone, transformed into managed woodlands or pastureland.

Black corvids had gained a bad reputation for fire-carrying, theft, and disturbance of crops. If in 1566 you brought three heads of 'Crowes Chawghes or Rookes' to your local churchwarden, you'd earn a penny's bounty; a 'Jaye' or raven was even more valuable at a penny a head. But with their intelligence and adaptability, most of Britain's blackbirds were able to deal with intensification of human use. A hundred years later Christopher Merrett could still write of the chough (perhaps meaning the jackdaw, as their names were conflated at that time) as found '*in omnibus oris maritimis a Cornubia ad Doroberniam*': on all coasts from Cornwall to Dover.

But the Cornish chough, dependent on cliff settings to raise its young, suffered from human intrusion and retreated to scattered coastal areas. Although in 1744 Irish naturalist Oliver Goldsmith ventured to assert choughs' positive qualities – 'They are sociable and harmless; they live only upon insects and grain, and wherever they are, instead of injuring other birds, they seem [s]entinels for the whole feathered creation' – he noted that choughs could only be found in the western coasts of England, even at that time. Other forces accelerated the chough's decline, leading these iconic black birds with their striking red beaks and legs to disappear gradually, gone from Sussex by 1830. The chough associated with King Arthur had finally vanished from Cornwall by about 1950.

Still living intimately with birds in their daily lives, medieval people drew them into symbolic and spiritual importance. But after medieval times, changing landscapes dramatically shifted daily life, disrupting the human connection with our ancestral avian companions. The demise of Cornish tin mining in the nineteenth century, followed by war-related tree-cutting in the twentieth, diminished remaining bird habitat. Now even more than in medieval times, remaining woodlands are disconnected from each other. Migrating birds in need of food-rich rest stops and specialist species who require a particular type of landscape have a difficult time. Birds who were once our everyday neighbours have become rare and exotic visitors. And some voices won't be heard again in British soundscapes.

Like our medieval forebears, we're inspired by birds' flight. We're awed by their migration and write poetry about their song. Also, like our ancestors, we're witnessing a world in which birds' native homes are being sacrificed for timber and development. In reshaping our places, we're also transforming the meaning for us of the winged creatures who call them home, who once brought magic and insight to earthbound humans.

Can we regain the past magic of birds now displaced, species erased? Might Gwrhyr return to speak birds' language? We don't often believe these days that we have been changed into birds or that birds can become humans. But I can now know birds intimately in new ways. I can pull up on my computer images of a living starling's brain as she responds to a Brandenburg concerto, or one by her own species. We've always been struck by corvids' intelligence; now we understand that behind those bright black eyes, ravens' brains have more neurons than a capuchin monkey's. More densely packed neurons mean that corvid brains sparkle with connections, yielding the cleverness that has awed people for millennia. Perhaps their brilliance is part of what has let us see ourselves in them, and them in us. Contemporary technology allows glimpses deep into birds' lives unimaginable to medieval people.

To gain the wisdom of birds on his quest, Culwych brought

Gwrhyr Ieithoedd, interpreter of all languages. Today, augury takes entirely new forms. Listening more carefully than ever before possible through bio-acoustic analysis, we now know exactly how hard rain shapes the night-time call of the tawny owl. We've learned that birds develop urban lingo; citified blackbirds sing at higher pitches so they can communicate effectively through traffic noise, and start their dawn chorus well before sunrise in electrified downtowns that never darken.

It's not only through laboratory technology that we contemporary people are connected to birds. Birdwatching is expanding as a hobby; every fortnight *6 million* Britons are out observing birds. Modern optics − binoculars and long-range camera lenses − have radically enhanced our ability to see birds in flight or forest, helping us learn to identify them and thus gain a deeper understanding of their behaviour and the ecology of their homes. Birding's long association with a dowdy, silver-haired population has transformed. Through school programmes like the Brighton-area Bird Buddies, children can rediscover awe of birds: 'Every bird is amazing,' wrote one student. And from this sense of wonder, participating teachers reported that their pupils' excitement spread to other children, who began reporting their own bird sightings. Students and staff alike are planning new gardens, ponds, woodlands for the birds. A new generation is becoming enchanted by these winged messengers of sky and shadow.

With the technology to understand birds' lives and the heart to care about them, scientists and other citizens are working together to return birds' magic to its ancestral land. In 1979, an astonished Norfolk farmer noticed three immense birds alight on his fields: the first cranes to winter in Britain since the seventeenth century. Three years later a pair of cranes successfully fledged the first crane chick Britain had seen in almost 400 years. Near my Luttrell ancestors' home in Dunster, cranes have adopted the Somerset Levels as a major new breeding ground, assisted by the introduction of ninety-three hand-reared common cranes as part of the Great Crane Project. As *Newsweek* writer Simon Barnes notes, collaboration among farmers, conservationists, and government is what has allowed the majestic, 'numinous' crane to appear winging through Britain's rewilded skies.

And what of that *incendaria avis,* Arthur's revenant alter ego, the chough? Plans were being hatched in 2001 to encourage the chough to return to Cornwall, with a captive-breeding programme and statistical analysis of likely suitable places to attempt establishment of a new colony. Researchers knew the chances were slim of choughs travelling on their own the 100-km-plus distance from the nearest known populations in Pembrokeshire – or farther, from Brittany or Ireland. Then one April day Alix Lord went walking along the cliffs of the Lizard Peninsula, perhaps during a brief sunbreak on a typical chilly, rainy day. I picture her astonishment when her ears caught the piercing, rattly call, when she finally saw the three black birds with their striking red beaks and talons. Ms Lord was thrilled to realise she was one of the first to hear and see the stunning return of the chough to Cornwall. Of their own accord, Arthur's once and future emblems had returned to resume their place of honour in his kingdom.

Beloved people: never despair.

EVELYN UNDERHILL

From *Practical Mysticism* (1915)

What would it mean for a soul that truly captured it; this life in which the emphasis should lie on the immediate percepts, the messages the world pours in on us, instead of on the sophisticated universe into which our clever brains transmute them? Plainly, it would mean the achievement of a new universe, a new order of reality: escape from the terrible museum-like world of daily life, where everything is classified and labelled, and all the graded fluid facts – which have no label – are ignored. It would mean an innocence of eye and innocence of ear impossible for us to conceive; the impassioned contemplation of pure form, freed from all the meanings with which the mind has draped and disguised it; the recapturing of the lost mysteries of touch and fragrance, most wonderful amongst the avenues of sense. It would mean the exchanging of the neat conceptual world our thoughts build up, fenced in by the solid ramparts of the possible, for the inconceivable richness of that unwalled world from which we have subtracted it. It would mean that we should receive from every flower, not merely a beautiful image to which the label 'flower' has been affixed, but the full impact of its unimaginable beauty and wonder, the direct sensation of life having communion with life: that the scents of ceasing rain, the voice of trees, the deep softness of the kitten's fur, the acrid touch of sorrel on the tongue, should be in themselves profound, complete, and simple experiences, calling forth simplicity of response in our souls.

DOROTHY WELLESLEY

'The Forest After Snowstorm' (1930)

The rabbits last night gave a dance.
They waltzed in circles as very clearly I see
In the snow-lighted radiance:
Pad-patterns, scissor-shape, yet in the spirit scamper;
The hare, the hawk, and the titmouse wee
Did polka together, John Peel in a jolly valiance,
Zigzagging in energy zealous all over the lea.

How many beasts, how many different birds
Danced here until dawn that from mortals hide;
I have found you out, wild ones! I know you for ever:
Fox went down slinkily, and fatty beaver,
To the Bad Brook to drink, the wild snowdrops beside.

Mysterious are they: but in the wood
Where, stacked along the deepening defiles,
Most lately the clean spiles
Of cloven chestnut shone
And, silver muskets of soldiers, together stood,
The carpets of the chestnut leaves are matted,
And crisp beneath the foot above the rut;
And, slung with small round leaves
Last evening wonted, singular to-day,
The peeling spirals of honeysuckles are plaited,
Strangling with several strands the hazel-nut.

But lately in the half-warm and the cold,
The long, proud catkin spent his pollen gold
Upon that rosy lady the nut-bloom gay:
Lovely for seeing eye is the forest way!
Mysterious the bypaths I knew yesterday;
Gone the guides I knew, and to-day do not know,
Save by some sober sign, toppled, half gone:
That sign of Socrates, the black hemlock,
Or this bright bilberry tangle feathered with snow,
That a magpie has curtsied on.

Or this sudden dark slab, this wall upright of rock,
Sloppy, toupéed with mosses green and grey,
Where, radiating like rain freshets, flow
The young wine-coloured hearts of the ivy spray.

'Moths' (1925)

Now with a humming from the greening skies,
Sphinx moths with course set true
Shoot forth, torpedoes with a spinning screw,
And bulbous lantern eyes.

Now hanging round the trumpet of the flowers
The Death's Head, hairy, squeaking as he comes,
A squeal of bagpipes and a blur of drums,
Seeks his black food, the Deadly Nightshade; scours
The garden like a vampire after prey,
And failing fades, an air machine, away.

Now those small moths that in their infancy

Feed on the wild sea spurge,

Growing above the surge

That creams the slate slabs of the Cornish sea,

Come for the honeysuckle swinging loose

On the brick summer house;

And Leopard Moths that feed upon the spindles

And lilac-bark in spring,

With dark blue spots upon a wedge-like wing,

Loving the lights, flying to cottage candles;

The Ghost Swift moth that feigns

Death in the capturers' net, with such deep arts;

And Gipsies horned and lean, straight showers of darts;

Dark Dagger from the plains;

And sweet Peach Blossom feeding on the brambles;

The small coquettish Puss;

And that great blunderbuss

That bumps on homing farmers and down drumbles

On footpaths through the midnight fields of May.

Blue moths that seek chalk hills above the leas,

And Scarlet Tigers in the apple-trees,

These are the moths that linger on the day.

But others will seek out the darkest hours,

To make their drunkard onslaught on the flowers;

Drab, stout, like little mice

Scampering after rice.

Fen moths that feed

On parsley, wild angelica, lucerne,

Companions of newt and leech and herne.

And Mottled Rustics that love teazel weed;

Waved Umber moth that in the forks of pears

Spins its soft silk cocoon,
Breaking to wing in the short nights of June
To feast upon dog roses and sweet briars;
The moth named Phoenix, symbol of the rest,
For all their brood
Were grubs that bred their beauty in a wood,
Freedom made manifest:
A faith assured hailed glorious in a husk,
Seen as a whirl of wings and windy lights
On hills, in hollows of soft earthly nights;
Ardent adventurers across the dusk,
That fly, fanatics freed, and reach a bed
Where above tapers tall
A dead man's shadow dances on a wall,
And shower their burning faiths above his head.

For they must travel far;
Out of the spreading south Spring Usher blew;
Tattered beside him flew
The Chinese Character, the Cinnabar;
The Brindled Pug, and the small Seraphim
Blew in with butterflies
Out of the tropic skies;
Sea-going beauties, that will lightly skim
Around the crows' nest, or the baking brasses,
Telling the sailor of the coastal walk,
Harebells on slopes of chalk,
Stillness of quaking grasses;
That will not rest, but wearily take flight
Into the ocean night;
Or, taking passage on an old tea clipper,

Seek hiding in the sails, and finding this,
Work round to England as a chrysalis:
The Painted Lady with the Dingy Skipper.

And many with wide wing and lustrous name
Blew once, in early times, across the sea:
Paphia, Silver Washed Fritillary,
And that imperial dame
Vanessa Atalanta, who was borne
In sunny splendour on an off-shore gale
From coasts of Africa, to meet the hail
Battering the Kentish pebbles in the dawn.

'Birds' (1925)

The branches shivered. The dawn wind went free;
    In darkness there was heard
    The small peep of a bird,
That woke his brother in a neighbouring tree.
Then palpitating, suddenly united,
They woke in garden and in field excited.

All little birds that bless men's homes around,
Singing each morning on their roofs and trees,
Gave praise in place of men. Not only these,
All birds in England kindled to the sound:

Snow buntings, called Snow Flakes upon the fells,
Who in the saltings on sea-asters feed;
And Woodlarks wintering in the shingle-reed,

Basking in stony outcrops of the hills;
Dishwashers who love water, but attend
On heels of ploughmen to the furrow's end;
The Chaffinches who flock along the shore,
To pick the tide-line and the wads of foam,
Or in fat hopfields stab the marl and loam,
And when replete till they can eat no more
Will fight their own reflections in a pane;
Linnets in hill scrub on the windy knolls,
Siskins who love Redpolls,
Blackbirds who pipe from lilacs sunk with rain,
Cross Philip Sparrows sparring in the hedges,
Who hate all yellow flowers, and tear in spite
The new-sprung crocus and the aconite,
Then sit all plumped and pleased on window ledges;
Green Linnet loving fields of charlock seed,
And haunting stackyards with the old bronze Pigeon,
Who bears him down in puffed and pompous dudgeon;
Hawfinches who in greed
Strew garden paths with gaping pods of peas,
And clean split cherry stones;
Crossbills who ardently dislodge the cones
To feast in the brown twilight of the trees;
The Mistle Thrush pecking at mistletoe,
Singing full voice in driving storms of snow;
The cat-faced Owl, horn-eared upon an oak
Against a cratered moon; men, homing late,
Will know him blindly wavering round a gate,
Or snoring in the eaves of narvish folk;
The Nightingale, who with slight-lifted wings
Through his whole body sings;

Magpies who courting speak in lowered tones;
The Wood Wren with his whistle;
And Sherriff's Man a-swinging on a thistle;
Jackdaws that hoard bright jewels and marrow
        bones;
Ravens that on the February braes
Slaughter the runts among the lambs and tear
Their entrails out, and line, year after year,
With human clothes their forts in Raven Trees;
Or from a scarp-face hung above the waves
Will scrap with passing Peregrines; the Choughs
Who on Carnarvon bluffs
Above the hollow suction of the caves
Build nests on ledges veined with red and blue,
And lit with inward light; all migrants who
Are killed by wires that whine mile after mile
Coastwise along the cliff-line and the crags;
And Cormorants who gather with the Shags
On far St Kilda or the Holy Isle;
Gulls who besiege broad boats with blubber loads,
And love the jumbled garbage of a port
Docking the world-going steamers, and consort
With the world's shipping riding in the roads;
Sea-Ducks asleep, tin toys upon the seas;
Stormy Petrels sliding down a wave; Wild Swans
Flying at sunset, gathering into clans,
Scattering round East Anglian estuaries,
Wing-beating raucous flocks,
Down sprinkling loose,
Off shore from Broad and Fen to Denver Sluice,
Dabbing at slippery tangles of the rocks,

For winkle and for frond
That stain and shadow low-tide pools to wine,
For spiders lurking in the corralline,
For kelp from deep storm-water flung beyond
The spring high-water mark,
Called the Black Tang by fishermen of Sark,
Where women in the shallows
At vraicking season with hook, horse and boat,
Work till the laden cart is half afloat,
Then spread the stinking sea-weed on the fallows.

The migrants reach the strands
To crowd, half dying, round the lighthouse flares,
But birds, while life is theirs,
Must take the sky-roads back;
The Fire-Crest,
Rose-Coloured Pastor, and the Yellow Hammer;
With what rash joy and clamour
Gathers the Dusky Warbler with Red Breast,
Mixing with modest birds about the shires,
Singing their waking song for the last time.
Rising from lawn and lime,
From piggeries, middens, byres,
From stooks and standing crops,
Till shooting suddenly with thrill and scream,
They join the Eastern stream:
Take flight for Asia from a Hampshire copse.

PHILLIS WHEATLEY

'A Hymn to the Evening' (1773)

Soon as the sun forsook the eastern main
The pealing thunder shook the heav'nly plain;
Majestic grandeur! From the zephyr's wing,
Exhales the incense of the blooming spring.
Soft purl the streams, the birds renew their notes,
And through the air their mingled music floats.
Through all the heav'ns what beauteous dies are spread!
But the west glories in the deepest red:
So may our breasts with ev'ry virtue glow,
The living temples of our God below!
Fill'd with the praise of him who gives the light,
And draws the sable curtains of the night,
Let placid slumbers sooth each weary mind,
At morn to wake more heav'nly, more refin'd;
So shall the labours of the day begin
More pure, more guarded from the snares of sin.
Night's leaden sceptre seals my drowsy eyes,
Then cease, my song, till fair *Aurora* rise.

ISABELLA WHITNEY

From 'The Admonition by the Author to All Young
Gentlewomen, and to All Other Maids, Being in Love' (1567)

Hero did try Leander's truth
before that she did trust;
Therefore she found him unto her
both constant true and just.

For he always did swim the sea,
when stars in sky did glide;
Till he was drowned by the way,
near hand unto the side.

She scratched her face, she tare her hair,
it grieveth me to tell,
When she did know the end of him
that she did love so well.

But like Leander there be few;
therefore, in time, take heed!
And always try before ye trust!
So you shall better speed.

The little fish that careless is
within the water clear,
How glad is he, when he doth see
a bait for to appear!

He thinks his hap right good to be,
that he the same could spy;
And so the simple fool doth trust
too much before he try.

O little fish, what hap hadst thou,
to have such spiteful fate!
To come into one's cruel hands,
out of so happy state.

Thou didst suspect no harm, when thou
upon the bait didst look:
O that thou had Lyceus's eyes,
for to have seen the hook!

Then hadst thou, with thy pretty mates,
been playing in the streams;
Where as Sir Phoebus daily doth
shew forth his golden beams

But sith thy fortune is so ill
to end thy life on shore;
Of this, thy most unhappy end,
I mind to speak no more.

But of thy fellow's chance that late
such pretty shift did make
That he, from fisher's hook did sprint
before he could him take.

And now he pries on every bait,
suspecting still that prick
For to lie hid in everything,
wherewith the fishers strike.

And since the fish, that reason lacks,
once warned doth beware:
Why should not we take heed to that
that turneth us to care.

And I who was deceived late
by one's unfaithful tears,
Trust now for to beware, if that
I live this hundred years.

NIC WILSON

'Snickets' (2019)[†]

> *All locales and landscapes are ... embedded in the social and individual times of memory. Their pasts as much as their spaces are crucially constitutive of their presents.*
>
> Christopher Tilley, A Phenomenology of Landscape

Snicket, n. – a narrow passage between walls or fences, origin obscure

There are many different types of snicket and each has its own story to tell. I surface in these riven-pathways early; they tower above my head. The stones at eye level jut out of the mortar and despite their unforgiving corners I'm compelled to run my fingers along the broken edges, remembering the reputation of slate – the letter-bearer, the nose-slitter. With a recent school trip to Beaumaris Gaol still raw in my memory, the subterranean passages behind my grandparents' house in Gyffin simultaneously draw and repel me.

Slate is a grotto stone, waiting damply for the unwary to slip and graze a knee or elbow. But I'm young enough, in my early snicket days, that there's always a rough hand holding mine, leading me up the steps from the musty utility room with its cavernous chest freezers and ham-radio desk to the square grey terrace and narrow snicket beyond the gate. I look up as I ascend, at the glossy slick on the undersides of the stones, the moisture collecting in ferny fingerpools which feed the liverwort crusting. Ivy-leaves of toadflax drip down the walls, smudging the yellow fumitory, and up by the fence red campion dots the colour of Welsh lanes onto the empty terrace: a place much celebrated by my grandpa for its horticultural barrenness.

But Granny belonged to the wild and it came for her, fed by the floods that gushed down the snicket in heavy rain, breaching the houses, sowing the cracks with soil and seed, floating the foliage of hart's tongue fern and maidenhair spleenwort. In this intractable, embedded space the gravitational pull of the earth was strong and there was no guarantee of finding a way out. Although my head eventually reached beyond the walls and my hands became the firm clasp around lithe fingers, I discovered a rootedness in those slate passages that has stayed with me as I've walked through the past forty years.

My daily journeys still connect me to the land: a morning run along Gypsy Lane, one of the ancient holloways carved into the chalk alongside the Roman villa at Purwell; visiting the lightning-blasted black poplar with its roots in the Ash Brook or walking back from the community garden fete with the children, exploring the old ways that used to mark the medieval field boundaries, now forgotten snickets, their entrances hidden behind brambles, buddleia and privet. Many of these ancient pathways survived in Hitchin as a result of the open-field system, which remained intact on the east side of the town well into the twentieth century, far longer than in many towns and villages where enclosures in the eighteenth and nineteenth centuries radically altered the structure of the landscape.

Overlaying an early sixteenth-century map onto Google Earth reveals little change to our local paths, field boundaries and lanes. As the area was developed, the estates, roads, even the railway was forced to fit into the existing field-strip framework and as ancient boundary paths were surrounded by houses, new snickets were born. These in-between spaces exist on the margins of everyday narratives; we merely pass through, leaving behind us memories of daily journeys and the seeds of our agricultural and horticultural heritage. Like the Dead Sea Scroll deciphered in 2018 by scholars using fragmented marginal notes, old pathways retain the scattered remnants of local histories even when the main body of the landscape has been erased and rewritten.

As I trace these porous paths on the school run, on my way to the train station or to the shops, I can feel the past seeping up through the cracks.

In the verges, deadly nightshade lifts its shadowy bells above the nettles, garlic mustard and cuckoo-pint, rising from its agricultural past as a nineteenth-century pharmaceutical crop and embracing the arable margins. Alpine clematis coils over the wall and tumbles into the snicket, freed from the rigours of trellis and twine. Its leaf-stalks tangle with its wild cousin, old man's beard, on a reverse mission to infiltrate the cottage borders from the hedgerows. At the back of the park beside the path, elm suckers have broken through a line of old fence panels and are busy creating thickets in an abandoned garden corner.

After years of walking the snickets, I am in step now, trodden into the upwelling of wild and cultivated, past and present, culture and landscape, all muddied and conjoined. I have become grounded in these everyday routes, now the runnels for my commonplace roots, like a network of veins feeding a living landscape.

VIRGINIA WOOLF

'Kew Gardens' (1919)

From the oval-shaped flower bed there rose perhaps a hundred stalks spreading into heart-shaped or tongue-shaped leaves half way up and unfurling at the tip red or blue or yellow petals marked with spots of colour raised upon the surface; and from the red, blue or yellow gloom of the throat emerged a straight bar, rough with gold dust and slightly clubbed at the end. The petals were voluminous enough to be stirred by the summer breeze, and when they moved, the red, blue and yellow lights passed one over the other, staining an inch of the brown earth beneath with a spot of the most intricate colour. The light fell either upon the smooth, grey back of a pebble, or, the shell of a snail with its brown, circular veins, or falling into a raindrop, it expanded with such intensity of red, blue and yellow the thin walls of water that one expected them to burst and disappear. Instead, the drop was left in a second silver grey once more, and the light now settled upon the flesh of a leaf, revealing the branching thread of fibre beneath the surface, and again it moved on and spread its illumination in the vast green spaces beneath the dome of the heart-shaped and tongue-shaped leaves. Then the breeze stirred rather more briskly overhead and the colour was flashed into the air above, into the eyes of the men and women who walk in Kew Gardens in July.

The figures of these men and women straggled past the flower bed with a curiously irregular movement not unlike that of the white and blue butterflies who crossed the turf in zig-zag flights from bed to bed. The man was about six inches in front of the woman, strolling carelessly, while she bore on with greater purpose, only turning her head now and then to see that the children were not too far behind.

The man kept this distance in front of the woman purposely, though perhaps unconsciously, for he wished to go on with his thoughts.

'Fifteen years ago I came here with Lily,' he thought. 'We sat somewhere over there by a lake and I begged her to marry me all through the hot afternoon. How the dragonfly kept circling round us: how clearly I see the dragonfly and her shoe with the square silver buckle at the toe. All the time I spoke I saw her shoe and when it moved impatiently I knew without looking up what she was going to say: the whole of her seemed to be in her shoe. And my love, my desire, were in the dragonfly; for some reason I thought that if it settled there, on that leaf, the broad one with the red flower in the middle of it, if the dragonfly settled on the leaf she would say "Yes" at once. But the dragonfly went round and round: it never settled anywhere – of course not, happily not, or I shouldn't be walking here with Eleanor and the children – Tell me, Eleanor. D'you ever think of the past?'

'Why do you ask, Simon?'

'Because I've been thinking of the past. I've been thinking of Lily, the woman I might have married … Well, why are you silent? Do you mind my thinking of the past?'

'Why should I mind, Simon? Doesn't one always think of the past, in a garden with men and women lying under the trees? Aren't they one's past, all that remains of it, those men and women, those ghosts lying under the trees,… one's happiness, one's reality?'

'For me, a square silver shoe buckle and a dragonfly—'

'For me, a kiss. Imagine six little girls sitting before their easels twenty years ago, down by the side of a lake, painting the water-lilies, the first red water-lilies I'd ever seen. And suddenly a kiss, there on the back of my neck. And my hand shook all the afternoon so that I couldn't paint. I took out my watch and marked the hour when I would allow myself to think of the kiss for five minutes only – it was so precious – the kiss of an old grey-haired woman with a wart on her nose, the mother of all my kisses all my life. Come, Caroline, come, Hubert.'

They walked on the past the flower bed, now walking four abreast, and soon diminished in size among the trees and looked half transparent as the sunlight and shade swam over their backs in large trembling irregular patches.

In the oval flower bed the snail, whose shell had been stained red, blue, and yellow for the space of two minutes or so, now appeared to be moving very slightly in its shell, and next began to labour over the crumbs of loose earth which broke away and rolled down as it passed over them. It appeared to have a definite goal in front of it, differing in this respect from the singular high-stepping angular green insect who attempted to cross in front of it, and waited for a second with its antennae trembling as if in deliberation, and then stepped off as rapidly and strangely in the opposite direction. Brown cliffs with deep green lakes in the hollows, flat, blade-like trees that waved from root to tip, round boulders of grey stone, vast crumpled surfaces of a thin crackling texture – all these objects lay across the snail's progress between one stalk and another to his goal. Before he had decided whether to circumvent the arched tent of a dead leaf or to breast it there came past the bed the feet of other human beings.

This time they were both men. The younger of the two wore an expression of perhaps unnatural calm; he raised his eyes and fixed them very steadily in front of him while his companion spoke, and directly his companion had done speaking he looked on the ground again and sometimes opened his lips only after a long pause and sometimes did not open them at all. The elder man had a curiously uneven and shaky method of walking, jerking his hand forward and throwing up his head abruptly, rather in the manner of an impatient carriage horse tired of waiting outside a house; but in the man these gestures were irresolute and pointless. He talked almost incessantly; he smiled to himself and again began to talk, as if the smile had been an answer. He was talking about spirits – the spirits of the dead, who, according to him, were even now telling him all sorts of odd things about their experiences in Heaven.

'Heaven was known to the ancients as Thessaly, William, and now, with this war, the spirit matter is rolling between the hills like thunder.' He paused, seemed to listen, smiled, jerked his head and continued:

'You have a small electric battery and a piece of rubber to insulate the wire – isolate? – insulate? – well, we'll skip the details, no good going into details that wouldn't be understood – and in short the little machine stands in any convenient position by the head of the bed, we will say, on a neat mahogany stand. All arrangements being properly fixed by workmen under my direction, the widow applies her ear and summons the spirit by sign as agreed. Women! Widows! Women in black—'

Here he seemed to have caught sight of a woman's dress in the distance, which in the shade looked a purple black. He took off his hat, placed his hand upon his heart, and hurried towards her muttering and gesticulating feverishly. But William caught him by the sleeve and touched a flower with the tip of his walking-stick in order to divert the old man's attention. After looking at it for a moment in some confusion, the old man bent his ear to it and seemed to answer a voice speaking from it, for he began talking about the forests of Uruguay which he had visited hundreds of years ago in company with the most beautiful young woman in Europe. He could be heard murmuring about forests of Uruguay blanketed with the wax petals of tropical roses, nightingales, sea beaches, mermaids, and women drowned at sea, as he suffered himself to be moved on by William, upon whose face the look of stoical patience grew slowly deeper and deeper.

Following his steps so closely as to be slightly puzzled by his gestures came two elderly women of the lower middle class, one stout and ponderous, the other rosy cheeked and nimble. Like most people of their station they were frankly fascinated by any signs of eccentricity betokening a disordered brain, especially in the well-to-do; but they were too far off to be certain whether the gestures were merely eccentric or genuinely mad. After they had scrutinised the old man's back in silence for a moment and given each other a queer, sly look, they went on energetically piecing together their very complicated dialogue:

'Nell, Bert, Lot, Cess, Phil, Pa, he says, I says, she says, I says, I says, I says—'

'My Bert, Sis, Bill, Grandad, the old man, sugar, sugar, flour, kippers, greens, sugar, sugar, sugar.'

The ponderous woman looked through the pattern of falling words at the flowers standing cool, firm, and upright in the earth, with a curious expression. She saw them as a sleeper waking from a heavy sleep sees a brass candlestick reflecting the light in an unfamiliar way, and closes his eyes and opens them, and seeing the brass candlestick again, finally starts broad awake and stares at the candlestick with all his powers. So the heavy woman came to a standstill opposite the oval-shaped flower bed, and ceased even to pretend to listen to what the other woman was saying. She stood there letting the words fall over her, swaying the top part of her body slowly backwards and forwards, looking at the flowers. Then she suggested that they should find a seat and have their tea.

The snail had now considered every possible method of reaching his goal without going round the dead leaf or climbing over it. Let alone the effort needed for climbing a leaf, he was doubtful whether the thin texture which vibrated with such an alarming crackle when touched even by the tip of his horns would bear his weight; and this determined him finally to creep beneath it, for there was a point where the leaf curved high enough from the ground to admit him. He had just inserted his head in the opening and was taking stock of the high brown roof and was getting used to the cool brown light when two other people came past outside on the turf. This time they were both young, a young man and a young woman. They were both in the prime of youth, or even in that season which precedes the prime of youth, the season before the smooth pink folds of the flower have burst their gummy case, when the wings of the butterfly, though fully grown, are motionless in the sun.

'Lucky it isn't Friday,' he observed.

'Why? D'you believe in luck?'

'They make you pay sixpence on Friday.'

'What's sixpence anyway? Isn't it worth sixpence?'

'What's "it" – what do you mean by "it"?'

'O, anything – I mean – you know what I mean.'

Long pauses came between each of these remarks; they were uttered in toneless and monotonous voices. The couple stood still on the edge of the flower bed, and together pressed the end of her parasol deep down into the soft earth. The action and the fact that his hand rested on the top of hers expressed their feelings in a strange way, as these short insignificant words also expressed something, words with short wings for their heavy body of meaning, inadequate to carry them far and thus alighting awkwardly upon the very common objects that surrounded them, and were to their inexperienced touch so massive; but who knows (so they thought as they pressed the parasol into the earth) what precipices aren't concealed in them, or what slopes of ice don't shine in the sun on the other side? Who knows? Who has ever seen this before? Even when she wondered what sort of tea they gave you at Kew, he felt that something loomed up behind her words, and stood vast and solid behind them; and the mist very slowly rose and uncovered – O, Heavens, what were those shapes? – little white tables, and waitresses who looked first at her and then at him; and there was a bill that he would pay with a real two-shilling piece, and it was real, all real, he assured himself, fingering the coin in his pocket, real to everyone except to him and to her; even to him it began to seem real; and then – but it was too exciting to stand and think any longer, and he pulled the parasol out of the earth with a jerk and was impatient to find the place where one had tea with other people, like other people.

'Come along, Trissie; it's time we had our tea.'

'Wherever *does* one have one's tea?' she asked with the oddest thrill of excitement in her voice, looking vaguely round and letting herself be drawn on down the grass path, trailing her parasol, turning her head this way and that way, forgetting her tea, wishing to go down there and then down there, remembering orchids and cranes among wild flowers, a Chinese pagoda and a crimson crested bird; but he bore her on.

Thus one couple after another with much the same irregular and aimless movement passed the flower bed and were enveloped in layer after layer of green-blue vapour, in which at first their bodies had substance and a dash of colour, but later both substance and colour dissolved in the green-blue atmosphere. How hot it was! So hot that even the thrush chose to hop, like a mechanical bird, in the shadow of the flowers, with long pauses between one movement and the next; instead of rambling vaguely the white butterflies danced one above another, making with their white shifting flakes the outline of a shattered marble column above the tallest flowers; the glass roofs of the palm house shone as if a whole market full of shiny green umbrellas had opened in the sun; and in the drone of the aeroplane the voice of the summer sky murmured its fierce soul. Yellow and black, pink and snow white, shapes of all these colours, men, women, and children were spotted for a second upon the horizon, and then, seeing the breadth of yellow that lay upon the grass, they wavered and sought shade beneath the trees, dissolving like drops of water in the yellow and green atmosphere, staining it faintly with red and blue. It seemed as if all gross and heavy bodies had sunk down in the heat motionless and lay huddled upon the ground, but their voices went wavering from them as if they were flames lolling from the thick waxen bodies of candles. Voices. Yes, voices. Wordless voices, breaking the silence suddenly with such depth of contentment, such passion of desire, or, in the voices of children, such freshness of surprise; breaking the silence? But there was no silence; all the time the motor omnibuses were turning their wheels and changing their gear; like a vast nest of Chinese boxes all of wrought steel turning ceaselessly one within another the city murmured; on the top of which the voices cried aloud and the petals of myriads of flowers flashed their colours into the air.

DOROTHY WORDSWORTH

From Journal, *Written at Alfoxden* (1798)

ALFOXDEN, January 20th 1798. The green paths down the hill-sides are channels for streams. The young wheat is streaked by silver lines of water running between the ridges, the sheep are gathered together on the slopes. After the wet dark days, the country seems more populous. It peoples itself in the sunbeams. The garden, mimic of spring, is gay with flowers. The purple-starred hepatica spreads itself in the sun, and the clustering of snow-drops put forth their white heads, at first upright, ribbed with green, and like a rosebud when completely opened, hanging their heads downwards, but slowly lengthening their slender stems. The slanting woods of an unvarying brown, showing the light through the thin network of their upper boughs. Upon the highest ridge of that round hill covered with planted oaks, the shafts of trees show in the light like the columns of a ruin.

21st. Walked on the hill-tops a warm day. Sate under the firs in the park. The tops of the beeches of a brown-red, or crimson. Those oaks, fanned by the sea breeze thick with feather sea-green moss, as a grove not stripped of its leaves. Moss cups more proper than acorns for fairy goblets.

22nd. Walked through the wood to Holford. The ivy twisting round the oaks like bristled serpents. The day cold a warm shelter in the hollies, capriciously bearing berries. Query: Are the male and female flowers on separate trees?

23rd. Bright sunshine, went out at 3 o'clock. The sea perfectly calm blue, streaked with deeper colour by the clouds, and tongues or points of sand; on our return of a gloomy red. The sun gone down. The crescent moon, Jupiter, and Venus. The sound of the sea distinctly heard on the tops of the hills, which we could never hear in summer. We attribute this partly to the bareness of the trees, but chiefly to the absence of the singing of birds, the hum of insects, that noiseless noise which lives in the summer air. The villages marked out by beautiful beds of smoke. The turf fading into the mountain road. The scarlet flowers of the moss.

24th. Walked between half-past three and half-past five. The evening cold and clear. The sea of a sober grey, streaked by the deeper grey clouds. The half dead sound of the near sheep-bell, in the hollow of the sloping coombe, exquisitely soothing.

25th. Went to Poole's after tea. The sky spread over with one continuous cloud, whitened by the light of the moon, which though her dim shape was seen, did not throw forth so strong a light as to chequer the earth with shadows. At once the clouds seemed to cleave asunder, and left her in the centre of a black-blue vault. She sailed along followed by multitudes of stars, small, bright, and sharp. Their brightness seemed concentrated, (half-moon).

26th. Walked upon the hill-tops; followed the sheep tracks till we overlooked the larger coombe. Sat in the sunshine. The distant sheep-bells, the sound of the stream; the woodman winding along the half-marked road with his laden pony; locks of wool still spangled with the dewdrops; the blue-grey sea, shaded with immense masses of cloud, not streaked; the sheep glittering in the sunshine. Returned through the wood. The trees skirting the wood, being exposed more directly to the action of the sea-breeze, stripped of the net-work of their upper boughs, which are stiff and erect, like black skeletons; the ground strewed with the red berries of the holly. Set forward before two o'clock. Returned a little after four.

27th. Walked from seven o'clock till half-past eight. Upon the whole an uninteresting evening. Only once while we were in the wood, the moon burst through the invisible veil which enveloped her, the shadows of the oaks blackened, and their lines became more strongly marked. The withered leaves were coloured with a deeper yellow, a brighter gloss spotted the hollies; again her form became dimmer; the sky flat, unmarked by distances, a white thin cloud. The manufacturer's dog makes a strange, uncouth howl which it continues many minutes after there is no noise near it but that of the brook. It howls at the murmur of the village stream.

28th. Walked only to the mill.

29th. A very stormy day. William walked to the top of the hill to see the sea. Nothing distinguishable but a heavy blackness. An immense bough riven from one of the fir trees.

30th. William called me into the garden to observe a singular appearance about the moon. A perfect rainbow, with the bow one star, only of colours more vivid. The semi-circle soon became a complete circle, and in the course of three or four minutes the whole faded away. Walked to the blacksmith's and the baker's; an uninteresting evening.

31st. Set forward to Stowey at half-past five. A violent storm in the wood; sheltered under the hollies. When we left home the moon immensely large, the sky scattered over with clouds. These soon closed in, contracting the dimensions of the moon without concealing her. The sound of the pattering shower, and the gusts of wind, very grand.

Left the wood when nothing remained of the storm but the driving wind, and a few scattering drops of rain. Presently all clear, Venus first showing herself between the struggling clouds; afterwards Jupiter appeared. The hawthorn hedges, black and pointed glittering with millions of diamond drops; the hollies shining with broader patches of light. The road to the village of Holford glittered like another stream. On our return the wind high a violent storm of hail and rain at the Castle of Comfort. All the Heavens seemed in one perpetual motion when the rain ceased; the moon appearing, now half veiled, and now retired behind heavy clouds, the stars still moving, the roads very dirty.

BIOGRAPHICAL NOTES

Kathryn Aalto is an American historian, designer, speaker, and author living in Devon. She has written three books including *Nature and Human Intervention* (2011), the *New York Times* bestseller *The Natural World of Winnie-the-Pooh: A Walk Through the Forest that Inspired the Hundred Acre Wood* (2015), and *Writing Wild: Women Poets, Ramblers, and Mavericks Who Shape How We See the Natural World* (2020). She is a writing mentor and co-founder of The Rural Writing Institute. She writes for *Smithsonian Magazine*, *Outside*, *Sierra*, and more. www.kathrynaalto.com and @kathrynaalto

Naoke Abe is a Japanese journalist and non-fiction writer. Since moving to London she has published five books in Japanese. Her biography of Collingwood 'Cherry' Ingram in Japanese won the prestigious Nihon Essayist Club Award in 2016. Her English-language adaptation of the book was published in 2020 and won the 2020 Award for Excellence from The Council on Horticultural and Botanical Libraries. She is a trained classical pianist and an advanced yoga practitioner.

Kitty Aldridge trained as an actor at Drama Centre London, and went on to work in theatre, film and television for sixteen years. Her novels have been shortlisted and longlisted for various fiction awards, and she won the Bridport Short Story Prize in 2011. She has recently completed the MSt in Creative Writing at Cambridge University.

Monica Ali, FRSL, is an award-winning, bestselling writer whose novels include *Brick Lane*, *In the Kitchen* and *Untold Story*. She was chosen as one of Granta's 2003 Best of Young British Novelists. Her work has been translated into 26 languages. Her fifth book, *Love Marriage*, will be published by Virago in 2022.

Elizabeth von Arnim (1866–1941), née Mary Annette Beauchamp, later Elizabeth Russell, Countess Russell, was an Australian-born British novelist. Publication of her first book introduced her to readers as Elizabeth, which she eventually became to her friends and finally even to her family. She used the pen name Alice Cholmondeley only for the novel *Christine*, published in 1917. Her best known work is *The Enchanted April* (1922).

Polly Atkin lives in Cumbria. Her first poetry collection *Basic Nest Architecture* (Seren, 2017) and third pamphlet, *With Invisible Rain* (New Walk, 2018) will be followed in 2021 by a second poetry collection *Much With Body*, and a biography focusing on Dorothy Wordsworth's later life. She is working on a memoir exploring place, belonging and disability.

Jane Austen (1775–1817), was an English writer who first gave the novel its distinctly modern character through her treatment of ordinary people in everyday life. She was known primarily for her six major novels, *Sense and Sensibility* (1811), *Pride and Prejudice* (1813), *Mansfield Park* (1814), *Emma* (1815), *Northanger Abbey* (1818) and *Persuasion* (1818) which interpret, critique and comment on the British landed gentry at the end of the eighteenth/start of the nineteenth centuries.

Anna Laetitia Barbauld, née Aikin (1743–1825), was a prominent English poet, essayist, literary critic, editor, and author of children's literature. Her work embraced political and social themes, promoting the values of the Enlightenment and of sensibility, while her meditative poetry made a founding contribution to the development of British Romanticism.

Cicely Mary Barker (1895–1973) Since their first publication in 1923, Cicely Mary Barker's *Flower Fairies* have enchanted both adults and children alike around the world. The botanically accurate drawings in 170 original illustrations, coupled with enchanting fairy images and poetry, appeal to our innate sense of magic and wonder.

Elizabeth Barratt Browning (1806–1861) was an English poet admired for the independence and the courage of her views. Her family were, historically, slave-owners and their wealth derived from the plantations of Jamaica. Barrett Browning campaigned for social justice throughout her life. While she lived her literary reputation surpassed that of her poet-husband. She had a wide following among cultured readers in England and in the United States.

Amy-Jane Beer is a biologist turned naturalist, conservationist and writer. In addition to books on natural history she writes regularly for a variety of magazines and newspapers, is a columnist for *British Wildlife* and a Country Diarist for the *Guardian*. She lives in rural North Yorkshire.

Isabella Mary Beeton, née Mayson (1836–1865), was an English journalist, editor and writer. She wrote the cookery column for her husband's publication:

The Englishwoman's Domestic Magazine using collected recipes, many of them sent in by readers. In 1859 a 48-page supplement to the magazine was published in 24 installments and it this which formed the original *Mrs Beeton's Book of Household Management* (1861), selling over 60,000 copies. Isabella Beeton was working on an abridged version of the book when she died of puerperal fever at the age of twenty-eight.

Gertrude Margaret Lowthian Bell, CBE (1868–1926) was an English writer, traveller, political officer, administrator, mountaineer and archaeologist who played an important role in establishing and helping to administer the modern state of Iraq. Bell was one of the leading women climbers of her day; the previously uncharted peak Gertrudspitze in the Swiss Engelhorner range was named in her honour. She scaled the Matterhorn in 1904 which she described in her memoir: *A Woman in Arabia: the Writings of the Queen of the Desert*.

Frances Bellerby née Parker (1899–1975) was a poet, novelist and short story writer. An athlete who played cricket, ran cross-country and won school colours for swimming and diving, Bellerby damaged her spine in a fall at Lulworth cliffs after which she struggled with ill health for the remainder of her life. *The Encyclopedia of British Women's Writing, 1900–1950* wrote of Bellerby: 'Her poetry is imbued with a spiritual awareness encoded through the natural environment while her political socialism is more evident in her prose'.

Claire-Louise Bennett grew up in Wiltshire and studied literature and drama at the University of Roehampton, before moving to Ireland where she worked in and studied theatre for several years. In 2013 she was awarded the inaugural White Review Short Story Prize and her debut book, *Pond*, was shortlisted for the Dylan Thomas Prize in 2016. Claire-Louise's fiction and essays have appeared in a number of publications including *White Review*, *Stinging Fly*, *gorse*, *Harper's Magazine*, *Vogue Italia*, *Music & Literature*, and *New York Times Magazine*.

Sharon Blackie is an award-winning writer and internationally recognised teacher whose work sits at the interface of psychology, mythology and ecology. As well as writing four books of fiction and nonfiction, her writing has appeared in the Guardian, the Irish Times, the Scotsman, and more. See www.sharonblackie.net

Enid Blyton (1897–1968) is one of the most popular children's authors of all time. Her books have sold over 500 million copies and have been translated into other languages more often than any other children's author. Born in London, Enid lived much of her life in Buckinghamshire and loved dogs, gardening and the countryside. She was very knowledgeable about trees, flowers, birds and animals. Dorset – where some of the Famous Five's adventures are set – was a favourite place of hers.

Tessa Boase is a journalist and writer interested in the connections between the land and society – food and commodity chains; our relationship with nature; our relationship with the rural past. As a social historian, she brings to life the stories of invisible women from the late nineteenth and early twentieth centuries.

Dorothy 'Dorf' Bonarjee (1894–1983) was born in India into a family of Christian Bengali brahmins. In 1914, while a student at the University College of Wales at Aberystwyth, Dorf won the college Eisteddfod, becoming both the first woman and the first non-British person to win the accolade. Much of her poetry was written while in Wales. She married an artist, Paul Surtel, and died in France in 1983.

Alison Brackenbury was born in 1953. Her work has won Eric Gregory and Cholmondeley Awards, and has frequently been broadcast on BBC Radio. *Gallop*, her 2019 Selected Poems, is published by Carcanet. New poems can be read on her website: alisonbrackenbury.co.uk

Kate Bradbury is a garden and nature writer, specialising in wildlife gardening. She has written three wildlife gardening books, along with her memoir, *The Bumblebee Flies Anyway*, which documents the transformation of her tiny paved courtyard into a thriving wildlife oasis.

Charlotte Brontë (1816–1855) was the third child of Patrick and Maria Brontë. Her father was curate of Haworth, Yorkshire. Her mother died when she was five. Charlotte worked as a teacher from 1835 to 1838, then as a governess, and in 1842 accompanied her sister Emily to study languages in Brussels, where she again worked as a teacher. Charlotte's first novel, *The Professor*, was not published until 1857. *Jane Eyre* was published under the pseudonym of Currer Bell in 1847 and achieved immediate success. Charlotte married the Revd A. B Nicholls, her father's curate, in 1854.

Emily Brontë (1818–1848) was the younger sister of Charlotte Brontë and the fifth of six children. Apart from a brief spell as a teacher, Emily spent the most part of her adult life at home, cooking, cleaning and teaching at Sunday school. In 1846 there appeared 'Poems by Currer, Ellis, and Acton Bell', the pseudonyms of Charlotte, Emily, and Anne Brontë. *Wuthering Heights* by Ellis Bell was first published in 1847 and is a classic of English literature. Emily Brontë died from tuberculosis in 1848.

Nancy Campbell is an award-winning writer. Her travels in the Arctic between 2010 and 2017 have resulted in several projects responding to the environment, most recently *The Library of Ice: Readings in a Cold Climate* (S&S), which was longlisted for the Rathbones Folio Prize 2019. Her previous book on the polar environment, *Disko Bay*, was shortlisted for the Forward Prize for Best First Collection in 2016. She has been a Marie Claire 'Wonder Woman', a Hawthornden Fellow and Visual and Performing Artist in Residence at Oxford University.

Keggie Carew won the Costa Biography Award in 2016 for her memoir, *Dadland*. In 2019 she published *Quicksand Tales*. 'The Heron Blood Tulips' is an extract from her forthcoming book on the relationship between humans and the creaturely world, which will be published by Canongate Books in 2022. See www. keggiecarew.com

Natasha Carthew is an award-winning country writer from Cornwall. She has written all her books outside, either in the fields and woodland that surround her home or in the cabin that she built from scrap wood. She has written two books of poetry and four acclaimed novels, *Winter Damage, The Light That Gets Lost* and *Only the Ocean*, which are all published by Bloomsbury, and her latest *All Rivers Run Free*, published by Quercus. Her new prose-poem 'Song for the Forgotten' was published by National Trust Books in 2020.

Margaret Cavendish, née Lucas, Duchess of Newcastle-upon-Tyne (1623–1673), was a philosopher, poet, scientist, fiction-writer, and playwright. Her first book *Poems and Fancies* was published in 1653. After the publication of *Observations upon Experimental Philosophy* (1666) she became the first woman invited to attend meetings at the Royal Society. Her fantastic fiction *The Description of a New World, Called the Blazing World* remains her most famous work.

Nicola Chester lives and writes in the North Wessex Downs. She is a tenant in a farm worker's cottage beneath the highest chalk hill in England. An 'early pioneer' of new women nature writers, she has been a columnist for The RSPB since 2003 and is a *Guardian* Country Diarist. See nicolachester.wordpress.com and @nicolawriting

Frances Cornford, née Frances Crofts Darwin, (1886–1960) was a poet. Her grandfather was Charles Darwin. Her first book of verse, containing the infamous 'To a Fat Lady seen from a Train', was published in 1910. Later volumes include *Spring Morning.*(1915), *Autumn Midnight*(1923), *Different Days* (1928), *Mountains and Molehills* (1934), and *Travelling Home* (1948). Cornford's *Collected Poems* appeared in 1954. She was awarded the Queen's Medal for Poetry in 1959.

Following two collections of short stories, **Linda Cracknell**'s novel, *Call of the Undertow* (2013) was set in coastal Caithness. Her non-fiction book *Doubling Back: Ten Paths Trodden in Memory* (2014) became a BBC Book of the Week. Short stories linked to a Perthshire woollen mill over two centuries are collected in *The Other Side of Stone* (Taproot Press, 2021). See www.lindacracknell.com

Anne Howard, née **Dacre**, Countess of Arundel (1557–1630), was an English poet and religious conspirator. She was devoted to her husband, Philip Howard, and to Roman Catholicism, the latter of which resulted in the life-long imprisonment of the former. Dacre was the mother-in-law of Aletheia Talbot, whose portrait introduces the Natura Exenterata and to which Dacre contributed several recipes, including one purportedly dictated by an angel.

Miriam Darlington is an author and naturalist who has been obsessively tracking wildlife and writing about it since childhood. She writes the Nature Notebook in *The Times* and her latest books are *Otter Country* and *Owl Sense*. She lectures in creative writing at Plymouth University and lives in Devon.

Kerri ní Dochartaigh is from the North West of Ireland but now lives in the middle, in an old railway cottage with her partner and dog. She has written for the *Guardian*, the *Irish Times*, *Winter Papers*, *Caught by the River* and others. She is the author of *Thin Places*. @kerri_ni

George Eliot was the pen name of Mary Ann Evans (1819–1880), an English novelist, poet, journalist, translator and one of the leading writers of the Victorian era. Eliot wrote seven novels, *Adam Bede* (1859), *The Mill on the Floss* (1860), *Silas Marner* (1861), *Romola* (1862–63), *Felix Holt, the Radical* (1866), *Middlemarch* (1871–72) and *Daniel Deronda* (1876).

Christine Evans has published seven collections of poetry, landscape pieces, stories and essays and a personal history of the Welsh island where she lives for half the year,

Bardsey. *Growth Rings* (2006) was shortlisted for Welsh Book of the Year. In 2012 she received a Society of Authors' Cholmondely award.

Margiad Evans, the pseudonym of Peggy Eileen Whistler (1909–1958), who had a lifelong identification with the Welsh border country, is best known for her border writing and *Country Dance* (1932) which features in the 'Library of Wales' series of classics, but she was also an extraordinary short-story writer, novelist, autobiographer and poet. She died aged 49 of a brain tumour, having suffered severe epilepsy for some time. She published four novels and was known for her brilliant descriptions of the natural world.

Sara Evans writes about the world's last wild places and the extraordinary flora and fauna that live in them. Her features have been published around the globe. She is also the author of *When the Last Lion Roars* (Bloomsbury) which details the majestic rise and tragic fall of the king of the beasts.

Celia Fiennes (1662–1741) travelled extensively through England, on horseback, over almost thirty years, when the roads could not have been worse. Sometimes she travelled with family, sometimes in the company of one or two servants. Fiennes kept detailed journals which she worked into a memoir in 1702 and which were finally published for a general readership in 1888. From a family of religious Non-conformists, she was the daughter of Colonel Nathaniel Fiennes and Frances née Whitehead.

Anna Fleming is a Scottish-based writer whose non-fiction work examines landscape, environment and ecology. In 2017 she completed a PhD on Wordsworth, Creativity and Cumbrian Communities with the University of Leeds. Her debut book, *Time on Rock: A Climber's Route into the Mountains*, will be published with Canongate in 2022.

Tiffany Francis-Baker is a nature writer and illustrator from the South Downs, Hampshire. She is the author of six books, including Dark Skies: A Journey into the Wild Night (Bloomsbury, 2019), a nature memoir about our relationship with the landscape after dark. www.tiffanyfrancisbaker.com

Elizabeth Cleghorn Gaskell (1810–1865) spent her formative years in Cheshire, Stratford-upon-Avon and the north of England. In 1832 she married Rev. William Gaskell. The mother of four daughters, Gaskell worked among the poor, travelled frequently and wrote. *Mary Barton* (1848) was her first success. In 1850 she began writing for Dickens's magazine, *Household Words,* to which she contributed for the next thirteen years, notably the industrial novel, *North and South* (1855). In 1850 she befriended Charlotte Brontë, later writing *The Life of Charlotte Brontë* (1857).

Josie George is a writer and visual artist. She spends her quiet days in the West Midlands with her son while her partner lives and works in Denmark. Her brave and lyrical memoir *A Still Life* unravels the depth and truth of her life with a disability. She is now working on a novel and shares artwork, observations and stories at bimblings.co.uk.

Chrissie Gittins's poetry collections are *Armature* (Arc), *I'll Dress One Night As You* (Salt) and *Sharp Hills* (Indigo Dreams). She appeared on BBC Countryfile with her fifth children's collection, *Adder Bluebell, Lobster* (Otter-Barry Books). Chrissie features on the Poetry Archive and is National Poetry Day Ambassador. See www.chrissiegittins.co.uk

Sinéad Gleeson's essay collection *Constellations* won Non-Fiction Book of the Year at 2019 Irish Book Awards and the Dalkey Literary Award, and was shortlisted for the Rathbones Folio Prize and the James Tait Black Memorial Prize. She is the editor of four anthologies of Irish short stories and is working on a novel.

As well as being a writer, **Sally Goldsmith** is an environmental campaigner, most recently in the fight to save Sheffield's threatened street trees. She is currently writing a book about the lure of the English countryside – a sort of Cobbetty rural ride on which she is accompanied by long-gone historical friends – walkers, artists, activists and labourers.

Eluned Gramich is a Welsh–German writer and translator. Her memoir, *Woman Who Brings the Rain*, won the inaugural New Welsh Writing Award and was shortlisted for Wales Book of the Year 2016. She has recently published a novella exploring the 1970s Welsh-language protests, 'The Lion and the Star', in *Wales: Hometown Tales* (Orion Books), and is currently completing a PhD at Aberystwyth and Cardiff University.

Jay Griffiths is the author of *Tristimania: A Diary of Manic Depression, Wild: An Elemental Journey; Pip Pip: A Sideways Look at Time; A Love Letter from a Stray Moon* and *Kith: The Riddle of the Childscape*. She won the Barnes and Noble Discover Award for the best new non-fiction writer in the USA, and the Orion

Book Award. She has also been shortlisted for the Orwell Prize and a World Book Day award.

Melissa Harrison is a novelist, nature writer, children's author and columnist. Her books have won the European Union Prize for Literature, been shortlisted for the Costa Novel of the Year Award and longlisted for the Wainwright Prize for Nature Writing and the Women's Prize for Fiction. She lives in Suffolk.

Hannah Hauxwell (1926–2018) was a Pennine hill farmer. She first came to the public eye when an ITV documentary, *Too Long a Winter* (1972), chronicled the almost unendurable winter conditions in which Hauxwell farmed, alone, without electricity or running water. After transmission 'the old lady in the Yorkshire Dales' received thousands of letters and donations from well-wishers around the world; a local campaign funded the running of electricity to her farm. Today, Hauxwell's unimproved upland hay meadows and grazing pasture are a Site of Special Scientific Interest. Hannah's Meadow Nature Reserve is managed by Durham Wildlife Trust.

Jacquetta Hawkes née Hopkins (1910–1996) is perhaps best known for her book *A Land* (1951). She was a prolific writer who was above all interested in discovering the lives of the peoples that were revealed by scientific excavations. Her works include *The World of the Past* (1963), *Prehistory (History of Mankind: Cultural and Scientific Development, Volume 1 Part 1)* (1963), *The Atlas of Early Man* (1976) and *The Shell Guide to British Archaeology* (1986).

Edith Blackwell Holden (1871–1920) was a British artist and art teacher. She was born in King's Norton, Birmingham. She became famous following the posthumous publication of her *Nature Notes for 1906*, in facsimile form, as the book *The Country Diary of an Edwardian Lady* in 1977, which was an enormous publishing success. These, and her life story, were later the subject of a television dramatisation.

Katie Holten (Dublin, 1975) is an artist. She represented Ireland at the 50th Venice Biennale. At the root of her practice she studies the inextricable relationship between humans and the natural world through excavating hidden histories, ecologies and stories. Interested in exploring possibilities for multispecies storytelling, she made a *Tree Alphabet* and the book *About Trees* (2015). She recently made a new *Irish Tree Alphabet* (2020). See www.katieholten.com and @katieholten

Olga Jacoby (1874–1913) was a German Jewish emigrée and the mother of four adopted children who lived in London. Terminally ill, she wrote a series of letters between 1909–13 published posthumously as *Words in Pain* (1919, 1920 and 2019). When her condition became unbearable Olga Jacoby took her own life, but it is her passion for living which exudes from these letters.

Kathleen Jamie is a multi-award winning poet and essayist who was born in the west of Scotland. Her writing is rooted in Scottish landscape and culture, and ranges through travel, women's issues, archaeology and visual art. She writes in English and occasionally in Scots. Kathleen Jamie's work includes, among others, *The Queen of Sheba* (1995), *The Tree House* (2004), *Findings* (2011), *The Overhaul* (2012), *Sightlines* (2012), *The Bonniest Companie* (2015) and, most recently, *Surfacing* (2019).

Poet, novelist, editor and translator, **Julith Jedamus** was born in Boulder, Colorado and has lived in London for the past twenty years. Her first book of poetry, *The Swerve*, was shortlisted for the Michael Murphy Prize and the Seamus Heaney Centre prize for best first collection.

Julian (or **Juliana**) **of Norwich** (1343–after 1416) was an English anchorite who lived in a cell attached to St. Julian's church in Norwich. She wrote the mystical *Revelations of Divine Love* which is the first book written in English by a woman. The work emerged from obscurity in 1901 when a manuscript in the British Museum was transcribed and published with notes by Grace Warrack. Julian is today considered to be an important Christian mystic and theologian. **Elizabeth Spearing** holds a D.Phil from the University of York. Besides her translation of Julian of Norwich, her publications include an anthology, *Medieval Writings on Female Spirituality*, an edition of *The Life and Death of Mal Cutpurse*, and articles on the *Amadis* cycle and on Aphra Behn.

Jackie Kay is a Scottish poet and novelist, and has been the National Poet of Scotland since 2016. She is the author of a number of works, including *The Adoption Papers*, *Trumpet* and *Red Dust Road*. The recipient of numerous prizes, she was also twice shortlisted for the Scottish Book of the Year Award. She is currently chancellor of the University of Salford, and divides her time between Glasgow and Manchester. @JackieKayPoet

Margery Kempe (*c.* 1373–after 1438) was an English Christian mystic known for writing through dictation *The Book of Margery Kempe* which is often referred to as the first autobiography written in English. It chronicles both the domestic and spiritual aspects of her eventful life, including her extensive pilgrimages to holy sites in Europe and the Holy Land and her mystical conversations with God. She is honoured in the Anglican Communion but, like her contemporary, Julian of Norwich, was never made a Catholic saint.

Louise Kenward is a writer, psychologist and visual artist living on the East Sussex coast. In 2014 Louise spent a year travelling with Victorian collector Annie Brassey, in a bid to reconnect with the world after a long period of illness. Louise is currently writing her first book based on this journey and a subsequent artist residency at Bexhill Museum, where Annie's collections now reside. Ongoing research interests engage with the interaction of objects, place and person, past and present. Louise has an MA in Fine Art from London Metropolitan University (2011) and an MSc in Criminological Psychology from Birmingham University (1997). She is usually by the sea. See @LouiseKenward and www.louisekenward.com

Linda Lear is an American environmental historian and biographer. A native of Pittsburgh, she received her A.B. from Connecticut College, her A.M. from Columbia University and her Ph.D. from the George Washington University. In addition to a life-long career in academia Lear is the author of *Rachel Carson: Witness for Nature* (1997) which won the Margaret W. Rossiter History of Women in Science Prize from the History of Science Society and *Beatrix Potter: A Life in Nature* (2007) which won the Lakeland Book of the Year, the Bookends Prize for biography, and the Delta Kappa Gamma literary prize.

Jessica J. Lee is the author of two books of nature writing, *Turning* and *Two Trees Make a Forest*, and winner of the 2020 Hilary Weston Writers' Trust Prize for Non-fiction. She is the founding editor of *The Willowherb Review* and a researcher at the University of Cambridge.

Rachel Lichtenstein is an author, artist, academic, co-director of Centre for Place Writing at Manchester Metropolitan University. Publications include *Estuary: Out from London to the Sea* (Penguin 2016), *Diamond Street: The Hidden World of Hatton Garden* (Penguin, 2012), *On Brick Lane* (Penguin, 2008) and *Rodinsky's Room* (1999, co-authored with Iain Sinclair).

Ann Lingard, novelist and writer of non-fiction, is a former scientist and lives on a small-holding in NW Cumbria within sight of the Solway Firth. Her latest (non-fiction) book is *The Fresh and the Salt: The Story of the Solway* (Birlinn, 2020). See www.thefreshandthesalt.co.uk and www.eliotandentropy.wordpress.com

Amy Liptrot grew up on a sheep farm in the Orkney islands, Scotland. Her bestselling memoir, *The Outrun* won the Wainwright Prize for nature writing and the PEN Ackerely Prize for memoir. She lives in West Yorkshire.

Karen Lloyd is the author of *The Gathering Tide: A Journey Around the Edge of Morecambe Bay* and *The Blackbird Diaries* both published by Saraband. Her new book *Abundance: Journeys into Restoration in the Natural World* is published by Bloomsbury in September 2021.

Jane Lovell is an award-winning poet whose work focuses on our relationship with the planet and its wildlife. She is Writer-in-Residence at Rye Harbour Nature Reserve. Her latest collection is the prize-winning 'God of Lost Ways' (Indigo Dreams Press). Jane also writes for *Dark Mountain, Photographers Against Wildlife Crime* and *Elementum Journal*. See janelovellpoetry.co.uk

Helen Macdonald is a writer, poet, illustrator, historian and affiliate at the Department of History and Philosophy of Science at the University of Cambridge. Her books include the poetry volume *Shaler's Fish* (2001) and the bestselling *H is for Hawk* (2014).

Sara Maitland is the author of numerous works of fiction, including the Somerset Maugham Award-winning *Daughters of Jerusalem*, and several non-fiction books about religion. Born in 1950, she studied at Oxford University and currently tutors on the MA in creative writing for Lancaster University. She lives in Galloway.

Mary Malyon is the eldest child of a third-generation Hampshire farming family, and home is still the North Wessex Downs. She's the Content Editor for Ordnance Survey's new Secret Stories app, and is also writing a book about endemic gender discrimination in Britain's agriculture and land-owning communities. Her writing was longlisted for Canongate Books' 2019 Nan Shepherd Prize for Nature Writing and Penguin UK's 2020 WriteNow programme. She's also published in the *Guardian, Wanderlust, The Big Issue* and more. See marymalyon.com @MaryMalyon

Pippa Marland is an author and academic based at the University of Bristol. Her research focuses on the nature writing genre, especially the representation of small islands and farming communities. Her creative writing has appeared in *Earthlines* and *The Clearing*, and her monograph *Ecocriticism and the Island: Readings from the British-Irish Archipelago* is published by Rowman and Littlefield. She is the co-editor, with Anita Roy, of *Gifts of Gravity and Light: A Nature Almanac for the 21st Century* for Hodder and Stoughton.

In 2017 **Bláthnaid McAnulty**, then aged seven, posted on her brother Dara's *30 Days Wild* blog for his website Naturalist Dara, 'a wee story about why I love climbing trees' called 'Climb trees to another world'. Bláthnaid lives in County Fermanagh, Ireland, with her mum, dad, and two brothers.

Zakiya Mckenzie is a writer based in Bristol where she is a PhD candidate with the Caribbean Literary Heritage project at the University of Exeter writing about the Black alternative press in post-World War Britain. In 2019, Zakiya was writer-in-residence for Forestry England. She works with the Black and Green Project at Ujima 98 FM Bristol.

Jean McNeil is the author of fourteen books. In 2016 she won the Banff Mountain Film and Book Festival's Grand Prize for her memoir Ice Diaries, based on a year spent as writer in residence with the British Antarctic Survey, and which was named by the *Guardian* as one of the best nature books of 2018. She lives in London and is Professor of Creative Writing at the University of East Anglia.

Charlotte Mew (1869–1928) lived in Bloomsbury all her life. Although much praised by her contemporaries for her short stories and poetry, increasing family and financial difficulties stifled her literary output and she eventually committed suicide. Her collections included *The Farmer's Bride* (1915) and *The Rambling Sailor* (1929). Unrivalled in her stark representation of human isolation, she has been described as 'an English Emily Dickenson'.

Alice Christiana Gertrude Meynell née Thompson (1847–1922) was a writer, editor, critic and suffragist. Born in London, her first poetry collection was published in 1875 and was praised by Ruskin. She converted to Catholicism and later married the Catholic newspaper publisher and editor Wilfred Meynell. Together they became the proprietors and editors of such magazines as *The Pen*, the *Weekly Register,* and *Merry England*. Meynell co-founded the Catholic Women's Suffrage Society and was twice considered for Poet Laureate, although the first woman to occupy that post would be Carol Ann Duffy in 2009.

Emma Mitchell is a designer-maker, naturalist, illustrator, and the author of *The Wild Remedy* (2019) and *Making Winter* (2017). She is a *Guardian* Country Diarist, has contributed creative projects to BBC *Countryfile Magazine, Country Living* and others. She lives on the edge of the Fens with her family and records her daily nature finds on Instagram @silverpebble2 and Twitter @silverpebble

Jan Morris (1926–2020) was born of a Welsh father and an English mother. She lived with her partner Elizabeth Morris in the top left-hand corner of Wales, between the mountains and the sea. Soldier, journalist, historian, author of forty books, including *Coronation Everest, Venice,* the Pax Britannica trilogy and *Conundrum,* Jan Morris led an extraordinary life, witnessing such seminal moments as the first ascent of Everest, the Suez Canal Crisis, the Eichmann Trial, and the Cuban Revolution. In 2018 she was recognised for her outstanding contribution to travel writing by the Edward Stanford Travel Writing Awards. Her final book, *Allegorizings*, was published posthumously, as was her wish.

Helen Mort is a poet and novelist. She is a five-times winner of the Foyle Young Poets award. Her books include Division Street (shortlisted for the Costa Book Awards and the T.S. Eliot Prize), *No Map Could Show Them* and *Black Car Burning*. In June 2018 she was elected Fellow of the Royal Society of Literature. She lectures in creative writing at Manchester Metropolitan University.

Elizabeth Rose Murray writes for children, young adults, and adults. Her books include the award-winning Nine Lives Trilogy and Caramel Hearts. Recent anthology/journal publications include The Elysian: Creative Responses, Reading the Future, Autonomy, Popshots, Banshee, Terrain, Not Very Quiet, Channel, South Circular, and Ropes. She lives in West Cork, Ireland. See www.ermurray.com

Stephanie Norgate's three poetry collections from Bloodaxe Books are *Hidden River* (2008, shortlisted for the Forward and Jerwood Aldeburgh first collection awards), *The Blue Den* (2012) and *The Conversation* (forthcoming in 2021). Her plays have been broadcast on BBC Radio 4. She often runs site-specific poetry workshops.

Annie O'Garra Worsley is a Professor of Environmental Change, crofter and writer who left full-time academia to live in the NW Highlands of Scotland. Her essays have been published by Elliott & Thompson, in *Elementum Journal,* and Harper Collins will publish her first book. Annie's blog can be found at https://redrivercroft.com/

Irenosen Okojie Irenosen Okojie is a Nigerian British writer. Her debut novel *Butterfly Fish* won a Betty Trask award and was shortlisted for an Edinburgh International First Book Award. Her work has been featured in *The New York Times*, the *Observer*, the *Guardian*, the BBC and the *Huffington Post* amongst other publications. Her short story collection *Speak Gigantular*, published by Jacaranda Books, was shortlisted for the Edgehill Short Story Prize, the Jhalak Prize, the Saboteur Awards and nominated for a Shirley Jackson Award. She was recently inducted as a fellow of the Royal Society of Literature as one of the Forty Under Forty initiative.

Deborah Orr was an award-winning journalist, whose work regularly appeared in the *Guardian*, the *Independent*, *The Sunday Times* and in many magazines including *Vogue*, *Grazia* and *Marie Claire*. She was a contributing editor to *Another Magazine* and was the first female editor of the Guardian's *Weekend Magazine* at the age of thirty. Deborah was a co-creator of 'Enquirer', a play commissioned by the National Theatre of Scotland, performed in London, Glasgow and Belfast, broadcast by Radio 4 and shortlisted for new play of the year in the Critics' Awards for Theatre in Scotland.

Alice Oswald lives in Devon and is married with three children. Her collections include *Dart*, which won the 2002 T.S. Eliot Prize, *Woods etc.* (Geoffrey Faber Memorial Prize), *A Sleepwalk on the Severn* (Hawthornden Prize), *Weeds and Wildflowers* (Ted Hughes Award), *Memorial* (Warwick Prize for Writing), and *Falling Awake*, which won the 2016 Costa Poetry Award and the Griffin Prize for Poetry. She was elected as the Oxford University Professor of Poetry in 2019.

Ruth Padel's twelve poetry collections include *Darwin, A Life in Poems*, on her great-great-grandfather Charles Darwin, nature and *Emerald*, exploring the green of nature and renewal. She is Professor of Poetry at King's College London, Fellow of both the Royal Society of Literature and Zoological Society of London. See www.ruthpadel.com.

Thomasine Pendarves née Newcomen (1618– after 1671) was born in Dartmouth, Devon, into a pious and wealthy family. She married John Pendarves, vicar of St Helen's in Abingdon, afterwards minister of a Baptist congregation. Although nominally a Baptist herself, Thomasine defended the political prophetess Elizabeth Poole and corresponded with the English Ranter, Abiezer Coppe. Her letters, which can be read either as profoundly spiritual or deeply erotic, and which embrace the natural world, were published by Coppe and attributed to 'T.P.'

Katherine Philips née Fowler (1631/2–1664), nom-de-plume Orinda, was an Anglo-Welsh royalist poet, translator, and woman of letters described by her contemporaries as both 'the Matchless Orinda' and 'the Incomparable'. She is best known today for her poems on friendship between women. She achieved renown as a translator of Pierre Corneille's Pompée and Horace, and for the posthumous editions of her work. She was highly regarded by many writers including Dryden and Keats.

Dorothy Pilley Richards (1894–1986) was a pioneering journalist, writer, & mountaineer. A co-founder of The Pinnacle Club – the world's first women's mountaineering club – Pilley climbed extensively in Europe, China & North America. In 1928, she made the celebrated first ascent of the north arête of The Dent Blanche, Switzerland, with Joseph & Antoine Georges and her husband, I. A. Richards – a feat brilliantly described in her marvellous memoir, Climbing Days (Bell, 1935). A biography written by Pilley's great-great-nephew, Dan Richards, was published by Faber in 2016.

Sylvia Plath (1932–1963) was one of the most dynamic and admired poets of the twentieth century. In the years following her suicide at the age of thirty Plath's work attracted the attention of a multitude of readers, who saw in her singular verse an attempt to catalogue despair, violent emotion, and obsession with death. Intensely autobiographical, Plath's poems explore her own mental anguish, her troubled marriage to fellow poet Ted Hughes, her unresolved conflicts with her parents, and her own vision of herself.

Poet and historian **Katrina Porteous** lives on the Northumberland coast and writes from a deep commitment to the ecology of place and local community. Her collections from Bloodaxe Books include *The Lost Music* (1996) and *Two Countries* (2014), and poems written for a planetarium, *Edge* (2019). See www.katrinaporteous.co.uk

Heather Ramskill is an Artist & Printmaker specialising in linoprint where she pushes the linocut process to its limits with delicate cutwork. She is influenced by the countryside around her North Yorkshire home. She works alongside her husband, Gary in their studio, where they are known as 'Little Ram Studio'. @littleRamstudio

Jini Reddy is an author and journalist. Her book *Wanderland* (2020) was shortlisted for the Wainwright Prize. Previously, she contributed to the anthology, *Winter* (2016)

and her first book *Wild Times* also came out in 2016. She has written widely for national newspapers and magazines and has been a National Geographic Woman of Impact.

Rachel Rooney's first poetry collection *The Language of Cat* won the CLPE Poetry Award and was long-listed for the Carnegie Medal. Her other collections, *My Life as a Goldfish* and *A Kid in My Class*, have both been shortlisted for the CLiPPA. She performs at festivals and for The Children's Bookshow. In 2017 she was the Chair of Judges for the CLiPPA and has judged the Betjeman Poetry Prize.

Devon-born **Lynne Roper** (1961–2016) began swimming outdoors at fifty while recovering from mastectomy. As a spokesperson for The Outdoor Swimming Society, she inspired a generation to 'read water' and take educated risks. For five years – until bedbound by a brain tumour – Lynne recorded adventures in over sixty breathtaking locations. In her last month, she met just once with fellow West Country writer Tanya Shadrick, who promised to publish the diaries as *Wild Woman Swimming*. The book was longlisted for the 2019 Wainwright Prize.

Christina Rossetti (1830–1894) was born in London to Italian parents. Her father was the poet Gabriele Rossetti; her brother the poet and Pre-Raphaelite painter Dante Gabriel Rossetti. Rossetti's first poems were written in 1842 and printed in the family press. She is best known for her ballads and mystical religious lyrics. *Goblin Market and Other Poems* (1862) established Rossetti as a significant Victorian voice. *The Prince's Progress and Other Poems* (1866) was followed by *Sing-Song* (1872), a collection of verse for children. She continued to write poetry and works of religious prose until her death in 1894.

Vita Sackville-West (1892–1962) was a novelist, a biographer, an historian, a travel writer and a journalist. But it is as a poet, for the world-famous garden that she made at Sissinghurst in Kent and for the deep friendship she formed with Virginia Woolf that she is remembered and celebrated.

Polly Samson's first novel, *Out of the Picture*, was shortlisted for the Authors' Club Award, and many of her stories, including those from her first collection, *Lying in Bed*, have been read on BBC Radio 4. A second collection, *Perfect Lives*, was a BBC Book at Bedtime. Samson has written an introduction for a collection of Daphne du Maurier's earliest stories and has been a judge for the Costa Book Awards. Her novel *The Kindness* was named Book of the Year by *The Times* and the *Observer*. She is currently writing the introductions to new editions of Charmian Clift's *Peel Me a Lotus* and *Mermaid Singing*. Samson has written lyrics for four number-one albums and is a Fellow of the Royal Society of Literature.

Anita Sethi is an award-winning writer and journalist who has written for national newspapers and magazines including the *Guardian* and *Observer, Sunday Times, BBC Wildlife, New Statesman, Granta*, and *Times Literary Supplement*. Her first book, *I Belong Here: A Journey Along the Backbone of Britain* is published by Bloomsbury, the first in her nature writing trilogy to be followed by *Nocturne* (June 2022) and *Forces* (April 2024).

Tanya Shadrick (born 1973) began her creative life after forty with *The Wild Patience Scrolls*: a mile of writing beside England's oldest outdoor pool. *Birds of Firle* is her latest durational work: a single, wordless book of twenty-one rook images. First released into the wild on New Year's Day 2020, it will continue going out and back until the end of the decade, gathering mixed-media responses on 'grief and hope as the things with feathers'.

Hilary Shepherd has lived in Wales since 1979, running an organic farm for twenty years and then as a woodworker making stairs and windows in oak. She is the author of three novels published by Honno: *Albi, In A Foreign Country* and *Animated Baggage*.

Nan (Anna) Shepherd (1893–1981). Closely attached to Aberdeen and her native Deeside, she graduated from her home university in 1915 and for the next forty-one years worked as a lecturer in English. An enthusiastic gardener and hill-walker, she made many visits to the Cairngorms with students and friends. She also travelled further afield – to Norway, France, Italy, Greece and South Africa – but always returned to the house where she was raised and where she lived almost all of her adult life, in the village of West Cults. To honour her legacy, in 2016, Nan Shepherd's image was added to the Royal Bank of Scotland five-pound note.

Mary Sidney, later Mary Herbert, Countess of Pembroke (1561–1621) was, in 1600, listed alongside her brother Philip Sidney, Edmund Spenser and William Shakespeare as one of the notable writers of the day (Bodenham, J., *Belvidere*). Her play *Antonius* revived interest in soliloquy based on classical models and is a probable source of both Samuel Daniel's *Cleopatra* (1594) and Shakespeare's *Antony and Cleopatra* (1607). She was also known for translating Petrarch's 'Triumph of Death', but especially for her lyrical translation of the Psalms.

Daniela F. Sieff is an author and scholar. She is fuelled by a desire to understand what shapes us as human beings. Daniela has a doctorate in anthropology from Oxford University. She is currently exploring emotional trauma and its healing and is author of *Understanding and Healing Emotional Trauma* (2015). Daniela is working on new books. See www.danielasieff.com

Ali Smith is a Scottish author, playwright, academic and journalist. *Hotel World* was shortlisted for the Booker Prize and the Orange Prize. *The Accidental* was shortlisted for the Man Booker Prize and the Orange Prize. *How to be both* won the Bailey's Prize, the Goldsmiths Prize and the Costa Novel of the Year Award, and was shortlisted for the Man Booker Prize. *Autumn* was shortlisted for the Man Booker Prize 2017 and *Winter* was shortlisted for the Orwell Prize 2018.

Charlotte Smith, née Turner, (1749–1806) was an English novelist and poet. Her celebration of the 'ordinary pleasures' of the English countryside has drawn comparison with William Cowper and her work was highly praised by Sir Walter Scott. Her radical attitudes to conventional morality and her ideas regarding class equality gained her notoriety. She moved to France and in 1787 left her husband, and his debts, and began writing to support their twelve children; the romantic novel provided her most lucrative source of income.

Florence Margaret Smith, known as **Stevie Smith** (1902–1971), was an English poet and novelist. Born in Hull, she lived much of her life in London. Her poetry appears in countless anthologies. She was awarded the Cholmondeley Award for Poets and won the Queen's Gold Medal for poetry. A play, *Stevie* by Hugh Whitemore (1977), based on her life, was the following year adapted into a film starring Glenda Jackson.

Jean Sprackland's latest book is *These Silent Mansions: A Life in Graveyards* (Cape, 2020). She was the winner of the Costa Poetry Award in 2008, and the Portico Prize for Non-Fiction in 2012. Jean is Professor of Creative Writing at Manchester Metropolitan University.

Jo Sweeting is a sculptor, letter-carver and printmaker. Travelling out from her home in Brighton she walks the Downs chalk paths. Noticing and collecting 'foundles' (anything found on a Sussex hillside, a word from Sussex dialect). These objects then inform carvings and woodcut works. They are collected in Wunderkammer (cabinets of curiosities) for future study See www.josweetingsculpture.com

Aletheia Talbot, Baroness Talbot, later Aletheia Howard, Countess of Arundel (1590–1654). *Natura Exenterata* (1655), which features Talbot's portrait on the frontispiece, is a collection of 1,720 recipes 'for the cure of all sorts of infirmities, whether internal or external, acute or chronical, that are incident to the body of man. Collected and preserved by several persons of quality and great experience in the art of medicine, whose names are prefixed to the book'.

Sarah Thomas was apprenticed to writing through six years spent living and loving in the Arctic. The resulting work was longlisted for the Nan Shepherd Prize. She has a PhD in creative writing from the University of Glasgow and is published in the *Guardian* and *Dark Mountain* among others. Currently found tramping the intertidal zone where Scotland and England mingle. See sarahthomas.net and @journeysinbtwn

Jessica Traynor is a poet, librettist and creative writing teacher. Her debut collection, *Liffey Swim*, was shortlisted for the Strong/Shine Award. Her second, *The Quick*, was a 2019 Irish Times poetry choice. Awards include Hennessy New Writer of the Year, the Ireland Chair of Poetry Bursary and the Listowel Poetry Prize.

Trileigh Tucker lives near the Salish Sea in West Seattle, Washington, USA, on unceded ancestral land of the Duwamish people. After a career teaching college environmental studies, she is now a writer, natural historian, artist, and nature photographer. She is currently working on a book about birds and environmental change.

Evelyn Underhill (1875–1941) was an Anglo-Catholic mystic, writer, teacher and pacifist known for her many works on religion and spiritual practice, including *Mysticism* (1911) although she also wrote novels and poetry. Underhill read history and botany at Kings College, London where she was made a fellow. She received an honorary Doctorate of Divinity from Aberdeen University, and was both the first woman to lecture in theology at an Oxford college and the first woman to lecture Anglican clergy.

Dorothy Wellesley, née Ashton, Duchess of Wellington (1889–1956) was a poet, water colourist and passionate gardener. She published sixteen collections of poetry including *Early Poems* (1913) and *Early Light* (1955) and was the editor and patron of the first series of Hogarth Living Poets, 1928–32. Wellesley was an intimate friend of

Vita Sackville-West, who dedicated *The Land* to her. W. B. Yeats hailed Wellesley as one of the best poets of her generation.

Phillis Wheatley Peters (1753–1784) was born in West Africa and enslaved and transported to Boston as a young child. She was enslaved by the Wheatley family where she learned to read and write, and to translate Latin and Greek. In 1773 Phillis Wheatley travelled with Nathaniel Wheatley to London in search of a publisher. *Poems on Various Subjects, Religious and Moral* (1773) brought her fame on both sides of the Atlantic. She was emancipated by the Wheatley family that same year. Following the Wheatleys' deaths Phillis married grocer John Peters. She died in poverty, aged thirty-one. Wheatley was the first published African American poet.

Isabella Whitney (born between 1546 and 1548, and died after 1624), grew up in Cheshire, and lived and worked in London. Whitney described herself as 'whole in body, and in mind,/ but very weak in purse' and is credited with being the first professional woman writer in England, observing: '…till some household cares me tie,/ My books and pen I will apply.' Arguably the first Englishwoman to have written and published secular poetry under her own name, *A Sweet Nosegay or Pleasant Posy, Containing a Hundred and Ten Philosophical Flowers* was published in 1573.

Nic Wilson is a writer and mum to two budding naturalists. She is a Guardian country diarist and writes for magazines including *Gardeners' World* and *BBC Wildlife*. Nic enjoys literary research and contributes to the *John Clare Society Journal*. She is currently writing a book about the nearby wild.

Virginia Woolf, née Stephens (1882–1941) is regarded as one of the most important modernist writers of the twentieth century, in particular for her use of stream of consciousness within the narrative voice. Woolf was educated at King's College, London. Following the death of her father the family moved to Bloomsbury where they established the Bloomsbury Group. Virginia married Leonard Woolf, who published all of her books through their imprint, the Hogarth Press. Woolf committed suicide in 1941.

Dorothy Mae Ann Wordsworth (1771–1855) was an English author, poet, and diarist. She was the sister of the Romantic poet William Wordsworth, and the two were close all their adult lives. Although unpublished during her lifetime, Wordsworth left behind numerous letters, diary entries, topographical descriptions, poems, and other writings. *Recollections of a Tour Made in Scotland* was published posthumously in 1874 and her *Grasmere Journal* in 1897 which reveal the influence of her writing on that of her brother.

ACKNOWLEDGEMENTS

Women on Nature has been made possible by the 842 people whose names are listed in this volume and who have supported the project from a time when it was simply an idea. My deep gratitude goes to the 119 extraordinary women, their literary estates and publishers, whose words and images comprise the collection. Many others have contributed significantly to enabling this book to become a reality: sincere thanks to Anna Simpson, my excellent editor at Unbound; to John Mitchinson, Mathew Clayton and Simon Spanton for commissioning the book, and for their support throughout; to Holly Ovenden, our brilliant cover designer, and art director, Mark Ecob; to David Atkinson, Catherine Best, Debbie Elliott, Catherine Emery, Lauren Fulbright, Becca Harper-Day, Caitlin Harvey, Julian Mash, Kate Quarry and Cassie Waters. To Todd Borlik, my PhD supervisor, for his guidance and forbearance. To Caradoc King and Millie Hoskins at United Agents for their care and commitment. To the British Library. To my dear family: Jean, John, Maria, Anna, Connor and Lauren Norbury, for being there. Finally, thank you to my husband Rupert Thomson and my daughter Eva Rae Thomson for their encouragement, their humour and their love.

COPYRIGHT ACKNOWLEDGEMENTS

Extract from *Writing Wild* by Kathryn Aalto © Kathryn Aalto, 2020, and reproduced by kind permission of the author.

Extract from *'Cherry' Ingram: The Englishman who saved Japan's Blossoms* by Naoko Abe © Naoko Abe, 2019, and reproduced by kind permission of Penguin Random House.

Extract from *Cryer's Hill* by Kitty Aldridge © Kitty Aldridge, 2007, and reproduced by kind permission of the author.

Extract from *In the Kitchen* by Monica Ali © Monica Ali, 2009, and reproduced by kind permission of the author.

The poem 'Fell' by Polly Atkin © Polly Atkin, 2021, and reproduced by kind permission of the author.

'The Daisy Fairy' by Cicely M. Barker © Cicely M. Barker, 1923, and reproduced by kind permission of Penguin Random House.

Extract from *The Flow* by Amy-Jane Beer © Amy-Jane Beer, 2001, and reproduced by kind permission of the author.

'All Soul's Day' by Frances Bellerby © Frances Bellerby, 1970, and reproduced by kind permission of the author's estate.

Extract from *Pond* by Claire-Louise Bennett © Claire-Louise Bennett, 2015, and reproduced by kind permission of the author's agent.

The poem 'Peregrina' by Sharon Blackie © Sharon Blackie, 2019, and reproduced by kind permission of the author.

Extract from *The Mountain of Adventure* by Enid Blyton © Enid Blyton, 1949, and reproduced by permission of Hodder Children's Books, an imprint of Hachette Children's Books, Carmelite House, 50 Victoria Embankment, London imprint, EC4Y 0DZ.

COPYRIGHT ACKNOWLEDGEMENTS

Extract from *Under the Opium Spell* by Sara Evans © Sara Evans, 2020, and reproduced by kind permission of the author.

Extract from *Dances with Hares* by Anna Fleming © Anna Fleming, 2018, first appeared on Caught by the River and reproduced by kind permission of the author.

'Gone to Earth' by Tiffany Francis-Baker © Tiffany Francis-Baker, 2021, and reproduced by kind permission of the author.

'Forest' by Josie George © Josie George, 2021, and reproduced by kind permission of the author and agent.

The poem 'Otter' by Chrissie Gittins © Chrissie Gittins, 2016, in *Adder, Bluebell, Lobster* (first published under the original title 'River Torridge' in 2006 in *I Don't Want An Avocado For An Uncle*) and reproduced by kind permission of the author.

'Islanded' by Sinéad Gleeson © Sinéad Gleeson, 2021, published by kind permission of the author.

'Caravan' by Sally Goldsmith © Sally Goldsmith, 2021, and published by kind permission of the author.

'The Flowers of Wales' by Eluned Gramich © Eluned Gramich, 2021, and published by kind permission of the author.

Extract from *Wild: An Elemental Journey* by Jay Griffiths © Jay Griffiths, 2006, and reproduced by kind permission of David Higham Associates.

Extract from *All Among the Barley* by Melissa Harrison © Melissa Harrison, 2019, and reproduced by kind permission of the author.

Extract from *A Land* by Jacquetta Hawkes © Jacquetta Hawkes, 1951, and reproduced by kind permission of the author's estate.

'Tree Alphabet' by Katie Holten © Katie Holten, 2020, and reproduced by kind permission of the author.

The poem 'Migratory III' by Kathleen Jamie © Kathleen Jamie, 2015, first published in *The Bonniest Companie* (2015), and reproduced by kind permission of the author.

COPYRIGHT ACKNOWLEDGEMENTS

Extract from *The School Run Instagram Project* by Mary Malyon © Mary Malyon, 2018, and published by kind permission of the author.

'Enlli: The Living Island' by Pippa Marland © Pippa Marland, 2021, and reproduced by kind permission of the author.

'Climb trees to another world' by Blathnaid McAnulty © Blathnaid McAnulty, 2017, and published by kind permission of the author.

'Memories Live in the Forest' by Zakiya Mckenzie © Zakiya Mckenzie, 2019, and publisged by kind permission of the author.

'Arboreal' by Jean McNeil © Jean McNeil, 2021, and reproduced by kind permission of the author.

'The Muntjac' by Emma Mitchell © Emma Mitchell, 2019, and reproduced by kind permission of the author.

Extract from *Wales: Epic Views of a Small Country* by Jan Morris © Jan Morris, 1986, and reproduced by kind permission of the Estate of Jan Morris.

The poem 'Barn Owl' by Helen Mort © Helen Mort, 2021, and reproduced by kind permission of the author.

'An Affinity with Bees' by Elizabeth Rose Murray © Elizabeth Rose Murray, 2021, and published by kind permission of the author.

The poem 'Jackdaws' by Stephanie Norgate © Stephanie Norgate, 2008, and reproduced by kind permission of Bloodaxe Books.

'An ancient royal fernery, August 2019' by Annie O'Garra Worsley © Annie O'Garra Worsley, 2021, and reproduced by kind permission of the author.

Extract from *Nudibranch* by Irenosen Okojie © Irenosen Okojie, 2020, and reproduced by kind permission of the publishser.

Extract from *Motherwell* by Deborah Orr © Deborah Orr, 2020, and reproduced by kind permission of Weidenfeld & Nicolson.

COPYRIGHT ACKNOWLEDGEMENTS

'Perseophone's Tor' by Daniela Sieff © Daniela Sieff, 2021, and published by kind permission of the author.

Extract from *Winter* by Ali Smith © Ali Smith, 2017, and reproduced by kind permission of Penguin Random House.

The poem 'Alone in the Woods' by Stevie Smith © Stevie Smith, 1930, and reproduced by kind permission of Faber & Faber.

The poem 'The Birkdale Nightingale' by Jean Sprackland © Jean Sprackland, 2007, and reproduced by kind permission of the author.

'An Island Ecology' by Sarah Thomas © Sarah Thomas, 2016, first appeared in *Drift Fish*, and reproduced by kind permission of the author.

The poem 'Apple Seed' by Jessica Traynor © Jessica Traynor, 2020, and reproduced by kind permission of the author, in 'Tree Alphabet' © Katie Holten, 2020.

'Arthur's Magic Birds: Once in Shadow, Future Bright' by Trileigh Tucker © Trileigh Tucker, 2021, and published by kind permission of the author.

'The Forest After Snowstorm', 'Moths' and 'Birds' by Dorothy Wellesley © Dorothy Wellesley, 1930, 1925, first published in *Deserted House* (1930) and *Lost Lane* (1925), later collected in Early Light (1955), and reproduced by kind permission of the Estate of Dorothy Wellesley.

'Snickets' by Nic Wilson © Nic Wilson, 2019, first published on the *Land Lines Project* and reproduced by kind permission of the author.

INDEX

unbound

Unbound is the world's first crowdfunding publisher, established in 2011.

We believe that wonderful things can happen when you clear a path for people who share a passion. That's why we've built a platform that brings together readers and authors to crowdfund books they believe in – and give fresh ideas that don't fit the traditional mould the chance they deserve.

This book is in your hands because readers made it possible. Everyone who pledged their support is listed below. Join them by visiting unbound.com and supporting a book today.

Kathryn Aalto

Clara Abrahams

Karissa Adams

Sonya Adams

Kitty Aldridge

Sheila Algeo

Julie Allan

Kim Allen

Lisa Allen

Louise Allen-Jones

Ines Anchondo

Michelle Anderson

Abi Andrews

Rachel Andrews

Louise Ankers

David Antrobus

C Appleby

Diane Archer-Henley

Alba Arikha

Jay Armstrong

John Ash

George Ashe

Kate Ashley

Alison Atkin

Will Atkins

Rachel Atkinson

Oliver Atwell

David Bailey

Jennie Bailey

Tamora Baird

Harriet Baker

Anna Barker

Caroline Barlow	Maggie Bissmire
Phil Barnard	Susan Bittker
Debbie Barnes	Sharon Blackie
Nick Barnes	Maud Blair
Sara Barratt	Cathy Blake
Bryan Barraza	Marga Blankestijn
Simon Barrett	Kate Blincoe
Sally Basile	Margaret Bluman
Jackie Bates	Amy Bogard
Luke Batts	Sheela Bonarjee
Ginny Battson	Clare Bonetree
Juliet Bawden	James Bonner
Emma Bayliss	Jeannie Borsch
Norfolk Bea	David Borthwick
Catherine Beard	Justine Bothwick
Jane Beaton	Helen Bown
Samuel Becker	Kate Bradbury
Louise Beckett	Helen Bralesford
Amy-Jane Beer	Vee Brannovic
Dawn Behan	Kelly Brenner
Bryony Benge-Abbott	Katie Bridger
Maria Benjamin	Easkey Britton
Melanie Benn	Maggie M. Broadley
Richard Benson	Sophie Bromley
John G Bernasconi	Alison Brown
Robert Berry	Caroline Brown
Karen Beynon	Martin Brown
Iain Biggs	Laura Buckley
Litsa Biggs	Yvonne Budden
Heather Binney	Holly Budge
Heather Binsch	Andrea Burden

Trudie Burge

Sarah Burgess

Lesley Burton

Alison Butcher

Tanya Butchers

Anna Caig

Fiona Caley

Louise Calf

Jacqueline Calladine

Dominique Cameron

Catriona Campbell

Nancy Campbell

Valerie Campbell

Caitriona Carlin

Gemma Carlin

Lorena Carrington

Sean Carroll

Cynthia Carson

Jane Carter

Richard Carter

Natasha Carthew

Catherine Casey

Alex Catherwood

Caught by the River

Zelda Chappel

Catherine Chapple Gill

Thalia Charles

Yung En Chee

Paul Cheney

Nicola Chester

Annie Cholewa

Tine Stausholm Christiansen

Beth Christie

Ian Christie

Helen Clancy

Becky Clark

Carolyn Clark

Caro Clarke

Jane Clarke

Daire Cleary

Lara Clements

Karina Clifford

Mel Coath

Gina Collia

Rachel Colson

Joanna Comino

Jennie Condell

Helen Conford

Alina Congreve

Wendy Constance

Patricia Coombe

Fiona Coombs

David Cooper

Fiona Cooper

Julie Cooper

Cassandra Cope

Ellie Cornell

Amanda Corp

Sally Cosstick

Glenda Cotter

Joy Coulbeck

Rob Cowen

Robert Cox

Tom Cox

Clare Coyne

CR

Susan Crawford

Vybarr Cregan-Reid

Anna Crilly

Elizabeth Cross

Jo Cross

Stephanie Cross

Julia Croyden

Lucy and Hattie Croyden

Curious Wild

Maryam D'Abo

Amanda Dackombe

Sue Dancey

Rosie Dastgir

Marita Davidson

Cathy Davies

Claire Davies

Harriet Fear Davies

Helena Davies

Nicola Davies

Jess Davies Porter

Ruth Dawkins

Jenny Day

Leslie de Bont

Rachael de Moravia

Anouk de Regt

Sarah Deakin

Claire Dean

Ayala Deasey

Jo deBank

Sarah Deco

Megan Delahunty-Light

Andy Delmege

Phoebe Demeger

Eleanor Dickenson

Rachel Dickenson

Jo Dickinson

Miranda Dickinson

Robert Dickinson

Valia Dikova

James Disley

Katherine Dixson

Jenna Dobson

Joanna Dobson

Melanie Doherty

Maura Dooley

Janeen Dorling

Inge Dornan

Linda Doughty

Amelia Dowler

Mary Doyle and David Austen

Mandy Drake

Jonathan Dransfield

Katy Driver

B A Benjamin du Bernard

Christine Duff

Natalie Duffy

Kate Dyer

Thom Eagle

Lakin Easterling

Jane Eastgate

Kathryn Eastman

Kim Eddy

Mel Ede

Jennifer Edgecombe

Juliet Edwards

Marti Eller

Cherie Ellis

Steffan Ellis

Helen M Elster Jones

Elisabeth England

Lucy Erickson

Anna Erkinheimo

Ilana Estreich

Cath Evans

Ieuan Evans

Jake Evans

Sara Evans

Tamara Fairbanks-Ishmael

Tilly Fairlie

Camilla Fanning

John Fanshawe

Charlotte Featherstone

Madeleine Fenner

Charles Fernyhough

Peter Fiennes

William Fiennes

Alexia Fishwick

Maria E. FitzGerald

Paul Fitzpatrick

Claire Flahavan

David Flusfeder

Cal Flyn

Hayley Flynn

Jean Forbes

Angela Ford

Anna Forss

Birte Förster

Charles Foster

Rebecca Foster

Bonnie Foulkes

Margaret Anne Fountain

Jessica Fox

Liza Fox

Gillian Foxcroft

Alexi Francis

Tiffany Francis-Baker

Sarah Franklin

Melissa Fu

Pamela Fuhrmann

Hero Fukutu

Katie Fuller

Saffron Uma Gardenchild

Ed Garland

Eileen Garner

Sarah Garnham

Laurie Garrison

Matt Gaw

Emma Geen

Alice Geldenhuys

Josie George

Joyce Gilbert

Matthew Gilbert

Sarah Gillett

Chrissie Gittins

Elizabeth Gladin

Laura Gladwin

Gus Glaser

Sinéad Gleeson

Jenny Glover

Georgina Godwin

Anne Goldsmith

Sophie Goldsworthy

Victoria Goodbody

Laura Gordon

Jackie Gorman

Karina Graj

Chris Gravatte

Heather Gray

Alex Green

Megan Green

Kay Greenbank

Jessica Groenendijk

Gus Grosch

Elaine Ground

Jamie Grove

Anisha Grover

Malcolm Guite

Stephen J Hackett

Caroline Hadley

Rob Haley

Rosalind Hallifax

Trish Halligan

With gratitude to
    Mary Hamilton

Joan Harcourt

Alison Hardy

Ange Harker

Joe Harkness

Ann Harman

Becca Harper-Day

Becky Harrington

John Harrington

Rachel Harrington

Francesca Harris

Janet Harris

Melissa Harrison

Sally Harrop

Celia Hart

Michelle Harvey

Katherine Hawes

Alex Hawthorne

Ashley Hay

Sue Hayes

Rebecca Hearle

Emma Heasman-Hunt

David Hebblethwaite

Sam Hedges

Alison Helm

Caspar Henderson

Tania Hershman

Cecilia Hewett

Leonie Hicks

Kirsten Higgins-Amor

Madame Hilaire

Jeremy Hill

Lynda Hillman

Karen Hinckley

Ali Hines

Jacqueline Hitt

Ben Hoare

Jennie Hobbs

Emily Hodder

Anne Hodgkins

Penny Hodgkinson

Susan Hodgkinson

Nicole Hodgson

Amelia Hodsdon

Gail E. Hofmar

Hayley G. Hofmar-Glennon

Susan H. Holland, Author of
   The Garden of Eaton: The
   Botanical Adventures of Mary
   Emily Eaton (1873-1961)

Holly Holmes

Marcelle Holt

Katie Holten

Antonia Honeywell

Marie Hood

Pamela Hopkins

Sharon Hopkinson

Justin Hopper

Rachel Hore

Julie Hotchin

Claire Houle

Susan Housley

Adrian Howe

Natalie Howell

Hugh Hudson

Theresa Hudson

Sara Hudston

Briana Huether

Bekah Hughes

Michael Hughes

Brian Human

Robin Hunt

Diane Husic

Lizzie Huxley-Jones

Anna Iltnere

Susan Iverson

Tanya Izzard

Steve Jackson

Christopher Jelley

Davina Jelley

Lyndsey Jenkins

Laura Jennings

Paul Jeorrett

Emily Joáchim

Joshua Johnson

Bronwen Jones

David Jones

Heather Jones

Helen Jones

Hollie Jones

Lucy Jones

Alice Jones Bartoli

Royce Kallerud

Stella Kane

Eileen Kaner

Milan Karol

Martha Kearney

Rym Kechacha

Jo Keeley

Frances Keeton

Andrew Kelly

Matt Kelly

Helen Kelsall

Christina Kennedy

Andrew Kenrick

Louise Kenward

Richard Kerridge

Heidi Kerrison

Rebecca Kershaw

Tim Kershaw

Anita Kerwin-Nye

Hannah Khwaja

Dan Kieran

Maureen Kincaid Speller

Ellia King

Catherine Kirkham

Jackie Kirkham

Blue Kirkhope

Paula Knight

Anna Koska

Sydney Kovar

Janna Krumm

Roxani Krystalli

Chris La Tray

Steve Lambert

Ruth Lampard and Ian Tattum

Felicity Lane

Bet LaRue

Diana Lempel

Chan Li Shan

Patrick Limb

Amy Liptrot

Shona Littlejohn

Ruth Livingstone

Karen Lloyd

Vikki Lloyd

Carly Lockett

K. M. Lockwood

Judith Loftus

Jackie Lomax

Angela Lord

Fraser Lovatt

Jane Lovell

Catriona M. Low

Sayling Low

Jen Lunn

Rachel Li-Jiang Luo

Christine Luxton

Caroline Lynch

Chantal Lyons

Alissa M

Kim M

Laura MacArthur

James Macdonald Lockhart

Karen Mace

Robert Macfarlane

Anna Mack

Seonaid Mackenzie-Murray

Katherine Mackinnon

Fi Macmillan

Deirdre Madden

Anthony Madigan

Catt★★ Makin

Michael Malay

Marion Malik

Vincent Malone

Mary Malyon

Trevor Mapstone

Naomi Markham

Roisin Markham

Pippa Marland

Sarah Marshall

Jim Martin

Catherine Mason

Lu Mason

Charlin Masterson

Diana and Hisham Matar

Justyna Matwiejczyk

Jos Mawdsley

Bev Maxted

Julia Maxted

Anne Maxwell

Claire Maycock

Rebecca Mays-Vandewater

Róisín McAnulty

Stephen McAteer

June McAvoy

Kari McBride

Douglas McCabe

Olivia McCarthy

Yvonne Carol McCombie

Megan McCormick

Margot McCuaig

Kate McDermott

Ian McDonald

Carol McGill

Rosie McIntosh

Tor McIntosh

Sarah McLoughlin

Ian McMillan

Jac McNeil

John McTague

John McVey

Simon Meacher

Inke Meier

Ineke Meijer

Susan Meikle

Meludom

Harriet Mercer

Susan Metcalfe

Kathrin Meyer

Victoria Mier

H Mikhail

Kizzia Mildmay

David Miller

Toby Miller

Kirsty Millican

Millie

Chris Mills

Sarah Mills

Joe Minihane

Andy Mitchell

Emma Mitchell

For Sarah Mitchell

John Mitchinson

Richard Montagu

Lucy Moore

Natalie Moore

Niamh Moore

Trevor Moore

Matt Morden

Ceri Morgan

Eleanor Morgan

Catherine Morris

Jackie Morris

Elaine Morrison

Stephen Moss

Mary Muir

Dipika Mummery

Wendy Murfitt

Hedvig Murray

Tiffany Murray

Gareth Mytton

Ana Nanu

Carlo Navato

Jenna Naylor

Vanessa Neat

Marie-Laure Neulat

Charlotte Newland

Jill Nicholls

Julie Nicholson

Oly Nicolaysen

Derek Niemann

Garth Nix

Ariel Noffke

Sabra Noordeen

Jean Isobel Norbury

John and Maria Norbury

Jo Norcup

Meredith Norwich

Linda Nowlan

James Nowland

Brighid Ó Dochartaigh

Grainne O'Toole

Jenny and Gerry O'Donovan

Orlagh O'Farrell

Mark O'Neill

Erika O'Reilly

Susan O'Reilly

Rick O'Shea

Ciara O'Sullivan

Kate Oakley

Sharon Oldham

Rebecca Olive

Helen Oliver

Kristina Olsson

Emily Oram

Deborah Orr

Lucy Oulton

Scott Pack

Helen Pallett

Abby Palmer

Emma L. Palmer

Alberthe Papma

Lev Parikian

Gail Parker

Steph Parker

Janice Parsons

Helen Patrice

Jaimie Pattison

Michelle Payne

Esme Pears

Marly Pehoviack

Jeremy Pettitt

Gemma Pettman

John Phelan

Sue Phelan

Crystal Phelps

Simon Phelps

Kyla Phillips

Helia Phoenix

Tara Physick

Juliet Pickering

Sophia Pickles

Teresa Pilgrim

Ruth Pimenta

John Pitchford

Nicola Pitchford

Aasheesh Pittie

Eleanor Platt

Anne Plouffe

Justin Pollard

Steve Pont

Emma Pooley

Beki Pope

Emily Porth

Gwen Potter

Hannah Powell

Rebecca Prentice

Alex Preston

Robert Preuss

Ruth N Price

Sandra Leigh Price

Siân Prime

Julie Procter

Amanda Pyron

Claudine Quarry

Joanna Quinn

Jennifer Racusin

Ravinder Randhawa

Miranda Rathmell

Kelvin Ravenscroft

Rebecca Read

Yvonne Reddick

Jini Reddy

Dahl Redman

Sula Lily Reed

Ashley Reedy

Katharine Reeve

Amber Regis
Lara Reid
Barbara Renel
Chris Rennard
Natasha Reynolds & Halil Sen
Dan Richards
Alexia Richardson
Susan Richardson
Colin Riley
Kerry Rini
Stefanie Rixecker
Jules Robbins
Jane Roberts
Mark Roberts
Caroline Robinson
Rachael Robinson
Rocky Mountain Land Library
Rocky Mountain Land
  Library Lee
Peter Rogers
Sarah Rogers
Ameena Rojee
Laurence Rose
P Rotterdam
Carol Rowntree Jones
Jane Rusbridge
Fiona Russell
Bryony Rust
Polly Samson
Claire Sargent
Claudia Karabaic Sargent

Mimi Saunders
Bettina Schlass
Lisa Schneidau
Lee Schofield
Janette Schubert
Anna Schulten
Bronwen Scott
James Scudamore
Paul Scully
Sophie Segura
Anna Selby
Karen Selley
Anita Sethi
Seven Fables Dulverton
Cate Sevilla
Emma Seward
Tanya Shadrick
Shantha Shanmugalingam
Victoria Shaw
Hilary Shepherd
Dearbhla Sheridan
Rachel Shirley
Daniela F. Sieff
With gratitude to Lily Sieff
  (1930-1997)
Lorna Simes
Duncan Simpson
Emily Simpson
Inga Simpson
Lorna Sixsmith
With gratitude to Ann Skinner

Jeanne Skotnicki

Katharine Slater

Sadie Slater

Tom Smail

Toni Smerdon

Gail Smith

Mark Smith

Michael Smith

Will Smith and Polly Atkin

Trudy Smoke

Carolyn Soakell

Nicholas Soar

Anna Souter

Simon Spanton

Helen Spicer

Lucinda Sporle

Nicola Spurr

Vimla Sriram

Kassia St Clair

Judith St Quinton

Camilla Stacey

Laura Stafford

Jan Stannard

Lucia Stanton

Jill Stanton-Huxton

Cate Steele

Mary Steele

Peggy Stella

Andrea Stephenson

Ruth Stevens

Katrina Stewart

Tracy Stillwater

Amanda Stone

Aurora J Stone

Isabella Streffen

Doris Stubbs

Nina Stutler

Fiona Stygall

Geoffrey Sullivan

Nike Sulway

Sasha Swire

Catherine Sykes

Eline Tabak

Leia Tait

Sarah Tanburn

Soulla Tantouri Eriksen

Romy Tappero

Anne Taylor

Henry Taylor

Paul Taylor

Louie Thomas

Mike Thomas

Pauline Thomas

Sarah Thomas

Dr Laura Thomas-Walters

Pierrette Thomet

Helen Thompson

Louisa Thomsen Brits

Eva Rae Thomson

Rupert Thomson

Adam Tinworth

Tracey Todhunter

Francesca Tondi	David Walsh
Lesley Totten	Meredith Walsh
Chris Townsend	Patrick Walsh
Cerys Trayner	Esme Ward
Lindsay Trevarthen	Miranda Ward
Trileigh Tucker	Taryn Ward
Ann Tudor	Caro Warner
Giles Turnbull	Deborah Warner
Annie Turner	Iona Wassilieff
Jo Turner	Paul Watson
Luke Turner	Rachel Watt
Jenny Turtle	Catherine Watts
Dom Tyler	Weaverbird
L. Tyler-Rickon	E Webb
Kat U	Sarah Webb
Julia Unwin	Catriona Webster
Anna Urbanetz	Liz Weldrake
Hannah Varacalli	Tracey Weller
Charlotte Varela	Jane Wellesley
Louise Vergette-Lynn	Amelia Wells
Sally Vince	Angharad Westmore
Sarah Vines	Jane Wheeler
Alexa von Hirschberg	Pam Whetnall
Elizabeth Wainwright	Emilie Whitaker
Cheryl Waitkevich	Dylan White
Mike Waldron	Jane White
Eloise Wales	Andrew Whitehead
Sir Harold Walker	Vicki Whitehead
Olivia Wall	Mark Whitley
Jamie Lee Wallace	Helena Wiklund
Catherine Walmsley	Susan Wilde

Anne Williams

Eley Williams

Jacqueline Williams

Jane Helen Williams

Matt Williams

Sioned Williams

Louise Williamson

David Willis

Laura Willis

Elizabeth Willow

Nic Wilson

Jo Wimpenny

Terri & Howard
    Windling-Gayton

Meryl Wingfield

Lucie Winter

Mike Winter

Judith Wise

Rachel Withey

Howard Wix

Chris Wood

Rebecca Wood

Alex Woodcock

Amy Woodhouse

With gratitude to Marion
    Woodman (1928–2018)

Pauline Woods

Charlotte Woodward

Michael Woolf

Annie Worsley

Georgina Wright

J L Yates

Anoushka Yeoh

Emma Yorke

Noel Young

A NOTE ON THE EDITOR

Katharine Norbury is the author of *The Fish Ladder* which was shortlisted for the 2016 Wainwright Prize, longlisted for the *Guardian* First Book Award and was a Book of the Year in the *Guardian*, *Telegraph* and *Observer* newspapers. She was the *Observer*'s Rising Star in Non-fiction in 2016, and has contributed to the *Guardian*, the *Telegraph*, *The Washington Post*, *Lonely Planet* magazine and Caught by the River.